CONTENTS

FROM JANET.

G, 14/1/2008

Pennine Perspectives

Aspects of the History of Midgley

Essays by members of
The Midgley History Group

Edited by
Ian Bailey, David Cant, Alan Petford and Nigel Smith

Midgley Books
2007

© 2007, The Contributors

Published by Midgley Books
Great House Barn
Towngate
Midgley
Halifax
HX2 6UH

Typeset in Palatino Linotype by Midgley Books

Printed and Bound in Great Britain by
The Amadeus Press
Ezra House
West 26 Business Park
Cleckheaton
BD19 4TQ

ISBN: 978-0-9554965-1-6

British Library Cataloguing-in-Publication Data:
A catalogue record for this book is available from the British Library

This book is supported by the Heritage Lottery Fund through the
Local Heritage Initiative

Preface

When Midgley's Post Office and general store closed in 2001, the village was left with no shop, pub, church or meeting facility. This prompted a committed group of local enthusiasts to organise the founding of a volunteer-run shop, Post Office and meeting room in order to promote a sense of community. The shop and Post Office opened in September 2003, followed by the meeting room in April 2004. Local history emerged as a favoured activity to utilise this new facility and a grant for over £16,000 was secured from the Local Heritage Initiative to run a project that was to be completed with this book.

The project began with a ten-week course in conjunction with the WEA, where participants were introduced to Midgley's rich local heritage and its sources of historical evidence. It proved so popular that two evening classes were required. Following this, the group proceeded with a series of research projects that included transcribing the census, transcribing wills and inventories as far back as 1531 and learning about architecture. This programme was complemented by a number of guided walks and guest lectures. The final phase of the project involved the researching and writing of this book. The aim was to cover a number of the many different facets of Midgley's rich history across a broad span of time, but not the definitive history of Midgley.

The group started by identifying the topics that individuals, pairs or teams would like to work on. The result is the series of illustrated essays that now follows from twenty-five contributors. Each chapter is written in its own style, reflecting the diversity of the project participants. Some have had previous experience in historical writing, whilst others are new to it. Some have a detailed local knowledge of Midgley, although several of the contributors are from outside the area. The result of this approach is a series of essays with differing styles.

Particular attention has been given to illustrating each chapter. We have been extremely fortunate in having access to a fabulous collection of photographs held by one of the group members. If you recognise anyone who is not named, please tell us. We have also been able to make extensive use of digital photography, both for illustrating the book and throughout all the research conducted on this project. There has been a major advance in this area in recent years, not just in terms of the technology available but in the facilities of the archives that hold our historical records. It has been possible to photograph any document that we have seen or arrange for it to be scanned.

The use of publicly available records has been at the core of this book. One of the motivations behind this entire project has been to promote awareness of the range and depth of sources that is freely available within the public domain. Attention has been given to the footnotes on each page of this book, in order to guide the reader clearly to any of the sources of our information. As such, it should be possible to access most of the original documents upon which our findings are based. Hopefully, this will inspire further interest in archived information, where a wealth of untapped resource awaits the potential researcher.

Throughout this project, we have used the facilities of a number of institutions: the National Archives, The British Library, The National Portrait Gallery, The Borthwick Institute at York University, the West Yorkshire Archive Service branches at Calderdale and Wakefield, the Bankfield Museum in Halifax, the Brontë Parsonage Museum in Haworth, the Yorkshire Archaeological Society in Leeds, the Halifax Antiquarian Society, Bradford Central Library and Halifax Central Library. We are extremely grateful to the staff at these institutions who have been so helpful in providing us with the information we required. We have also received the generous help of a number of individuals who are referred to in the footnotes throughout the book and the list of illustrations at the back.

The largest group of documents that we have used has been the John Murgatroyd & Son collection held by the Calderdale branch of the West Yorkshire Archive Service. This is one of the country's most comprehensive collections from a textile mill and the estate of its owners. Thanks to the foresight of the Murgatroyd and Wade families, who have preserved and made this available to the public, this book has been richly enhanced.

This has been a tremendously enjoyable and rewarding project. It has demonstrated the wealth of information that is available to us and the light that it can shed on the rich heritage of our local communities. Above all, it has highlighted the talents that exist amongst our neighbours and how working together can result in such impressive creativity.

Ian Bailey, Midgley, April 2007

Introducing Midgley

Lawrence Sullivan

Midgley is a village on a lofty eminence and a mountainous moorland township, containing a scattered population, and parts of the villages of Mytholmroyd, Luddenden and Luddenden foot[1]

We are standing at the bottom of the Calder Valley whose steep sides have been carved out by the River Calder, which shares the space with a road, a canal and a railway. We are about a mile downstream from Mytholmroyd, where the valley floor widens into a flood plain which, until the introduction of a flood prevention scheme a few years ago, flooded regularly, damaging property and blocking the road through the valley. Westwards, the valley becomes narrower and narrower until a few miles upstream at Hebden Bridge it is so narrow that the river, canal, railway and road criss-cross in a fight for space in what by then has become a gorge which continues on to Todmorden and beyond. Further downstream to the east, the valley widens but never loses its confined sense until many miles downstream beyond Halifax. Hebden Bridge and Todmorden recently suffered flooding in spite of massive flood defences. We will return to the power of the river, but for now it is time to start moving uphill.

We are going to climb up the north side of the valley via Midgley and out onto the moor. We are also going to take it slowly, not just to admire the ever changing view, but because we are facing a climb of nearly 1,000 feet in a little over a mile. Due to the steepness, Midgley and the moorland beyond are out of sight, but in any case trees often obscure the view until we reach the edge of the terrace which lies above the steep valley side and below the moor above. Leaving the valley floor, our way goes up by ancient paths enclosed by dry stone walls. Underfoot are so called flagstones which are made from the same material as the walls, namely Millstone Grit, the predominant stone of the area. Direct paths upwards are so steep at times that the flags give way to steps; their hollowed form a testimony to the wear and tear by so many feet, long before roads through the valley were built. The steep slope eventually

---

[1] *Post Office Directory of the West Riding of Yorkshire*, London: Kelly & Co., 1861, p557

gives way to the much gentler slope of the terrace as we emerge from the trees and it is time for a well-earned rest as we contemplate the scene.

Below us the river is still visible, but the views up and downstream are much clearer and we can see the gorge-like shape of the valley, which twists and turns its way westwards towards Todmorden, a contrast with the more gently winding course eastwards towards Halifax. Surrounding us are fields enclosed by dry stone walls and scattered farms and old buildings all built from the same Millstone Grit. The stone is dark and in poor light may appear forbidding, but if you break a piece in half it reveals a beautiful golden interior and it is this which over time reacts with the atmosphere and changes colour. It was thought that the dark shade was due to smoke blackening and in days gone by that was certainly an influence but not any more. A road goes along the edge of the terrace and it is on this terrace, going east and west, that the village of Midgley is built.

Figure 1   Midgley village and its surroundings, seen from the Warley hillside

We are at a height of about 700 feet above sea level as we cross the road to begin our final climb up towards the moor. We leave the village behind and are soon on a rough track and past the last of the dry stone walls before the open moor. This particular way goes up the side of a small ravine known as Coal Dike where a small seam of coal was found. Grass and moss gradually give way to heather and with a final steep climb we are at last on the top of the moor, the height of which varies from 1,250 feet to 1,400 feet hereabouts. This time we are going to have a longer rest while we take in the scene.

If this is your first visit what did you expect to see? A grim, bleak, forbidding landscape of the type portrayed in films about the Brontës with valleys full of Blake's Dark Satanic Mills? Well, Haworth and the 'Brontë' moors are only five miles away and it is still possible to see the odd relic of a mill chimney in the valleys if you look hard enough. As for grim and bleak, well it certainly can be, especially on a cold, wet and misty day. But then again so can any city centre. Perhaps you thought that the smoke from a thousand chimneys would engulf the valley and blacken the sheep and all around us? Well you would be quite right if you went back a mere fifty years before the Clean Air Act, when coal was used for fuel in every house and mill. If you did think along those lines you might be astonished at the scene before you now. It is an ever changing scene just like that of any upland area, sometimes obscured by mist and driving rain; conditions to be avoided or enjoyed as wild and romantic? Sometimes the moor bakes under a cloudless sky, with birdsong in the spring and a honey-flavoured atmosphere in autumn when the heather blooms, or you may be lucky and have a day of such rain-washed clarity that beyond the rolling moorland you can see the hills of the limestone Yorkshire Dales to the north, or the Bowland fells beyond the Ribble Valley or even, if you wander over the moor a little higher, the Lakeland fells away to the north west. Nearer to hand the moors go on for mile after heather-coated mile, full of peat bogs, the odd rocky outcrop and very few footpaths. To the east the moors slope gradually down and down to the vasty fields of Yorkshire, while looking westwards there is a sharp drop to the Lancashire plain.

On 24 January 2006, the London-based media were much exercised by the revelation that it was the most depressing day of the year. That same day on Midgley moor you would have had your spirits lifted by the sight of an early frost followed by a hazy sun and a gentle ripple of colour through the heather as a breeze arrived. The valley mist, now no longer polluted by smoke, gradually dispersed, and it was impossible not to feel moved by the enormous sense of space as the Pennines marched away, valley after valley, to the north and south, encompassing so much of our history. Six weeks later the first curlews arrived back on the moor with their first bubbling 'curlee' call and you knew that spring had arrived.

Man has exploited these hills since the first nomadic people passed through and it can be said that much of local history is due to the shape of our hills and valleys and the way man has exploited it. The next step is to ask the question: how did it all come about? Time to ask the geologists.

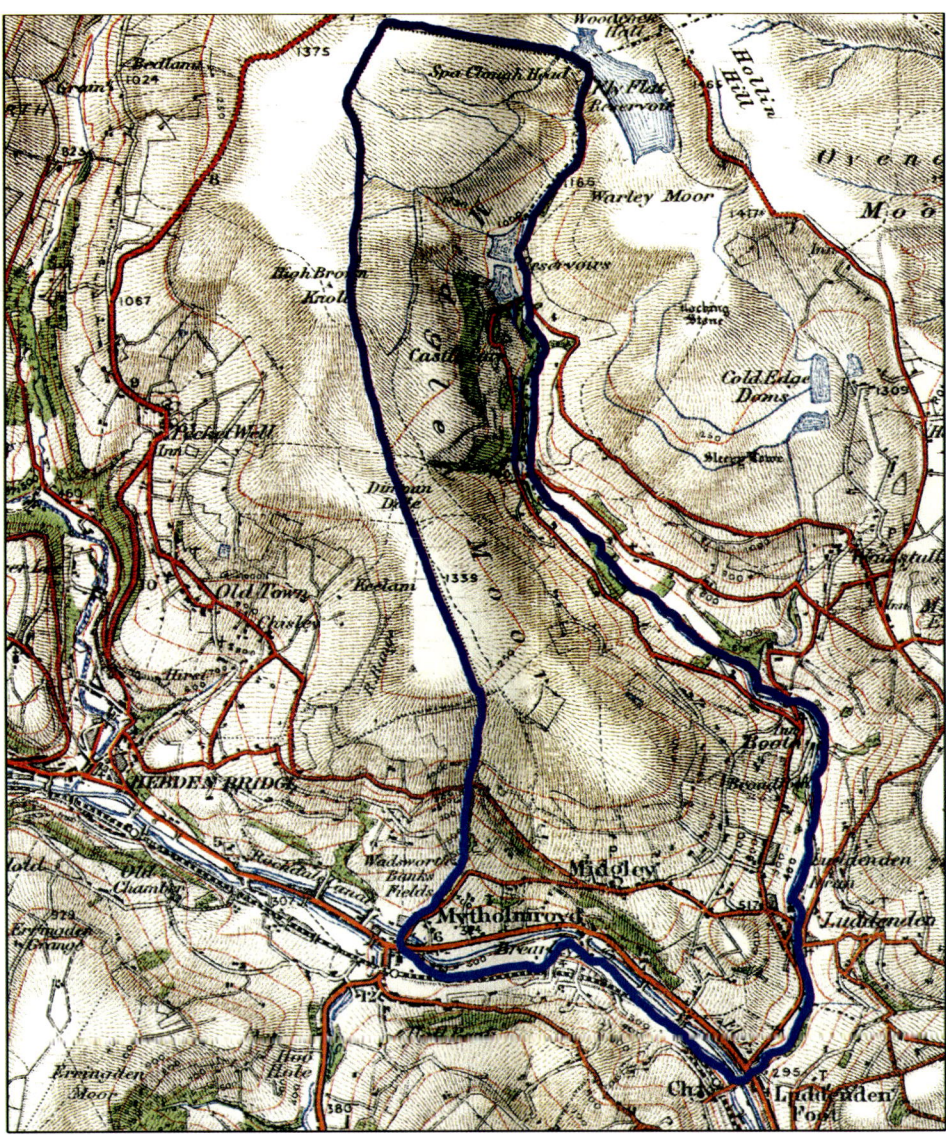

Figure 2   An extract from the Ordnance Survey Map, scale one inch to one mile, sheet 30, published 1913, with Midgley township bordered in blue

CHAPTER 1

The Geology which Shaped Midgley

Lawrence Sullivan

The geology of the British Isles is said to be the most complex in the world for its area. To put the particular circumstance of Midgley and its place in the Pennines into context, does require a look back in time, unimaginable years of it, to see how we got here.

> And the sun grew round that very day.
> So it must have been after the birth of the simple light
> In the first, spinning place…

There are different theories about how our world came into being but Dylan Thomas' poetic description is not a bad way for us to start. Whichever theory for the beginning one favours, geologists agree that we are looking back about 4,500 or 4,600 million years ago to that 'first spinning place'. Thereafter it took roughly 4,000 million years for the land mass to form from a volcanic soup bombarded by meteorites into a reasonably stable crust. Trying to imagine such lengths of time is an impossible task for most of us but there are various tricks to get it all into proportion, such as measuring out a distance and dividing it into chunks of time. Geologists are unlikely to say 'chunks of time'. They think in specific eras and periods which we will touch on later.

The land masses formed into various continents but it wasn't until 1912 that the theory of Continental Drift was first suggested. A German called Wegener pointed out that our continents fit together like pieces in a jigsaw and must therefore once have been joined together. Initially, his theory was ridiculed and it took fifty years before it became accepted. It is now generally recognised that the Earth's crust or outer shell is composed of separate plates moving independently of each other, which is now known as the theory of Plate Tectonics.

Million Years Ago	Period	Era	Mountain Building
Present	Quaternary		
	Pliocene		
	Miocene	Tertiary	
	Oligocene	(Cainozoic)	Alpine Fold
	Eocene		Mountains
100			
	Cretacious		
	Jurassic	Mesozoic	
200			
	Triasic		
	Permian		Heroynian/ Armorican Progenesis
300	Carboniferous	Upper Paleozoic	
	Devonian		
400			Caledonian Orogenesis
	Silucian		
	Ordovician	Lower Paleozoic	
500			
	Cambrian		
600			
	Pre-Cambrian		
7,600			

Figure 1   *Geological time-scale*

About 500 million years ago a continent, called Avalonia, contained the area which would one day become the southern part of the British Isles. What would become the northern part was on another continent, Laurentia. They were both in the southern hemisphere. Subsequent northward movement saw these two continents join about 400 million years ago during the period known as Devonian, to form the super-continent of Pangea. This period lasted about forty-six million years before we enter the period of great significance for Midgley and surrounding areas, namely the Carboniferous.

Thus far in the Earth's history, every kind of climatic condition had occurred, from deserts similar to the Sahara of today through arctic conditions to tropical temperatures. Between 363 million years ago and 290 million years ago a shallow, tropical sea invaded the land. During this period tiny shell fish thrived, died and the shells which then gathered on the bottom of the sea were compressed over time and became the limestones of the Dales. This is known as the Dinantian Period (Figure 2). This was succeeded by the Namurian Period (Figure 2) during which rivers flowing in from the north formed an enormous delta in which were deposited sand particles. As the sea level fluctuated and weathering

Million Years Ago				Local Significance
290	Westphalian		The Coal Measures (with mudstones, siltstones, sandstones and coal seams	Lower Coal Measures occur chiefly to the east of Halifax/ Hebble Brook (and in Rossendale)
	Namurian	Yeadonian Marsdenian Kinderscoutian Other Sandstone Grits/ Shales e.g. Pendle Grit	Millstone Grit Group Rough Rock Middle Grits Kinderscout	Chiefly in South Pennines between Todmorden and Halifax (Gritstones, Flagstones and Shales with thin seams of coal).
360	Dinantian		Carboniferous or Mountain Limestone	Limestone with some Sandstones and Shales (in Yorkshire Dales and White Peak areas).

Figure 2   Classification of carboniferous rocks

changed the nature of the uplands from which the rivers flowed, so too did the consistency of the particles of sand being deposited. If you go onto the moor the day after heavy rain you can see by paths and water courses where the sandstone has been washed into miniature versions of the delta effect mentioned above. By gently scraping the surface all kinds of sandstone particles will be revealed from fine shales to coarse grit. As one layer superseded another, so the lower level was compressed to form the layers of different sandstones we see today. Perhaps the most famous of these is Millstone Grit, the coarse texture of which made it ideal for millstones as well as providing a magnificent building material from which many local houses and many buildings further afield were built. The specific type of millstone grit found locally is Midgley Grit which forms the moor itself and, at a slightly lower level, the Scotland Flags which have been much quarried. The village of Midgley sits on the Upper Kinder Scout band of rocks. When the sea periodically receded, tropical rain forests thrived and when the sea returned another cycle of sand deposits began. The trees and vegetation were in turn compressed into layers and became coal. These are known as the Coal Measures. Immediately below the Coal Measures, can often be found a band of Seat Earth which has been formed from the soil in which the tropical vegetation grew and which sometimes contains deposits of iron ore such as outcrop in the Luddenden valley.

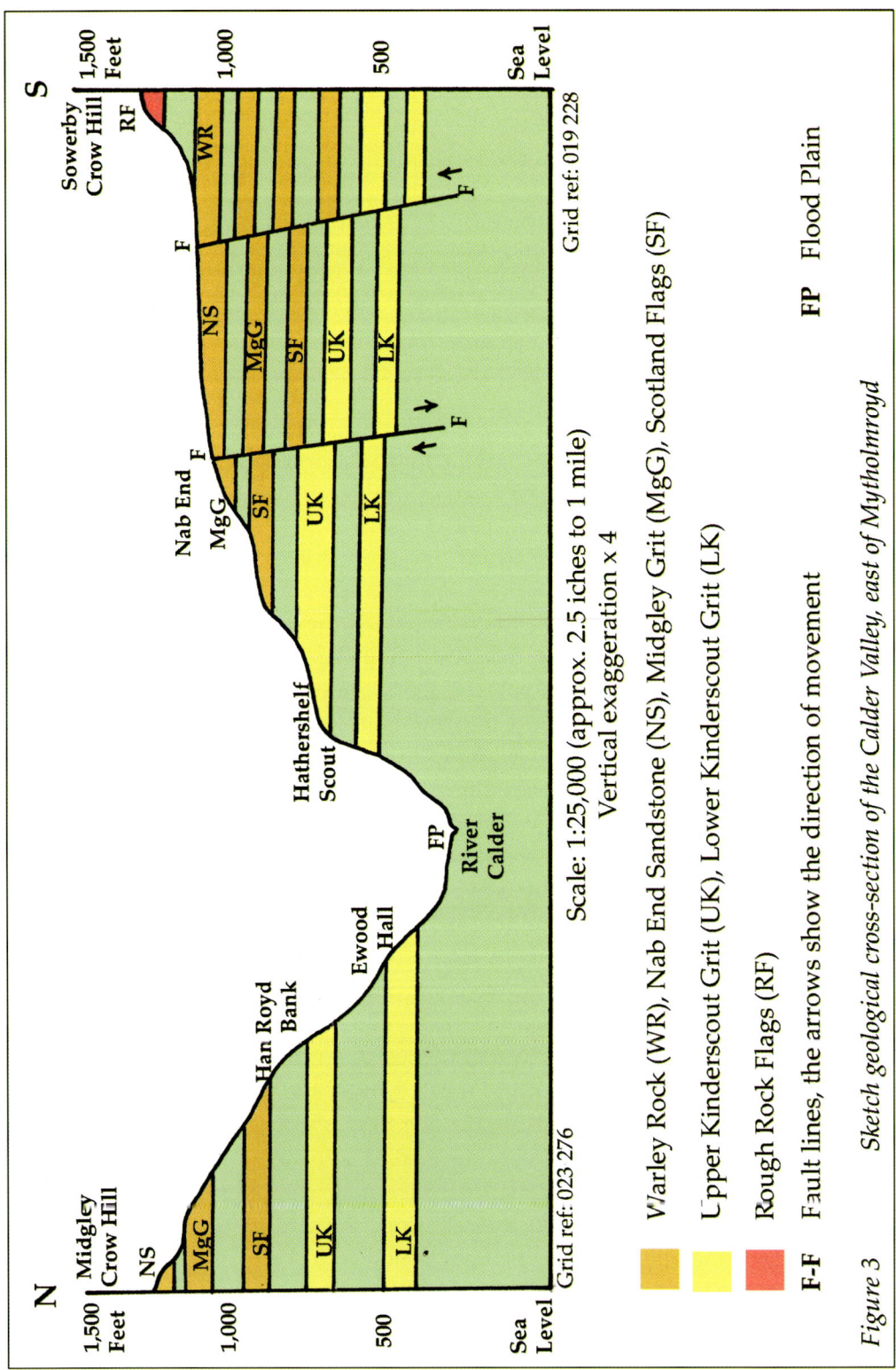

Figure 3   Sketch geological cross-section of the Calder Valley, east of Mytholmroyd

Scale: 1:25,000 (approx. 2.5 iches to 1 mile)
Vertical exaggeration x 4

Warley Rock (WR), Nab End Sandstone (NS), Midgley Grit (MgG), Scotland Flags (SF)

Upper Kinderscout Grit (UK), Lower Kinderscout Grit (LK)

Rough Rock Flags (RF)

F-F   Fault lines, the arrows show the direction of movement

FP   Flood Plain

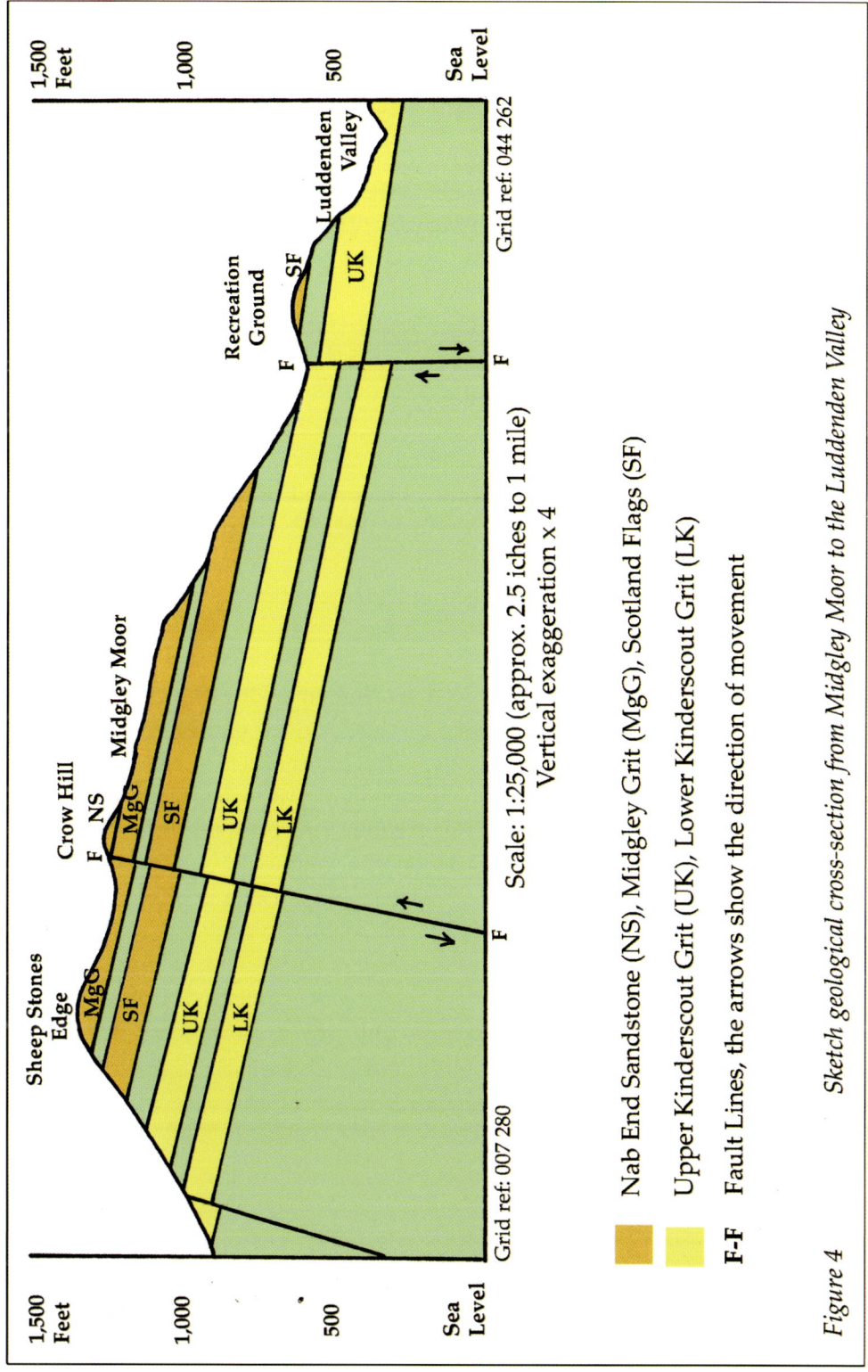

Figure 4   Sketch geological cross-section from Midgley Moor to the Luddenden Valley

Nab End Sandstone (NS), Midgley Grit (MgG), Scotland Flags (SF)

Upper Kinderscout Grit (UK), Lower Kinderscout Grit (LK)

F-F   Fault Lines, the arrows show the direction of movement

Scale: 1:25,000 (approx. 2.5 iches to 1 mile)
Vertical exaggeration x 4

By the end of the Carboniferous Period, the three basic rock structures of the Pennines, namely sandstones, coal and limestone formed as deposits at the edge of a sea. However, about 280 million years ago the land began to rise above sea level due to the compressional forces imposed by the movement of the Tectonic Plates. The super-continent Pangea began to break up and slowly assume the continental shapes we see today. These compressional forces are known as the Variscan or Amorican orogeny. The effect of them in the north of England was quite complex. Broadly speaking, the land rose up rather in the way that a piece of paper does if you push it from both ends. Geologists describe this folding of the land as an anticline; therefore, we are looking at the Pennine Anticline. However, unlike your bit of paper the curvature is not regular, being steep to the west and gradual to the east. This is why it is known as an asymmetrical anticline or monocline. In the immediate vicinity of Midgley the rocks all dip eastwards (Figure 4). Perhaps the really staggering thing about all this is the height of the hills formed by the Variscan orogeny. The land uplifted to a height of 12,000 to 14,000 feet, roughly the height of the Alps today, and over the ensuing millions of years has eroded to the present height of some 1,250feet to 1,400feet and further afield to almost 1,700ft on Boulsworth Hill (Grid reference: SD 929 356).

This dramatic erosion, which reduced the height of the Pennines by some 10,000 feet, took place in a variety of ways and had the effect of removing the upper layers first and subsequently exposing lower levels to either side. This resulted in the lowest deposits, the Millstone Grits, now being on the surface and if you look at a geological map they run north and south down the spine of the Pennines flanked either side by the coalfields of Lancashire and Yorkshire. The detail of this situation for the Midgley area is shown in Figure 5.

While all that was going on, the plate movements continued. One important implication for the local landscape was that these movements during the Tertiary Era caused or reactivated fault lines, such as those between Midgley and Luddenden (Figure 5).

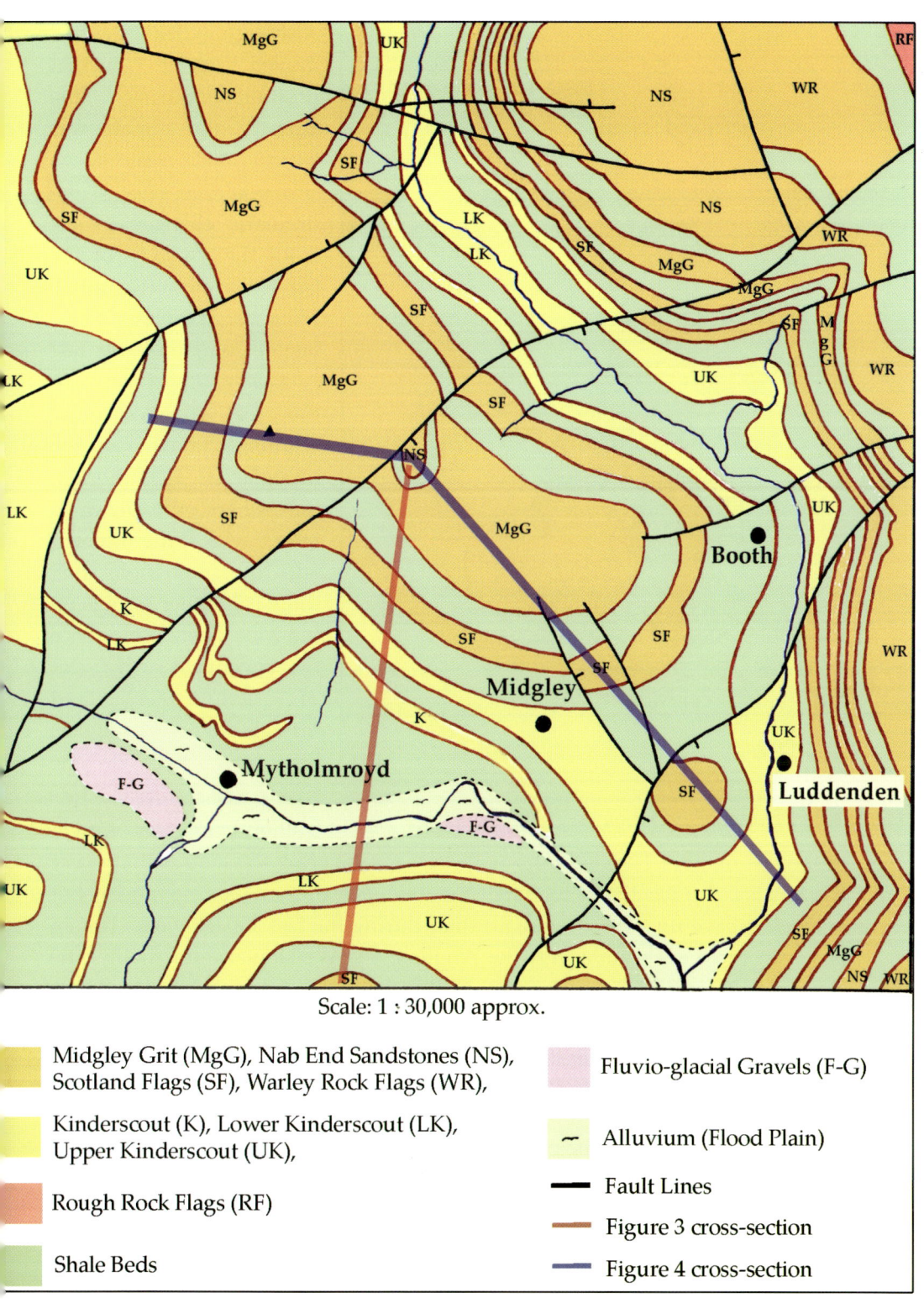

Scale: 1 : 30,000 approx.

Midgley Grit (MgG), Nab End Sandstones (NS),
Scotland Flags (SF), Warley Rock Flags (WR),

Kinderscout (K), Lower Kinderscout (LK),
Upper Kinderscout (UK),

Rough Rock Flags (RF)

Shale Beds

Fluvio-glacial Gravels (F-G)

~ Alluvium (Flood Plain)

━ Fault Lines

━ Figure 3 cross-section

━ Figure 4 cross-section

Figure 5   Geological sketch map of the Midgley area

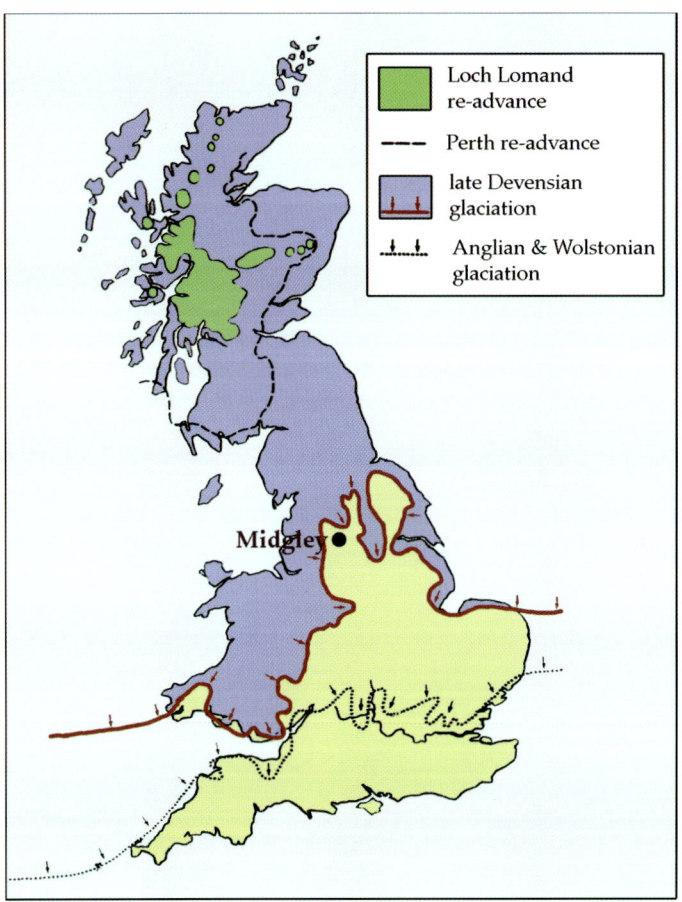

Loch Lomand re-advance

‒ ‒ ‒ Perth re-advance

late Devensian glaciation

Anglian & Wolstonian glaciation

Midgley

Figure 6   Extent of glaciation

Although Britain had moved to its current position during the Tertiary, the climate was warm and humid, a situation that was to see dramatic changes as we enter the ice ages of the Quaternary Era (Figure 7). However, the climate also began comparatively fast cyclical changes between the ice advances and warming known as the interglacials. It is thought that we are probably in an interglacial at the moment and it is possible that there is another ice age on the way. There is evidence that seventeen such cycles of ice ages and interglacials are known to have occurred in the British Isles in the last two million years, ten of them in the last million. The difficulty with ice caps covering the land is that every advance of the ice tends to wipe out evidence of previous advances, but geologists have uncovered evidence that during the last 300,000 years Britain has seen three such advances, the Anglian, the Wolstonian and finally, the Devensian (Figure 6). Not surprisingly, it is this last one which has shaped the British landscape into more or less what we see now. The two earlier glaciations covered the whole country and reached as far south as the Thames valley. The Devensian was less extensive and, whilst it reached the Pennine watershed locally, it did not actually enter the Calder valley although, as we shall see, its effect was to be quite dramatic in shaping our valley.

The Devensian advance reached its peak between 23,000 and 18,000 years ago but by 13,000 years ago it had all but disappeared. Sadly, global warming has become a political football as politicians vye with each other to present their 'green' credentials. That mankind must find a way to manage finite resources and refrain from destroying the environment goes without saying. However, there is nothing new in global warming nor on the consequences to wildlife. From 13,000 years ago a rapid warming began. In one period of 100 years the temperature rose 10ºC, the summers were warmer then than they are now, and the retreating ice left deep mud over the permafrost which could collapse if for example, mammoths walked across it. Fossils of mammoths have been found in Shropshire and have been subject to radio carbon dating and a date of 12,700 years ago established.

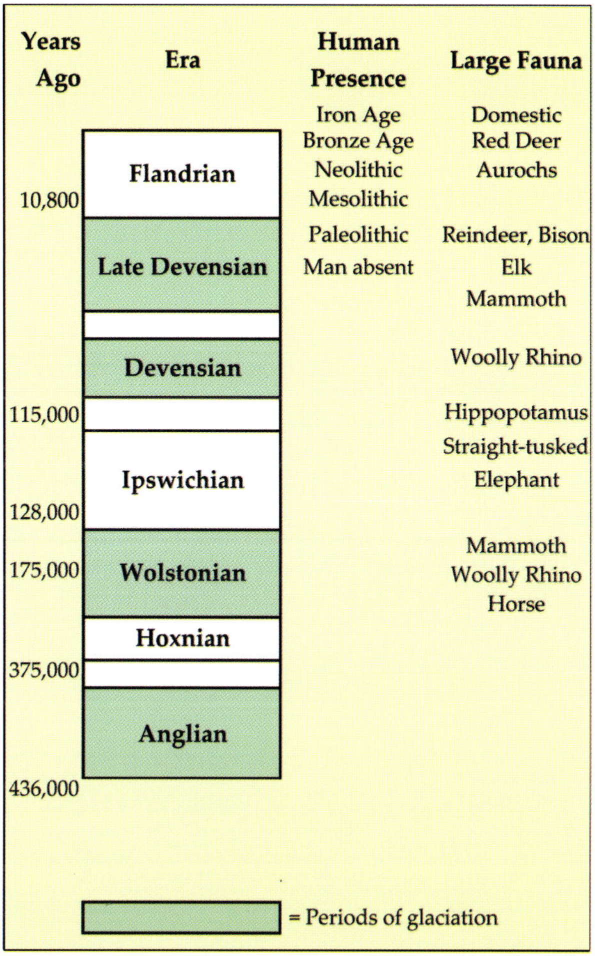

Years Ago	Era	Human Presence	Large Fauna
10,800	Flandrian	Iron Age Bronze Age Neolithic Mesolithic	Domestic Red Deer Aurochs
	Late Devensian	Paleolithic Man absent	Reindeer, Bison Elk Mammoth
	Devensian		Woolly Rhino
115,000			Hippopotamus
	Ipswichian		Straight-tusked Elephant
128,000			
175,000	Wolstonian		Mammoth Woolly Rhino Horse
	Hoxnian		
375,000			
	Anglian		
436,000			

☐ = Periods of glaciation

Figure 7   *A chronology of the Quaternary Era*

Ten thousand years ago another rapid warming occurred and the glaciers disappeared from Britain. Glaciers had covered an area from the Lake District, down over the plains of Yorkshire, Lancashire and Cheshire but not into the valley of the Calder. The margin of the ice ran along the Pennine watershed to the west at the head of the Cliviger and Walsden gorges. It is generally supposed that as it melted large lakes formed. The valley downstream which was to become the Calder had the appearance of a gentle curve linking the higher moorlands on either side. The vast quantity of melt water from the ice fields had nowhere to go but down and cut through the floor of the valley, carrying all before it until it reached somewhere near the level of the present valley floor.

Geologists give the word 'erratic' to rocks which are, as it were, in the 'wrong' place. In the river bed east of Mytholmroyd, and in the valley bottom below

Midgley, erratics have been found which began life in the Dales and the Lake District. It is quite a thought if you are ever on the moor in conditions mentioned earlier where in the blue distance the fells of the Lakes can be seen, to realise just how far the erratics have travelled. These erratics are the most obvious evidence of the deposits carried here by water from the glacial overflow channels to the west. Less obvious evidence of these deposits are the terraces by the side of the river Calder, notably at Caldene, Mytholmroyd (Grid reference: SE 010 260) and less prominently in the vicinity of Brearley Old Hall, in Midgley township (Grid reference: SE 031 259).

The sides of the valley into which the 'V' is cut became a terrace on which Midgley and other hill villages now sit; a site made all the more attractive by the springs which emerge at the junction between the Kinder Scout Grit on which Midgley is built and the overlying shales (Figure 6). Yet another effect of the carving out of the valley was the creation of steep tributary valleys which naturally cut down to the now lower valley bottom. It was the consequent water power that these side valleys provided which had such an influence on the growth of early textile mills but that, and man's exploitation of the local environment, is another chapter in history.

Further reading

N. Aitkenhead, *The Pennines and Adjacent Areas,* 4th ed., Nottingham: British Geological Survey, 2002

A. Hunter and G. Easterbrook, *The Geological History of the British Isles,* Milton Keynes: The Open University, 2004

G. Sellers, Walking in the South Pennines, Milnthorpe: Cicerone Press, 1991

P. Toghill, The Geology of Britain: an Introduction, Shrewsbury: Swan Hill Press, 2002

Acknowledgements
With thanks to David Uttley for his advice and supply of illustrations.

CHAPTER 2

Prehistory in the Midgley Area

Dave Shepherd

The prehistoric context

Ten thousand years ago Calderdale was largely covered in primary forest, north European jungle, in which lived bears, beavers, wolves, wild boar, aurochs[1] and red deer. On higher ground, above around 300m, the oak, beech and lime cover gradually gave way to hazel, rowan, birch and pine, and the high tops bore scrub and grass. There was no peat or heather for the climate was somewhat warmer and drier. There were very few people, perhaps a few thousand in the whole country, who followed a seasonal round in tribal and family groups, governed by the migrations of prey animals and the ripening of wild food sources.

Over many years these Mesolithic hunter-gatherer groups began to domesticate animals and plants, and more permanent dwelling-places developed from the ancestral campsites. The Neolithic brought an increase in population, a greater social elaboration, and a sense of place rather than of

Figure 1   *Mesolithic Microliths from High Brown Knoll on Midgley Moor. These are all 'narrow blade' types from the later Mesolithic period (6600 - 3500 BC). Very small blades and points, which are typical of the economical use of a scarce and heavy resource.*

---

[1] Very large, wild cattle

passage, of territory held and possessed. The farmers and part-time hunters of the late Neolithic and early Bronze Age, some four thousand years ago, had cleared much of the land suitable for grazing their cattle, sheep and goats, and for growing their oats, rye and emmer wheat. Trackways now crossed the Pennines linking the navigable rivers to east and west; goods and ideas passed between Ireland and mainland Europe. People lived in permanent settlements within regional hierarchies; this was perhaps the beginning of the settlement that later became Midgley. Around two thousand five hundred years ago the climate began to deteriorate to that which we experience at present. There was a retreat from what had become marginal land and thus there is little evidence of Iron Age activity in the immediate area.[2]

An Approximate Chronology for British Prehistory

Mesolithic (middle stone age)	Neolithic (new stone age)	Bronze Age	Iron Age	Romano-British
10,000 to 5,000 years ago	5,000 to 3,000 years ago	3,000 years ago	From 2,500 years ago	2,000 years ago

This enormous sweep of time, from the end of the most recent Ice Age to the Roman invasions, encompasses some of the most fundamental advances that people have ever made and this chapter is concerned with the surviving vestiges of this period around Midgley. The divisive labels applied in the table above can be misleading and it should be borne in mind that all the changes must have been slow and piecemeal; it is only our vantage point so far in the future that can lend a false foreshortening. There was, of course, no place called Midgley and this account necessarily includes some features and sites that lie outside the modern boundary but which would have been familiar to the people living here.

---

[2] This general account of the context is drawn from several sources.
    a. R. Bradley, *The Significance of Monuments*, London: Routledge, 1998
    b. M. Edmonds and T. Seaborne, *Prehistory in the Peak*, Stroud: Tempus, 2001
    c. A. Gibson and A. Sheridan (eds), *From Sickles to Circles*, Stroud: Tempus, 2004
    d. T. Manby, S. Moorhouse and P. Ottaway (eds), *The Archaeology of Yorkshire*, Leeds: Yorkshire Archaeological Society, 2003. (Y.A.S. Occasional Paper No 3)
    e. P.A. Spikins, *Prehistoric People of the Pennines*, Leeds: West Yorkshire Archaeology Service, 2002
    f. R. Young (ed.), *Mesolithic Lifeways*, Leicester: University of Leicester, 2000. (Leicester Archaeology Monographs No 7)

Finds and features around Midgley

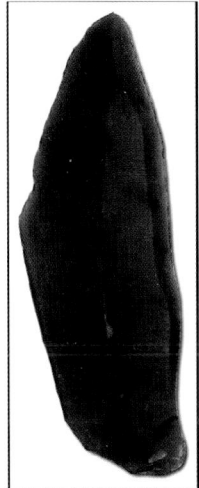

*Figure 2
Blade: Neolithic
and later.
General purpose
blade which
might be hafted
with wood or
bone. It has an
edge like a
modern craft
knife.*

In following this discussion it will be helpful to refer to the gazetteer at the end of this chapter. Figure 1 shows a group of edges and points known as microliths from their small size. Typically around 15-20mm long, these were once known as pygmy flints from erroneous assumptions made about their makers. In the Middle Stone Age small, very finely-worked shards and splinters of flint were set into wood, bone or antler to make composite implements in preference to using larger pieces of flint; thus, for example, an arrow would have a point and barbs attached to the shaft separately rather than a single arrowhead. Apart from the typical flint scatters found where implements were made or maintained there is at present no actual evidence for Mesolithic activity in the area. Transient hunters utilising temporary shelters leave little trace even after prolonged, traditional use of a particular place[3] and finding hearths and the sites of 'benders', portable shelters supported on flexible poles, would actually be a rare, nationally-significant event. In the later Stone Age and Bronze Age, flint was worked in larger pieces.

All of the artefacts illustrated came from a 300 x 300 metre area close to the Limers Gate packhorse route, adjacent to the trig point and the panels of rock art at High Brown Knoll (21).[4] Flint and chert debitage was found along with the 'tools', indicating that manufacture was taking place at this site.[5] This last is important because the acidic soil of the moorland leaves little or no trace of any organic matter; wood, leather, bone and pottery can all vanish completely and finding artefacts alone could mean that they are all that remains of a burial or ritual deposition. The waste flakes and chips make that less likely.

The Neolithic and Bronze Age sites and features that remain are largely confined to the higher, unimproved land; later farming and settlement are likely to have obliterated any traces on lower ground. We have therefore a rather skewed picture, where funerary and ceremonial sites, which may well

---

[3] Spikins, *Prehistoric People of the Pennines,* Chapter 3

[4] These numbers refer to the gazetteer at the end of this chapter

[5] Ilustrations of flint artefacts from Brian Howcroft's extensive collection from sites all over the South Pennines. Debitage is the term used for the fragments left from the creation of these artefacts.

have been set apart anyway, can still be examined, but dwelling areas, level spots with a water supply and warm aspect, are likely to have been built upon and may be marked now by the oldest farmsteads.

Figure 3   *Scrapers: Neolithic and later. Used in processing hide for removing the fatty layer from the inside surface of animal skins.*

Studies in the better-explored and better-preserved Peak District[6] have indicated a typical layout of late Neolithic and early Bronze Age settlements in very similar upland areas. Burials were commonly placed above dwelling areas and out of sight of them, but within pastoral areas, perhaps so that the ancestors could watch over, and signify ownership of, the grazing grounds and herds – the wealth and tangible assets of the extended family to which they belonged. This is arguably supported by the burials at Heights Clough and Shore End Top, which are likely to be the funerary or ancestral areas for family groups living lower down in the Luddenden valley. By analogy, it seems likely that what is now moorland above Midgley formed, for several thousand years, an area of pasture for sheep, goats[7] and cattle, conveniently bounded on three sides by deep valleys.

It should be borne in mind that, in a period at least twice as long as recorded history, there will have been changes in familial groupings, tribal allegiance and possession of land. Much of this is inaccessible now but, as elsewhere, there is evidence in the single cairns of varying sizes (4, 5, 6, 12, 13, 14, 19, 22), the enclosed cemeteries (1, 2) and the unenclosed cairnfields (8, 20, 23) of changes in funerary tradition[8] and the re-definition and re-owning of territory. Similarly the clearance cairns (14, 23), the Neolithic walling (11, 15, 23) and, possibly, the embanked stone circle (9) may indicate an earlier phase of land-use where crops were raised on the lower shelf of the moor, before the climate began to deteriorate.

---

[6] J. Barnatt, 'To Each Their Own: Later Prehistoric Farming Communities and their Monuments in the Peak', *Derbyshire Archaeological Journal*, 2000, 120, pp1-86

[7] Sheep and goats are difficult to distinguish in prehistoric terms, because they are physically and genetically so similar.

[8] T. Taylor, *The Buried Soul*, London: Fourth Estate, 2003

Robin Hood's Penny Stone (Figures 6 and 7) is a large, detached block near the crest of the moor with a mass of some eight to ten tonnes; the bedding runs vertically and is well-exploited by weathering. The rock type, Huddersfield White Rock, occurs as a degraded outcrop some 300m south west. It may possibly have been moved by glacial action although its altitude argues against this. The stone would appear to have been manoeuvred into its present position by being stood upright from a more natural horizontal orientation and it could have been moved a short distance across the hill.

Miller's Grave (Figure 5) consists of a large, split, earthfast boulder of the same rock type as the Penny Stone. It has been closely enclosed and concealed from view by a substantial circular bank of earth and stones approaching 2m in height. The earthfast and outcropping rock around these features is Midgley Grit, a darker and browner gritstone contrasting in both colour and eroded texture with the paler Huddersfield White Rock; the possible significance of this is discussed below in relation to rock art.

These two features form prominent points on the skyline of the moor. When viewed from the Penny Stone the midwinter sun rises exactly beyond the Miller's Grave. The prehistoric importance of such solar alignments are dealt with elsewhere[9]; it is most unlikely to be accidental but its significance for, and relationship to, the other monuments on Midgley Moor is not clear at this stage. There are examples of similar enclosed boulders in Cumbria[10] but Miller's Grave seems unique in the South Pennines. Although it is possible to describe what remains, the meaning is inaccessible.[11]

Figure 4   *Barbed and tanged arrowhead: early Bronze Age. Possibly a hunting loss or a ceremonial deposition*

---

[9] D. Shepherd, 'Stand By Your Stone', *Northern Earth*, 2006, 107, pp17-21. A full-length paper can be found on The Megalithic Portal (www.megalithic.co.uk) as 'Standing For What? Standing Stones of the South Pennines'

[10] P. Rodgers, personal communication

[11] Bradley, *The Significance of Monuments* and also C. Tilley, *A Phenomenology of Landscape*, Oxford: Berg, 1994 are useful in considering the defensible extent of conjecture.

A final account of the prehistory of a place is only possible when it is utterly destroyed; that is, when the buildings and vegetation are removed, the soil stripped away and the whole excavated down to undisturbed subsoil. This happens only in large civil engineering projects. In the case of Midgley we can at best gather clues and accumulate evidence that can be compared with features elsewhere in similar situations and contexts. It must be remembered that the land is a palimpsest, that people have continually affected it and continue to do so. For example there are cairns and stones on Midgley Moor with an historic origin; they mark the contentious boundary between Midgley and Wadsworth. Small-scale stone extraction has left holes not unlike prehistoric pit alignments. Management of the moor for shooting, too, has a very real effect with heather burning and regrowth alternately revealing and obscuring potentially important features. Ultimately the prehistory of Midgley involves revisiting and re-reading the landscape.

Figure 5   *Miller's Grave with Robin Hood's Penny Stone on the skyline.*

The vestiges of prehistoric activity in and around the area of the Midgley township contain elements that are both typical and unique within the South Pennines. Similar late Neolithic and early Bronze Age flint assemblages, burials, standing stones, field boundaries, circular features and rock art can be found on other moorland and rough pasture areas between the M62 and the Aire Gap south of Skipton.[12] It seems reasonable to assume that life was lived around Midgley much as it was lived right across the uplands. However, there are monuments in Midgley that have not, so far, been located elsewhere.

These last and most enigmatic features, Robin Hood's Penny Stone, the Miller's Grave, and the rock art, underline perhaps the most significant point about the first people who lived around Midgley. They were physically and intellectually indistinguishable from us, they made sophisticated use of a comparatively restricted technology and set of resources, they lived here successfully for some thousands of years, and yet their conception of reality and their rationalising of existence were quite alien to our own.

The term rock art is used to describe a variety of carvings on stone and well-known examples exist in northern Spain, Ireland, Scotland, the Scandinavian seaboard, Northumberland, the North York Moors and Ilkley Moor.[13] Although figurative and representational forms are known abroad, what might be termed British and Irish rock art is thought to be symbolic and a range of motifs has been described, including rings, spirals, zigzags and cups. The panels of rock art around the summit of High Brown Knoll and across the Luddenden valley at Dean Head consist of hemispherical depressions - cup-marks - hammered and ground into flat areas of bedrock. The reason and purpose for this carving, what it represents and what it signified, are not known.[14] Interestingly the main rock outcrop at Dean Head, which extends across Warley Moor, is Huddersfield White Rock and is devoid of carving. The panels of cup-marks are found only on an outlier of Midgley Grit[15]; this might be an indication of preference for a rock type and further work is being undertaken to seek other examples.

---

12 D. Shepherd, 'Prehistoric Activity in the Central South Pennines', *Transactions of the Halifax Antiquarian Society*, 2003, 12, pp13-38

13 K. Boughey and E. Vickerman, *Prehistoric Rock Art of the West Riding*, Leeds: West Yorkshire Archaeology Service, 2003

14 The best short resume of the welter of theorising around rock art in this country is in P. Brown and G. Chappell, *Prehistoric Rock Art in the North York Moors*, Stroud: Tempus, 2005, Chapter 7: A Search For Meaning

15 See Chapter 2; N. Aitkenhead, *The Pennines and Adjacent Areas*, 4th ed., Nottingham: British Geological Survey, 2002

Figure 6   *Midwinter sunrise over Miller's Grave seen from the Penny Stone. Note that the notch in the top edge of the stone complements the outline of Miller's Grave - out of which the sun appears to rise.*

Figure 7   *The same view as Figure 6, but showing the sun just beginning to catch the small pool in the top of the Penny Stone.*

*Figure 8   General view of one of the cupmarked slabs at Dean Head. Miller's Grave and the
Penny Stone are on the skyline across the valley*

'igure 9   Han Royd earth circle showing as an elliptical form of darker vegetation

In considering the prehistoric monuments above Midgley, it is also necessary to take into account the existence of trade routes crossing the Pennines, linking the navigable rivers to east and west and enabling travel between Ireland, Cumbria, the more populated Aire and Wharfe valleys around Ilkley and Baildon, the important areas of Thornborough and Ferrybridge, regionally significant as meeting places or religious centres[16], and the northern continental coast. The deep valleys, filled with marshes, dense woodland, dangerous animals and spirits would be avoided. One obvious line across the immediate hills would take the level of the Long Causeway, the Heptonstall spur, the flat land of lower Midgley Moor then on to Mount Tabor. A north-south line would include the old, Mesolithic routeways along Blackstone Edge, Great Manshead and on over High Brown Knoll toward Chellow Heights. This is not to imply that the area of Midgley formed a crossroads as

---

[16] T.G. Manby, A. King and B. Vyner, 'The Neolithic and Bronze Ages: a Time of Early Agriculture', in Manby, Moorhouse and Ottaway, *The Archaeology of Yorkshire*, Chapter 6

such, but it seems very likely that many travellers would pass through the area. This is supported by the existence of later trackways and packhorse routes on obviously practical lines of travel that may well have had a prehistoric origin and circumstantially by locations of surviving sites and hoards.

Gazetteer

This is not a complete listing of all the prehistoric features to be found around Midgley. There are two reasons for this. The first is brevity; it seems unnecessary for the present purpose to list, for example, separate references for the dozen or so slabs bearing cup-marks on High Brown Knoll because they are all close together conveniently near the path and the trig point, or to similarly list each of the small cairns in the cairnfield since they are all similar and within a few metres of each other. The second, much more important reason is that most of the moor is blanketed in dense heather which makes fieldwork - or indeed movement - problematic. Some features which were easily visible five years ago after an extensive fire are now very hard to find, and equally there may yet be more features still concealed. A conclusive search of the heaviest areas of growth is still in progress and it is hoped to undertake an intensive survey in the near future. The features are listed geographically, moving west to east over the lower moor and then north, rather than by category since precise ascriptions are difficult in some cases. The grid references[17] and descriptions provided are sufficiently accurate for them to be located and examined. Since no modern excavation has taken place the datings offered are arrived at simply by analogy with similar features in other areas.

---

[17] References were all derived from Garmin Geko 301 Global Positioning System (GPS) readings with EGNOS differentiation, giving 2m accuracy

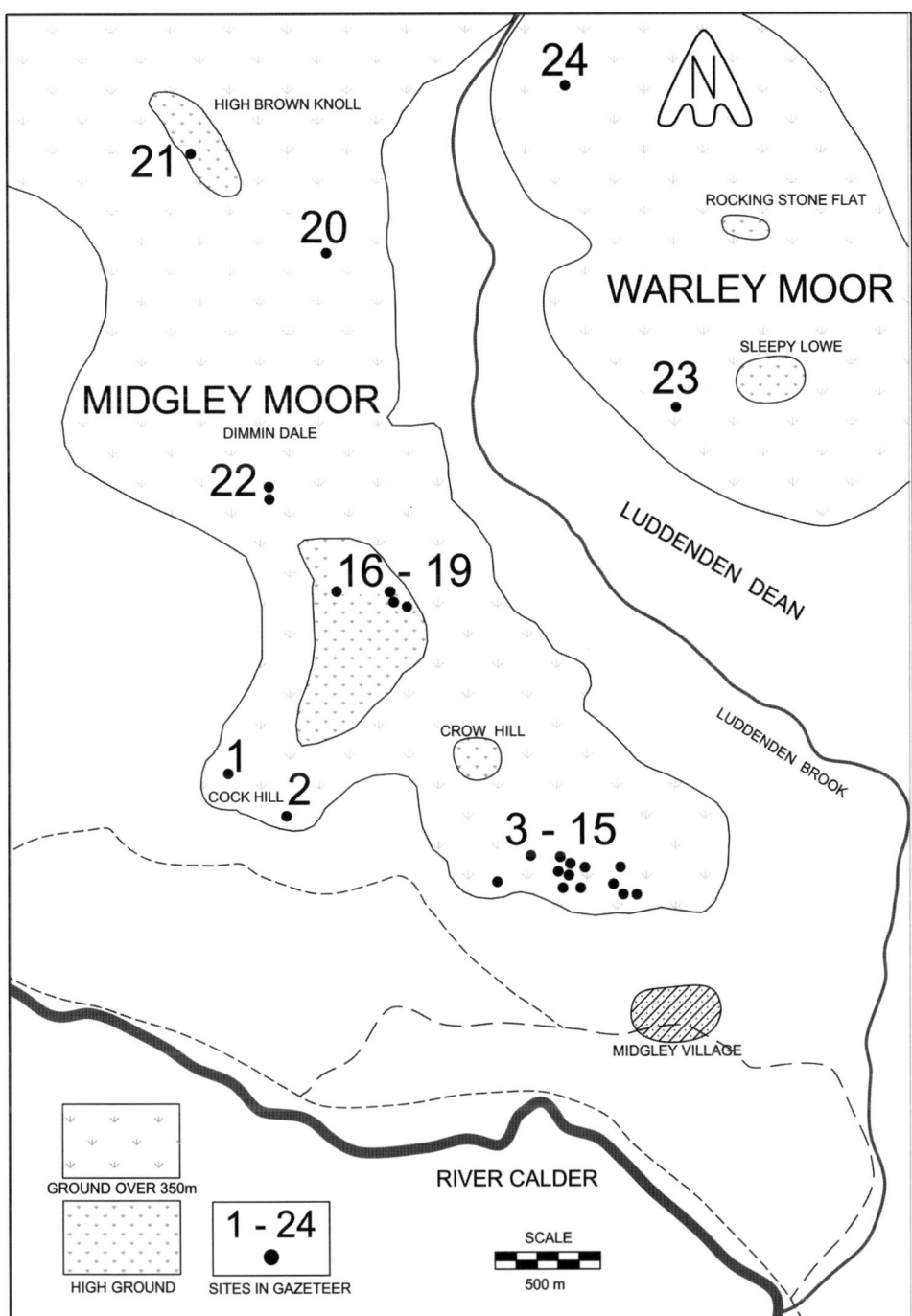

Figure 10   *The general locations of prehistoric sites around Midgley.*
                    Numbers refer to the gazetteer, where the grid references are
                    given

1: Cock Hill earth circle: SE01052.27590

Half of this feature remains above the quarry which first exposed it and the stone and subsoil construction can be seen at the quarry lip. Urns and human remains were apparently revealed at the time of the quarrying.[18] 20m in diameter with a bank 1.5m wide and 30cm high, no sign of a ditch. Bronze Age.

2: Wicken Hill earth circle: SE01336.27390

This is the feature referred to on early Ordnance Survey maps as 'British Camp'. 40m in diameter with a bank 2m wide and 30-40cm high. It appears to be a Bronze Age urnfield enclosed by a roughly circular bank; probing suggests there may have been an internal ditch. Digging in 1897 produced burnt human bone and fragments of prehistoric pottery, and the excavation of a central mound in 1933 turned up half a quern.

3: Han Royd earth circle or ring cairn: SE02341.27082

This is rather an anomalous feature, differing somewhat from the circular forms at Wicken Hill (1) and Cock Hill (2). Again there is a low bank of earth and stones but it is smaller, 14m diameter, 1m wide and 30cm high, and there is a 4m break in the bank on the SE side. A well-defined internal ditch runs continuously around the whole circle. There is a low 1.5m diameter cairn in the middle and the central area may have been levelled. Possibly a modified early Bronze Age feature.[19]

4: robbed cairn: SE02500.27204

This is a large, 15m diameter cairn that has had much of its stone removed in the past through a gap on the W side to leave a 1m high circular bank. A pile of uncarted stone near the middle resembles a cairn.

5: oval cairn: SE02641.27198

The burrowing of rabbits has thrown up the clay, subsoil and small stones of which this cairn seems to be composed. Long axis E-W, 3m long, 1m wide, 35cm high.

---

[18] H. Ling Roth, *The Yorkshire Coiners 1767-1783 and Notes on Old and Prehistoric Halifax*, Halifax: F. King & Sons, 1906. Hebden Bridge Local History Society Archive, *Proposed publications*, n.d, HBLSS14a Chapter 2

[19] The Han Royd feature may well have been altered more recently. 'Cock-fighting as an organised game had ceased by the time I was a boy, (he was born 1886) but it had been practised in Midgley, and I was told of many a gory contest held in the earth rig on Midgley Moor above Coal Dike, used in my time as a breaking-in ring for young horses (many of which I have witnessed).' H. W. Harwood, *Glimpses of Midgley History*, n.d., West Yorkshire Archive Service (Calderdale), MISC 78/54. This may account for the clarity of the internal ditch, and also its continuity. Similar circular ditches exist on Aaron Hill across the valley.

6: large cairns: SE02689.27167 and SE02682.27112

These two features are relatively prominent although completely overgrown with heather and appear to be composed of stones. They are described together since they are so similar and lie only 25m apart. 6 to 8m diameter, 1.5m high.

7: small standing stone: SE02632.27130

An erect slab 60cm high, 30cm long, 20cm thick, just inside thick heather cover that obscures its possible relationship to other features.

8: cairnfield: SE02758.27149

Eight small sub-circular cairns typically 1.5m diameter and 30cm high, composed of subsoil and small stones. Groupings of unenclosed funerary cairns are likely to be Bronze Age.

9: embanked stone circle: SE02654.27053

A circular, stony bank 8m in diameter and 30-40cm high with three stones visible set into the internal face of the bank, blanketed in heather and difficult to distinguish. Possibly late Neolithic. John Barnatt, Archaeologist for the Peak District National Park, felt that it was very similar to features in the gritstone upland of Derbyshire. First noted after fires in 1995.[20]

10: standing stone: SE02738.27053

A low slab adjacent to a yet unexplained line of stones at turf level. 40cm high, 90cm long, 15cm thick.

11: field boundary: SE02892.27071

First located after fires in 1995, (see 9). Noted by John Barnatt during a field visit as possibly Neolithic. Low (30cm) linear arrangement of stones traced for around 12m.

12: cairn: SE02978.27022

1.5m diameter, 40cm high, just above the main break of slope and adjacent to the oval cairn (below), composed of small stones and subsoil.

13: oval cairn: SE02951.27023

Long axis E-W, 2m long, 1m wide, 35cm high, similar position to the cairn above, small stones and subsoil.

14: cairn: SE02925.27150

Set back from the break of slope, more likely to be a clearance cairn (John Barnatt). 2m diameter, 65cm high, overgrown with heather but appears to be composed of stones. Late Neolithic, if associated with the field boundary.

---

[20] J. Billingsley and P. Bennett, 'Recent Fieldwork on Midgley Moor', *Northern Earth*, 1996, 65, pp15-17

15: field boundary: SE02093.28300

Similar to the other linear feature (11) although more extensive, with some 15-20m being visible. There may be a right-angled junction and possibly a gate-space or passage way. Although similar in construction to (11) the right-angled junction may indicate a date in later prehistory.

16: Miller's Grave: SE01912.28369

A circular bank of stones 2m high and 15m across enclosing a large split boulder. Does not fit easily into any category of prehistoric monument. Possibly originally Neolithic.

17: standing stone: SE01849.28391

Low, possibly fallen, block, now 1.8m long and 40-50cm high and wide.

18: Robin Hood's Penny Stone: SE01832.28439

Large, possibly erratic boulder, 2m high, 2.5m long and 1.5m thick.

19: cairn: SE01576.28441

1.5m diameter, 50cm high, composed of stones.

20: Shore End Top SE01534.30025

A fin-like standing stone 2m long, 1m high and 30cm thick, associated with three to five denuded cairns all deep in vegetation or peat. Early Bronze Age.

21: High Brown Knoll: SE00885.30490

Several panels of rock art along the south and west facing edges of the moor-top, comprising varying sizes of cup-mark and some apparently modified natural basins. Rock art is usually taken to be late Neolithic or early Bronze Age.

22: Old Hold Edge: SE01258.28916 and SE01256.28931

Two 1.5m diameter denuded cairns in a recently burned patch.

23: Heights Clough: SE032.293

A multi-period site with small (1m diameter by 30cm high) Bronze Age burial cairns, a wall remnant similar to the other two field boundaries noted (11 and 15), clearance cairns and a bank, possibly Iron Age or Romano-British, enclosing a rectilinear area.

24: Dean Head Stony Edge: SE02677.30807

Several panels of rock art comprising various sizes of cup-mark with some associated scored grooves. Again, probably late Neolithic or early Bronze Age.

Acknowledgements

I am indebted to Frank Jolley for his excellent map, to Brian Howcroft for the photographs of artefacts from his extensive collection, and to John Billingsley for his advice on an earlier draft and the provision of additional information.

CHAPTER 3

Finding the Past

John Billingsley

In this chapter we look at the history of Midgley Moor's sites in terms of their re-incorporation into local knowledge - what we might call the 'rediscovery' of local prehistory.

The 1:25000 Ordnance Survey map tells the visitor little; on it appear two prehistoric sites, an 'earthwork' above Wicken Hill (2) and the Miller's Grave tumulus (16).[1] The former requires some familiarity with archaeological sites to recognise it, and has not, to the author's knowledge, been reused for any purpose, nor appeared in local folklore. Awareness of the Miller's Grave, however, goes back at least to the eighteenth century; it also features prominently in a folk tale that appears to date from the end of that century. According to this legend, a miller who committed suicide was interred in the tumulus, which is how it acquired its name. At that time, on the evidence of the legend, it was seen as a place outside Christianity, implicitly acknowledging its pagan past. Robin Hood's Pennystone (18) is not marked as an archaeological site (though we think it should be acknowledged as a prehistoric landmark), but its name implies that, like the Miller's Grave, it found a place in local folk tradition.

Surprisingly, no Midgley sites feature in Watson's monumental work of 1775, 'The History and Antiquities of the Parish of Halifax', and the first textual reference to a prehistoric site on Midgley Moor concerns the half-vanished earth circle among the quarries above Mount Skip (1). The discovery of this site, as described by Ling Roth (Figure 1), is revealing:[2]

> In May, 1897, a grave was discovered at a quarry above Mount Skip Inn. The first indications were the rolling down of pieces of urns which the delvers called flower pots. Then in digging a hole to fix the leg of a crane, human bones were discovered.

---

[1] The sites referred to in this chapter are referenced to the map and gazetteer in Chapter 2

[2] H. Ling Roth, *The Yorkshire Coiners, 1767-1783, and Notes on Old and Prehistoric Halifax*, Halifax: F King and Sons, 1906, p306

There is no reason why quarrymen should have recognised Bronze Age funerary urns, but neither had they recognised the circular earthwork that they were about to dig into, nor that the 'flowerpots' had any funerary significance at all - until, as work carried on around the broken pottery, the bones were found, and a simple excavation followed. We might then assume that quarrying carried on, as the report goes on to say:

> There were originally three rings formed by means of a circular vallum of earth at Wadsworth Cockhill, but two have been destroyed by quarrying; the third the largest is still there

Crossley Ashworth, a year after the find and excavation, remarked that 'in quarrying two of these rings have been destroyed'. It had been subsequently assumed that the third ring referred to was the Wicken Hill earth circle (2), and that the damaged circle mentioned above had been lost to the quarry. This assumption was perhaps confirmed by Abraham Newell in 1923, when he wrote archaeological notes for a Hebden Bridge Local History Society project that went unpublished; he speaks of 'the two earth circles ... on Wadsworth Moor and one on Midgley moor' (though without more detailed location descriptions - there were no Ordnance Survey grid references then - we cannot be sure of this). It therefore seems that one other circle may have disappeared in the quarrying, but there is ambiguity in Newell about the fate of other sites; speaking to Crossley Ashworth, 'he tells us of the ashes of burnt wood being still there'.[3] This ambiguity took the author to Cock Hill in 2004, where, searching the tops of the existing quarries, he found a semi-circular bank abutting on to a deep quarry, and fitting the description of the disturbed burial site. In other words, when the burial was discovered, quarrying at that place was halted. Why? Was it archaeological or sentimental sensitivity? Pressure from local antiquarians? Economic reasons? Or was it a superstitious response to disturbing the dead?[4]

Interest in prehistory was proceeding in other ways, however. Flint-hunting was a nineteenth-century pursuit. Given impetus by both antiquarian interests and the practical need for gunflints, the practice has extended, albeit rather diminished, to the present day. It was a common practice for people such as

---

[3] Hebden Bridge Local History Society Archive, *Proposed publications*, n.d, HBLSS14a Chapter 2

[4] A number of pot sherds, and also charred wood, were found from this site, and whether they still even exist is unknown. Newell mentions a 'little more than half of a primitive red earthenware urn' that was found by Thomas Greenwood of Shawcroft Hill and passed on to Bankfield Museum; this may have been among the local council's prehistory collection that was made over in its entirety to the Tolson Museum, Huddersfield. (See Ling Roth, p306, and HBLHS archive notes in previous reference).

reservoir keepers, gamekeepers, naturalists and walkers to scour erosion patches on the moors in search of both flint implements and waste material. There are several very important collections now stored in local museums, and much more material in private hands, some of which is probably lost to the archaeological community. Brian Howcroft knew some of the flint-hunters, having met them as old men, and he has himself spent some thirty years building up an impressive assemblage of Mesolithic, Neolithic and Bronze Age material from the South Pennine uplands. During the early 1970s he field-walked High Brown Knoll and the surrounding area and photographs of his finds are included in Chapter 2, Figures 1 to 4. Other finds from this period include a Mesolithic scatter from an area just north of High Brown Knoll and a tentative report from the early twentieth century of a Paleolithic blade found somewhere on Midgley Moor.

However, no actual sites appear to have been described in the literature until 1979, when the author was walking across Midgley Moor above Han Royd in the face of a hailstorm. Walking with my head down out of the hail, I came across what seemed to be a sunken track, and followed it thankfully. When I realised I was being led around in an arc, I looked up and recognised it to be the ditch of another earth circle (3).

A surprise was that it was not on Ordnance Survey maps or the Sites and Monuments Record at the time, though being an obvious and visible feature; the reason for both its visibility and perhaps its omission as an archaeological site might well be that it appears to have been re-used for more recent purposes, including cock-fighting and horse training, as noted in Chapter 2 - this would account for the clarity of the internal ditch, and also its survival.

So here, at the Cock Hill quarry and the Han Royd earth circle, are two examples where later land use has contributed to the knowledge of Midgley Moor's prehistory; the first directly, the second indirectly. The sites themselves may have even affected that land use, in the first case by possibly influencing the quarrying activity, in the second by providing a ready-made venue. The last point might also be made of the Miller's Grave, if indeed the legendary reburial of the suicide victim really took place.

The same element of land use can be seen in the rediscovery in 1995 of the main area of Midgley Moor's archaeology so far identified; the cluster of sites to the SE of Crow Hill.[5] These latest sites were only located because of heather burning, a practice designed to renew heather growth for the purposes of grouse management, and because of field walking, which can reveal to the enquiring eye not only archaeological remains but other sites of antiquarian interest.[6] The importance of field walking in locating lost traces of the past cannot be sufficiently emphasised, and it is something which is not restricted to specialists. What is needed is a basic familiarity with archaeological traces and an eye to recognise minor features in the landscape. It is this mixture that has led Brian Howcroft to build up his collection of flints. External factors like low-angled light, seasonal variation in vegetation and grazing can help when surveys are being made. In moorland areas particular and timely attention should be paid to burnt areas; subsequent regrowth can hide sites once more, as has already happened with much of the area of the 1995 finds.

The internet is also opening up new possibilities for preliminary research. One potential resource is aerial photography, although Google Earth is less useful than it might be because it provides vertical rather than oblique views. Aerial views in general, however, offer a different perspective to the inevitably 'horizontal' one encountered in walking, and certain features can stand out as worthy of further investigation on the ground.

In recent years, we have come across other sites on Midgley Moor, which are listed in the previous chapter, as well as other possible archaeological remains both here and elsewhere, and have been working with archaeological and historical agencies to establish an empirical record.[7]

Yet we are aware that recording the basic facts of sites leaves a gap of interpretation, and that most people want interpretation with their evidence. We are ourselves not immune, of course, from the same preference. This is especially true in a climate where archaeology has become extremely popular. There are many reasons for today's enthusiasm for archaeology, which ranges from the alternative archaeology movement that emerged in the 1970s, that shows how non-specialists can have a role to play in the understanding of Britain's past, to mainstream TV programmes like 'Time Team', that put non-specialists in their proper place in the friendliest manner possible.

---

[5] See J. Billingsley and P. Bennett, 'Recent Fieldwork on Midgley Moor', *Northern Earth*, 1996, 65, pp15-17

[6] D. Shepherd, 'The Neo-Antiquarian Prospect', *Northern Earth*, 2004, 100, pp20-22

[7] D. Shepherd, 'Prehistoric Activity in the Central South Pennines', *Transactions of the Halifax Antiquarian Society*, 2003, 12, pp13-38

Both ends of the spectrum attempt interpretation, and they are both influenced by what they know and what they feel - just like the reburiers of the tragic miller, or the quarrymen. One of the finders of the Crow Hill cluster was later to write of one of the large cairns (4) that it was 'probably the burial place of a shaman-king figure', although there is no excavation or other evidence that could substantiate this assertion.[8] However, it is clear that such a leap of faith reflects contemporary predilections tending to read shamanism into a wide range of sites and practices,[9] and while such associations may not be incorrect, they are hard to justify without evidence.

Equally, there appears to be no firm indication of a deliberate practice of ley-line style site alignment at any stage of the upper Calder valley's prehistory; though several claims of leys have been made, they do not rest on the archaeological and historical evidence as required by the pioneer of alignment research, Alfred Watkins.[10] However, there may be other alignments - one possible astronomical alignment has been identified on Midgley Moor to date, and has been discussed in Chapter 2. In addition, there are orientational alignments in cases of enclosure entrances and predominant views.

Whatever our opinion of any hypothesis or suggestion, academic or otherwise, we should be careful not to accept or discount it without assessing the evidence put forward. There are many possible interpretations and many possible uses of any site or archaeological landscape, and they are not always exclusive, especially when separated by a gulf of many centuries. Historical sites are always simultaneously historical and contemporary, loaded with assumptions and preferences, and it can be hard to steer a way between competing narratives, and even harder to bear in mind that there is no single definitive story of prehistory. Where prehistory is concerned, none can claim a final word, nor assume intellectual ownership; and there is always further evidence to be found, by whoever happens to be in the right place at the right time. We look forward to future discoveries in the Upper Calder valley that will help shed further light on the ancient past of our area.[11]

---

[8] P. Bennett, *The Old Stones of Elmet,* Milverton: Capall Bann, 2004, p93

[9] Some of the sites on the moor have been used in recent decades for contemporary neo-pagan rituals, further demonstrating issues of interpretation and contemporary relevance.

[10] A. Watkins, *The Old Straight Track,* London: Sphere, 1974

[11] The Hebden Bridge Local History Society has a sub-group specifically concerned with prehistory, and would welcome information relating to local prehistory.

Figure 1   *Ling Roth, curator of the Bankfield Museum in the early twentieth century*

CHAPTER 4

Medieval Settlement

Nigel Smith

Midgley township today contains a mix of clustered and scattered settlements. The village itself is a clustered, or nucleated, settlement that lies on one of the terraces that characterise the sides of the Upper Calder valley. Scattered, or dispersed, settlement has spread along this terrace to the township boundaries on either side, being particularly extensive along the slope above Luddenden Dean. Larger nucleated settlements at Mytholmroyd, Luddenden and Luddenden Foot are located on the valley floors. This chapter will examine the available evidence for the development of this settlement pattern, focusing on the medieval period.

As with other Calderdale settlements, the first record we have of Midgley's existence is in the Domesday survey of 1086. Listed as Micleie, it was one of nine berewicks of the Manor of Wakefield.[1] A berewick was a dependent settlement of a manor[2] and is defined by the Oxford English Dictionary as a demesne farm. Demesne means held directly by the Lord of the Manor but it is thought that by at least 1186 it had become a sub-manor held by an undertenant, Adam de Birkin.[3]

Indications of the growth of Midgley in the early medieval period can only be gleaned from Domesday and early taxation assessments. The population information in Domesday has limitations because it was not primarily a census of people, but rather a record of land tenure and land values. However, it identifies the landholders of the West Riding in 1086, together with certain other miscellaneous persons, as being 3,190 in number, of which the Manor of

---

[1] A. Williams and G.H. Martin (eds), *Domesday Book: a complete translation*, London: Penguin, 1992, pp788-789. For a facsimile of the original text and a literal translation see C. Spencer, *The History of Hebden Bridge*, Hebden Bridge: Hebden Bridge Literary and Scientific Society, 1991, pp1-2

[2] D. Hey (ed), *The Oxford Companion to Local and Family History*, Oxford: Oxford University Press, 1996, p39

[3] M.L. Faull and S.A. Moorhouse (eds), *West Yorkshire: an Archaeological Survey to A.D. 1500*, Wakefield: West Yorkshire Metropolitan County Council, 1981, p455 and map 22

Wakefield only had thirty (including three priests).[4] Maxwell has shown that this equates to 0.3 recorded population per square mile in the Calderdale area compared with a maximum density of 4.8 per square mile further east.[5] He suggests a multiplication factor of four or five in order to approximate dependants. This gives the total population of land-holding families for the Manor as being only around 120 to 150 people.[6] However, this provides no record of the servile class who owned no land and who probably formed the bulk of the population.

The earliest surviving tax returns for the area are those for the Lay Subsidy of 1332-33, so called because the Church was taxed separately. Only the relatively well off were taxed and there were five taxpayers in Midgley paying a total of 8s, with very similar numbers of taxpayers and amounts paid elsewhere in the Calder Valley. The tax system changed in 1334 to one based on township quotas and Midgley then paid 13s. The levels for the rest of the Calder Valley townships ranged from a mere 11s for Halifax and Heptonstall combined, to 16s in Wadsworth. However, these are very small amounts compared to Ripon and Wakefield who paid £6 or more.[7]

In 1377, a poll tax was assessed at a flat rate on everyone over the age of fourteen who was not a mendicant (pauper).[8] Unfortunately, only the receipts survive but these record that in Midgley forty-nine taxpayers paid 16s 4d.[9] However, the detailed roll exists for another poll tax in 1379 in which twenty-one taxpayers paid 7s 4d.[10] The tax was now graduated according to means and payable by everyone above the age of sixteen who was not a pauper.

---

[4] H.C. Darby and I.S. Maxwell (eds), *Domesday Geography of Northern England,* Cambridge: Cambridge University Press, 1962, p37

[5] Darby and Maxwell (eds), *Domesday Geography of Northern England,* p38 Fig 11

[6] Darby and Maxwell (eds), *Domesday Geography of Northern England,* p36. See P. Laslett and R. Wall (eds), *Household and family in past time,* Cambridge: Cambridge University Press, 1972 for a discussion of the problems in determining mean household size using multipliers. For the period since the late sixteenth century, Laslett's research shows a fairly constant size of 4.75 persons per household but he cautions against assuming that this can be used for the Middle Ages; see pp48 and 126.

[7] B. Jennings, *Pennine Valley: a History of Upper Calderdale,* Otley: Smith Settle, 1992, p42, National Archives E179/206/47 and E179/206/17

[8] C.C. Fenwick (ed.), *The Poll Taxes of 1377, 1379 and 1381,* Oxford: Oxford University Press, 1998. Part 1: Bedfordshire Lincolnshire. Records of Social and Economic History, New Series 27, p xiv; National Archives E179/206/44/31

[9] C.C. Fenwick (ed.), *The Poll Taxes of 1377, 1379 and 1381,* Oxford: Oxford University Press, 2005. Part 3: Wiltshire-Yorkshire. Records of Social and Economic History, New Series 37 p262

[10] J. Lister and J.H. Ogden, *Poll Tax (Lay Subsidy) 2 Richard II (1379): Parish of Halifax, in the Wapontake of Morley,* Halifax: Halifax Antiquarian Society Record Series, n.d., vol 1, p15; National Archives E179/206/49

Unlike the 1377 assessment, married women were not taxed, although in the West Riding they were usually listed against a husband's name. It is thought that the 1377 lists were therefore used to levy the 1379 tax.[11] Sixteen couples are listed and five single persons. Based on the size of families in the 1801 Census, Lister assumed that each family had three children under sixteen years of age. He therefore calculated that the total population for Midgley in 1379 was eighty-six, comprising the sixteen named couples, forty-eight assumed children under sixteen, five named single persons and one assumed mendicant.[12]

By 1524, a different tax system applied with liability starting on annual income from land of £1, or on moveable goods worth £2 or more. Fifteen taxpayers in Midgley were assessed under these thresholds.[13] In 1545 the minimum liability threshold for both goods and land was reduced to £1. The tax was collected in three unequal instalments over three years, but Henry VIII asked for an early collection of the third payment in June 1545 for those assessed at more than £10 in goods or £5 in income from land. The final assessment for those less wealthy took place in October of that year. The number of Midgley taxpayers in both groups rose to forty, paying a total of 75s in the third instalment.[14]

Although these figures are not directly comparable, we can at least be certain that the minimum population in 1332-33 was five taxpayers and their families, perhaps twenty-five people. If Lister's assumptions are correct, this had increased to eighty-six by 1377. Based on the taxation records and other documents, Jennings estimates that taxpayers in 1545 were about 46 per cent of the number of households, which would therefore have totalled eighty-seven. On the basis that the dual economy households would have been 'a little larger', he uses a multiplier of five to estimate the total population.[15] This provides an estimate of 435 inhabitants for Midgley in 1545.

---

[11] Fenwick, *The Poll Taxes of 1377, 1379 and 1381*, Part 1: Bedfordshire-Lincolnshire, p xiv and p255-256

[12] Lister and Ogden, *Poll Tax (Lay Subsidy) 2 Richard II (1379): Parish of Halifax, in the Wapontake of Morley*, p40

[13] J. J. Cartwright (ed.), 'A Subsidy Roll for the Wapentake of Agbrigg and Morley of the 15th Henry VIII', *Yorkshire Archaeological Journal*, 1873, 2, pp43-60. The original documents are in the National Archives at E179/207/130 and a summary explanation is available on the E179 database accessible via the National Archives website

[14] 'Lay Subsidies, co. York, West Riding, Wapentakes of Aggbrigg and Morley, Anno 1545', *Publications of the Thoresby Society*, 1899, 9, pp311-16; 1904, 11, pp101-129, 333-368. The original documents are in the National Archives at E179/207/186 and a summary explanation is available on the E179 database accessible via the National Archives website. See also B. Jennings, *Pennine Valley: a History of Upper Calderdale*, Otley: Smith Settle, 1992, pp48-49

[15] Jennings, *Pennine Valley: a History of Upper Calderdale*, p48

However, research in the parish registers suggests that that this may be an overestimate. Based on the numbers of Midgley baptisms and assuming that there were 30 births per 1,000 of the population in each year, the average population was 344 in the decade between 1547 and 1556.[16] If we take Jennings' figure of eighty-seven households for 1545 and use a multiplier of four instead of five the result of 348 provides a close corroboration of the baptism estimate.[17] During the next two centuries the population increased rapidly. According to Crabtree, the Easter books of the Vicar of Halifax in 1764 record that there were 217 families in Midgley, which gives an estimated population of 1,031 using a multiplier of 4.75.[18] By 1801 the population had increased to 1,209 inhabitants according to the census of that year.[19]

How did settled sites develop to accommodate this increasing population?[20] Documentary evidence of properties in Midgley reveals that Gate House existed as an occupied site in 1392.[21] Oats Royd is first documented in 1452[22] while Ewood and Brearley are first mentioned in the 1470s, although they may well have existed prior to that. However, a survey in 1309 of part of the Manor of Wakefield shows that Saltonstall on the Warley side of Luddenden Dean was in existence then as a demesne cattle farm or vaccary.[23] Indeed, it would seem that settlement had already spread up Luddenden Dean as far as Upper Heys on the Warley side by 1308. In that year William de Sounderland paid '3s. 4d. for 9 acres of land in Saltonstall near the Overheyng', a reference interpreted by Jennings to be Upper Heys.[24] Although on the Midgley side of the valley the earliest documented occupation date we have is Arrowbutt Lee

---

[16] I am indebted to Ian Bailey for the analysis of the data researched by Mary Browne and Janet Speak. See Chapter 6

[17] It should be borne in mind that Laslett based his finding of an average multiplier of 4.75 on data between 1574 and 1821. See footnote 6 above. This reminds us that any multiplier used is only an estimate.

[18] J. Crabtree, *A Concise History of the Parish and Vicarage of Halifax*, Halifax: Hartley and Walker, 1836, p311-312

[19] Crabtree, *A Concise History of the Parish and Vicarage of Halifax*, p313. The original documents can be found in *1801 Census: Abstracts of the Answers and Returns: Enumeration. Part I England and Wales*, British Parliamentary Papers 1801, VI (140), 813

[20] See the O.S. map of 1851 at the end of the book for the location of the various settlements mentioned

[21] H.W. Harwood, 'Booth Farm and the Midgleys', *Transactions of the Halifax Antiquarian Society*, 1964, pp17-29 at p19

[22] T. Sutcliffe, 'Oats Royd in Midgley', *Transactions of the Halifax Antiquarian Society*, 1920, pp63-82 at p64

[23] J. Lister, *The Extent (or Survey) of the Graveships of Rastrick, Hipperholme and Sowerby, 1309*, Halifax: Halifax Antiquarian Society Record Series vol 2, 1914, p31

[24] W.P. Baildon (ed.), *Court Rolls of the Manor of Wakefield* vol 2, 1297 to 1309, Leeds: Yorkshire Archaeological Society Record Series, 1906, vol 36, p176; Jennings, *Pennine Valley: a History of Upper Calderdale*, p32

in 1526,[25] it seems reasonable to assume that settlement had extended as far as Castle Carr by around 1300 at the latest, based on the Warley evidence. Further documentary evidence shows Hawksclough being occupied in 1541.[26]

Many of the houses surrounding the village have a first documented date in the sixteenth century. For example Dean House in 1526,[27] New Heath Head in 1541,[28] Ellen Royd and Mill Field End in 1555.[29] On the western side of the village, Hanroyd existed in 1506.[30] Further down the slope towards the valley bottom, Upper White Lee is recorded in 1548[31] while Broadfold in Luddenden Dean is 1587[32] and Booth is 1614.[33]

Bearing in mind that the first dates of occupation were almost certainly earlier than the dates recorded in surviving documents, it seems likely that by around 1300 settlement on both the Warley and Midgley sides of Luddenden Dean had already reached the limits that we see today. Certainly, by the end of the sixteenth century there is no doubt that habitation in the township had spread to its present extent. By the end of the seventeenth century, nearly all of the individual settlement sites that we see today were occupied.[34] Indeed examination of the Manor Map of 1806[35] shows surprisingly little additional settlement had occurred during the eighteenth century (Figure 1). The map marks individual settlements and shows that 200 years ago Midgley village only contained twenty places of habitation along Towngate. Comparing the 1806 map with the modern Ordnance Survey map, nearly all the additional settlement since 1806 has occurred in the valley floor settlements of Mytholmroyd, Luddenden Foot and Luddenden as well as Midgley village itself.

---

[25] G. Dent, 'Ewood in Midgley', *Transactions of the Halifax Antiquarian Society*, 1939, pp7-70 at p12

[26] Harwood, 'Booth Farm and the Midgleys', p19

[27] Dent, 'Ewood in Midgley', p12

[28] Harwood, 'Booth Farm and the Midgleys', p19

[29] T. Sutcliffe, 'A Tour in Midgley', *Transactions of the Halifax Antiquarian Society*, 1928, pp113-157 at pp117-118

[30] Sutcliffe, 'Oats Royd in Midgley', p67

[31] I. Bailey and A. Petford (eds), *Midgley Probate Records 1531-1731*, Midgley: Midgley Books, 2007, p7. The original wills are held at the Borthwick Institute of Historical Research, University of York.

[32] Harwood, 'Booth Farm and the Midgleys', p19

[33] Harwood, 'Booth Farm and the Midgleys', p20

[34] See the table of Midgley settlement dates at the end of the chapter

[35] West Yorkshire Archive Service (Calderdale), Manor of Midgley Records 1764-1897, *Plan of the manor*, 1806, Misc:329/2

Having explored how settlement spread within the township of Midgley, it is time to consider some of the reasons behind this settlement pattern. The Domesday records of landholders in the Manor of Wakefield comprised four villeins, seven sokemen and sixteen bordars.[36] A villein held his land by providing agricultural services, whereas a bordar was a smallholder who cleared and farmed land on the edge of settlements. A sokeman was a free peasant tenant who paid customary dues to the lord of the manor.[37] As we have already seen, these figures do not represent the whole population and their interest here lies in the proportions of different types of land tenure. The ratios of 'tenant types are 1 villein: 1.75 sokemen: 4 bordars and these can be contrasted with the ratios for the whole of the West Riding of 6.14 villeins: 1 sokeman: 3.71 bordars.[38] The small number of villeins and the greater proportion of bordars in the Wakefield population profile is significant because it implies that creation of individual land holdings through clearance from moor and forest was a more common activity than elsewhere in the Riding.

This clearance is a process known as assarting. Whilst no records exist for assarting in Midgley, there is plentiful evidence in the adjacent townships of Warley and Sowerby, which together with Erringden and Soyland formed the Graveship of Sowerby. Unlike Midgley, the Graveship was land held directly by the Lord of the Manor and the Manor Court Rolls are full of references to payments for permission to assart. Between 1274 and 1329 the rolls show that 585 acres were assarted of which 237 acres were recultivations of previously abandoned land.[39] The abandoned land was taken into cultivation first, largely between 1274 and 1298, as this would have been easier land to clear. The reasons for abandonment and subsequent recultivation can only be guessed at, but Stinson points out that, in marginal land areas, land will tend to go in and out of use depending on pressure on available resources.[40] The assarting process typically results in small irregularly-shaped fields which can sometimes still be seen in the landscape.[41]

---

[36] A. Williams and G.H. Martin (eds), *Domesday Book: a complete translation*, London: Penguin, 1992, p789

[37] Hey, *The Oxford Companion to Local and Family History*

[38] Darby and Maxwell, *Domesday Geography of Northern England*, p37

[39] M. Stinson, 'Assarting and Poverty in Early-Fourteenth-Century Western Yorkshire', *Landscape History*, 1983, 5, pp53-67 at p54 Table 1

[40] Stinson, 'Assarting and Poverty in Early-Fourteenth-Century Western Yorkshire', p57

[41] C. Taylor, *Fields in the English Landscape*, London: J M Dent, 1975, pp95-96, 99-100 and Figure 13

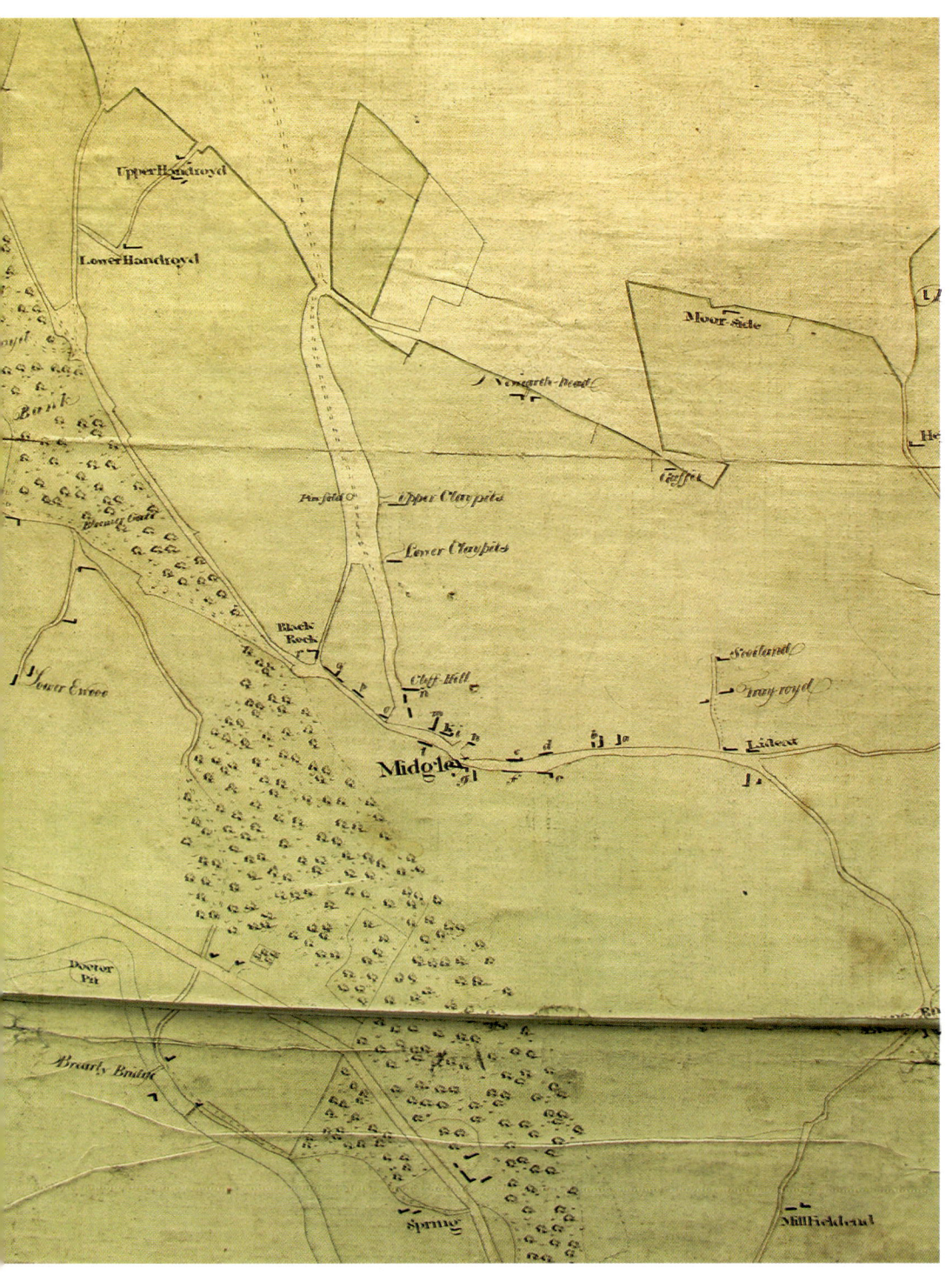

Figure 1   *A section of the Manor Map of Midgley, 1806*

It seems reasonable to assume that a similar process would have been happening in the Midgley sub manor, though on a much smaller scale. Some evidence for this is provided by place names. *Royd* is a very common Calder Valley place name element that means a clearing in a wood.[42] On the 1806 Manor map of Midgley there are four names with such elements: 'Handroyd', 'Stony royd', 'Tray royd' and 'Oats royd', all in fairly close proximity to Midgley village. *Leah* is another Old English word element that occurs frequently in Calder Valley place names and can perhaps best be translated as a natural clearing in woodland.[43] Midgley itself means a 'midge-infested clearing or glade'.[44] Midgley Manor Map also has five names with this element: Whitelee, Harabut Lee (later Arrowbut Lee), West But Lee (later Goosenest), Fearnley Lee (Fearney Lee), and Brearley. It is significant that these *leah* names all occur further away from Midgley village than the *royd* names. These place name elements indicate a possible sequence of events initiated by settlement in a clearing that eventually became Midgley village. Initial growth of the settlement was by man-made clearances surrounding the village, with eventual use of more natural clearings beyond. Unfortunately, visible evidence of assarts is not easily identifiable in Midgley, probably because such initial clearances took place in the central portion of the settled area and have been replaced by later field boundaries. There are later place names containing *royd* such as Ellen Royd and Green Royd and an analysis of field names in Midgley in 1866 shows that fourteen of the fields had *royd* names, including Stoney Royd, Little Royd, Great Royd and Hay Royd.[45] Whether *royd* is retaining its original meaning in such names is unclear.

Thirsk points out the impact on colonisation made by the custom of partible inheritance, which would have resulted in the division of the original holding equally between the children. Such subdivision would have created pressure to clear more land as the population grew.[46] That the practice of partible inheritance was customary in Midgley is demonstrated by various wills between 1542 and 1571 where property is frequently divided with one third to the wife and the rest divided equally between the children.[47]

---

[42] A.H. Smith, *English Place-Name Elements: Part 2*, Cambridge, Cambridge University Press, 1956, p86. (English Place-Name Society vol 26)

[43] Smith, *English Place-Name Elements: Part 2*, pp18-19

[44] A.H. Smith, *The Place-Names of the West Riding of Yorkshire: Part 3 Morley Wapentake*, Cambridge: Cambridge University Press, 1961, p132. (English Place-Name Society vol 32)

[45] West Yorkshire Archive Service (Calderdale), *Wadsworth and Midgley Valuations*, 1833, SU: 406

[46] J. Thirsk, 'The Common Fields', *Past and Present*, 1964, 29, pp3-25 at pp13-14

[47] Bailey and Petford, *Midgley Probate Records 1531-1731*, pp5,12,13,14

We can then characterise early settlement in Midgley as a gradual process of expansion from individual clearings. As the land was progressively subdivided, more land was cleared to compensate. Expansion to higher ground in the north was limited by the poorer soils of the moors. Expansion downslope into the valley encroached on valuable woodland and expansion west was limited by steep slopes and the western boundary of the township. There must have been a natural tendency to expand eastwards following the terraced shelf round above Luddenden Dean with the result that probably by around 1300 settlement had already spread as far as it is today. The majority of today's settlement sites were occupied by the end of the seventeenth century. Expansion in later centuries was limited to a small number of these sites whose location and growth was determined largely by mill and factory.

Midgley sites with documentary or building evidence dating to 1700 or earlier.

Date	Site	Source Reference
1392	Gate House	THAS 1964 p19
1452	Oats Royd	THAS 1920 p64
1471	Ewood	THAS 1939 p7
1474	Brearley Lower	THAS 1922 p128
1506	Hanroyd Lower	THAS 1920 p67
1526	Arrowbutt Lee	THAS 1939 p12
1526	Dean House	THAS 1939 p12
1541	Hawksclough	THAS 1964 p19
1541	New Earth Head	THAS 1964 p19
1545	Mytholm	YAS Record Series Vol 2 p119
1548	White Lee Upper	Wills p7
1555	Ellen Royd (alias William Royde; Boggard House)	THAS 1928 p117
1555	Mill Field End (alias Robert Royd)	THAS 1928 p118
1555	High Lee Head	Wills p11
1587	Broadfold	THAS 1964 p19
1587	Scout	Wills p22
1589	Tray Royd	THAS 1939 p214
1599	Great House	THAS 1954 p69
1599	Kershaw House	Saxton Map 1599
1599	Lane House	Saxton Map 1599
1600	Dry Carr	Personal communication
1600	Hoyle House	Personal communication
1601	Cliffe Hill	Building
1604	Acre	THAS 1920 p69
1605	High House	Building

1607 or 1609	White Lee	Building
1610	Stoney Royd	THAS 1964 p21
1611	High Lees Upper	THAS 1939 p257
1614	Booth	THAS 1964 p20
1615	Ferney Lee	THAS 1939 p21
1623	New House	CA:SH4/VL 1623
1627	The Milne (Dean)	THAS 1964 p20
1634	Lord Nelson (Luddenden)	Building
1646	Thorney Lane	THAS 1928 p128
1649	Castle Carr	THAS 1921 p99
1653	Ewood Little	THAS 1939 p31
1654	Greave House	THAS 1928 p151
1655	Hanroyd Upper (alias Hanroyd Green)	THAS 1939 p27
1655	Mill or Milne House	THAS 1939 p33
1659	Upper Foot	THAS 1939 p33
1660	Pepper Hill	THAS 1928 p153
1664	Green House or Calling	THAS 1928 p153
1666	Brownhill	THAS 1914 p266
1666	Buttrice	THAS 1914 p266
1666	Ewood Lower	THAS 1939 p53
1666	Whitehill Bank	THAS 1914 p266
1672	Stocks or Lacey Hey	Building
1673	Bloomer Gate (Wood End)	THAS 1939 p49
1676	Head House	CA:CAC2
1693	High Lees Head	THAS 1939 p257
1693	Scotland	THAS 1939 p242
1706	Height	Personal communication
1706	Stoney Spring	Building

Abbreviations

CA = West Yorkshire Archive Service (Calderdale)

Personal communication = Private papers inspected by David Cant

THAS = Transactions of the Halifax Antiquarian Society

Wills = I. Bailey and A. Petford (eds), *Midgley Probate Records 1531-1731*, Midgley: Midgley Books, 2007

YAS = Yorkshire Archaeological Society

Saxton map = C. Saxton, *Map of the course of the Luddenden brook from Luddenden to Luddenden Foot*, 1599

This table is based on information kindly provided by David Cant

CHAPTER 5

Farming before the Nineteenth Century

Nigel Smith

Landscape history is the interpretation of the landscape that we see today, using both visual and documentary evidence, in order to piece together its evolution. As Richard Muir so aptly describes it, the landscape historian is a detective dealing with many different types of evidence. These evidential pieces are often thin and the historian must, like a police detective, juggle with the probabilities and seek interpretations that seem to fit best.[1] The story presented may well change as new evidence and interpretations are put forward over time.

This particular story is an attempt to explain how land has been used for farming in the township of Midgley over the centuries. The aim is to provide a framework, albeit necessarily tentative, for explaining the form of agriculture practised up to the start of the nineteenth century when the first official records were compiled. Unfortunately Midgley is a township for which relatively little documentation survives prior to 1800. Comparative evidence of other areas must therefore be utilised to help inform the local picture. This evidence may be local, as in the rest of the Calder Valley, regional as in the rest of Yorkshire, topographical as in the northern upland areas, or ultimately national. Midgley cannot be viewed in isolation but must be considered as an individual expression of wider environmental and social influences. Space precludes considering many of the formative factors such as the interplay between textiles and farming and its effect on land use, or the impact of national agricultural crises and revolutions. Instead our focus will be on the key outline themes of the type of agriculture practised by its inhabitants and the techniques used.

Agricultural practice

The mean annual temperature decreases by roughly 6.5°C every 1,000 metres of altitude, so that Midgley is nearly 2°C colder than temperatures at sea level. As the growing season contracts by about one day for every fifteen metres in altitude, Midgley has a shorter growing season by around two weeks than

---

[1] R. Muir, *Landscape Detective: Discovering a Countryside*, Macclesfield: Windgather Press, 2001, p1

areas at sea level. In consequence, not only is the output of upland pastures one third to one fifth lower than lowland pastures but above 245 metres the 'frequency of harvest failure increases exponentially'.[2] While temperature decreases with altitude, rainfall increases. With a mean annual rainfall of around 100cm,[3] Midgley and the rest of the Upper Calder Valley have less sunshine than the lower rainfall areas to the east. The rain results in leaching of nutrients from the soil which in turn increases the acidity of the soil.[4] High acidity reduces the nitrogen available for plants and limits what can be grown.[5]

The soils on the Midgley shelf are typical brown earths which are classified as having moderately or moderately-severe limitations that restrict the choice of crops. These are limited to grass, with cereals as possible alternatives if carefully managed.[6] In the further reaches of Luddenden Dean beyond Castle Carr the soils are stagnopodzols, an acidic infertile soil with severe or very severe limitations whose use is limited to pasture or rough grazing.[7] On the higher ground of Midgley Moor, the soil is poorly drained with a peaty surface and stony subsoil also limited to rough pasture use.[8]

Midgley's climate and soil profile are therefore determining factors in the type of agriculture that can be practised. Not surprisingly, settlement and agriculture is limited to the brown earth areas of the township. The observations above suggest that agricultural capabilities are restricted to pastoral activity with limited crop growing. We must now look at the documentary evidence available to see whether this is supported historically.

In an analysis of Yorkshire inventories for 1678 and 1679, Long showed that in the Industrial West Riding over 42 per cent of the valuation of thirty-three wills was in cattle. This exceeded the valuations of all other items and led him to conclude that 'cattle formed the backbone of the farming of the times'.[9] The next highest value was in corn at 21 per cent while nearly 5 per cent was in

---

[2] D. Grigg, *English Agriculture: an Historical Perspective*, Oxford: Blackwell, 1989, p230

[3] M.L. Faull and S.A. Moorhouse (eds), *West Yorkshire: an Archaeological Survey to A.D. 1500*, Wakefield: West Yorkshire Metropolitan County Council, 1981, Vol 4, Map 2

[4] D.M. Carroll, R. Hartnup and R.A. Jarvis, *Soils of South and West Yorkshire*, Harpenden: Soil Survey of England and Wales, 1979, p36. (Soil Survey Bulletin No.7)

[5] Grigg, *English Agriculture: an Historical Perspective*, p231

[6] Carroll, Hartnup and Jarvis, *Soils of South and West Yorkshire*, pp56-66

[7] Carroll, Hartnup and Jarvis, *Soils of South and West Yorkshire*, pp69-74

[8] Carroll, Hartnup and Jarvis, *Soils of South and West Yorkshire*, pp81-86

[9] W. Harwood Long, 'Regional Farming in Seventeenth-Century Yorkshire', *Agricultural History Review*, 1960, 8(2), pp103-114 at p112

hay. Horses accounted for over 10 per cent while sheep were valued at 9.5 per cent of the total.[10] The numbers of sheep in this area were the lowest of all the Yorkshire regions analysed with an average of 19.3 per farm as opposed to 54.2 per farm in the Dales and 96.3 in the Wolds.[11] In fact, only seventeen out of the thirty-three West Riding farms had sheep at all.[12] The farms without sheep had slightly more cattle, an average of ten per farm as opposed to nine on those with sheep. They also had less oats at eight quarters per farm, in contrast to the twelve quarters on farms with sheep. The implication is that farms with sheep pursued a more mixed form of farming than those without sheep.[13]

Long does not define the area that he calls the Industrial West Riding but clearly it covers lowland areas to the east as well as the Pennine uplands. These figures may therefore hide significant differences in farming between those two topographic areas. Whether the presence of sheep is an indicative factor of lowland or upland farms is unfortunately not clear. However, the Midgley probate records from 1531 to 1587 and from 1691 to 1731 have no mention of sheep at all (Figure 1). Thirteen of the twenty-five inventories between 1691 and 1731 had agricultural goods and only two of those thirteen did not have cattle. More than half (eight) had horses or galloways while three had pigs. No other livestock is mentioned.[14]

Between 1274 and 1297, cattle occur in the Wakefield Court Rolls on forty two separate occasions in Sowerby Graveship, while horses occur twenty-three times and pigs ten times. Sheep are only mentioned three times.[15] Because these mentions in the Rolls are in connection with misdemeanours by the owners of the animals, such as escapes into the lord's land, these figures only give an indication of livestock proportions. But the fact that the rough proportions of cattle to horses to pigs is the same as in the eighteenth century Midgley wills suggests, not only that cattle farming predominated, but that the pattern of livestock farming may have remained fairly constant over the centuries.

---

[10] Long, 'Regional Farming in Seventeenth-Century Yorkshire', p105 Table 1
[11] Long, 'Regional Farming in Seventeenth-Century Yorkshire', p106 Table 2
[12] Long, 'Regional Farming in Seventeenth-Century Yorkshire', p111 Table 5
[13] Long, 'Regional Farming in Seventeenth-Century Yorkshire', p112 Table 6
[14] I. Bailey and A. Petford (eds), *Midgley Probate Records 1531-1731,* Midgley: Midgley Books, 2007. The original wills are held at the Borthwick Institute of Historical Research, University of York.
[15] W.P. Baildon (ed.), *Court Rolls of the Manor of Wakefield* vol 1, 1274 to 1297, Leeds: Yorkshire Archaeological Society Record Series, 1900, vol 29

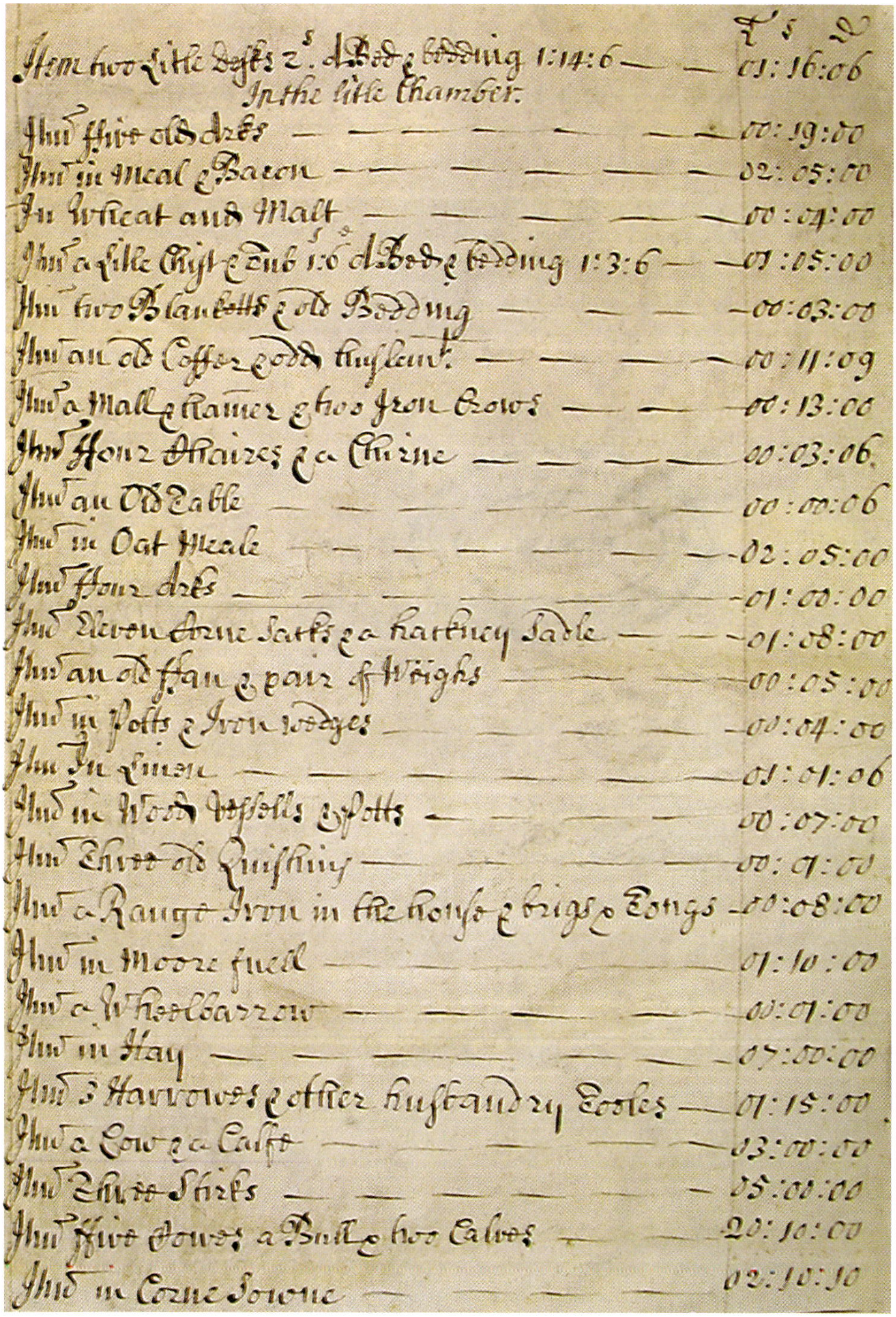

£ s d

Item two little desks 2s & Bed & bedding 1:14:6 — — 01:16:06
In the little Chamber.

Item five old Arks — — — — — — — — 00:19:00
Item in Meal & Bacon — — — — — — — 02:05:00
In Wheat and Malt — — — — — — — 00:04:00
Item a little Chist & tub 1:6 & Bed & bedding 1:3:6 — — 01:05:00
Item two Blanketts & old Bedding — — — — 00:03:00
Item an old Coffer & other husslm. — — — — 00:11:09
Item a Mall & Ramer & two Iron Crows — — — 00:13:00
Item four Chaires & a Chirne — — — — — 00:03:06
Item an Old Table — — — — — — 00:00:06
Item in Oat Meale — — — — — — — 02:05:00
Item four Arks — — — — — — 01:00:00
Item eleven Corne Sacks & a hackney Sadle — — 01:08:00
Item an old ffan & pair of Weighs — — — — 00:05:00
Item in Potts & Iron woodges — — — — — 00:04:00
Item In Linen — — — — — — — 01:01:06
Item in Wood vessells & potts — — — — 00:07:00
Item three old Cuishins — — — — — 00:04:00
Item a Range Iron in the house & briggs & Tongs 00:08:00
Item in Moore fuell — — — — — 01:10:00
Item a Wheelbarrow — — — — — — 00:01:00
Item in Hay — — — — — — — 07:00:00
Item 3 Harrowes & other husbandry Tooles — 01:15:00
Item a Cow & a Calfe — — — — — 03:00:00
Item three Stirks — — — — — — 05:00:00
Item five Cowes a Bull & two Calves — — 20:10:00
Item in Corne Sowne — — — — — 02:10:10

Figure 1   An extract from the inventory of John Turner of Midgley, 1703

There is, however, some further evidence as to the existence of sheep farming. John de Miggeley ought to have received sixteen sheep as part of the chattels of Hugh de Barkeshere in 1274.[16] In 1314, Adam Attetownend de Miggeley, who had been the lord's stockkeeper at the vaccary at Saltonstall, was found guilty of keeping '11 sheep on the lord's hay during the winter' at the vaccary.[17] Kendall quotes a number of instances in wills of the late sixteenth century where sheep are bequeathed. In 1562, Richard Greenwood of Over Baitings bequeathed a cow and forty sheep to Robert Royde; twenty young wethers to two of his servants; and a cow and ten sheep to another. Although Greenwood was clearly a large-scale farmer, smaller farmers also had some sheep. Richard Crabtree of Heptonstall in 1581 desired his son to allow his mother pasture for two cows and twenty sheep.[18] Balancing the evidence it seems reasonable to surmise that livestock farming was largely cattle based, but that a small number of farmers did keep sheep, a practice that may have become less common as time went on.

The nature of arable farming is rather more clear cut, at least at the turn of the eighteenth century. The 1801 crop returns for the parish of Luddenden, which includes Midgley as well as half of Warley, record that 91 per cent of arable land was under oats, 5 per cent under wheat and 4 per cent under potatoes (Figure 2). Very similar figures were supplied by Sowerby with 92 per cent of arable being cultivated for oats. However, further east the lower altitude area of Elland only had 60 per cent in oats with 26 per cent in wheat and 6 per cent in barley. Small amounts of peas, turnips and rye were cultivated in addition to potatoes. Even further east, Rastrick had only 35 per cent devoted to oats, 32 per cent under wheat and 14 per cent under barley. Clearly, while the uplands of the Calder Valley were almost a monoculture of oats, the further east and the lower in altitude one went, the more mixed the arable farming became.[19]

Unfortunately, there is little other earlier evidence as to what crops were being grown in the Calder Valley, but what there is tends to confirm oats as being a monoculture. Between 1274 and 1309 all the references in the Wakefield Court Rolls to named crops are to oats with two references to rye. Across the whole manor, oats were being sold, stolen, damaged by animals, or being taken in

---

[16] Baildon, *Court Rolls of the Manor of Wakefield* vol 1, 1274 to 1297, p94

[17] J. Lister (ed.), *Court Rolls of the Manor of Wakefield* vol 3, 1313 to 1316 and 1286, Leeds: Yorkshire Archaeological Society Record Series, 1917, vol 57, p72

[18] H.P. Kendall, 'Gleanings from Local Elizabethan Wills', *Transactions of the Halifax Antiquarian Society*, 1915, pp113-148 at p126

[19] National Archives, Home Office, *Parish acreage returns*, 1801, HO 67

distress for debts.[20] Long's analysis of probate records in 1688 and 1689 showed that, in the Industrial West Riding, 21 per cent of the valuation per farm was in corn.[21] Frequency distributions provided Long with a 'model' farm for each Yorkshire farming area. The Industrial West Riding model farm without sheep had eight quarters of oats while those with sheep had twelve quarters.[22] No wheat or barley was recorded.

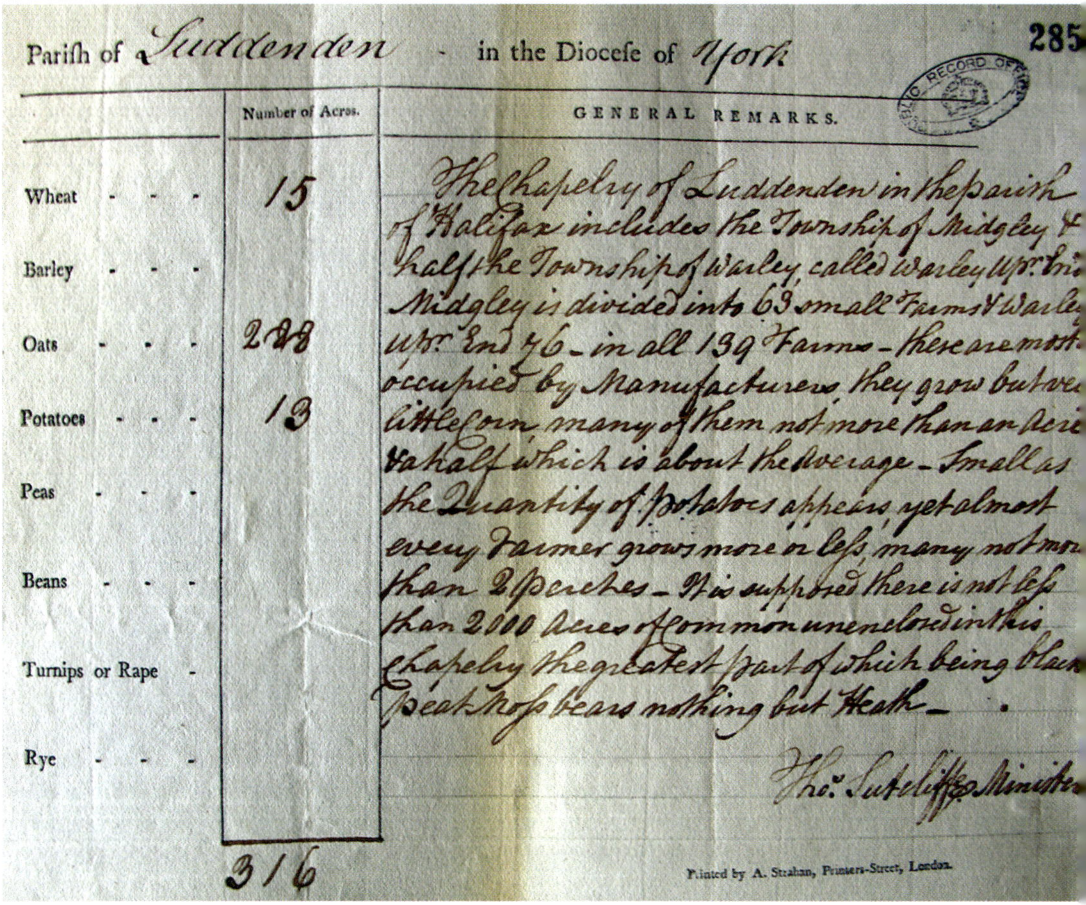

| Parish of *Luddenden* | in the Diocese of *York* | 285 |

	Number of Acres.	GENERAL REMARKS.
Wheat	15	
Barley		
Oats	288	
Potatoes	13	
Peas		
Beans		
Turnips or Rape		
Rye		
	316	

Printed by A. Strahan, Printers-Street, London.

Figure 2   *The Crop Return for Luddenden, 1801*

Unfortunately, the extent of arable land is not well documented. Based on very incomplete records of a survey of Hipperholme made around 1608,

---

[20] Baildon, *Court Rolls of the Manor of Wakefield* vol 1, 1274 to 1297; W.P. Baildon (ed.), *Court Rolls of the Manor of Wakefield* vol 2, 1297 to 1309, Leeds: Yorkshire Archaeological Society Record Series, 1906, vol 36

[21] Long, 'Regional Farming in Seventeenth-Century Yorkshire', p105 Table 1

[22] Long, 'Regional Farming in Seventeenth-Century Yorkshire', p112 Table 6

François suggested that 'the land used for livestock and hay may have amounted to more than twice the amount used to raise corn and other foodstuffs'.[23] By 1801, Thomas Sutcliffe commented in the Midgley agricultural return that:

> Midgley is divided into 63 small farms … these are mostly occupied by manufacturers. They grow but very little corn, many of them not more than an acre & a half which is about the average. Small as the quantity of potatoes appears, yet almost every farmer grows more or less, many not more than 2 perches.[24]

Further research in original documents is continuing and may eventually throw more light on the changing amount of arable land. In the meantime, it seems reasonable to assume that, as income from textiles grew in Midgley over the centuries, less emphasis was placed on arable crops. Indeed, given the climatic and environmental factors mitigating against crop growing, the growth of the dual economy was probably fuelled by the inability of the land to provide more than basic levels of subsistence. As the 1801 Ripponden agricultural return pointed out, 'the keeping of milk cows for family use is preferred to the growing of corn.'

From about 1100 to 1300 there is evidence that temperature averages were about 1.5ºC warmer than today while summer rainfall was around 15 per cent lower than it is today. In these circumstances growing oats would have been more productive than in later centuries. Between 1300 and 1630 the average temperature fell steadily before rising slightly again to present levels.[25] It is suggested therefore that the extent of arable reached its zenith during the medieval warm period or shortly thereafter, gradually declining to the level indicated by Thomas Sutcliffe in 1801. This is reflected in the records for assarting or land clearance, which peaked by the early years of the fourteenth century.[26] As the land grew less productive, so there was more pressure to find alternative sources of income through textiles.

From the available evidence we can provide a tentative model of agricultural practice in Midgley between 1274 and 1801. As elsewhere in the Upper Calder

---

[23] M.E. François, 'The Social and Economic Development of Halifax 1558-1640', *Proceedings of the Leeds Philosophical and Literary Society: Literary and Historical Section*, 1966, 11(8), pp217-280 at p254

[24] National Archives, Home Office, *Parish acreage returns*, 1801, HO 67. See also Figure 2

[25] Faull and Moorhouse, *West Yorkshire: an Archaeological Survey to A.D. 1500*, p48

[26] M. Stinson, 'Assarting and Poverty in Early-Fourteenth-Century Western Yorkshire', *Landscape History*, 1983, 5, pp53-67 at p59. See Chapter 4 for a discussion of assarting

valley, Midgley farming was predominantly pastoral. During the whole period cattle were the principal livestock with probably a small minority of farmers keeping a few sheep. Arable cultivation was overwhelmingly devoted to oats and it seems likely that its greatest extent occurred in the more favourable growing conditions between 1100 and 1300. By 1801, Robert Webster was commenting in the agricultural return for Ripponden that 'the land is chiefly cultivated and most adapted to the production of grass'.[27] We must now turn to examining the techniques used to maintain these forms of agriculture.

Agricultural techniques

We have already seen in Chapter 4 that land was cleared through a process of assarting. Bishop suggests that 'assarts are centred upon and subsidiary to a core of open-field land' and quotes evidence of a land grant of one third of the vill of Sowerby that carried with it 'one third of the assarts apurtenant to the vill'.[28] Locally these open or common fields were called town fields[29] and there is evidence that they existed in 1297 although their origin is likely to have been much earlier.[30] That they existed in Midgley is shown by the will of John Ferrer in 1579 where he bequeathed to his brothers 'all my messuages landes tenements rentes and hereditaments with all and singular their appurtenances scituate lyinge and being within the towne feildes territorie of Midgley'.[31] This reference is particularly interesting as it implies that town fields were considered to be an area surrounding or at least adjacent to the settlement, rather than a discrete parcel of land.

Usage and location of town fields

How might these town fields have been used? Open-field farming has been defined by Thirsk as comprising four essential elements. Both arable and meadow are divided into separate unfenced strips, the occupation of which may be scattered through the field. Secondly, the livestock of the occupiers are pastured on both fallow areas and on areas that have been harvested or mown. Thirdly, there is additional common pasture for grazing outside the field as well as waste that is used for other resources such as peat. Lastly, there

---

[27] National Archives, Home Office, *Parish acreage returns*, 1801, HO 67

[28] T.A.M. Bishop, 'Assarting and the Growth of the Open Fields', *Economic History Review*, 1953, 6(1), pp13-29 at p18

[29] A.R.H. Baker and R.A. Butlin, *Studies of Field Systems in the British Isles*, Cambridge: Cambridge University Press, 1973, p46

[30] Baildon, *Court Rolls of the Manor of Wakefield* vol 2, 1297 to 1309, p18

[31] Bailey and Petford, *Midgley Probate Records 1531-1731*, p20

is some form of regulation of this common agricultural activity, usually by the manorial court.[32] Using comparative evidence from Europe, Thirsk goes on to argue that not all four elements were always universally present and that common fields evolved gradually, varying in their features depending on place and time.

The classic expression of open-field farming is known as the Midland system after the area in which it predominated. In this system the strips were grouped into two or three sectors or fields, one of which was used as fallow grazing land each year. Fox argues that it was the requirements of fallow grazing that underlay this grouping rather than crop rotation.[33] Where available grazing land was limited to that within the field system, as in many places in the Midlands, there would have been a far greater need for control of the animals.[34] Moving animals between scattered bits of fallow in an open field would have been inconvenient and controlling them from breaking into crops growing in other strips difficult. It would have been far easier to control the collected animals of the cultivators in one fallow field.

The same principle of fallow grazing was followed in upland areas but in a rather different way. We have already seen that local environmental factors limited arable options to a virtual monoculture of oats and favoured pastoralism as the predominant form of agricultural activity. The hill farming year was therefore geared to maximising grazing opportunities. Based on research into manor court records from the Central and North Pennines, the Lake District and the Borders, Winchester has identified the simplest form of land management in the hills as the 'head-dyke model'. The head dyke was a permanent physical boundary, such as a bank and ditch, separating the cultivated land from the moorland waste. The farmland, or 'inbye', not only contained the limited arable but also hay meadows to provide winter fodder. It was critical to keep the animals out of the crops and meadows. The year was therefore divided into an 'open' season when animals were allowed within the head dyke, and a 'closed' season when they were excluded.[35]

The closed season started around April when the ground began to be prepared for the crops and grass growth started to increase. Stock were then

[32] J. Thirsk, 'The Common Fields', *Past and Present*, 1964, 29, pp3-25 at p3

[33] H.S.A. Fox, 'Approaches to the Adoption of the Midland System', in T. Rowley, *The Origins of Open-Field Agriculture*, London: Croom Helm, 1981, pp66-67

[34] Fox, 'Approaches to the Adoption of the Midland System', p94

[35] A.J.L. Winchester, *The Harvest of the Hills: Rural Life in Northern England and the Scottish Borders, 1400-1700*, Edinburgh: Edinburgh University Press, 2000, p52

Figure 3   Possible head dyke boundary on Workhouse Lane

pastured on the moors outside the head dyke. After the hay had been gathered in early August, some stock were allowed back inside the head dyke to graze the secondary growth of grass known as 'fog'.[36] The stubble of the oat fields was also available from September and the open season started properly around October. As the weather worsened, cattle were either housed indoors or pastured close to the farm, where grazing could be supplemented with hay. Winter fodder was also supplemented by tree branches, especially holly.[37]

To what extent can this head-dyke model be identified in Midgley? It is suggested that Workhouse Lane running behind New Heath Head is the higher edge of a head dyke, formed here by the bank separating the lower fields from the rougher ground above (Figure 3). The most obvious western boundary is Coal Dike, the clough leading into Chapel Lane, which provides a deep ditch boundary to the fields. A possible eastern boundary is provided by Scotland Lane, the footpath and track running down to Scotland and Tray Royd. Both the 1835 map by Myers and the 1851 Ordnance Survey map show

[36] Winchester, *The Harvest of the Hills: Rural Life in Northern England and the Scottish Borders*, p56. See also Bailey and Petford, *Midgley Probate Records 1531-1731*, p29 where 'fogge' is stored in the barn.
[37] M. Spray, 'Holly as a Fodder in England', *Agricultural History Review*, 1981, 29(2), pp97-110; Winchester, *The Harvest of the Hills: Rural Life in Northern England and the Scottish Borders*, pp56-57

both these eastern and western boundaries as providing stock access routes, or driftways, onto the moors.[38] In the middle of this area, two long narrow strip fields extend almost unbroken down to the west side of Great House (Figure 4). In 1452, the inquisition post mortem (inquest on the extent of an estate) of Robert Ferror of Otesroyd recorded him as owning 'a certain parcel of land in the north field of Miggeley'.[39] It is suggested that the area between Workhouse Lane and Towngate described above is likely to have been this North Field. Locational names were frequently used for town fields. For example a plan of Heptonstall drawn in 1835 shows a group of fields called South Fields as well as South Field Meadow and Long South Field.[40] Another form of locational name is illustrated in a 1750 plan showing the boundaries of Elland town fields and their names as Lowest, Middlemost and Highest Townfields.[41]

igure 4   Possible remains of strip fields above Great House, Midgley

---

[38] See O.S. map of 1851 and Myers' map of 1835 at the end of the book: Winchester, *The Harvest of the Hills: Rural Life in Northern England and the Scottish Borders*, p111

[39] T. Sutcliffe, 'Oats Royd in Midgley', *Transactions of the Halifax Antiquarian Society*, 1920, pp63-82 at p65

[40] West Yorkshire Archive Service (Calderdale), *Heptonstall Township Map*, 1833, MP 15

[41] West Yorkshire Archive Service (Calderdale), *A Plan of Eland with the Townfields and Crofts Adjoining*, 1750, MISC 393

Below Towngate remnants of strip fields can be identified with an access route provided by the stretchergate.[42] This area extends down towards Naylor Lane and is protected on its south western boundary by the escarpment above Brearley Wood which is continued by a curving high wall bank down into Naylor Lane. In 1556, Richard Thomas sold a 'parcel or "doole" of land called Syfdhill, lying in the Mylne Fyelde under Mydgelay'.[43] A 'dole' is defined by the Oxford English Dictionary as a portion of a common field and, according to Moorhouse, it is nearly always found describing the meadows in a common field.[44] A 'mylne' field is a mill field and the location of the present habitation of Mill Field Ends on Naylor Lane lends further credence to the suggestion that the area between here and the village is likely to have been the town field called Mill Field. Myers map of 1835 shows Mill Field Ends as Middle Field Ends.[45] This is likely to have been a mistranscription by Myers as it contradicts the 1556 deed and it is the only extant map showing this form of name. However, the name does make more sense than Mill Field as there is no record of any mill in the vicinity. The existence of a lidgate (as in the place name Lydgate) in the north eastern corner confirms the likelihood of this area being part of the town fields. A lidgate was a gate across a path or lane to prevent cattle wandering on to the arable and meadow areas within the town fields.[46] In addition the township pinfold was located in Coal Dike.[47] The pinfold was an enclosure used to impound stray and trespassing animals, a further integral part of stock control within the head dyke to protect crops and meadows.[48]

The 1851 Ordnance Survey map also shows further access routes onto the moors provided by Far Lane to the west of Han Royd, by Radcliffe Lane leading to High Lees Head, and by Acre Lane.[49] Whether the blocks of land in between these access routes were part of the town fields is not clear. A further possible part of Midgley town fields area can be identified as the flat summit of the promontory between Midgley School and Greave House, part of which is now the Recreation Ground. The D shaped perimeter is entirely bounded by

---

[42] Midgley's stretchergate is the grass lane leading downhill from the bus terminus, which is believed to have been used for stretching warps by the village's handloom weavers

[43] W. Brown (ed.), *Yorkshire Deeds*, Leeds: Yorkshire Archaeological Society Record Series, 1909, vol 39, pp115-116

[44] Faull and Moorhouse, *West Yorkshire: an Archaeological Survey to A.D. 1500*, pp657, 669

[45] See Myers' map of 1835 at the end of the book

[46] Faull and Moorhouse, *West Yorkshire: an Archaeological Survey to A.D. 1500*, p645

[47] West Yorkshire Archive Service (Calderdale), Manor of Midgley Records 1764-1897, *Plan of the manor*, 1806, Misc 329/2

[48] Faull and Moorhouse, *West Yorkshire: an Archaeological Survey to A.D. 1500*, pp725-726

[49] See the O.S. map of 1851 at the end of the book

a wall bank and a field access road runs through the middle of it. It is thought that wall banks were a means of protecting arable fields from the depredations of stock and wild animals.[50] It is possible that this may have been a 'South Field' part of the Midgley town fields (Figure 5).

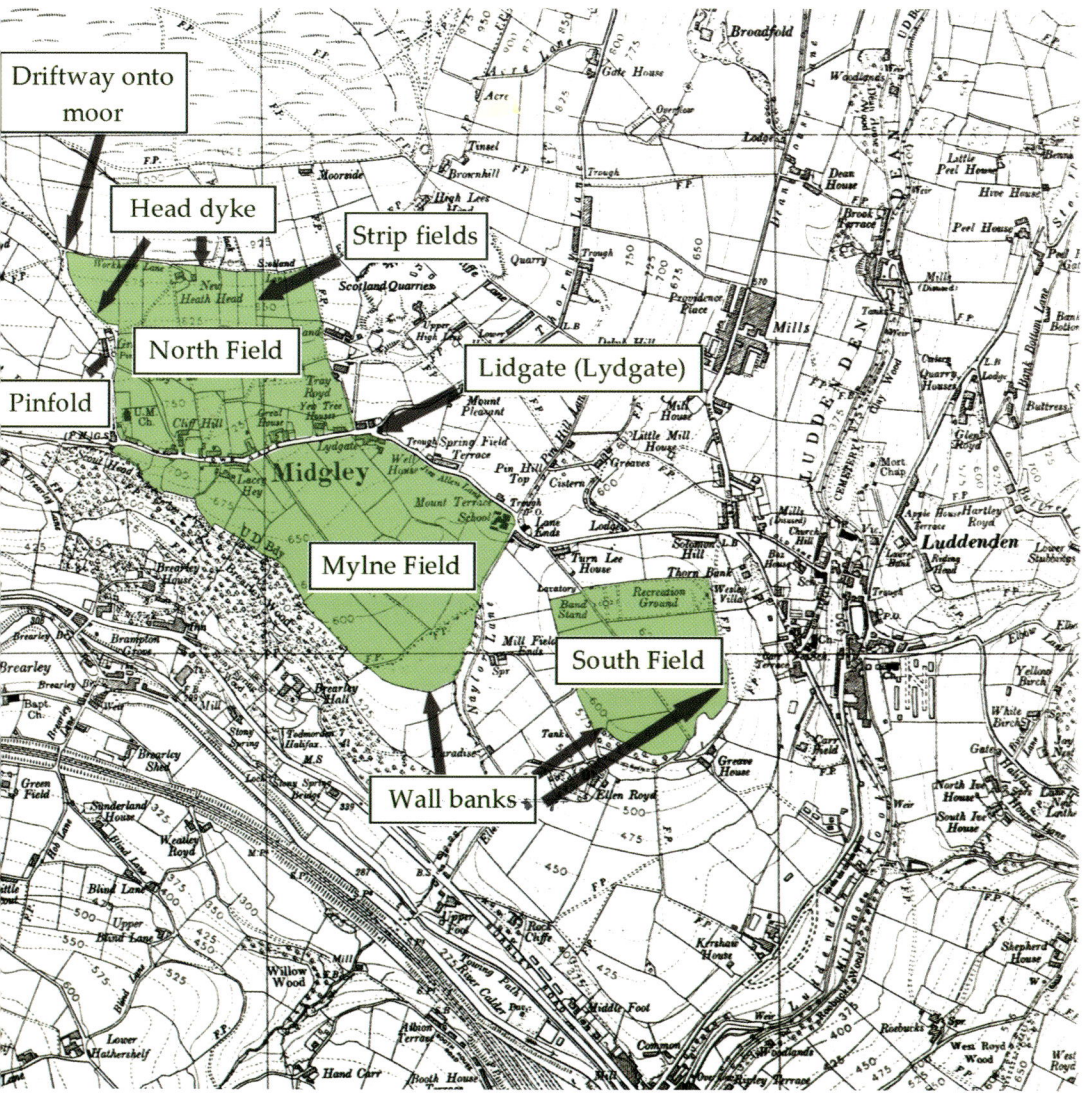

igure 5   Suggested town field areas of Midgley

---

[50] N. Smith, 'Fields and boundaries in the Upper Calder Valley', forthcoming

Turning the soil

The restricted growing season meant that crops were likely to be limited to a single crop of spring sown corn.[51] Termed 'half year lands' by Youd, this meant that the arable was in cultivation for six months and was then available for fallow grazing for the six months between harvest and the next spring sowing.[52] If the hypothesis that such a limited arable regime existed is true, then it is perhaps likely that there would be relatively limited investment in husbandry implements. This is borne out by the Midgley probate records. It is striking that there is only one reference to ploughing in the forty-five wills and inventories that have been transcribed between 1531 and 1731. In his will dated December 1572, William Ferrar of Ewood left his son 'all my ploughe geare, … and all other the thinges belonginge to husbandrye'.[53] It is generally assumed that oxen were typically used as plough beasts so it is also striking that oxen are only mentioned once, in the 1716 inventory of William Shackleton of Mill House who owned two of the beasts.[54] In contrast Kendall mentions two Upper Calder valley wills that contain references to ploughs and oxen. In 1590, Thomas Shackleton of Walshaw left his son his 'wains, ploughs, yokes and all tools as belong to oxen only' while in 1566 John Horsfall of Stoodley bequeathed all his gear belonging to his oxen.[55]

The wills of both William Ferrar and William Shackleton clearly indicate that they were both engaged in farming enterprises that were relatively large for this locality. We can therefore postulate that it was only the large-scale farmers who could justify the investment in ploughs and oxen. Analysis of national data by Langdon suggests that there was a relationship between the size of the holding and the size of the plough team, with only demesne and the largest peasant farms using the classic eight ox team.[56] If this is true, what were the smaller agriculturalists using to cultivate their arable? Langdon's data leads him to surmise that the plough teams used by smallholders with less than fifteen acres, such as many of those in the Calder Valley, may possibly only

---

[51] The Oxford English Dictionary explains that 'As a general term the word includes all the cereals, wheat, rye, barley, oats, …. Locally, the word, when not otherwise qualified, is often understood to denote that kind of cereal which is the leading crop of the district; hence in the greater part of England "corn" = *wheat*, in North Britain and Ireland = *oats*'

[52] G. Youd, 'The Common Fields of Lancashire', *Transactions of the Historical Society of Lancashire and Cheshire*, 1961, 113, pp1-41 at pp21, 33

[53] Bailey and Petford, *Midgley Probate Records 1531-1731*, p16

[54] Bailey and Petford, *Midgley Probate Records 1531-1731*, p53

[55] Kendall, 'Gleanings from Local Elizabethan Wills', p126

[56] J. Langdon, *Horses, Oxen and Technological Innovation: the Use of Draught Animals in English Farming from 1066 to 1500*, Cambridge: Cambridge University Press, 1986, pp234-244

have consisted of two animals.[57] Thirteenth century records indicate that the peasant would plough with whatever animals were available. That horses were used is shown by an entry in the Court Rolls for 1297 in which John de Mora was accused by William the Goldsmith of seizing a 'mare out of his plough' for arrears of rent, it being quite clear from the record that the plough was already yoked.[58] Also in 1297, Matthew de Thohill was fined for harnessing a borrowed heifer to a plough – not because heifers should not be used for ploughing but because the heifer was in calf.[59]

Although this provides a reason for the lack of oxen, it does not explain the scarcity of references to ploughs in the Midgley probate records. However, it has already been suggested that arable cultivation was at its greatest extent by around 1300 and that it slowly declined thereafter. The availability of ploughs would inevitably have followed the same pattern. Furthermore, medieval ploughing practices were usually a communal activity between groups of neighbours, with implements being shared. As the amount of land being used for arable decreased, it is also possible that it no longer made economic sense to plough using traditional methods. By the seventeenth century, a manual process known as 'graving' was clearly being pursued in the Calderdale area. As described by Watson in 1775, graving was 'performed by one man's cutting the ground in a right line, to a certain depth, with a spade contrived for the purpose, and another's pulling the earth over with an instrument called a hack, and so making a furrow'.[60] Crump records finding a graving spade listed in a Bingley inventory in 1638, but they usually seem to be lumped together with other implements under the heading of 'husbandry tools'.[61] It is thought that the narrow lines of ridge and furrow in the fields that can be seen below Oats Royd and above Dean House may be relics of graving (Figure 6).

The number of harrows in the Midgley inventories is just as striking as the absence of ploughs. Nearly half of the thirteen inventories listing agricultural goods had harrows, although only three had both husbandry tools as well as harrows listed.[62] Harrowing is a process of breaking the clods on turned soil, so the lack of ploughs together with the presence of harrows may well indicate

---

[57] Langdon, *Horses, Oxen and Technological Innovation: the Use of Draught Animals in English Farming from 1066 to 1500*, p242

[58] Baildon, *Court Rolls of the Manor of Wakefield* vol 1, 1274 to 1297, p297

[59] Baildon, *Court Rolls of the Manor of Wakefield* vol 2, 1297 to 1309, p7

[60] J. Watson, *The History and Antiquities of the Parish of Halifax in Yorkshire*, London: Lowndes, 1775, p9

[61] W.B. Crump, *The Little Hill Farm*, London: Scrivener Press, [1951], p43

[62] Bailey and Petford, *Midgley Probate Records 1531-1731*

Figure 6   *Ridge and furrow in the field above Dean House. This may be the result of graving*

that graving rather than ploughing was the usual method of turning the soil. Horses are traditionally used as traction for harrows and are recorded locally as being used for harrowing as early as 1297.[63] Horses were owned by eight of the testators with agricultural goods in the Midgley probate records and four of those also had harrows.[64] This probably indicates the multi-purpose use of horses for hauling and carrying as well as harrowing.[65]

Convertible husbandry

The lack of crop rotation suggested by a half-year land system and the relative abundance of pasture meant that there was no need for complex field systems in small upland settlements such as Midgley.[66] Their biggest problem was not

---

[63] Baildon, *Court Rolls of the Manor of Wakefield* vol 1, 1274 to 1297, p274; Langdon, *Horses, Oxen and Technological Innovation: the Use of Draught Animals in English Farming from 1066 to 1500*, p112

[64] Bailey and Petford, *Midgley Probate Records 1531-1731*

[65] Langdon, *Horses, Oxen and Technological Innovation: the Use of Draught Animals in English Farming from 1066 to 1500*, p113

[66] Fox, 'Approaches to the Adoption of the Midland System', pp85, 93

providing sufficient controlled grazing land as in the Midland system, but maintaining the fertility of their relatively poor soils. Youd suggested that the half-year lands were cropped every year, but it has been pointed out that even this was probably too intensive a regime for relatively poor soils and that 'plots were cropped either intermittently or for a period of years before being allowed to revert to pasture.' In other words arable cultivation was not restricted to set areas but was shifting cultivation 'according to rhythms based on differing fertilities.'[67]

Experiments at Rothamsted and at Woburn begun in the nineteenth century showed that if land was continuously cultivated, whether for corn or hay, yields rapidly declined with nitrogen being the first nutrient that became exhausted.[68] Adding nitrogen rapidly increased yields. The medieval farmer had two means of adding nitrogen. The first was to return nitrogen to the soil by adding manure, the second was to increase nitrogen by using nitrogen fixing plants.[69] The relatively random application of manure by animals in the open season was a key factor in helping to maintain soil fertility and doubtless was an originating reason for such a custom. However, a far more consistent method was allowing land to periodically revert to natural pasture which, according to the Rothamsted experiments, increased nitrogen fixation three times more than if the land were arable.[70] According to Clark, medieval yields on arable would have been equivalent to six bushels of wheat per acre whereas an acre of converted (ploughed up) pasture would have produced about seventeen bushels.[71]

Such a system is known as convertible or alternate husbandry. As it takes time for arable land to revert to grass, the timescale of the rotation was measured in periods of years rather than single years. In fact nitrogen is released very slowly at a rate of between 2 and 5 per cent per year[72] thus encouraging long rotations. Elliott points to the variable length of the rotation in the north west, quoting Cumberland evidence of a cultivation period of nine to twelve years

---

[67] E. Miller, 'Farming in Northern England during the Twelfth and Thirteenth Centuries', *Northern History*, 1975, 11, pp1-16 at p10. See also G. Elliott, 'Field systems of Northwest England', in A.R.H. Baker and R.A. Butlin (eds), *Studies of Field Systems in the British Isles*, Cambridge: Cambridge University Press, 1973, pp56-57

[68] J. Broad, 'Alternate Husbandry and Permanent Pasture in the Midlands, 1650-1800', *Agricultural History Review*, 1980, 28(2), pp78-89 at p85; G. Clark, 'The Economics of Exhaustion, the Postan Thesis, and the Agricultural Revolution', *Journal of Economic History*, 1992, 52(1), pp61-84 at p62

[69] Clark, 'The Economics of Exhaustion, the Postan Thesis, and the Agricultural Revolution', p63

[70] Clark, 'The Economics of Exhaustion, the Postan Thesis, and the Agricultural Revolution', p64

[71] Clark, 'The Economics of Exhaustion, the Postan Thesis, and the Agricultural Revolution', p65

[72] Clark, 'The Economics of Exhaustion, the Postan Thesis, and the Agricultural Revolution', pp73-74

followed by seven to nine years in grass as well as Westmorland evidence of four years in cultivation and seven in grass. In Lancashire the cultivation period ranged from three to five years, with five to six years in grass.[73]

There is some limited evidence for the use of convertible husbandry in the Calder Valley. One of the earliest pieces of evidence for such changes between pasture and arable is provided by an entry in the Wakefield Court Rolls for 1332 where 'six tenants of Saltonstall gave the lord 40d fine for licence to take 18 acres of arable land inside their hedge at Saltonstall'.[74] It would seem that this was the same hedge that in 1309 was recorded as surrounding the meadow and pasture areas of the cattle farm or vaccary.[75] Further confirmation of this theory of land being used for a dual purpose is provided by a 1608 survey for the graveship of Sowerby described by Franççois. She notes that the survey rarely distinguishes between pasture and arable. On the grounds that, where there was a distinction, pasture was the land type identified, she comments that 'this may indicate that most of the land was thought of as having a dual purpose.'[76] Of the classified land 73 per cent was pasture and arable land, 12 per cent was meadow, 3 per cent was pasture and 12 per cent was 'untilled but enclosed'. Youd found evidence that 'in some common fields in this district [upland Lancashire], a form of convertible husbandry was practised, the fields being used for grazing and for arable in turn.'[77] Sheppard notes that a variant of the normal rotation system in parts of Yorkshire was 'the devotion of parts of each field to grass leys lasting several years, whilst adjacent land was being cropped'.[78] Crump confirms that newly turned land in the Calder valley would be sown to oats but that 'it was usually turned down to meadow, though it might be kept under oats or other crops for a few years.'[79]

Control of grazing

The long rotations between pasture and arable demanded by convertible husbandry would have encouraged the development of permanent

---

[73] Elliott, 'Field systems of Northwest England', pp63-64

[74] S.S. Walker (ed.), *The Court Rolls of the Manor of Wakefield from October 1331 to September 1333*, Leeds: Yorkshire Archaeological Society, 1983. Wakefield Court Rolls vol 3, 1982, p130

[75] J. Lister, *The Extent (or Survey) of the Graveships of Rastrick, Hipperholme and Sowerby 1309*, Halifax: Halifax Antiquarian Society Record Series, 1914, vol 2, p31

[76] François, 'The Social and Economic Development of Halifax 1558-1640', p255

[77] Youd, 'The Common Fields of Lancashire', pp30, 34

[78] J.A. Sheppard, 'Field systems of Yorkshire', in A.R.H. Baker and R.A. Butlin (eds.), *Studies of Field Systems in the British Isles*, Cambridge: Cambridge University Press, 1973, p153

[79] Crump, *The Little Hill Farm*, p45

boundaries. In the traditional open-field system, land use rotated each year, the only fencing required being for temporary stock control. Such fencing typically consisted of banks topped with 'dry' hedging in which stakes were interwoven with brushwood.[80] Such a hedge required constant maintenance and it would have made sense to construct boundaries that demanded the least amount of attention where they were required for long periods of time as in convertible husbandry. The use of 'quick' or live hedging and stone walls resulted in the head dyke form of land management evolving into an 'enclosed pasture' model.[81] Such a model not only offered fertility benefits but made it easier to prevent cattle straying and provided a means for controlling grass growth by enabling the movement of animals from field to field as required.

The control of grazing was not only an issue within the town fields. It was also essential that common grazings on the moor were managed to prevent over stocking. Winchester describes the origin of these rights as being the renting of manorial waste on the upland areas of the Forests which gradually transformed into rights of common adjunct to the land holdings of local tenants.[82] Not only were these rights restricted to landholders within the manor, but the numbers of stock that could be grazed were limited. Such numerical limits were known as stinting and probably arose either as a result of a reduction in grazing land available or because of an increase in numbers of stock in the township.[83] Stints were expressed in units of beastgate or cattlegate, the right to graze one horned beast.[84] Another method was the rule of levancy and couchancy by which stock that could be grazed on the common were limited to no more than could be kept during the winter on the fodder produced by the farm.[85] Unfortunately, no known records survive that inform us of how limits were imposed in Midgley or indeed the period when they might have formed part of local agricultural practice. We do know, however, that stinting was used in the Calder Valley as late as 1781 as a document of that year lists the gates on Langfield Outpasture. Forty-eight landholders held a total of 318½ gates, ranging from seventeen to one gate each. The average was six and a half gates each.[86]

---

[80] Winchester, *The Harvest of the Hills: Rural Life in Northern England and the Scottish Borders*, pp62-63

[81] Winchester, *The Harvest of the Hills: Rural Life in Northern England and the Scottish Borders*, p52

[82] Winchester, *The Harvest of the Hills: Rural Life in Northern England and the Scottish Borders*, p32

[83] Winchester, *The Harvest of the Hills: Rural Life in Northern England and the Scottish Borders*, pp82-84

[84] Winchester, *The Harvest of the Hills: Rural Life in Northern England and the Scottish Borders*, p71

[85] Winchester, *The Harvest of the Hills: Rural Life in Northern England and the Scottish Borders*, p79

[86] 'An Account of the Gates on Langfield Out Pasture May 12, 1781', Todmorden and Hebden Bridge Almanack 1885, p95

As there was no permanent boundary marking the edges of Midgley township on the moor, it is unsurprising that grazing disputes arose with neighbouring townships. Around 1594 Sir George Savile, Lord of the Manor of Wadsworth, entered an action in the Star Chamber against John Lacy, Lord of the Manor of Midgley concerning trespasses between the commons of each manor and the enclosure of waste in Midgley. A compromise was entered into in 1597 by which the boundaries were redefined, Lacy granted Savile his lands to the west of the current boundary while the freeholders of Wadsworth paid Lacy £150 for common of pasture in Midgley.[87] This appears to represent an 'intercommoning' agreement, a not infrequent arrangement whereby use of pastures crossed administrative boundaries.[88] A map drawn by Christopher Saxton in 1594 that probably relates to this dispute shows a pinfold on the joint township boundary in Foster Clough below Crow Hill.[89] Pinfolds were used to impound 'foreign' stock trespassing on the commons and drives of the common were occasionally done to identify such stock.[90]

Another method of controlling grazing was the seasonal use of summer pastures known as shielings. These exploited grazing land at a distance from the farm and typically boasted temporary huts for the herdsmen so that the stock could be tended over the summer. Some of these eventually became permanent settlements.[91] Towards Castle Carr, the Luddenden valley has a number of place names that may indicate that this end of the valley was used for summer shielings.[92] 'Booth' is the modern form of Old Danish *both* meaning 'temporary shelter'[93] and is an example of Scandinavian word elements being taken into the dialect rather than an example of Scandinavian settlement. It survives not only in the hamlet of Booth but also in Arrowbutt Lee, a corruption of Herribothlee or Harribut Legh. As explained in Chapter 4 'lee' is derived from *leah*, a clearing, and Smith suggests that the name originated as 'Harry's booth in the clearing'.[94] On the Warley side there is Summer Booth Fold and Winter Booth Lee.

---

[87] J.H. Ogden, 'A Moorland Township: Wadsworth in Ancient Times', *Transactions of the Halifax Antiquarian Society*, 1904, pp37-51 at pp38-39

[88] Winchester, *The Harvest of the Hills: Rural Life in Northern England and the Scottish Borders*, p78

[89] C. Saxton, *A plat of the bounders of the Manner of Waddesworth*, 1594. British Library Add.MS 63751A. Illustrated in Chapter 9, Figure 2.

[90] Winchester, *The Harvest of the Hills: Rural Life in Northern England and the Scottish Borders*, pp116-117

[91] Winchester, *The Harvest of the Hills: Rural Life in Northern England and the Scottish Borders*, pp84-93

[92] Faull and Moorhouse, *West Yorkshire: an Archaeological Survey to A.D. 1500*, p761

[93] A.H. Smith, *English Place-Name Elements: Part 1*, Cambridge, Cambridge University Press, 1956. English Place-Name Society vol 25, p43

[94] A.H. Smith, *The Place-Names of the West Riding of Yorkshire: Part 3 Morley Wapentake*, Cambridge: Cambridge University Press, 1961, p132. (English Place-Name Society vol 32)

As we have seen, the town field areas are likely to have been gradually surrounded by assarts. All assarts had to be enclosed by law.[95] A case in the Wakefield Court Rolls in 1325 states that 'all lands of this kind of tenure have, from time immemorial all the year and at all seasons of the year, been enclosures.'[96] The size of these early clearings was typically under two acres with the majority only being of an acre or less.[97] This process of enclosure continued right up to the Parliamentary enclosures of the mid-nineteenth century. Winchester notes that there was a significant expansion in enclosure in the uplands during the sixteenth and seventeenth centuries.[98] For example, in 1565 a special commission reported that 239 acres had been taken in from the waste in Sowerby since 1509, one of the largest amounts in the area.[99] In a 1589 Halifax survey, 48 out of 201 copyholders were listed as holding recently enclosed land.[100] There is evidence that the size of enclosures had increased by the sixteenth century, with a 1602 map of Wadsworth 'intakes' typically averaging 11.5 acres.[101] The sizes of the Midgley fields with 'royd' (clearing) in their name in 1833 average 4.1 acres and are roughly one third of the size of the 1602 Wadsworth enclosures.[102] Possibly this may have been a typical size of subdivision within the 1602 enclosures.

The sixteenth-century enclosure process included attempts by lords to separate off areas of the commons as private pastures.[103] The Lacy family, as lords of the manor of Midgley, are recorded as enclosing a large area of Midgley Moor during the sixteenth century extending from Low Brown Knoll to near White Hill, and from Luddenden Brook as far as Deer Stones Edge.[104] Smaller blocks of grazing, appropriated from the moor by individuals or groups of individuals, acted as an intermediate grazing zone between the moor and the inbye land within the head dyke. These 'cow pastures' are typified by the enclosures between the moor and Workhouse Lane extending

---

[95] Faull and Moorhouse, *West Yorkshire: an Archaeological Survey to A.D. 1500*, p662

[96] J.W. Walker (ed.), *Court Rolls of the Manor of Wakefield* vol 5, 1322 to 1331, Leeds: Yorkshire Archaeological Society Record Series, 1944, vol 109, pp72-73

[97] Stinson, 'Assarting and Poverty in Early-Fourteenth-Century Western Yorkshire', p61

[98] Winchester, *The Harvest of the Hills: Rural Life in Northern England and the Scottish Borders*, p68

[99] M.J. Ellis, 'A Study in the Manorial History of Halifax Parish in the Sixteenth and Early Seventeenth Centuries', *Yorkshire Archaeological Journal*, 1960, Part 1 pp250-264; Part 2 pp420-442 at p424

[100] Ellis, 'A Study in the Manorial History of Halifax Parish in the Sixteenth and Early Seventeenth Centuries', p425

[101] C. Saxton, *A plat of Wadsworth Common*, 1602. British Library Add.MS 63751B

[102] West Yorkshire Archive Service (Calderdale), *Wadsworth and Midgley Valuations*, 1833, SU 406

[103] Winchester, *The Harvest of the Hills: Rural Life in Northern England and the Scottish Borders*, p68

[104] Ogden, 'A Moorland Township: Wadsworth in Ancient Times', p38; C. Saxton, *A plat of the bounders of the Manner of Waddesworth*, 1594. British Library Add.MS 63751A

from Coal Dike to Brownhill (Figure 7). Further indications of such intermediate enclosures are provided by the place names of High House Pasture and Pasture between the moor and High House Lane. Typically these were stinted pastures with a tendency for ultimate subdivision of the enclosure between those holding stints.[105]

Figure 7   Cow pasture above Workhouse Lane

---

[105] Winchester, *The Harvest of the Hills: Rural Life in Northern England and the Scottish Borders*, pp68-71

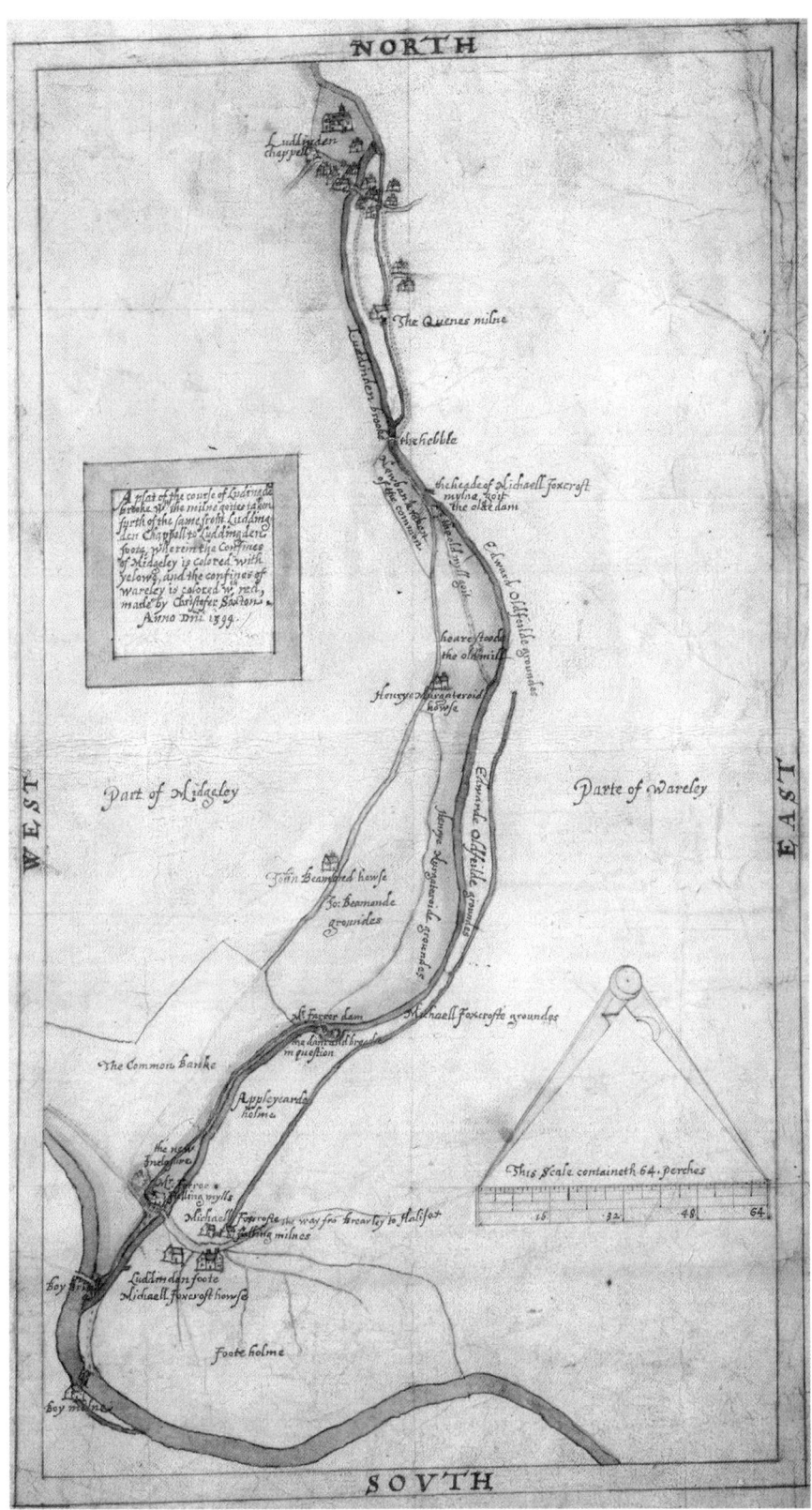

Figure 8   Saxton's map of Luddenden Foot, 1599 (not to scale)

Enclosure was also happening downslope as well as upslope. The Saxton map of 1599 shows that common grazing was also available along the banks of Luddenden Brook (Figure 8). Not only is there an extensive area called 'the Common Banke' in the triangle of land between Luddenden Brook and the Calder, but also two enclosures along the Midgley banks of Luddenden Brook. One of these is labelled as 'New bank taken of the common'.[106] Following Winchester's description of 'banks' in Cumbria as being prime pasture areas for milk cattle, it is possible that the term 'bank' was used to describe similar land in the Calder valley.[107]

The small field enclosures of Midgley and elsewhere in the Upper Calder valley originated in the process of clearing the land through assarts and continued right up until the nineteenth century. It seems that as agricultural practice increasingly focused on pastoralism, enclosure began to have a dual purpose of both protecting crops and meadows as well as controlling grazing areas. Certainly, by the eighteenth century the landscape appears to have reached a similar appearance to that of today. Writing in 1720, Defoe found that in the Halifax area the land was 'divided into small enclosures, that is to say, from two acres to six or seven acres each, seldom more.'[108]

The evolution of the Midgley landscape, from the time of the earliest evidence in Domesday in 1086 to the first agricultural survey in 1801, is a story that shows a change of land use from a relatively mixed form of agriculture up to the fourteenth century into a predominantly pastoral form of agricultural economy based on cattle thereafter. The agricultural techniques adopted, such as convertible husbandry and graving, provide an interesting example of adaptability to the local environmental constraints of climate, soil and altitude. In 1788 Marshall, referring to areas such as the Calder Valley, asserted that 'no country entirely mountainous, nor one which is disturbed by manufacture, can be a fit subject of study for rural knowledge.'[109] In contrast, this study demonstrates that the South Pennines area that includes Midgley has much to offer in terms of an historical 'rural knowledge'.

---

[106] C. Saxton, *Map of the course of the Luddenden brook from Luddenden to Luddenden Foot*, 1599, National Archives MPC 1/111/1

[107] Winchester, *The Harvest of the Hills: Rural Life in Northern England and the Scottish Borders*, pp110-111

[108] D. Defoe, *A tour through England and Wales*, Vol.2, London: J.M. Dent, 1928, p193. (Reprint of original edition 1724-1726)

[109] W. Marshall, *The Rural Economy of Yorkshire*. London: T. Cadell, 1788, vol 1, p10

CHAPTER 6

Population and People

Ian Bailey, Mary Browne and Janet Speak

Introduction

During the late winter of 1516, William Rokeby, Vicar of Halifax, prepared to visit London once again to officiate in his capacity as Archbishop of Dublin at the christening of the newly-born Princess Mary, only surviving child of King Henry and Queen Catherine. The princess had been born at the palace at Greenwich and was to be christened amidst much splendour and rejoicing at the Chapel of Observant Friars in Greenwich. We are told the 'church was hung with needlework, enriched with precious stones and pearls', whilst 'a canopy was carried by four knights, under which walked the Countess of Surrey with the Princess in her arms'.[1] Ahead of the procession waited the Archbishops of Armagh and Dublin, ready to officiate at this joyous and harmonious celebration.

William Rokeby was familiar with such splendid occasions as he had already 'played a prominent part in the gorgeous pageantry of Henry VIII's reign.' But the august clergyman so favoured his position in Halifax that, on his death in 1521, he directed that his heart should be buried in the choir of the parish church. Whilst Rokeby returned to end his days in Halifax, the life at the Tudor court had become increasingly sinister and turbulent, the effects of which were felt by everyone in England, including the inhabitants of Midgley.

This investigation is based primarily on parish registers, probate documents and taxation records which cover the brutal period of history when five monarchs ruled: Henry VIII, his heirs Edward VI, Mary and Elizabeth I; followed by James I (VI of Scotland). The Reformation, following Henry VIII's break with Rome and culminating in the first Act of Supremacy in 1534, brought about a turbulent period of religious and political intrigue between Protestant and Catholic factions. Probably the most notable Midgley figure to fall foul of the religious climate of the time was Robert Farrer, Bishop of St

---

[1] T.W. Hanson, 'Archbishop Rokeby, Vicar of Halifax 1502 – 21', *Transactions of the Halifax Antiquarian Society*, 1918, pp141 – 164 at pp149-150

David's, who was born at Ewood and died a martyr, burnt at the stake for his Protestant beliefs in Carmarthen in 1555.[2]

People and Places

At the beginning of the sixteenth century, the lordship of the manor of Midgley was held by the Lacey family, who lived at Brearley Old Hall. The manor mills for corn and fulling were on the River Calder nearby. The Laceys were a family of aristocratic Norman descent who had been awarded lands in Lancashire after the conquest. The heiress of the manor of Midgley, Isabel Sotehill, had married Gilbert, second son of John Lacey of Cromwell Bottom, around 1500. His son, Hugh, was Lord of the Manor at the time of the reformation.[3]

In 1588 a levy was raised to oppose the Armada. This was set at 2s 8d in the £ on land or 1s 8d on goods – no one paid on both.[4] The returns for families of Midgley were as follows:

	£	s	d
John Lacie, Knight, in land	2	13	4
Henry Ferror, in land	1	9	4
John Deyne, in land		6	8
Gilbert Lacie, in land		5	4
John Padget, in land		4	0
Edward Bannister, in land		4	0
John Haldesworth		2	8
Richard Helliwell		2	8
John Beaumonte		2	8
Henry Ferror of Old Roide		2	8
Henry Ferror senior		2	8
R Smith		2	8
Henry Murgatroyd		2	8
Robert Deane		2	8
	6	6	8

---

[2] R. Bretton, 'Bishop Robert Ferrer', *Transactions of the Halifax Antiquarian Society*, 1934, pp193-198 at p193

[3] T. Sutcliffe, 'The Brearley Halls in Midgley', *Transactions of the Halifax Antiquarian Society*, 1922, pp125– 160 at p128

[4] W. Brigg, 'Lay Subsidy 1588', *Thoresby Society*, 1909, 15, pp132-151 at p141

John Lacey of Lower Brearley Hall and Lord of the Manor of Midgley was the richest man in the Parish of Halifax according to this 1588 levy. John was the grandson and Gilbert the second son of Hugh Lacey. Gilbert married Maria Murgatroyd in 1563, and one of their daughters married James Murgatroyd, a man renowned for building fine houses in the area.[5]

Henry Farrer and his son William, of Ewood, were members of another important family, which was accumulating wealth through the cloth trade, with a stall at the great fair of St Bartholomew in London. Also of importance were the Deans of Dean House; William Farrer and John Dean each married a daughter of Hugh Lacey – together these families formed an influential triumvirate in the area. John Dean acted as constable for several years, and was often called upon as a witness, supervisor and scribe of his neighbour's wills.

One name missing from this list is that of Midgley itself, and there can be few farmsteads in the area which have not been connected at some time with that family, who take their name from their place of origin. The oldest inscribed tombstone in Halifax records the resting place of

Richard Midgley of
Brodefould in Midgley
Hark, Hark, I hear a trumpet sound
Arise ye dead out of the ground
1587

Another member of the family, also a Richard, was Vicar of Rochdale for thirty-four years from 1561 and was famed for his fiery eloquence, piety and puritan zeal. He was succeeded there by his son, Joseph. Appropriately for a puritan, Richard was largely instrumental in founding the Grammar School in Rochdale. Henry Tilson, son of Henry Tylson de Midgeley, born in 1577, also served Rochdale for twenty years from 1615 and later became Bishop of Elphin in Ireland. Another notable cleric from Midgley was Robert Farrer of Ewood, who has already been mentioned on page 71.

As there were few opportunities for education in the parish of Halifax in the sixteenth century, it may be surprising that Midgley was able to send out such a number of notable clerics. At the time only a minority of people could read or write, even to sign their name. There was a close connection between

---

[5] T Sutcliffe, 'A Tour in Midgley' *Transactions of the Halifax Antiquarian Society*, 1928, pp113 - 160

religion and education, and locally the thirst for education was reflected in a petition to Queen Elizabeth for a charter to found a grammar school in Halifax. Henry Farrer was a principal contributor and also gave two acres of land for the school in Skircoat. In 1600, 'The Free Grammar School of Queen Elizabeth' was finally opened. It was later known as Heath Grammar School, because of its location on the heath to the south of Halifax. John Lacey of Brearley, gentleman, Henry Farrer of Ewood, gentleman, and John Dean of Dean House, yeoman, were all on the first governing board. Midgley people contributed £3 16s 4d in subscriptions and a further £1 16s 4d in small donations.[6]

In the early seventeenth century, the Farrer family acquired the lordship of the manor from the Laceys and the manor court was transferred to Ewood. The Laceys continued to live at Brearley as tenants until 1620. Records of this period in Midgley are sparse, but the life of Henry Farrer had a dramatic conclusion when he was murdered in 1610 while attending a lawsuit at the Star Chamber. His assailant, Thomas Oldfield of Warley, was hanged, and Henry was buried in St Margaret's, Westminster.[7]

Wills

Seventy-three wills survive for Midgley township in the period 1531-1635, the first twenty of which have been transcribed. The opening clauses, sometimes written in Latin, name the testator and give the date the will was drafted. During this period it was usual for a will to be made shortly before death, as is evidenced by the inclusion in many of the wills of a clause similar to the one drafted for William Pighilles in 1542:

> I william pighilles of migeley within the parish of Halifax seke in bodie hool
> of mynd and of goode and perfect memorie laud be god…[8]

This clause also gives the all-important evidence that he was compos mentis. Subsequent clauses deal with the testator committing his soul to God and stating his preferred place of burial. It may be that the testator also leaves money to the church for building work or the clergy to say masses for his soul.

---

[6] T. Cox, *A popular history of the Grammar School of Queen Elizabeth at Heath, near Halifax*, Halifax: F. King, 1879, pp115, 117

[7] G. Dent, 'Ewood in Midgley', *Transactions of the Halifax Antiquarian Society*, 1939, pp7–70 at p16

[8] I. Bailey and A. Petford (eds), *Midgley Probate Records 1531-1731*, Midgley: Midgley Books, 2007, p4. The original wills are held at the Borthwick Institute of Historical Research, University of York.

It is in the clause for the commendation of the soul that we find the influence of the church, Catholic or Protestant, most in evidence, as can be seen from the following two wills. The Catholic emphasis prevalent at the beginning of the period is reflected in the early wills. The introduction to these wills often refers to 'the blessed virgin' or ' sancta marie' as in this will of Gilbert Shawe written in 1537:

> Fyrste and principallie I bequethe my soule to god almightie, to the blessed virgine our ladie sancta marie and to all the holye sainctes in heven…[9]

It remains a matter of debate how far these religious clauses reflect the views of the will writer or the testator, but since the will had to be read out to the testator then at least he or she must have acceded to the phrase.

Wills written after the accession of Protestant Queen Elizabeth in 1558 assume an entirely different tone, as in this will of 'Edward Bannester of yatehouse in the town shippe of miydgley', drafted in 1587:

> …ffirst and principallie I commend my soule into the hands of almyghtie god my most lovinge and most mercyfull father assuredlie belevinge to have forgivness of all my syns throwe his great love in the merits and Desertes of Jesus Christ his sonne my alone saviour and redeemer who is dead for my synes and Risen for my justifiacacon.[10]

A very clear demonstration of the protestant belief in salvation by faith in Christ alone.

The majority of those whose wills have been examined were buried in Halifax, with the exception of William Midgley, and Henry and William Farrer of Ewood, who were buried at Heptonstall. Three quarters left a mortuary. This suggests that these testators were men of some substance as a mortuary was a traditional 'gift' to the church, only payable when the goods of the deceased amounted to a total of ten marks or more (£6 13s 4d).[11]

Few women made wills, as a married woman had to seek the permission of her husband, who could revoke the will at any time. However, many acted as executors, alone or in conjunction with their children, and could clearly be left in sole charge to manage their husband's estate. Interestingly, after 1574

---

[9] Bailey and Petford, *Midgley Probate Records 1531-1731*, p3-4
[10] Bailey and Petford, *Midgley Probate Records 1531-1731*, p22
[11] The act which prescribed the sliding scale on which mortuaries were levied was passed in 1529: *An Act Concerning the Taking of Mortuaries*, 21 Henry 8, c.6

burials of married women are registered as 'widow' or 'wife of' rather than in their own name.

It was the custom to divide the estate into three parts, one third to the widow, one third to the children and the remainder distributed according to the deceased's wishes. Many wills follow this pattern:

> …my wyffe to have her thride onelie accordinge to the lawe and Custome of the Countrie and my seaven children to have the two partes equallie Devided Emonges them…[12]

Most married daughters were deemed to have had their share of the estate upon marriage:

> …Isabell and agnes my doghters which are maryd and had thir chilid porcions afore my deth have all my apparel belonging to me thai wilbe contented ther with withowt ony more besines and els I will thai hayff noyn of my guddes at all…[13]

Clothes were of sufficient value to be left individually in some wills, as for example Edward Sladen who left Gilbert Sladen 'my beste jacket and ii jerkins', Randall Breer 'my jacket and beste but one sherte my beste shoes' and William, his son, 'my clothe cloke'.[14]

Equally, furniture was sometimes specifically itemised and bequeathed individually – Edward Sladen left Gilbert 'one bedd, my chiste and my presser' and Margaret, his son's wife, 'my longe chiste'.

One interesting bequest was 'two greate Irone chimneys' by Hugh Lacey of Brearley to his son John, who also inherited his father's best apparel together with all his 'amor, harness and weapons, excepte the best steile coite of plaite and the best steil cappe or scolle which I will that my sonne Gilbert lacye shall have'.[15]

Most animals came under the general heading of 'cattelles', but Edward Sladen left Gilbert 'two stirkes, my horse, sadle and bridle'. Unfortunately, in the Diocese of York, no inventories were preserved during the sixteenth century, which makes it difficult to assess the number of animals at this time.

---

[12] Bailey and Petford, *Midgley Probate Records 1531-1731*, p14
[13] Bailey and Petford, *Midgley Probate Records 1531-1731*, p1
[14] Bailey and Petford, *Midgley Probate Records 1531-1731* pp19-20
[15] Bailey and Petford, *Midgley Probate Records 1531-1731*, p18. The chimneys appear to be stoves.

Charitable bequests were made to benefit the locality. For example, John Whiteheade left 5s in 1536 'unto the hallowing of the chapel of sainte Marie at Lodyngdeyne' and Gilbert Shawe in 1537 left £3 6s 8d 'to the reconciling of the chapel of Luddingden'.[16] These indicate the length of time it was taking to establish and consecrate the chapel of ease at Luddenden, for a licence was granted in 1496. It was not formally consecrated for births, marriages and deaths until 1624.[17]

Other bequests in wills include 12d 'unto xx power neighbours everie one' by Edward Sladen in 1575, and 20s 'to the poure of the Chappelrie of Sowerbie ... 20s to the poure of halifax' by Edward Bannester in 1581. William Farrer of Ewood left 6s 8d 'to every one of my servintes, prentizes and maydes', and Edward Bannester of Y(G)atehouse gave 5s 'to evrie servant in the house'.[18]

Parish Registers

Paradoxically, one of the effects of this period of change was the order of 1538 requiring churches to keep parish registers, which record the unchanging tempo of life. Exceptionally, the registers for Halifax survive from the very first year of their inception.[19] For the purpose of this study it was also possible to include those few Midgley residents who appear in the Heptonstall register, which survives from 1594. Over the thirty-year period from the start of the Heptonstall registers, only 7 per cent of the total baptisms of Midgley infants took place there. As St Mary's, Luddenden was granted the rights of baptism, marriage and burial in 1624, and many Midgley people are likely to have been registered there, the detailed analysis we were able to undertake had to end in that year. Sadly, the early Luddenden registers have not survived.

By comparing the names of those buried with the names of those who left wills, the proportion of those leaving a will can be determined.

Between 1538 and 1624, there were 614 burials of Midgley residents. Of these 233 (38 per cent) were noted as being someone's child. Assuming this indicates

---

[16] Bailey and Petford, *Midgley Probate Records 1531-1731*, p3-4

[17] J.A. Heginbottom, *The Parish Church of St Mary the Blessed Virgin, Luddenden with Luddendenfoot: A brief history and guide*, Luddenden: Tonyprint, 1984; available from the church.

[18] Bailey and Petford, *Midgley Probate Records 1531-1731*, pp17, 19, 22

[19] West Yorkshire Archive Service (Wakefield), *Halifax, St John the Baptist, Parish Records*, WDP53, Registers of Baptism, Marriage and Burial. For a transcription of the registers from 1538 – 1593 see Yorkshire Archaeological Society Parish Registers Series 37 (baptisms) and 45 (marriages and burials).

that they were unmarried and living with their parents, 381 adults were buried. With three exceptions, all those who made wills were men, presumably reflecting their position as the head of the household and that they left their property to children rather than their wives. So, just taking the adult men into consideration, there were approximately 190 heads of household that formed the potential 'will-making' inhabitants of Midgley. The number of men that left a will during the same period was forty-eight, just over one quarter of the total (Figure 1), which compares with similar findings elsewhere. This suggests that it would be a mistake to assume that only the wealthy made wills. It is worth noting that many of those who died were unmarried, a reflection of the high child mortality rate.

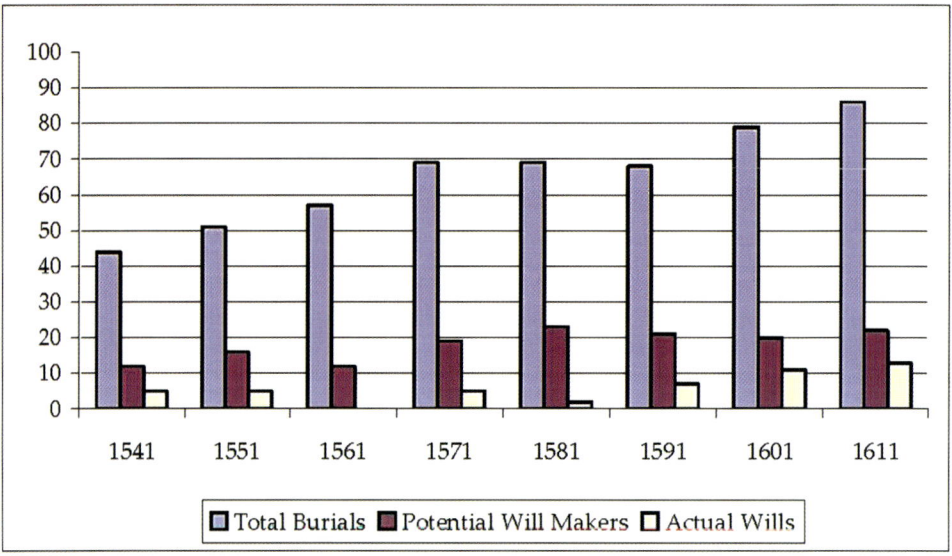

Figure 1   *Comparison for Midgley people of burials, wills proven and an estimate of those who could have made a will 1541 -1620*

Names

There were 939 names, 502 males and 437 females on the baptism registers for the period 1538-1624. A total of 154 surnames were recorded. The spelling of both personal and place names was idiosyncratic in this period, suggesting that they were being recorded phonetically by the incumbent or clerk. The surname Pickles is a good example of this. Appearing ten times, the name is spelt variously as Pighels, Pyghels, Pygheles, Pyghylles and Pyghyllys. An unusual form of the name Whitaker appears just once as Qwittagar.

Surnames

Whilst some family names appear only once or twice, certain names predominate at this time. Not surprisingly, Midgley is the most frequently found, appearing 96 times. The following table records the number of occurrences and variations in spelling of each of the 'top ten' names.

Surname	No.	Variations
Midgley	96	Miggelay, Midgelei, Mydglay, Midgeley, Midgelaye, Mydghlah, Midglye, Midley
Farrer	62	Farror, Faraw, Ferher, Farrar, Farrow, Farrowe, Ferrer, Farer
Smith	48	Smyth, Smythe, Smithe
Thomas	37	Thoms
Dean	30	Deyne, Dayn, Dayne, Deane
Townend	29	Townehe, Townehende, Townehend, Townend, Towend, Townede, Townende, Townhend
Oldfield	28	Oldefield, Oldefeld, Holdefield, Oldfield, Oldefelde, Oldfild, Oldfeld, Olphield, Oldfeeld
Lacey	25	Lacy, Lace, Lacye, Lassye
Holdsworth	19	Haldesworthe, Haldeworth, Holdesworth, Holdesworthe, Haldisworth, Haldsworth, Holdsworthe, Haldworth, Haldesworth
Ingham	19	Iggan, Yngga, Inggam, Ynggam, Ingam, Ingham, Inghu~, Ingho, Ingu~, Ingh~

Noticeably absent from this list is Murgatroyd, of which there are only eight recorded, although many more were to be found across the boundary in Warley. Other names prevalent in the area today, which appear less frequently at this time, include Greenwood, for example, which in this study numbered just fourteen whilst occurring 253 times in the Census of 1841.

Christian names

As may be expected many of the Christian names given at this time are biblical. From the Old Testament, Genesis is represented in the name Eden, mentioned three times between 1569 and 1583, Isaac, son of Abraham and Sarah, all of which were popular names of the time. Also recorded is a Bethsabee (1584), most likely a derivation of Bathsheba, wife of David and mother of Solomon. Ruth, Ester, Jacob and Samuel are also represented. Popular amongst the New Testament names are Mary, Elizabeth, James and

John, these also being the names of monarchs. Before 1570, Elizabeth often appears as Elsabeth. Names reflecting other influences and sources include Katherine, Joyce, Gennet and Agneta amongst the females with males being given such names as Anthony, William, George, Francis, Hugo and percivall (always appearing with a small p).

Christian names of Midgley infants in the baptism registers

Males	Number of times	Females	Number of times
John	100	Mary	88
Richard	41	Grace	64
Thomas	36	Susan	37
Henry	31	Anne	36
Samuel	30	Sara(h)	27
Abraham	28	Elizabeth	26
William	28	Margaret	16
Johes	26	Agnes	15
James	18	Isabel(la)	14
Michael	16	Jane	14

Christian names of Midgley residents in the burial registers

Males	Number of times	Females	Number of times
John	50	Mary	24
Richard	33	Margaret	17
William	28	Agnes	16
Thomas	28	Elizabeth	15
James	19	Isabel	14
Johes	18	Grace	12
Henry	13	Genet	10
Michael	11	Anne	10
Samuel	10	Alice	7
Robert	10	Susan	6
Edward	10	Sarah	5

A comparison of the two tables suggests the relatively constant repetition of names down the generations. The names Samuel, Edward, Robert and Alice are exceptions, appearing in the burial register but less frequently in baptisms.

George Redmonds has pointed out that during this time children were more likely to be named after a godfather than the father.[20] In the absence of recorded godparents, no evidence was found to suggest this was the case in Midgley, although it was interesting to note that out of approximately 500 male baptisms only eighty-six were named after the father. In puritan circles, godparents were often family members, a reflection perhaps of the puritan emphasis on the family as well as a suspicion of the essentially Catholic institution of godparent.

In the earliest register, the influence of the Latinate scholarship of the clergy of this period can be seen; for example, Henricus, Ricus, Gilbtus, Edwardus, Robtus, Jacobus, Isabella, Alicia and Johana. There are also examples of the name Christopher, Christ For Us, as Xpoferus, Xpofer and Xpofori.

Whilst recording of the males was very thorough throughout the registers, that of the females was less so. Only the father's name appears in the baptism register, unless the child was a bastard, in which case the mother's name is given and, on occasion, also that of the father. The women also remain relatively anonymous in much of the burial register, appearing under their own name only if no husband or father existed. In most instances, particularly after 1574, women are referred to simply as widow, wife or child of the male protector.

Population: An Overview of the Population of Midgley, 1500 to 2001

In 1500, England was very thinly populated compared to today. The population was so checked by high mortality that it did not expand at all. The total population in 1548 was estimated to have been just 2.8 million, about half that it had been 200 years earlier on the eve of the Black Death. However, over the next eighty years it had grown faster than ever before, reaching 4.7 million by 1630. The parish of Halifax had expanded at double this rate during the same time, from 8,500 to 20,000.[21]

It is possible to estimate the population of a parish by reference to the annual number of baptisms. It has been estimated that there were 30 births per annum for every 1,000 inhabitants. Using baptisms as a proxy for births, all that is required is the average number of baptisms recorded in the parish

---

[20] Personal communication. George Redmonds, Lecture to Hebden Bridge Local History Society, October 2006

[21] J.A Hargreaves, *Halifax*, Edinburgh: Edinburgh University Press; Lancaster: Carnegie Publishing, 1999, p25

register. Fortunately, parish registers for Halifax not only exist from 1538 but also record the township of the parents. Using this method, the population of Midgley in 1548 was 335. By 1630 this had grown to 431, a rise of 29 per cent (Figure 2).[22] This is half the rate for England and one fifth of that for Halifax Parish. In other words, Midgley's small population did not match the rapid population expansion of the whole parish of Halifax.

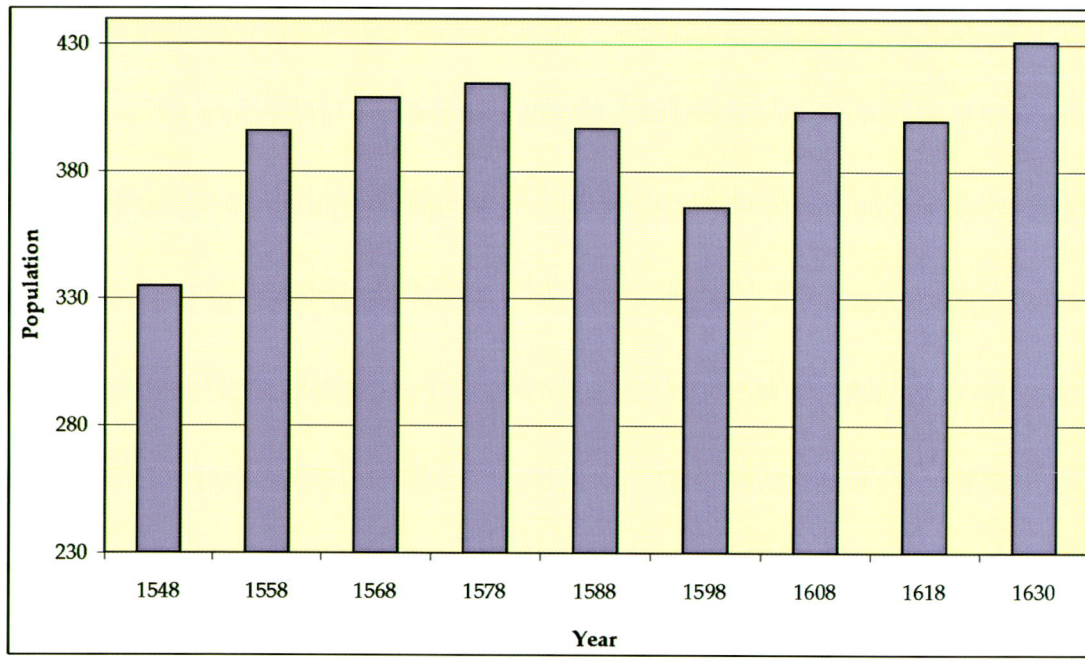

Figure 2   *Population estimates for Midgley Township based on baptisms during the Tudor and Stuart Period*

Mortality

Premature death was commonplace in Tudor and Stuart times. In the burial section of the Halifax parish register, references to the nature of death and the character of the deceased can occasionally be found as notes alongside the burial record. Typical of the comments of Vicar Favour, and perhaps a reflection of his puritan predilections, are these remarks in 1600. John Pillinge was described as 'a most wicked and incorrigible drunkard died miserably in want' and Sarah Ferrensyde 'had fyve bastards, a most damnable wicked queane'.

---

[22] The latest date that can be estimated from baptisms is 1623. The estimate for 1630 assumes the same rate of growth for the next seven years as had been the case for the previous seven years

The only notes that relate to Midgley are in 1551 when seven people were noted as dying from 'sweating sickness'. Evidently, there was an outbreak in the parish as over forty people died in total in this year. It can also be deduced

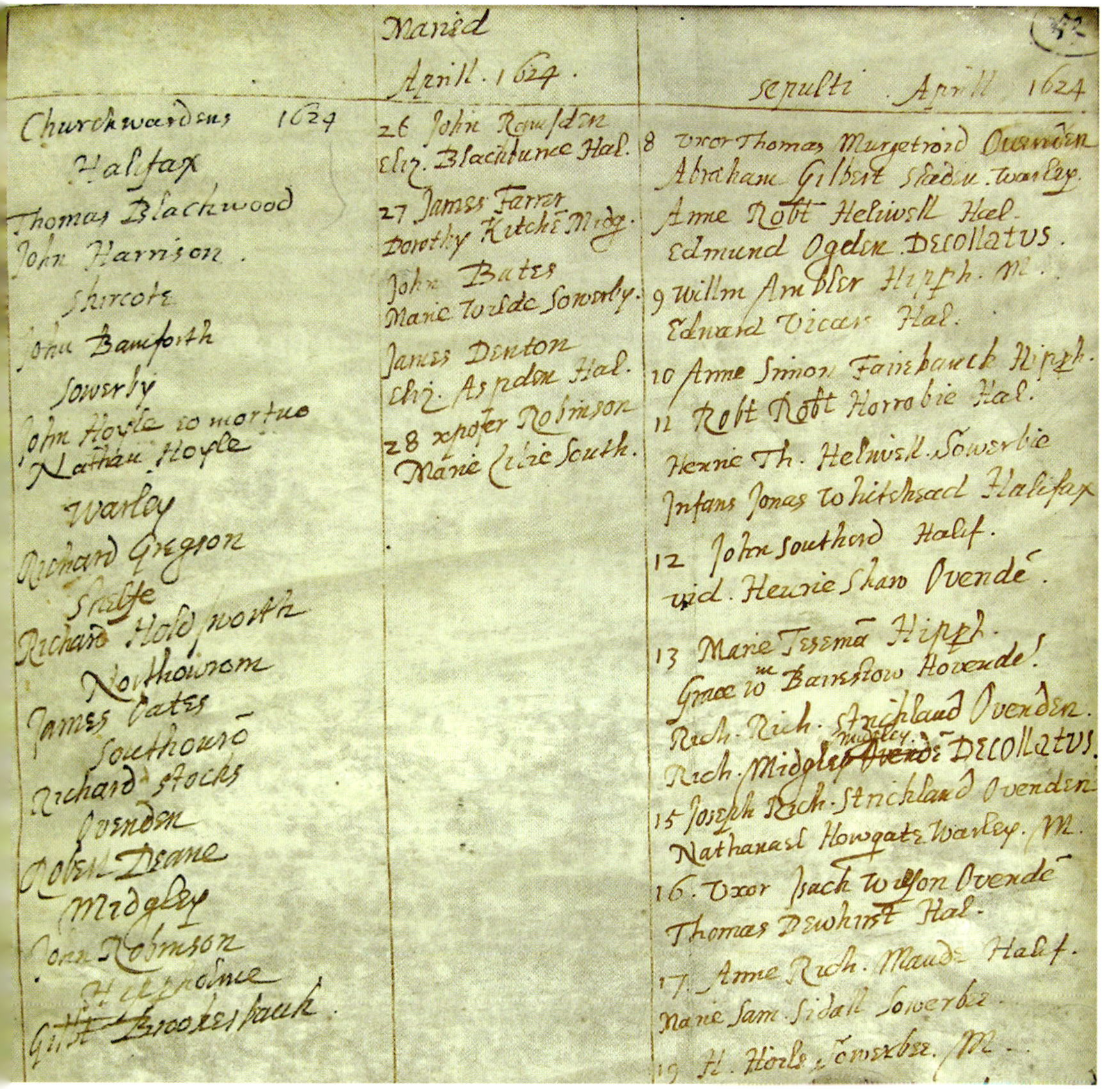

Figure 3   An extract from the Halifax parish register of April 1624. The Midgley Churchwarden is John Robinson (left column, near the bottom) whilst Rich[ard] Midgley of Midgley is shown to be 'DECOLLATUS' (right column, last entry on the 13th)

that it was likely to have been contagious, as in many cases more than one member of the same family died. In Midgley, three of the unfortunate victims were Laceys and two were Drapers.

There is one other death in Midgley during this period where the cause is certain. On 13 April 1624, Richard Midgley was recorded as 'DECOLLATUS' – he was decapitated on the Halifax gibbet (Figure 3).

In 1587 and 1623, there were two or three times more deaths than in the years around them. This characteristic is regarded by population historians as an indication of a population crisis. Interestingly, there were no observations noted in the parish register on either occasion. Furthermore, it is estimated that the population of Midgley in the sixteenth century peaked in 1586, the year before the first of these crises, but fell thereafter for the rest of the century and did not recover until after 1623. So what happened to cause such crises and population decline and why did it not prompt the vicar of Halifax to note it in the parish registers?

This phenomenon was first noted for 1623 in Lancashire by a WEA class in Bolton.[23] It was also noted in an academic study on Cumberland and Westmorland for both 1586 and 1623.[24] The Midgley characteristics are consistent with the findings of both these studies: a large increase in recorded burials, a fall in baptisms and hardly any noted observations.

Furthermore, it was demonstrated that the crises began in the autumn, worsened through the winter and recovered completely in the spring. Deaths were also less likely amongst infants, usually just one person per household was affected and upland parishes were far harder hit than lowland ones. These findings are not consistent with any contagious disease that was common during the times. Outbreaks of plague and cholera were usually well documented, anyway. The weather of the early 1620s had been noted as creating 'wet, rainy, scarce dear years'[25] and we know that harvests had been poor for three consecutive years by the autumn of 1623. Both studies concluded that the most plausible explanation for this crisis was the cumulative effect of malnutrition.

---

[23] C.D. Rogers, *The Lancashire Population Crisis of 1623*, [Manchester]: Department of Extra Mural Studies, University of Manchester, 1975

[24] A.B. Appleby, *Disease or Famine? Mortality in Cumberland and Westmorland 1580-1640*, Economic History Review, 1973, 26(3), pp403-432

[25] T. Short, *A Comparative History of the Increase and Decrease in Mankind*, London: W. Nicholl, 1767, p82

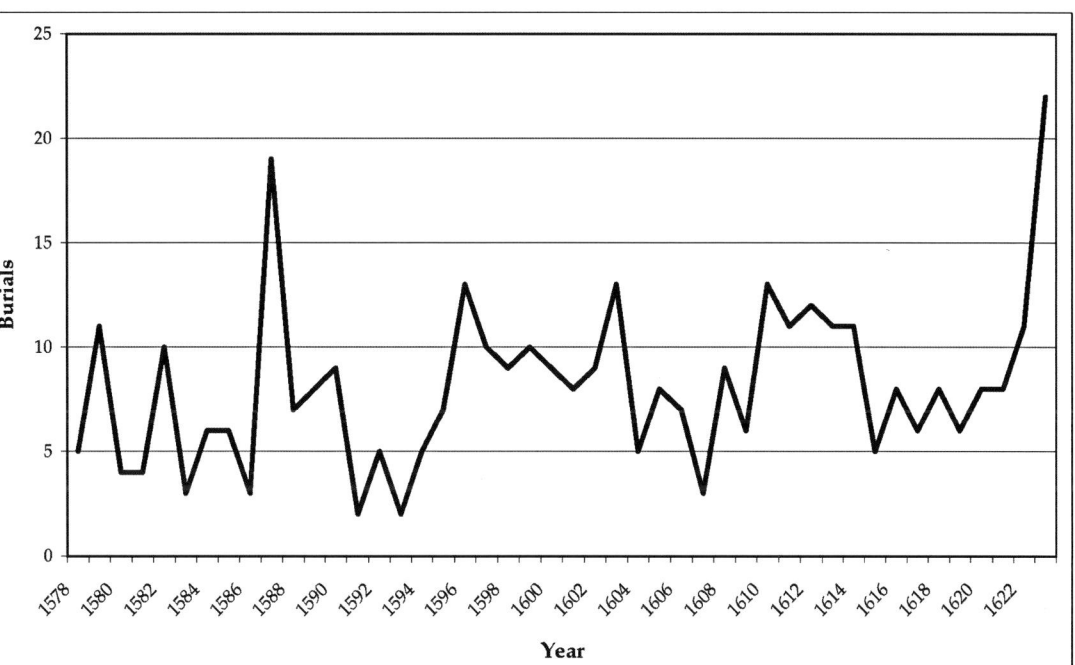

igure 4   Burials of people from Midgley Township, 1578 to 1623

It seems likely, therefore, that in both 1587 and 1623, the inhabitants of Midgley were struggling to feed themselves sufficiently. It is also possible that, due to the high, exposed moorland location, Midgley was worse affected than much of the rest of Halifax parish, its crops being more sensitive to the vagaries of the weather than those in less exposed locations. This would explain the comparatively low population growth during this period.

The next source from which the population of Midgley township can be derived is the Visitation Returns of 1743, which provide the number of households for Luddenden Chapelry, which includes Upper Warley.[26] There were 311 families, of which 154 are estimated to have been in Midgley.[27] Using a multiplier of 4.75 people per household, the estimated population is 733.[28] In

---

[26] S.L. Ollard and P.C. Walker, *Archbishop Herring's Visitation Returns, 1743 Vol II*, Leeds: Yorkshire Archaeological Society Record Series, 1928, vol 72, p149

[27] This is based on the same proportion of farms that were returned for Luddenden Chapelry in the Agricultural Returns of 1801 when 63 out of 139 farms were in Midgley

[28] See note 6 in Chapter 4 for a discussion of multipliers

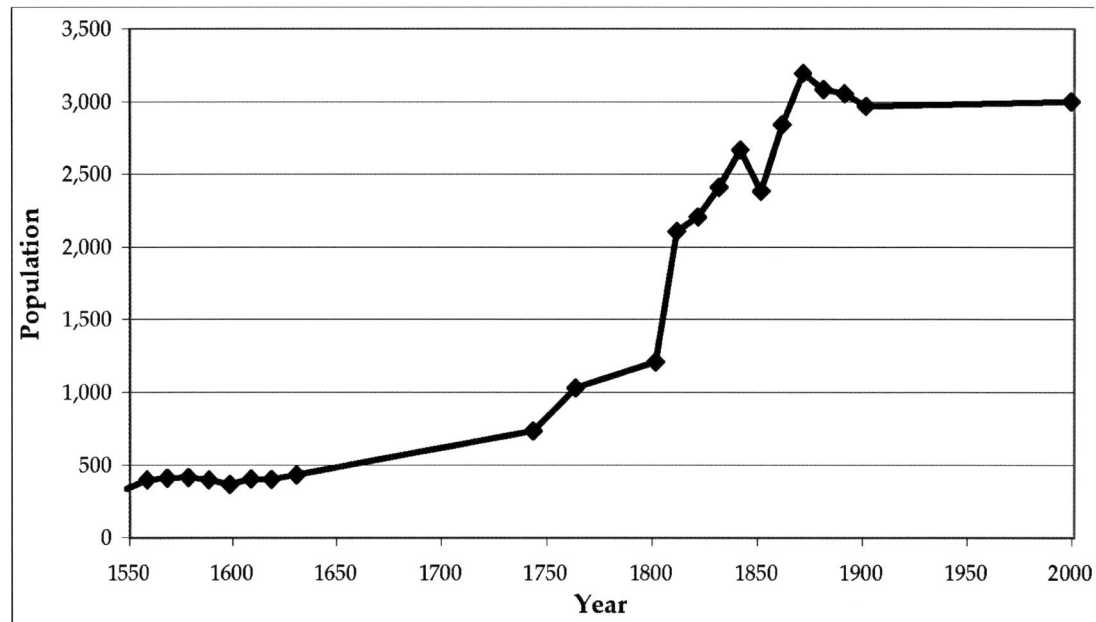

Figure 5   The population of Midgley township from 1550 to 2001

1764, further returns gave the number of households in Midgley as 217, suggesting that the population had risen to 1,031.[29] The first census was completed in 1801 and has been carried out every ten years since, with the exception of 1941. The population of Midgley township expanded rapidly during the nineteenth century and peaked in 1871 at 3,193. The total population is similar today.

---

[29] J. Crabtree, *A Concise History of the Parish and Vicarage of Halifax*, Halifax: Hartley and Walker, 1836, p311-312

CHAPTER 7

Of Meres and Bounders:
Disputes, Maps and Boundaries

Alan Petford

One of the most interesting features of Myers' map of the Parish of Halifax, so far as it concerns Midgley, is the legend 'Disputed Ground' (Figure 1).[1] This appears at the very northern boundary of the township where it reaches its highest point and adjoins Oxenhope. Like its neighbours, Wadsworth and Warley, Midgley is a long narrow township stretching northwards from the flood plain of the Calder, up the valley side, and on to the moor. This gives the township a good cross-section of different types of land.

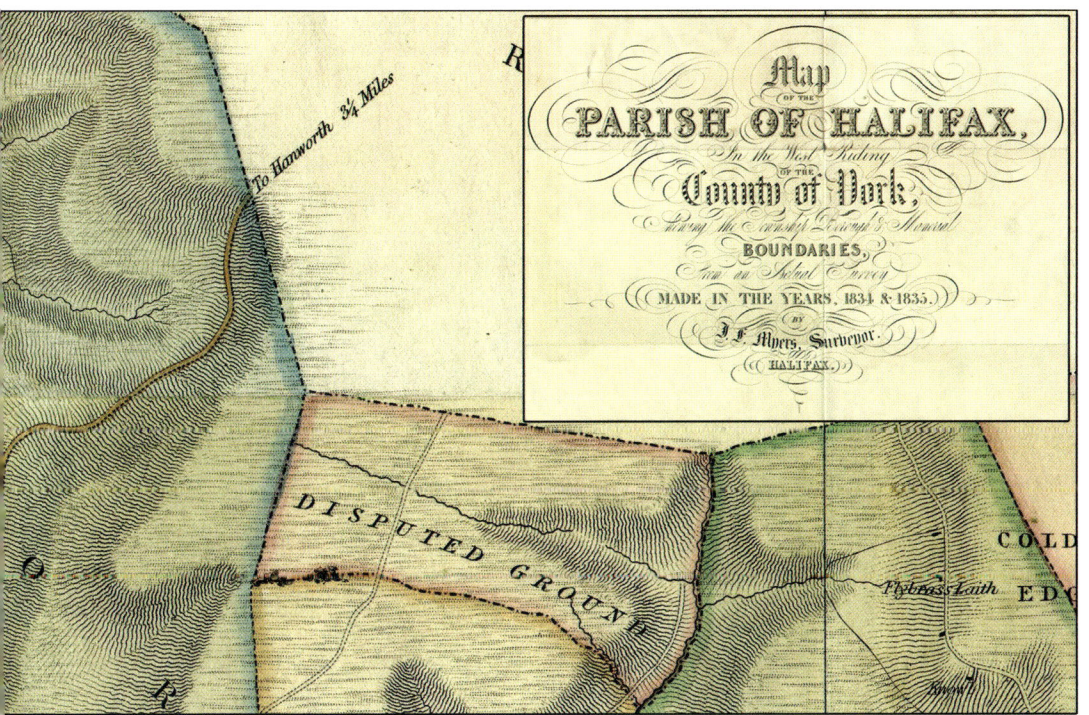

Figure 1   *An extract from Myers Map (1834 -1835), scale 2½ inches to 1 mile, showing the disputed ground on the northern boundary of Midgley Township*

---

[1] The full map is reproduced at the end of the book

In its lower reaches it is very likely that the boundaries of Midgley had been defined quite early because of pressure on valuable lowland resources. In contrast, in the moorland areas, there had probably been a good deal of shared use between the neighbouring townships. This is suggested by the note just below Foster Clough Head on Christopher Saxton's 1594 map of Wadsworth which reads: 'Here haith bene a pinfould in the devision betwixt Midgley and wadesworth'.[2]

However, by the late sixteenth century the expanding population of Midgley and its adjacent townships was putting pressure on resources. Inevitably, townships and individuals wanted to define the common and territorial rights they possessed. As a result there was a series of disputes about water rights, commoning and boundaries. In this, Midgley was no different to scores of Pennine townships.[3] What is unusual about Midgley is that two of these disputes resulted in the production of five maps between 1594 and 1602. Even more interesting is the fact that four of the maps were made by Christopher Saxton, perhaps the leading cartographer of his generation.

The earliest of these maps is that of Wadsworth, referred to above, which was produced as a result of a case brought in the Court of Star Chamber by Sir George Savile, Lord of the Manor of Wadsworth, against John Lacy, Lord of the Manor of Midgley. There appear to have been three points at issue. Firstly, an encroachment by John Lacy, whose new enclosure crossed the boundary into Wadsworth Township. Secondly, the trespass of Wadsworth commoners into Midgley and thirdly a dispute over rights of turbary. Matters were resolved by defining the boundaries between Midgley and Wadsworth. In addition, the Wadsworth commoners were allowed to continue to use the Midgley commons in return for a payment of £150. The newly defined boundaries are shown on a map of Wadsworth Common made by Christopher Saxton in 1602 (Figure 2).[4] As can be seen from the title, this map was primarily concerned with plotting the old and new enclosures but its delineation of the Wadsworth - Midgley boundary follows exactly that agreed in January 1597. The agreement, as described by J. H. Ogden, reads:

> Beginning at Foster Clough, alias Fostal Clough, thence going northwards to all
> such meres as are now, to one heap of stones or law then newly made called

---

[2] See Chapter 5, Figure 2, page 108

[3] A. J. Petford, 'The Process of Enclosure in Saddleworth, 1625 – 1824', *Transactions of the Lancashire and Cheshire Antiquarian Society*, 1987, 84, pp78-117; G. H. Tupling, *The Economic History of Rossendale*, Manchester: Manchester University Press, 1927

[4] C. Saxton, *A plat of Wadsworth Common*, 1602. British Library Add.MS 63751B

Foster Clough Head, thence to one lawe or heap of stones now called Savile's Law, from thence to one heap hill or moss hill, newly called Blether Hill, thence to one lying stone, newly named Greenwood Stone, and so to another stone newly called Resby Mere, thence to another stone newly called Farror's Bounder, also to the heap of stones which hath been in ancient time called Lad or Law, or the Low Brown Knowl, thence to the heap of stones newly called Wadsworth Law or High Brown Knowl, and from thence all along the west side of one enclosure, late taken in by the said John Lacy, up to the end of the ditch thereof pointing northwards, and so to one great stone anciently called Hoyland, alias Hoyning Stone, and so to one law or heap of stones at or near South Strine Head.[5]

The number of places in this agreement that are newly named is striking. It very much suggests that, in order to define the boundary, hitherto anonymous land marks were given names. Many of these names have survived to the present day and the boundary survived into the nineteenth century to be marked on Myers' map. However, in 1891, with the creation of Mytholmroyd Local Board, Foster Clough ceased to be the western boundary of Midgley from the Calder, but the line of 1597 remained from Savile's Law (Churn Milk Joan) northwards.[6]

The other two Saxton maps associated with Midgley relate to a dispute over water rights in the Luddenden valley (Figure 3).[7] This complex dispute has been written about elsewhere.[8] It occasioned not only the production of Saxton's maps but also one by John Bell, a map maker of York, which has been reproduced here for the purpose of comparison with the Saxton maps (Figure 4).[9]

These maps show that as the resources of the area came under pressure in the late sixteenth century, conflicts arose which required rights to be defined. More than in most places, in Midgley maps were being used as a means of illustrating evidence, resolving disputes and recording decisions.

[5] J.H. Ogden, 'A Moorland Township: Wadsworth in Ancient Times', *Transactions of the Halifax Antiquarian Society*, 1904, pp37-51

[6] Ordnance Survey 6 inch to 1 mile, Yorkshire (West Riding) Sheet 230, 1894

[7] C. Saxton, *A plat of Mychaell Foxcrofte groundes with his house, Milnes, goite, or dames*, 1601, National Archives MPC 1/111/2; See also Chapter 5, Figure 8, page 69

[8] H.P. Kendall, 'A Local Feud', *Transactions of the Halifax Antiquarian Society*, 1923, p21

[9] J. Bell, *A Platt of Luddington brooke from the Hebble brigg downe to the milnes in Varyance between mr fferrer and michael foxcroft*, 1602, National Archives MPC 1/111/3

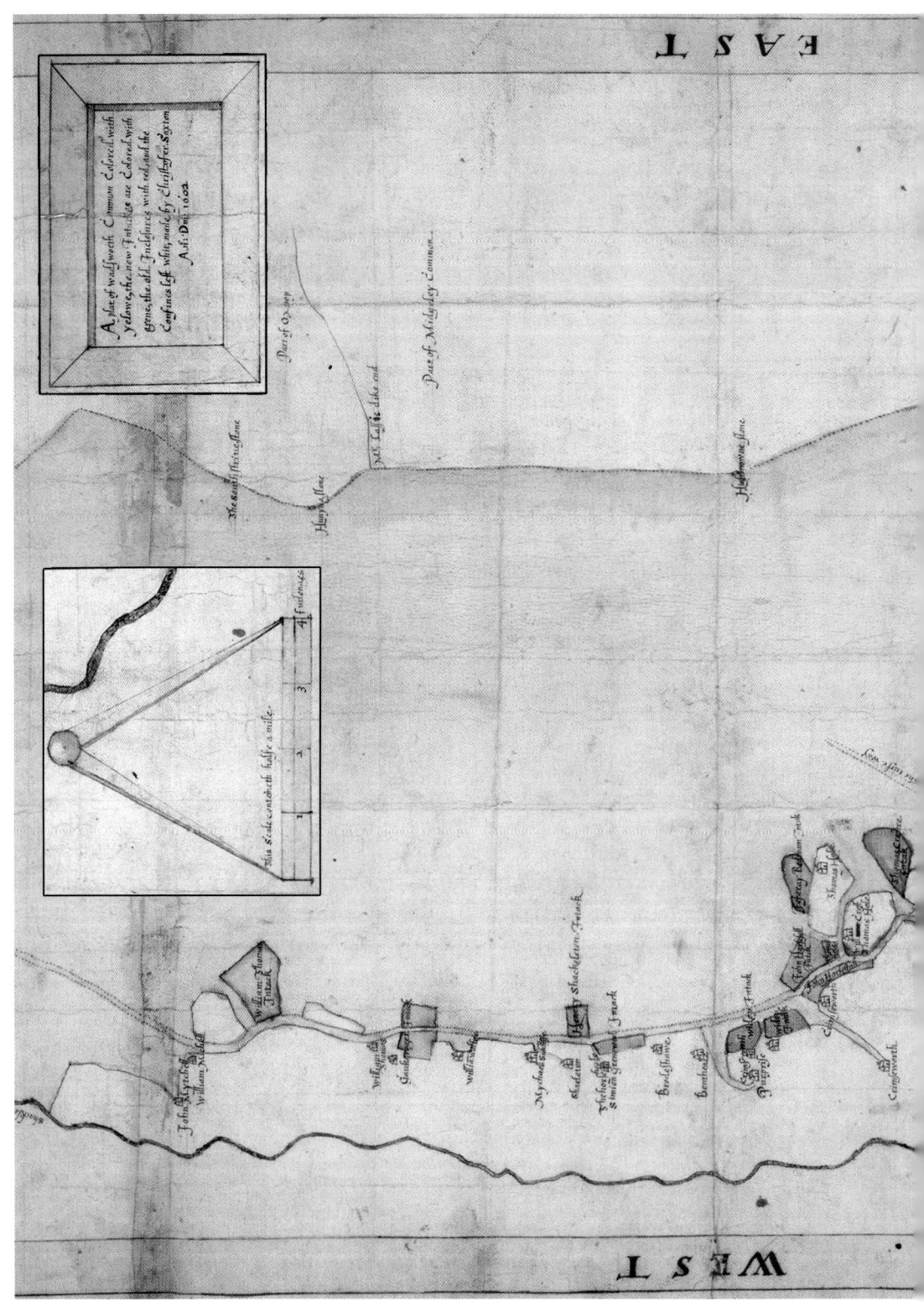

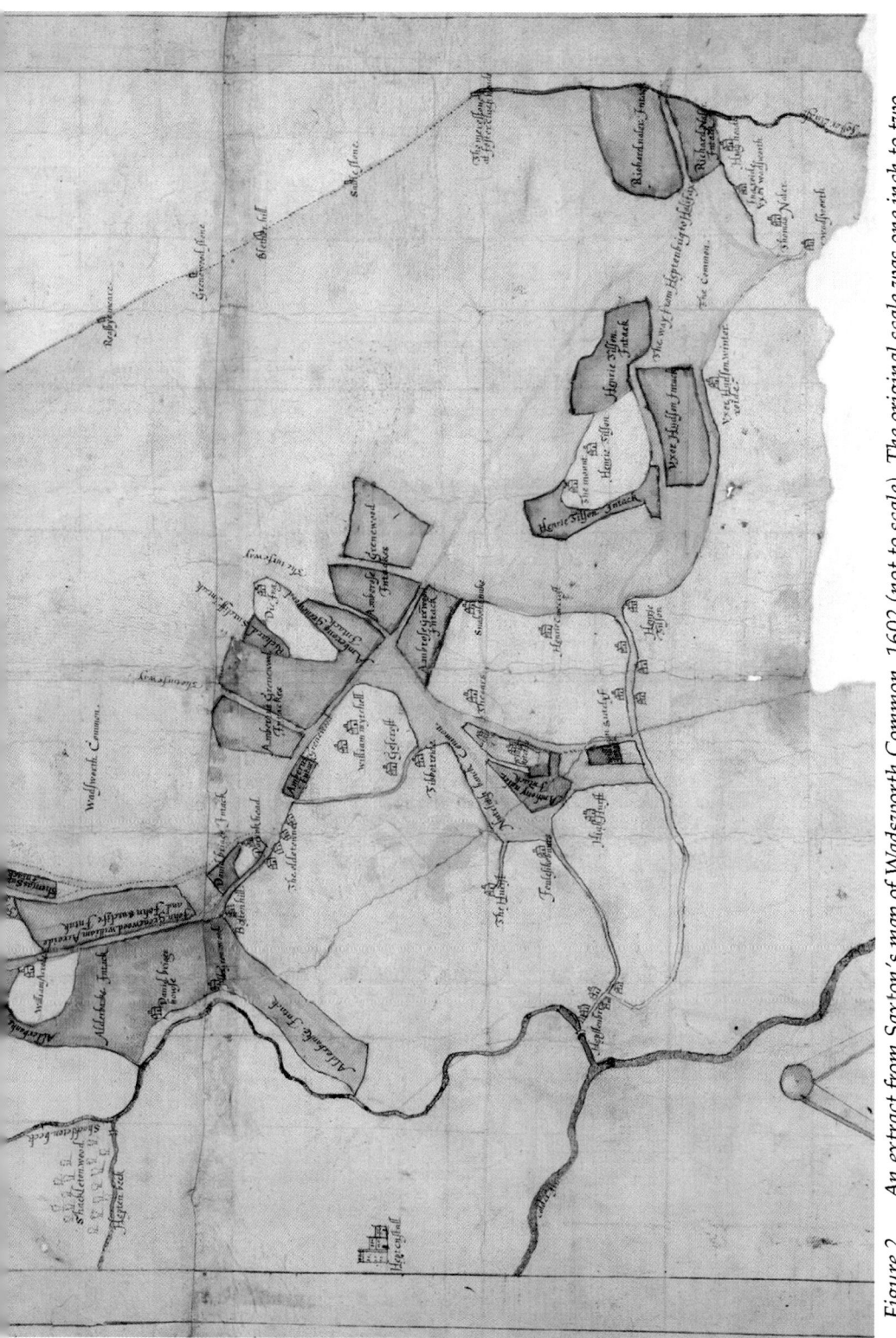

Figure 2   An extract from Saxton's map of Wadsworth Common, 1602 (not to scale). The original scale was one inch to two furlongs (quarter of a mile) . The title and scale have been transposed onto this extract.

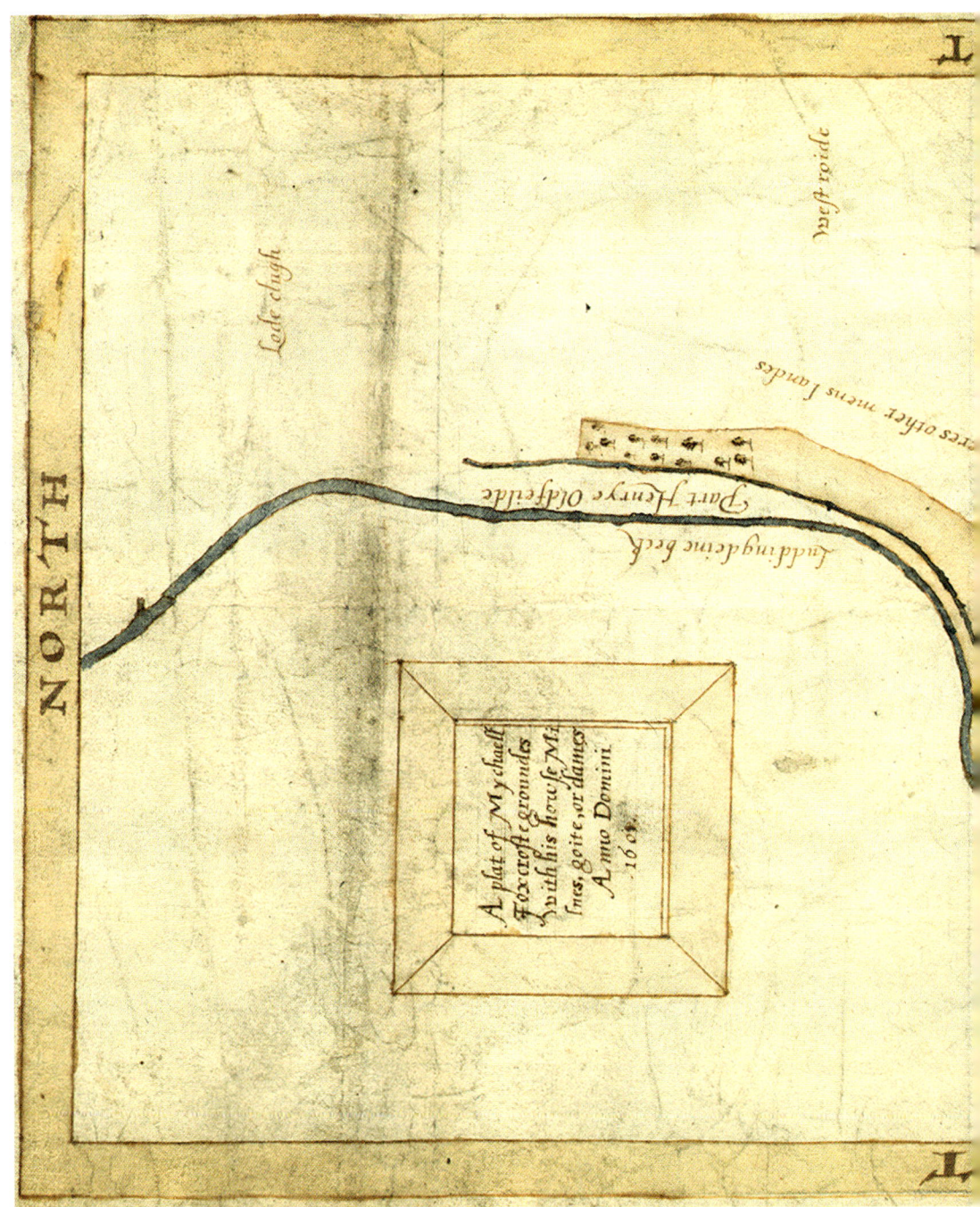

Figure 3   Saxton's map of Luddenden Foot, 1602 (not to scale). The original scale was one inch to sixteen perches. (303 perches to one mile).

Figure 4   *Bell's map of Luddenden Foot, 1602 (not to scale). The original scale was one inch to twelve perches (303 perches to one mile)*

CHAPTER 8

Sports and Pastimes

P. Horsfield and Sue Slater

Pastimes are among the forgotten footnotes of history, swept aside in the rush to explain, analyse and measure the past, yet they are important. This chapter attempts to illustrate some of the ways in which Midgley people spent their leisure time, based on the recollections of elderly people recorded in the 1970s.[1]

Billeting and Knur & Spell

Two sports which were very popular with the men of the area were billeting and knur and spell. These sports required reasonably level ground on which the billets and knurs could be found once they had been hit. Both games attracted many players and numerous spectators, especially when a local hero was taking part. Henry Horsfield (Harry Cock'oil) was one such man, a quarryman who lived at Stocks Farm. He used to practice his sport in the fields above the farm.

Figure 1   A billet match on Midgley recreation ground, Jack Horsfield is about to strike; Kenneth Smith is holding a coat to shield the billet from the wind

---

[1] Hebden Bridge Local History Society Archive, *Midgley Oral History Recordings 1977*, OH 1 to OH 11

The aim of the game was to hit the billet as far as possible. The billet was placed in the groove in the pummel head at the end of the stick, tossed into the air and hit as it descended. The distance was measured with a chain, twenty yards in length and the contestant's strike was gauged by how many twenty-yard lengths or 'scores' he could hit. Henry Horsfield could occasionally strike the billet up to twelve score.

The sticks and billets were usually made by the players themselves. The sticks were about four feet long with a shaft made of two pieces of hickory or ash spliced together and glued with gutta percha. This was melted into the joint and the stick was bound with string to give a firm grip. The pummel head was made of holly and had a carved notch where the billet rested before being tossed into the air. The billets were four to five inches long and were made of box wood. The five-inch ones were usually curved (Figure 2).

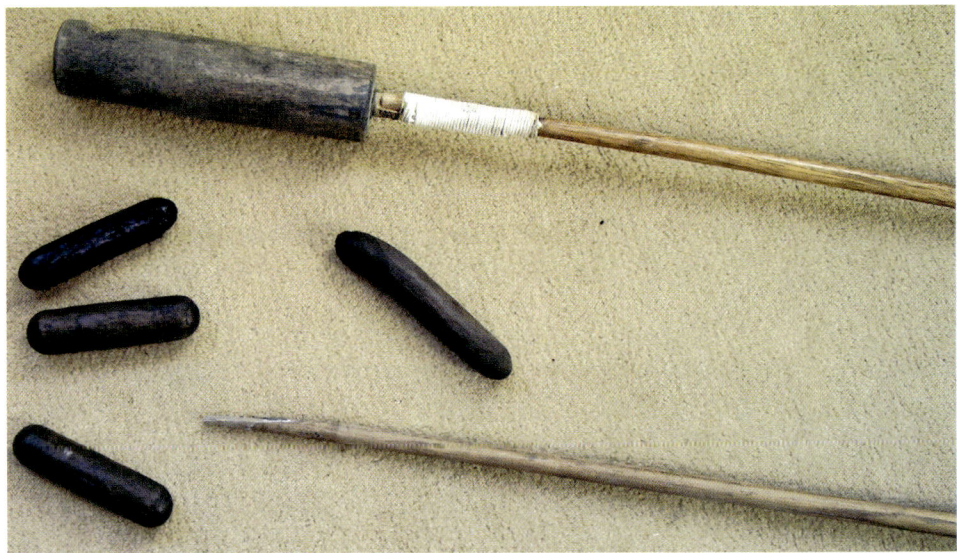

Figure 2   Two sticks and four billets – the stick without a head belonged to Harry Horsfield. The curbed billet was made by Allan Greenwood

Henry Horsfield was the champion billeter of Midgley but Alan Greenwood was the expert billet-maker. According to Fred Prior in his recorded account of billeting, Alan's billets were much sought after. To see one X-ing (revolving and twisting through the air like a propellor, pronounced 'exing') after being hit was 'a sight to behold'.

Knur and spell was also a popular game which was similar to billets. The sticks were not much different in length but they had a shorter pummel head, which was thicker and had one flat side. The early knurs were made of clay or sometimes of wood, while later the knurs were pot (earthenware). All were the shape of small balls approximately one inch in diameter (Figure 3).

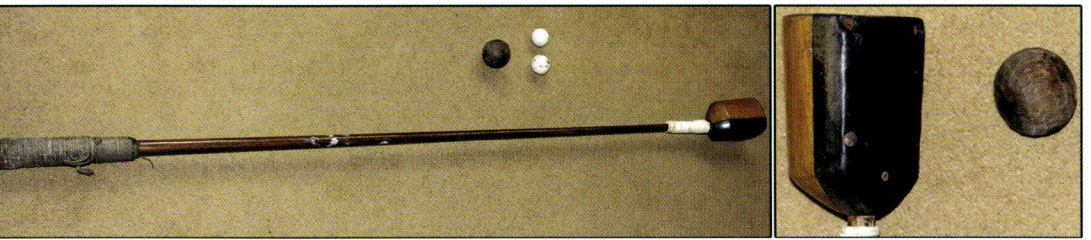

Figure 3   *A knur stick, two pot knurs and a wooden one, made from hard, dense, heavy wood from the tropics of America*

The knurs were hit in different ways. They were placed in a sling hanging from a pole inserted into the ground at an angle, or alternatively a spell board was used. This consisted of a flat board with spikes at each corner which were pushed into the ground. On the other side was a spring contraption with a cup shape where the knur was placed, the spring was set and the player then hit the spring, thus projecting the knur into the air (Figure 4).

Figure 4   *A Spell Board*

Both these games were usually organised by the customers of public houses and stakes of anything up to £100 were put on each side. Two individuals or two teams played against each other. Games usually consisted of ten rises (strokes) for each side but this varied. Instead of aggregate scores, a game would sometimes be decided on the longest knock or a series of long knocks. Both games had been played for many years. Knur and spell was referred to in

1665 in a diary kept by a squire, Thomas Beswicke.[2] In the Midgley area, both games were played in the nineteenth and early twentieth centuries but died out after World War II. Two local sayings come from the playing of these games: 'Get out o't spell 'oil' - meaning get out of the way and 'pummel'- meaning a good hit.

Lark-singing Competitions

Lark-singing competitions took place in public houses around the area in the late nineteenth and early twentieth centuries. The aim of these competitions was to find out which lark sang the most sweetly and for the longest length of time. Alice Craven recalled how her father, Frank Schofield, the last clogger in Midgley and usually referred to as 't'clogger', was one of the competitors. He went onto the moor to capture young larks and 'train' them to sing. She described how as a small child she went with her father onto the moor, where he observed the larks and located their nests. He was then able to pick up perhaps one or two chicks from each nest. These chicks were taken home and put in boxes which had fine white sand spread on the floor - this sand was also collected from the moor. The chicks had to be fed at four-hourly intervals with a special treat of mealy worms in between feeds. Frank's wife and daughter were 'roped in' to feed the chicks and also to listen to the larks when they began to sing, so helping Frank to determine which was the best singer.

Another Midgley resident, Jack Ingham, nick-named 'Larky' because of his involvement with larks, said that he had learnt all that he knew about the birds from Frank Clogger. He described how they were fed. The food consisted of hen's eggs, well beaten and made into a soft paste by mixing them with pea-meal, then baked in the oven for an hour. Hemp seeds were added and the whole mixture was crushed up finely. It was then fed to the birds on the end of a stick. The mealy worms were produced by putting oatmeal into a jam jar with damp cotton wool, the lid was replaced and left for ten days or so, by which time a good supply of worms had appeared.

When the larks had developed their flight feathers, they were taken in a closed box for a few hours each day to a place where they could hear the adult birds singing. After these 'lessons', they were then put into cages with cloth tops which were positioned on windowsills or similar places. The lark's natural instinct is to sing when the day dawns and at the same time rise into the air,

---

[2] H.W. Harwood, *Glimpses of Midgley History*, n.d., West Yorkshire Archive Service (Calderdale), MISC 78/54, Chapter 21, p11

hence the cloth top to the cage, preventing damage to the feathers. Hen birds were released back into the wild together with any cock birds which didn't come up to scratch with their singing.

Jack related how he had, while living at The Lord Nelson at Scout Head, taken some young birds from a nest and put them into a hat. He then proceeded to move the hat very gradually nearer to the house each day, until he had placed it on the windowsill. The adult birds had continued to feed the chicks as usual. He was very proud of this achievement and brought Frank to watch the chicks being fed by their parents. Jack said he had never competed with the birds he had trained because the 'sport' had died out and was illegal.

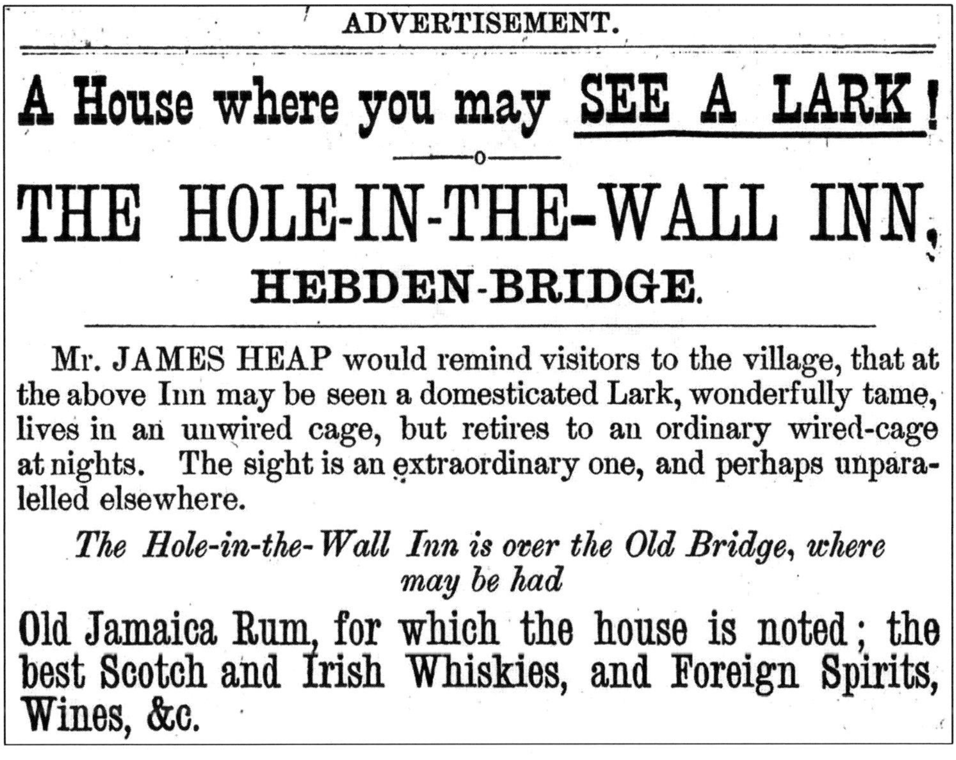

ADVERTISEMENT.

A House where you may SEE A LARK!

—o—

THE HOLE-IN-THE-WALL INN,

HEBDEN-BRIDGE.

Mr. JAMES HEAP would remind visitors to the village, that at the above Inn may be seen a domesticated Lark, wonderfully tame, lives in an unwired cage, but retires to an ordinary wired-cage at nights. The sight is an extraordinary one, and perhaps unparalelled elsewhere.

The Hole-in-the-Wall Inn is over the Old Bridge, where may be had

Old Jamaica Rum, for which the house is noted; the best Scotch and Irish Whiskies, and Foreign Spirits, Wines, &c.

Figure 5   Advert for lark singing from the 1890s – who captured the lark?

In the nineteenth century, competitions were held throughout the Calder Valley and beyond. First prizes were awarded to the lark which sang the longest, and usually this would be a copper kettle or some such. Drinking and betting were all part of the event and doubtless the landlord's profits would increase considerably on competition days.

Cock Fighting and Wrestling in the Circle

The 'earth circle' on Midgley Moor is hardly distinguishable now, but if one looks carefully one can see a ring of raised earth with heather growing on top, situated in the V shape formed by the junction of the Calderdale Way and the footpath leading from the top of Coal Dike to Foster Clough Delves.[3] There have not been any recent findings in the area to indicate why or how it came to be there. However, it has had many uses. Cock fighting took place in the 'circle', although it seems to have died out by the end of the nineteenth century. A family who lived at the Rough went to Brough Fair, Westmoreland, and bought horses, then brought them back to Midgley and used the 'circle' for breaking-in the horses. Another pastime which might have been practiced in the 'circle' was wrestling, but this is only conjecture. Certainly there were wrestling matches in the area - Sam Broadbent (Figure 6) was landlord of the Royal George, Midgley, and one of the photographs was taken at High Lees Head.

Figure 6   Sam Broadbent with wrestlers at High Lees Head

---

[3] Illustrated in Chapter 2, Figure 9

Cricket

H. W. Harwood records that cricket was played on the moor.[4] It hardly seems possible but the pitch was on a level piece of ground just above 'Th'acker' (Acre). He also said that cricket was played on 'Wark'us' (Workhouse) Rough. This seems even less likely as there is no area of level ground to be seen. We must presume that the cricket played on these two patches of ground was nothing like the game of cricket that we play today, but was undoubtedly the forerunner of cricket clubs which later formed in Booth and Luddenden.

Hound Trailing

Hound trailing, to quote Harwood, 'was promoted by local inns'.[5] Jack Ingham who lived at the Lord Nelson, Scout Head said he had been told of trailing taking place from there. Shortly before the event took place, a man would run over the course of two or three miles trailing a highly-scented rag, usually aniseed. This completed, the dogs were released to follow the trail up the Coal Dike onto the moor above Foster Clough delves and circling back to the starting point. The barking of the dogs, the shouting of spectators, the excitement of the chase and the run down the last few hundred yards were all watched by the village children.

Figure 7   Dogs and hound trailers outside the Grove Inn, Brearley

---

[4] Harwood, *Glimpses of Midgley History*, Chapter 21, p14
[5] Harwood, *Glimpses of Midgley History*, Chapter 21, p18

The last trail from Scout Head was held in February 1927. Hound trailing was a gambling sport, one of many carried out at High Lees Head, which was known locally as the Bird i'th'and or Monte Carlo. Ned Carter, another old Midgley resident, told the tale of watching the trail hounds starting at Queensbury and running to finish the trail at High Lees Head. There are graves of famous or well-loved dogs at The Withens and at the last house over Cockhill Moor, Keepers Lodge.

Another game played at various venues on the moor was pitch and toss. This was also an illicit gambling game and was played well away from the public eye. Today, we do not have any of these gambling games on the moor but it is still used for many leisure activities such as fell racing, orienteering, rambling and grouse shooting. Lark fanciers have been replaced by twitchers, there being a wealth of birds on the moor e.g. twite, snipe, golden plover.

The Grouse Moor

Midgley moor's history as a grouse moor dates back over a hundred and sixty years. In 'The Little Hill Farm', W. H. Crump says that by the 1850s grouse were of more value to the large landowners than sheep.[6] This led to the gradual restriction of grazing rights. When the moors were sold on the death of their owner, Mr Thomas Denton, at auction as part of the Castle Carr Estate on 15 April 1802 at The White Lion in Hebden Bridge, they were described as the extensive commons of the Manor of Midgley. Attention was drawn to the fact that the occupiers of the Castle Carr Estate had grazed over four hundred sheep a year on the moors.[7] When the moor came into the hands of John Murgatroyd in 1895, they were described as being the finest grouse moors. This shift in emphasis in the use of the land can be seen in material printed to advertise yet another sale of the moor (Figure 8). Now there is no mention of sheep but of the moor as being 'noted for the good bags obtained'. In 1949 the moors were on sale again as part of the Castle Carr Estate owned by John Murgatroyd.

---

[6] W.H. Crump, *The Little Hill Farm*, London: The Scrivener Press, [1951], p65
[7] T. Sutcliffe, 'Castle Carr', *Transactions of the Halifax Antiquarian Society*, 1921, pp97-108 at p101

YORKSHIRE GROUSE MOOR.

CROSSLEY, CROSLAND & UTTLEY

Are instructed to offer for **SALE BY AUCTION**, at the

LAW SOCIETY'S ROOMS, Hopwood Hall, Halifax,

On Wednesday the 12th day of JUNE, 1940,

At 4 p.m.

Subject to the general Conditions of Sale of the Law Society and
such Special Conditions as will be then produced, **The Valuable**

Freehold GROUSE MOOR

called "MIDGLEY MOOR"

containing an area of about 1,200 acres, situate in West Riding of Yorkshire,
together with SMALL HOLDING adjoining called "Rough Farm," comprising Keeper's House, Farm Buildings and Land, containing 12a. 3r. 5p.,
and Pasture Land adjoining called "Nelmires," containing 26a. 2r. 25p.,
and Land at Warley called "Haigh Cote Allotment," containing 21a. 0r. 18p.

Included with the sale is the Manor or reputed Manor and Lordship of
Midgley.

The Estate is Freehold, and contains valuable beds of Building Stone.

The Moor, which is noted for the good bags obtained, adjoins the well-known
Castle Carr and Lord Savile's Wadsworth Moors and is situate 1 mile from
Mytholmroyd, two miles from Hebden Bridge, six miles from Halifax, and
easy of access by good roads to other important towns in Yorks. and Lancs.

VACANT POSSESSION of the MOOR

WILL BE GIVEN ON COMPLETION.

Further particulars may be had from the Auctioneers, 1, Lord Street, Halifax ; Mr.
R. EDGAR HORSFALL, Chartered Surveyor, Linden Lodge, Halifax ; or

SUTCLIFFES, JACKSON & CO.,

Solicitors, HEBDEN BRIDGE.

JACKSON & CLAYTON, PRINTERS, HALIFAX.

Figure 8   Notice of auction for the sale of Midgley Moor, 1940

The foreword in the auction catalogue contains the following paragraph highlighting the sporting merits of the moorlands of Midgley, Warley and Oxenhope.

> The moors which adjoin the park are well clothed with heather and bilberry, abound with springs of the purest water, and afford excellent sport. Their large area, rich in indigenous cover, combined with their accessibility to so many important manufacturing towns and the increasing scarcity of really good grouse shooting will alone recommend this property to the notice of sportsmen.[8]

During John Murgatroyd's ownership, the moors were looked after by the gamekeeper, Mr Stansfield Boulton. He lived at Rough Farm until he retired in the late 1950s. He continued to live locally until his death in the late 1960s and was a well-known figure at the Mount Skip public house. When H. W. Harwood was alive he experienced many 'opening days' (12 August) in Midgley, probably overseen by Mr Boulton. Harwood tells how the first shoot of the year caused a tangible air of excitement in the village even though the people were only allowed at the edges of the moor to watch the proceedings. There were two main grouse shooting parties in action. The party covering

Figure 9   An example of an early shooting box - Crow Hill

---

[8] Auction Catalogue 1949

Figure 10   An example of a modern shooting box - Crow Hill

Midgley Moor was the Riley party from Ewood Hall while the Oxenhope and Wadsworth moors were covered by the Murgatroyd party from Broad Fold.[9]

There are several ways of hunting grouse. Formal driven shooting came to the fore in the mid to late nineteenth century.[10] This method was used on Midgley moor and continues to this day. Here shooting butts, known locally as 'shooting boxes', were used and were some of the first in this part of Yorkshire. There were rows of butts built with rough stone walls and covered with earth sods and heather (Figure 9). The shooting parties hid in these shelters waiting for the 'drivers' (the local word for the more usual 'beater') to carry out their part of the procedure. Each 'driver' carried a small flag and Harwood, who took part himself on several occasions, notes that the men often had a sprig of lucky white heather from the moor tucked into their lapels. The 'drivers' fanned out across the moor in a wide arc almost a mile wide and then moved forward. The grouse were raised and, flying low over the butts, were dispatched by the waiting guns. There were five or six 'drives' on a successful opening day and Harwood counted as many as 120 brace of

---

[9] Harwood, *Glimpses of Midgley History*, Chapter 22, p22
[10] http://www.basc.org.uk/content/grouseshooting [Accessed on 8 April 2007]

birds. Volunteer drivers were always to be found even if it meant taking time off work and they would earn 5s a day.[11]

Today, some people born in Midgley still remember the grouse shooting on the moor in the 1950s. One ex-Midgley resident, David Fisher, recalls when he was about fourteen taking days off school to go beating. There would be an 8 o'clock pick up of about twenty volunteers organised by the gamekeeper, Stansfield Boulton. The flags used would be homemade and there would be about eight or nine 'Shots' (men with guns). The drivers would be in two groups working towards each other on the moor. Lunch was eaten in a room in the gatehouse at Castle Carr and consisted of sandwiches made by the lad's mother.[12] The liquid refreshment was a highlight of the day as a small barrel of beer was provided. Our Midgley lad was told that there was once a hut at Shore End Gate for the use of beaters but this was before his time. The bags in his early beating days numbered over one hundred brace. His wage for a day started at 5s and gradually rose over the years to the princely sum of 12s 6d.

Today Midgley moor continues as a grouse moor with the shooting rights being owned by a syndicate. As with all grouse moors there is the rotational burning of strips of heather to increase the availability of young heather shoots. These are a highly nutritious source of food for the grouse. A by-product of this burning is that the land is laid bare and stone formations and other interesting features can be more easily seen.

---

[11] H. W. Harwood, *Glimpses of Midgley History*, Chapter 22, p22
[12] Private communication from David Fisher, 2006

CHAPTER 9

Common Rights on Midgley Moor

Sue Slater

Common land belongs to the Lord of the Manor, but his ownership is not absolute; he has to permit those living in the manor to use the common in certain well-defined and specific ways.

The most important of the common rights on Midgley moor was the right of grazing. Surprisingly, although all farmers in Midgley must have exercised this right at one time, little documentary evidence has as yet been found. By comparison with other Pennine townships, we might assume that the grazing was strictly regulated, with each farm being allowed a certain number of 'beast gates' to graze cattle or sheep.[1] The physical evidence of this regulation still survives in the form of the Midgley pinfold, a stone-walled circular enclosure on the edge of the moor, just off Chapel Lane.

Figure 1   Midgley Pinfold in 1977

---

[1] See Chapter 5, p65

Figure 2   *Saxton's map of 1594 showing 'turf pittes' on the Midgley Wadsworth boundary*

June the 10th 1717

A Division of the Turberie on Midgley Moor from the High browr knowl Stone to the Rams-Cloughhead devided by the ffreeholders of the mannor of Midgley by Lot according to the Poundrate of their Estates by order of James Farrer Esqr Lord of ye sd Mannor being agreed that every person Shall gett or Cutt their pitt or pitts to the Bottom

No.		yards
1	Saml ffletcher for Lydiat	13
2	Thomas Siddal of Midgley	14
3	Jonas Bordal for Whitelee	16
4	Henry Helliwell for ye same	16
5	William Eastwood of Greave	16
6	Henry Plurit for Brayroyd	20
7	Richard Eastwood for Greavehous	13
8	David Brigg of Midgley	5
9	Jonas Turner of Breacley	30
10	William Lockwood for Whitelee	16
11	John Shackleton for Millhouse	22
12	John Murgatroyd for Oates Royd	21
13	John Shaw for Lucy ffaeme	12
14	John Lockwood of Swood	55
15	James Farrer Esqr	65

No.	the later Division	
1	John Shaw	4
2	Saml ffletcher	5
3	John Shackleton	10
4	Richard Eastwood	5
5	Henry Helliwell	6 ½
6	John Murgatroyd	10
7	David Brigg	1 ¼
8	William Eastwood	7
9	Jonas Turner	13
10	Jonas Bordal	6 ½
11	William Lockwood	6 ½
12	Thomas Siddal	6
13	James Farrer Esqr	30
14	Henry Plurit	8
15	John Lockwood	28

Figure 3   *Division of the Turbary on Midgley Moor*

A pinder was appointed by the township whose duty was to regulate the grazing on the common. If he found animals on the common that were not supposed to be there, he impounded them in the pinfold and charged for their release. It is significant that the pinfold is placed on Coal Dike, one of the old routes onto the moor. Pinfolds are often found in this type of location.[2] We do not know how long the pinfold has been there, but it is marked on the township map of 1806. The last pinder was John Scott, who died in 1869.

If grazing was the most significant common right then the most ubiquitous was the digging of peat for fuel. This is known as the right of turbary and was practised by all inhabitants of the township, for there were few alternative sources of fuel. Many Midgley inventories contain references to peat or turf as fuel, indicating widespread use.[3] It is clear that by the late sixteenth century peat was being dug from Midgley Moor in some quantity and the resource was under pressure.

---

[2] R Eccles, 'Local Pinfolds', *Transactions of the Halifax Antiquarian Society*, 1936, pp153-162 at p154

[3] I. Bailey and A. Petford (eds), *Midgley Probate Records 1531-1731*, Midgley: Midgley Books, 2007. The original wills are held at the Borthwick Institute of Historical Research, University of York

Significantly, at this time there was a dispute between Wadsworth and Midgley townships about their respective rights of turbary. In the course of this dispute, Christopher Saxton was commissioned to draw a map which is reproduced in Figure 2.[4] The eighteenth century division of turbary rights suggests that pressure continued on this valuable resource (Figure 3).[5]

That the getting of peat continued through the eighteenth century, is shown by the accounts of the Overseers of the Poor of Midgley for 1772 , where one entry reads, 'Eight cartfull of peats getting for the workhouse, 4s'.[6] It is likely that the workhouse had turbary rights, so that the 4s paid was the cost of digging and transporting the peat.

Peat in the southern Pennines can be found to a depth of six feet or more and the layers are known as 'mosses'. The thin layers of turf covering the peat was removed by paring using a flaight spade (Figure 4). The person using this spade would use an action similar to that used by a gardener to lift turf. The thin layers are known as 'flaights', 'flaughts' or 'flaghts'. In the inventory of David Crossley, taken in 1712, 'Coales, Turfes and Flaghts' are valued at 8s 6d and the context makes clear that they were being used as fuel.[7]

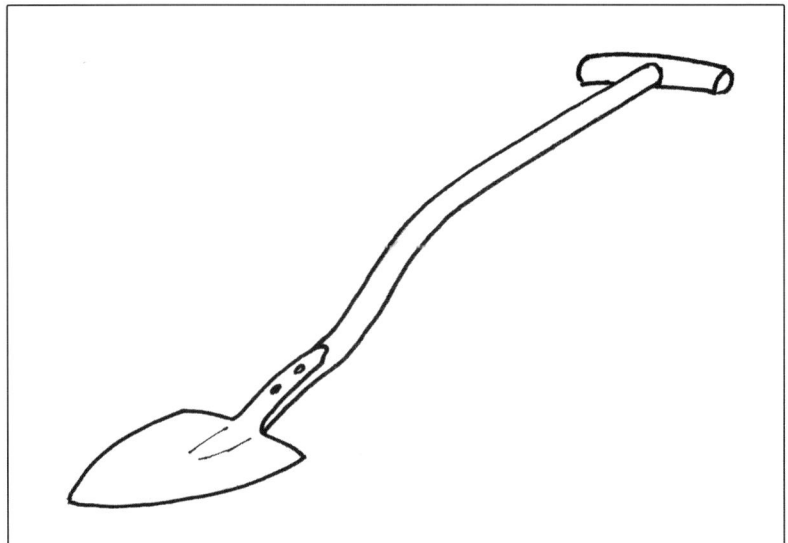

Figure 4   A flaight spade

[4] C. Saxton, *A plat of the boundaries of the Manner of Waddesworth*, 1594. British Library, Add.MS 63751A
[5] West Yorkshire Archive Service (Calderdale), *Midgley and Wadsworth deeds 1615 – 1872*, MW 42
[6] H.W. Harwood, 'Four Midgley Farms', *Transactions of the Halifax Antiquarian Society* 1939, pp213-263 at p240
[7] Bailey and Petford, *Midgley Probate Records 1531-1731*, p49

Once revealed, the peat can be dug with a special spade (Figure 5).[8] This has a straight wooden shaft with a long wooden blade which tapers slightly. A steel cutting blade is nailed to it and bent at right angles at the right hand edge in order to cut two sides of the peat block at one stroke. Peat spades tend to vary slightly in their construction in different parts of the country.[9]

We do not know when peat was last dug on Midgley Moor, but it is likely to have been towards the end of the nineteenth century when the influx of cheap coal diminished its value as fuel.

The moor also helped provide for the everyday needs of the local population. There were bilberries, crowberries and cowberries to be collected in season. The bilberries are still plentiful near the Midgley reservoirs and Slack Lane. It was the custom for bilberries to be collected from Wakes week onwards and regular pickers are still to be found as soon as the fruit ripens. In H.W. Harwood's day a pint of bilberries could be sold for 4d.[10]

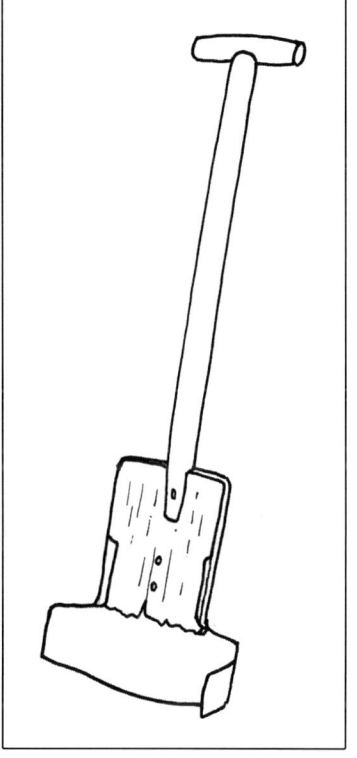

Figure 5   A peat spade

Heather is the ubiquitous moorland plant and this has provided well for people over the centuries. Both H.W. Harwood and W.B. Crump write about the continuing uses of heather during their lifetimes and in the generations before. The dead or burnt remains of heather are known as 'collon' or 'collin' bobs. These were gathered and stored in outhouses to use for kindling to light the very necessary house fires. Harwood reports that the 'collons' were collected right into the late nineteenth century when he was a lad.[11] The heather was also fodder for animals along with the gorse tops which in times of extreme winter weather, such as in 1697 to 1698, could be made palatable to animals by bruising the tops in troughs.[12] Bracken, now confined to some of

---

[8] W.B. Crump, *The Little Hill Farm*, London: Scrivener Press, [1951], p45

[9] There are several interesting photographs of these spades collected by P.C. Dorrington at
http://www.antiquefarmtools.info/index.htm [Accessed on 26 March 2007]

[10] H. W. Harwood, *Glimpses of Midgley History*, n.d., West Yorkshire Archive Service (Calderdale), MISC 78/54, Chapter 22, p8

[11] Harwood, *Glimpses of Midgley History*, Chapter 22, p7

[12] C. Jackson (ed.), Diary of Abraham de la Pryme, *Publications of the Surtees Society*, 1869, Vol 54

the edges of the moor, and rushes were sources of bedding for livestock. Moss from the moor was used to pack the gaps between the roofing slates on the older buildings; for example Peter Pickles was paid 10s for 'mossing House and lathe' in Midgley in 1776. [13]

The moor was also the place to find sand. One use for this is mentioned in 'Little Hill Farm' by W. B. Crump.[14] He tells how, at a talk he gave at Hebden Bridge, he met a man who remembered being sent as a boy up to the moor to Churn Milk Joan where he gathered a bag of sand. This was then used on a farm labourer's 'strickle'. A 'strickle' was the tool used to put a sharp edge on a scythe. It was a wooden strop with four faces which were coated before use with grease or fat and then dipped in or 'strinkled' with fine sand.

Bracken's Folly

During the economic depression of 1826 a committee was formed in Midgley to help the poor and unemployed. Another aim was to grow badly-needed food. Jonathan Bracken, who owned the paper mill at Booth, was one of the committee of seventeen which met on the first and third Friday in the month. This is an extract from one of the reports of the committee:

> We have hitherto sufficient out-post work in repairing roads, getting and braking stone and we have in contemplation to enclose a piece of waste ground, with the consent of the lord of the manor, and break it up for use of the town in order to find employment.[15]

As a result Folly Field, to the east side of Crow Hill on Midgley Moor, was cut from the moor. The precise location of the field may well have been determined by the spring shown on the first edition six-inch Ordnance Survey map.[16] A wall was built around the area and a stone cabin constructed where the men could shelter from the elements. It is said that one shilling a day was paid to those who helped to break up the moor.

Ultimately, the idea did not work out as far as cultivation was concerned. The land was barren and exposed to wild weather and the site was also too far from habitation. Jonathan Bracken eventually rented the field for a long time and it was during this period that it acquired the name Bracken's Folly. We do

---

[13] Harwood, 'Four Midgley Farms', pp240-241

[14] Crump, *The Little Hill Farm*, p57

[15] H.W. Harwood, 'Midgley Records, Third Series', *Transactions of the Halifax Antiquarian Society*, 1942, pp139-150 at p144

[16] See Ordnance Survey map of 1851 at the end of the book

not know how long it was used for agricultural purposes, but in the late nineteenth and early twentieth centuries illegal activities such as pitch and toss and cock fighting took place in the field. Crow Hill made a good lookout post when gambling was taking place.

In the latter part of the nineteenth century, a house was constructed in the middle of the field for the Eastwoods of Mill House, who for forty years or so tenanted the field. One wonders who lived in such an isolated place. The house was used as a shooting lodge. David Fisher, when reminiscing about his boyhood and Midgley Moor, said 'it was somewhere to explore, especially the cellar.'[17] Now all that remains is a pile of stones.

Figure 6   Bracken's Folly

It is probable that the path which leads from High Lees Head to the south east corner of Folly Field was the way used by pedestrians and horses while work was in progress. Nowadays, the path and the field have almost disappeared. Heather, cotton grass, and bilberry have almost reclaimed the land.

---

17 Private communication from David Fisher, 2006

Rights of Way

Up until the nineteenth century, Midgley people seem to have had unrestricted access to the moor. However, it is clear that by the early decades of the century this was being contested.

H.W. Harwood has called attention to a right of way dispute of 1849 when the question arose as to whether Radcliffe Lane was a public road to the moor.[18] In a document dated 24 June 1849 a resident, John Radcliffe, swore that the lane was not for general use. He said that the occupiers of High Lees Head Farm could give permission for the lane to be used and that the other person with full rights of use was the occupier of Brown Hill Farm. In fact these two farmers were responsible for the care and upkeep of the lane. People living in Mill House, Oats Royd and Mill Field End had the right to take peat for fuel from the moor down the road in the summer. If these people wanted to take sand or gravel down the road they had to seek permission. John Radcliffe also stated that in his father's day a lock was put on the gate at the top of the lane and the key was kept at High Lees Head which meant that the resident of Brown Hill had to fetch it each time he needed access.

Another right of way dispute arose when Joseph Priestley Edwards bought the Castle Carr estate in the 1850s and acquired the rights and privileges that went with it. In effect he gained control of the upper part of the Luddenden valley and moors. He closed packhorse routes and footpaths on the Midgley side of the valley that local people had used for centuries to gain access to the moor to exercise their common rights. The Midgley Local Board offered little opposition to what was happening and the main person to make a stand was William Howarth of Thorney Lane.[19] He was a working man with limited finances. In the 1861 Census, a William Howarth, aged forty-six, was the head of the household at 26 Thorney Lane. His occupation was recorded as a 'worsted weaver by power loom'. He is probably the William Howarth in question. Eventually the dispute centred on the route up the valley, past Castle Carr, towards Oxenhope. The outcome of this dispute was that Edwards paid £100 to the Midgley Local Board and promised to provide an alternative right of way. The road past Castle Carr was duly closed but an alternative road was never built.

---

[18] Harwood, 'Four Midgley Farms', p213

[19] T. Sutcliffe (ed.), *Newspaper cuttings Vol 2*, [the author, n.d.]. Held in the Local Studies Collection, Halifax Reference Library.

In the process of buying the land around Castle Carr, Edwards had acquired not only the farms but also their common rights. In 1895, the Estate was sold to Mr John Murgatroyd of Broadfold, owner of Oats Royd Mill. He felt justified in preventing others from using the moor. In 1897, the case of Murgatroyd v Murgatroyd was fought over this issue. The local papers of the time relate the progress of the case.[20] Samuel Murgatroyd, a Warley local councillor had been walking over the moor at Castle Carr to check on notice boards which had been erected threatening trespassers with prosecution. He was met by John Murgatroyd, junior, who was accompanied by two gamekeepers and was asked to turn back. He refused and was then threatened with prosecution for trespassing if he did not apologise to the owner. He refused again and the battle lines were drawn.

The case aroused considerable local interest and, at a meeting in Wainstalls before the case came to court, Mr James Brotherton, who was presiding, voiced support for the councillor. During the course of his speech he spoke about fishing for trout in his youth when he was able to work his way right up to where the Fly Flats embankment was later built.

> I mention the fishing rights only to show the tendency when the land becomes the property of one owner, the people's rights are gradually taken away; first, the sporting rights go, and then the roads and footpaths are attempted.

Ultimately the case went to the High Court in London and was tried by Judge Kekewich. Reading the newspaper reports one would have expected the defendant to have won the day. As a case of trespass it was expected that the plaintiff, Mr John Murgatroyd, would have to prove his case, but the judge threw the responsibility of proof onto the shoulders of Councillor Murgatroyd. He was able to produce some documentary evidence and some of the older residents could confirm the long-standing use of the disputed footpaths.

So did Samuel Murgatroyd win the day? Unfortunately he did not. To pay the costs of over £1,000, Samuel Murgatroyd's furniture and effects had to be sold; a man financially ruined for standing up for the rights of the common man.

> He has spent his whole substance in prosecuting a public claim and is convinced that the public have been unjustly deprived of their rights.[21]

---

[20] Sutcliffe, *Newspaper cuttings Vol 2*
[21] Sutcliffe, *Newspaper cuttings Vol 2*

Many of the small landowners had moor rights written into their deeds. These rights gradually dwindled as leases ran out and it suited the major landowner not to renew. A considerable change took place in 1965 with the Commons Registration Act. This required local authorities in England and Wales to establish registers of common land and town and village greens within their areas. The registers were to record the extent of the land, the owners and any rights of common held. Oxenhope, Midgley Moor and Dimmin Dale were among the commons registered in West Yorkshire.[22] Those landowners with moor rights were obliged to define their rights and to represent themselves at a tribunal. A local farm owner recalls that some of the locals did not do this and so forfeited rights. Few landowners continue to exercise moor rights on Midgley Moor in the twenty-first century apart from Rough Farm, which is in the old township of Wadsworth.[23] This may be a survival of the practice of intercommoning, when townships shared adjacent moorland for grazing. The Rough Farm sheep still graze on the moor and in harsh weather can be seen seeking cover in Foster Clough Delf.

---

[22] Conclusive Map of Registered Common Land and Open Country (2004), Countryside and Rights of Way Act 2000, Section 9

[23] Personal communication from Mrs J. Horsfield, Rough Farm, 2006

CHAPTER 10

Quarrying on Midgley Moor

P. Horsfield

The first quarrying in and around this area was probably to find thackstones, or, as they are known today, grey slates. Any stone for building purposes was picked up as land was cleared for cultivation. Early houses were largely built of timber, the thackstones being used for roofing. The early quarries were situated on the edges of the valley where the stone outcrops. In Midgley township, as early maps show, these sandstone quarries were roughly on the edges of the moor and were referred to as delves.[1]

It seems likely that owners and occupiers of land on the moor edge employed delvers to extract the stone required which was then sold to the builders in the area. In the case of the Midgley family, many of whom were prominent quarrymen, they used the stone to help with the building of the Congregational Church at Booth and to build houses. Some of the houses on Booth Street, for example, were built by the Midgleys. An advertisement in the Halifax Guardian in 1869 reads 'Delvers tenders are invited for delving and getting of stone'.[2]

Extracts from the Census Enumerators' Returns illustrate the growth of the quarrying industry in the township; mills were being built, houses were needed for the workforce, roads were being made and repaired. Midgley had its own township quarry, below Lower Hanroyd, where the road bends. It has now been filled in and looks like an ordinary field.

---

[1] See Ordnance Survey map of 1851 at the end of the book
[2] *Halifax Guardian*, 26 April 1869

Extracts from Census Enumerators' Returns[3]

1841	5	Delvers in the township of Midgley
1851	7	Delvers in the township of Midgley
	1	Quarryman and farmer, John Walton of Midgley
	1	Stone mason and farmer, Henry Fletcher of Midgley
1861	9	Delvers in the township of Midgley
	1	Stone merchant and farmer, John Walton, Upper Hanroyd
	2	Stone masons and farmers
1871	17	Delvers or quarrymen
	1	Stone merchant and farmer, John Walton, Upper Hanroyd
	1	Quarryman and farmer, Robert Midgley of Booth
1881	32	Quarrymen
	13	Stone masons
1891	39	Quarrymen
	4	Masons
1901	63	Quarrymen
	13	Stone masons

Two quarries which grew to occupy a large area by the mid-nineteenth century were at Foster Clough, known locally as Walton Edge Delves, and between The Slack and High House Pasture in the Luddenden Valley. There is little evidence to show who did the delving at the latter but since Murgatroyds had the two reservoirs built on the site we might assume that they were the owners. Amongst the Murgatroyd papers there are specifications and bills of quantities for these reservoirs dating from 1856. The contractors were Bower and Bower of Halifax.[4] The Census Enumerators' Returns indicate that there were only nine delvers in the township in 1861 and these may have been working at Walton Edge or High House Pasture. With the Murgatroyd papers is a small drawing headed 'A baring set out on High House Pasture for Mr William Dennett, 11 February 1873' (Figure 1).[5]

---

[3] This information is from the Census Enumerators' Returns, held at The National Archives, Series RG. Microfilm copies are available locally in Halifax Central Library

[4] West Yorkshire Archive Service (Calderdale), *John Murgatroyd & Son, Luddenden, Worsted Spinners and Manufacturers, Estate Records 1846 – 1925*, JM547-8

[5] West Yorkshire Archive Service (Calderdale), *John Murgatroyd & Son, Luddenden, Worsted Spinners and manufacturers, Estate Records 1846 – 1925*, JM547-8. A 'baring' is made when the topsoil is removed prior to a quarry being dug.

The Dennetts were quarrymen who lived in Midgley, so it seems likely that Mr Dennett was leasing the land for quarrying. In Kelly's Directory of 1877, William Dennett, quarryman and farmer, lived at Scotland Farm.[6] Local residents can remember this man's son, 'Willy' Dennett, who worked in Scotland quarries and lived for some time before his death in a small cottage behind Tray Royd. He was quite a character and was better educated than most of the quarrymen. Many of his fellow workers went to the Sportsman Inn and the Working Mens' Club at Springfield to hear him read the newspapers.

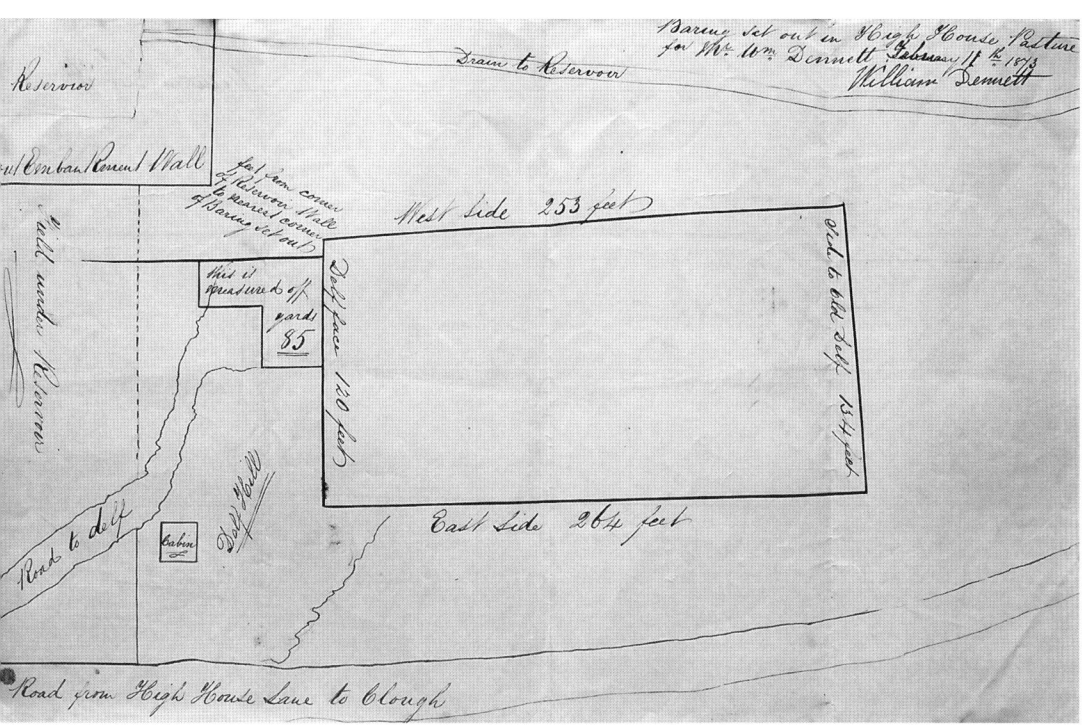

Figure 1   Plan of a baring set out in High House Pasture, 1873

The workings at Walton Edge were named after the Waltons, who lived at Upper Hanroyd, and later moved to Cliffe Hill in Midgley village. There are three Waltons mentioned in the 1851 Census: John Walton, aged forty-four, quarryman and farmer and David and Frank Walton, brothers, aged fifty and forty-two respectively, both stone delvers. It is tempting to assume that all these Waltons were working at Foster Clough Delves. Some of the Midgley family from Booth were also connected to theses delves.[7]

---

[6] *Post Office Directory of the West Riding*, London: Kelly & Co., 1877
[7] Personal communication from the late Arnold Midgley

Figure 2   *Workmen at Walton Edge, with a crane in the background*

Figure 3   *A stone waggon coming down from Walton Edge Delves*

The stone was brought down from the quarries by large, heavy four-wheeled waggons, pulled by two or three horses (Figure 3). There were brakes on all wheels, and wedges hanging from chains which could be used to prevent the waggons running away. Edward Crowther, who lived as a boy at Mill House Farm, could remember hearing the screech of the waggons on the other side of the valley descending Stocks Lane.[8]

Scotland is the quarry we know most about, and would seem to have been the most successful. There was a farm at Scotland before any quarrying took place. The earliest known deed for Scotland is dated 1693, but Harwood has suggested that there was settlement about Scotland, Trayroyd, Moorside and High Lees Head much earlier than this. He also claimed that the land was free of tax, hence its name Scot (free) land. Quarrying started here sometime before 1756. In papers dated 1756, where the fields of Scotland are mentioned by name, one is called the 'Delf Field'.[9]

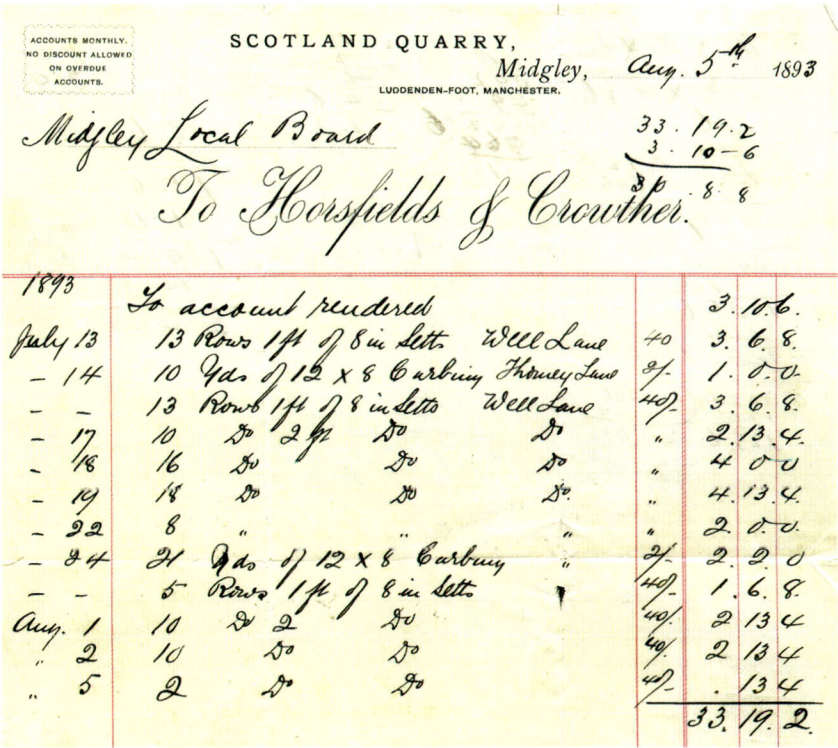

Figure 4   A bill for stone bought by Midgley Local Board

---

[8] Hebden Bridge Local History Society Archive, *Midgley Oral History Recordings 1977*, OH 1 to OH 3
[9] H.W. Harwood, 'Four Midgley Farms', *Transactions of the Halifax Antiquarian Society*, 1939, 213-260 at p255

J. & J. SCHOFIELD, QUARRY OWNERS,

Quarries :
Scotland & Thorney Lane, Midgley.

Telephone 26,
Luddenden Foot.

LUDDENDEN FOOT, YORKS.

Figure 5   *A bill head relating to the time when J. & J. Schofield were quarrying at Scotland.*

In 1858, Isabella Horsfield of Lydgate bought Trayroyd, Scotland and Moorside from the Roughtons.[10] Isabella had many children: Jonathan, who lived at Newhouse and was a cattle dealer; Thomas, who lived at Scotland; Harry who lived at Greenroyd and Christopher, a woolsorter, who also lived at Newhouse. One daughter, Mary, married William Crowther. He and Thomas ran the quarry business for several years until J. & J. Schofield purchased Trayroyd, Scotland and Moorside in 1895.

In tape recordings made in 1977, several references were made to the quarry at Scotland and the men who worked there.[11] Donald Craven's father, John, and his grandfather Illingworth both worked in the quarry. Illingworth Craven, who, according to Donald had been to America twice, came to work as a stone dresser at Scotland. He lived in Heaton near Bradford and from Monday to Saturday lunchtime he worked in the quarry, lodging at the Sportsman Inn. On Saturday he walked back to Bradford, returning to Midgley on Sunday, to be ready for work on Monday morning. How long this went on we do not know, but he eventually came with his family to live at Lower High Lees and was there when the Census was taken in 1891.

During his time at the quarry one of the crane cabins fell into the delf. Illingworth and one of his workmates broke up the cabin with maul hammers and rescued the trapped man. The wooden shaft of John Craven's hammer had indentations where his fingers had worn away the wood. One of John Craven's jobs at the quarry was to make and construct water tanks in various locations in the area. These tanks consisted of one flag stone, which formed the base, with four more flags for the sides. When the flags had been taken to the site it was then John's job to place the flags in position, fasten them together with iron bands and seal the joints with clay. Donald said that, as a boy, he had gone into the quarry on Saturday mornings, his job being to sweep up all the chippings left by his father during the previous week.

---

[10] Harwood, 'Four Midgley Farms', p255

[11] Hebden Bridge Local History Society Archive, *Midgley Oral History Recordings 1977*, OH 6, track 17

Hillary Shackleton (nee Cox) related how her grandfather, Frank Wilkinson, had come from Cleveland with his family of nine to work at Scotland Quarry. He had worked in the mines and had fifteen years experience of blasting. His help was required at Scotland. He and his family came by train to Mytholmroyd and walked up to Midgley. They apparently had relations living in Mytholmroyd, for they borrowed an old perambulator to carry the youngest child, who was only two years old, and their belongings up the Scout to Midgley. They came to 'Th'acker' (Acre), which then belonged to Murgatroyds, and the two eldest children went to work in the mill at Oats Royd. Frank worked in the quarry until he had time off to await the arrival of the doctor who attended his wife at the birth of their tenth child, Elsie. He was given the sack and was out of work for some time, but finally found employment as one of the maintenance staff at Oats Royd Mill.

Figure 6   *Herbert Horsfield and Jack Chisholm have a break from stone dressing at Scotland Quarry*

Joan Hayward (nee Horsfield) told of her father, Herbert, and her two elder brothers, Jack and Frank living on Thorney Lane and working at Scotland Quarry. They started work early, especially in summertime, came home for breakfast and then went back to work. They came home again for dinner, then worked until 5 or 6 o'clock in the afternoon, returning home again expecting another meal. 'My mother was worked to death' said Joan. She would of course be cooking with a fire oven, no electricity and perhaps only one gas ring. All water for laundry, washing, cleaning and personal hygiene would have been heated in a set pan at the side of the fire opposite to the oven.

Frank Ball came to live at Greenroyd, his family having moved to Midgley from Staffordshire so his father could seek work in this area. In 1937, at the age of fourteen, Frank went to work at Scotland Quarries. He recalled how he worked six and a half days for 12s. His duties when he first started were to make tea for the delvers, keep their workspace tidy and take their tools to and from the blacksmith when they needed to be sharpened. He was apprenticed to John Broadbent who taught him his trade and declared him to be his best pupil ever. The blacksmith, Joe Dennison, had his shop in the quarry alongside Radcliffe Lane. Also on the site were an office, stables, three cranes and a stone crusher.

Figure 7   Frank Ball and Jimmy Hall dressing stone at Scotland Quarry

These cranes were at first powered by steam. Frank reckoned that there were at least thirty men working at the quarry during this period. Not only were the cranes driven by steam but the first powered vehicle to come to Midgley was a steam lorry, driven by Welcome Farmer, who was also a quarryman.

J. & J. Schofield were very progressive in their business. They built the top two houses at Scotland as well as making a new road leading up to the quarry, avoiding the narrow bend at Tray Royd, which was awkward for waggons. It has been said that the large stone which forms the roof of the porch at Broadfold was quarried at Scotland. When it was transported from the quarry it got stuck at the corner between Tray Royd House and the barn, and the corner of the building had to be taken away.

Figure 8   Frank Ball, Jimmy Hall and Jack Horsfield dressing
                  stone at Scotland Quarry

As well as sending stone far and wide to all parts of the country, the Schofields installed a crusher. This machine crushed all waste stone into different grades of grit. Some was sold on, but some was retained by the quarry for making concrete curb edges and curved sides for silos. Women were employed to do some of the work with the crusher. In 1950, J. & J. Schofield sold the business to Farrer and Son. Shortly after Mr Farrer took over, a bulldozer and mechanical digger were used to make a new baring on the left hand side of Radcliffe Lane, but no useful stone was found. The quarrying gradually stopped, but Mr Hornby, who was employed at the quarry and lived at High Lees Head, dressed stone which was brought in from other quarries. Tipping rights were also obtained by Mr Farrer and infilling of the huge excavations began. Mr Hornby, as well as dressing stone, supervised the tipping process - old tyres and asbestos waste from Old Town was tipped there.

Figure 9   *A new use for Scotland quarry as a dump for tyres and asbestos waste*

The next owners, Walker May, continued to tip using large lorries which caused congestion and road safety problems. Eventually, after councillors, politicians, road safety and environmental health officials had been drawn into the dispute between the public and Walker May, a Public Enquiry was held at the Town Hall in Halifax in 1993. Tipping had to stop, the land had to be levelled out and grass sown, thus bringing the land back to something near its original state. The tipping did stop, but unfortunately all the land has not yet been reclaimed.

CHAPTER 11

Water from The Moor

P. Horsfield and Sue Slater

First impressions suggest that there is no water on Midgley Moor. However, even in a dry spell in summer time there are areas, such as that beside the footpath from Shore End Gate to Pasture, which are swampy, with coarse green grasses and ferns. These 'springs', between the 1,000 and 1,200 feet contour lines, indicate the edge of the water table. Rain water has soaked through the peat and soil, met the bedrock and found its way to the edge of the hillside. Closer investigation has revealed that this supply of water has been used for many generations.

The abundance of water is one reason why Midgley developed as a permanent settlement. Wells and watercourses provided a water supply to the fields and farms. Apart from drinking water, it was needed in the domestic textile industry from the early fourteenth century. It was water power that drove the first fulling mills from the same period. In the last one hundred and fifty years, the moor has served as a catchment area for reservoirs to serve the local industries and a wider population.

One good example is the way John Murgatroyd of Oats Royd Mill harnessed water and built reservoirs to meet the needs of his thriving business in the Luddenden valley. Two reservoirs were built above Slack Lane (also known as Sandy Lane). Although the water from these reservoirs no longer supplies the mill, it continues to be the sole supply for local properties. Nineteenth century maps show the development of these reservoirs and the Murgatroyd archive holds further evidence.[1]

Before the first reservoir was built, samples of water from six springs were tested. The water was 'all found to be suitable for steam manufacturing and for domestic purposes ', but water from two of them was 'inferior to the rest'. A contract was signed on 4 May 1868 by David Brook, Samuel Mann and

---

[1] West Yorkshire Archive Service (Calderdale), *John Murgatroyd & Son, Luddenden, Worsted Spinners and Manufacturers, Estate Records 1846 – 1925*, JM 547

Wardle Mann of Halifax, to construct a reservoir according to plans and specifications prepared by Edward Bull, engineer.

Figure 1   The reservoir of 1868 at High House Pasture

The reservoir was in High House Pasture and was to cost £1,370. It was to be completed on or before 31 October 1869. Conditions attached to the agreement were strict - the contractors were to forfeit £10 a week if they failed to adhere to the terms of contract. Other contracts at this time for locally-built reservoirs stipulated that the contractor was to find '… all planks, barrows and shovels, mattocks, scaffolding and all other necessary tools requisite for making the above named reservoir'. [2]

Around 1900, more water was required, and plans were made for a 'reservoir and diversion of catchwater conduit, Midgley moor, Luddenden, for Messrs John Murgatroyd and Sons'. The detailed specifications drawn up by John Judson and Hudson, architects and surveyors, were for a storage reservoir to supply Oats Royd Mill. Strict conditions applied; for example the contractor had to obtain Portland Cement of the highest quality from makers of known repute.

---

[2] West Yorkshire Archive Service (Calderdale), *John Murgatroyd & Son, Luddenden, Worsted Spinners and Manufacturers, Estate Records 1846 – 1925*, JM 547/1

The agreement was signed on 9 June 1905 in a contract drawn up with Bower Brothers, Halifax and it was to cost £8,300.[3] With hindsight, a significant clause in this contract, was 'Works to be completed and maintained in a perfect and watertight condition for a period of twelve calendar months from the date of such completion as hereinafter provided '.

In fact this reservoir has never held water to any great depth, and it is said that the contractors were never paid. A long-standing Midgley inhabitant recalls swimming here as a lad - the only rule imposed by his elders was that the boys should not swim near a square structure in the base of the reservoir. Exactly what purpose this structure served was not explained but it was evidently dangerous.

In the 1905 contract, the diversion of the catchwater appears to have been necessary because John Murgatroyd had built the original drain across land belonging to the Titterington family without permission. The Titteringtons waited until the job was complete and then destroyed it. Murgatroyds found a solution by having a syphon constructed across their own land. This runs down from behind Clough Cottage to a chamber just above Upper Mytholm.

Figure 2   The reservoir of 1905 at High House Pasture

---

[3] West Yorkshire Archive Service (Calderdale), *John Murgatroyd & Son, Luddenden, Worsted Spinners and manufacturers, Estate Records 1846 – 1925*, JM 547/5

The course of the syphon follows the line of Wood Lane, past Dry Carr, before rising to Slack Lane to a small stone shed and up into the reservoir. When in full working order, the water in the syphon was under considerable pressure. The system no longer works, but the remains of the outlet can be seen.[4]

Figure 3   High House Pasture looking South East showing the 1868 reservoir, with the dry 1905 reservoir immediately in front of it

Catchwater drains feed into both reservoirs, although they are now of limited use as upkeep is minimal and heather is filling the structures. A Midgley resident, who was one of the maintenance team for the Murgatroyd estate, recalled the water courses were cleared on Saturdays in the 1950s by members of the maintenance team working overtime. Included in this team were Irwin and Fred Wilkinson, who also farmed at Hoyle Bank and Height. One drain which required regular maintenance at that time rises from the moor above

---

[4] Private communication from David Broadbent and Mike Denton, both of Midgley

'Th'acker' (Acre). It runs along the moor edge and then descends to the reservoir and runs under the wall by the gates.

On a larger scale the catchwater drain for Fly Flatts (Warley Moor reservoir) comes across Midgley moor. It was built in the 1850s and is mentioned in 'Spring-time Saunter' by Whiteley Turner.[5] A little closer to Midgley are the reservoirs at Castle Carr - Dean Head (Upper), Dean Head (Lower) and Castle Carr. The three reservoirs together hold 124 million gallons and are now operated by Yorkshire Water. They were built between 1864 and 1872 by Halifax Corporation to gather water from the surrounding moorland. As Joseph Priestley Edwards had bought the Castle Carr Estate with a number of farms and rights to the extensive moorland in the 1850s, he was in a powerful position to dictate terms for the construction of the reservoirs.[6] They were to be fenced and there were to be no fewer than six bridges every mile across the catchwater drain.

The original Castle Carr reservoir was to have been built opposite the new mansion, but the site was found to be unsuitable. In the belief that time and money would be saved, Halifax Corporation agreed to buy further land from Mr Edwards for £4,000, with a further sum of £500 to be spent on 'ornamental waters and cascades'. The latter sum of money was increased substantially following a High Court action, resulting in the installation of the Castle Carr fountains which were said to rise over 100 feet. As part of the agreement, Halifax Corporation, and latterly Yorkshire Water, have been responsible for the considerable cost of maintaining the fountain and its workings.[7] The fountain can still be seen playing on special open days held at the discretion of the present owner, Mr F. Scholefield.

The Edwards family also specified that any buildings erected as part of the waterworks should be built in an ornamental style in keeping with their large new mansion, which had been begun in 1859. Examples of this style of building are the former reservoir keeper's house at Heights Lodge on the Wainstalls side, and Lower Lodge, part of which once housed a small gas works, on the Midgley side.

---

[5] W. Turner, *A Spring-time Saunter: round and about Bronte land*, 3rd ed., Halifax: Halifax Courier and Guardian, 1913, p48

[6] T. Sutcliffe, 'Castle Carr', *Transactions of the Halifax Antiquarian Society*, 1921, pp97 – 108 at p104

[7] H. Armitage, 'Castle Carr Deal with J.P. Edwards', *Evening Courier* 26 August 1978

Another man-made feature is the water tunnel which runs under Dimmin Dale. It is part of a conduit bringing water from Widdop, Gorple and Walshaw Dean reservoirs to the Albert water treatment works in Halifax. The tunnel under the Wadsworth and Midgley moors is the eastern end of a syphon system which brings water down into the Crimsworth valley and then up to Dimmin Dale. The only visible signs of this tunnel are the two inspection towers near the path across Dimmin Dale. The Wadsworth tunnel was constructed in the 1870s and renewed in the 1950s.

Figure 4   Inspection towers for the water conduit under Dimmin Dale

With the growing demand for water, the importance of Midgley Moor as a water catchment area has increased. Water from the moor not only supplies local properties but also some of the needs of the Halifax area. Although agricultural and industrial use has diminished, domestic needs have expanded, particularly with the re-occupation of formerly deserted farmsteads near the moor.

CHAPTER 12

Families, Friends and Neighbours:
Folklore and Cultural Tradition in Midgley

John Billingsley

The township of Midgley, indeed the whole of the Upper Calder valley, is rich in a wealth of folklore that binds the communities of the past with those of today. Throughout history, in any culture or society, the interaction of constituent elements has created patterns of behaviour, rhythms of celebration, networks of belief and experience and compromises of aspiration that are rarely written down, but nonetheless constitute the binding element in a boundlessly varied mix. Folklore, as will become clear in what follows, is not a collection of quaint bygones and strange fancies. It is the everyday life of communities, the ideas we share in common with neighbours, relations and members of our other peer groups.

A more descriptive term for folklore may be 'cultural tradition'. Any time that people form a group for some purpose, and that group achieves a degree of longevity, then an accepted set of ideas, customs, language, sayings and other shared knowledge is generated. It is, for that group, literally 'common sense', and their own sub-cultural tradition. Groups might include a family; a school, or a school class; worshippers at a chapel, or followers of a particular sect; members of a society or gang; regulars at a pub; residents of a neighbourhood, village, town, county and so on. The list of the groups we form around activities, beliefs and lifestyles is endless. A characteristic of a culture in such constant regeneration is that it is part of the shared and accepted personality of the group. As it is rarely seen as anything special, it is rarely thought especially important in the way that, for example, a spectacular one-off event may be remembered and recorded. A side-effect is that the traditions may not be noticed until they are gone; but the dynamics that create cultural tradition are still present, and in some cases the traditions themselves still, happily, persist alongside more recent customs.

Cultural tradition appears clearly in this township in the annual rhythm of festival. Midgley is particularly fortunate in having one of Britain's most celebrated calendar customs, the Easter Pace-Egg Play,[1] the survival of which is a heart-warming tale of doggedness and the happily coincidental presence of people who recognised the value of the custom both as an event in itself and, more importantly, as a community 'identifier'. They recognised that the Pace-Egg was part of Midgley life, and thus part of its social being, i.e. it 'belonged' and still belongs to Midgley, wherever else the particular Midgley version may be performed. The play is more fully described elsewhere in this volume (Chapter 13), but Midgley has stamped its own character on the event, as mumming plays of this sort were more usually associated with Yuletide. Their origins, though obscured by some rather fanciful and quasi-mystical theories emerging from Victorian observers, are generally nowadays considered an amalgamation of very real human and social concerns. They are now perceived as a communal celebration of a point in what we might call the ritual year, together with a bit of fun and entertainment, and the chance to earn a few useful coppers. In other words, things to make the holy day more of an event for all the community; something to look forward to, something to share with one's neighbours and something to look back on.

So we begin the Midgley year with the season of new life, and the celebration of one of Christianity's principal festivals; albeit remembered most strongly in a play that few would regard as in any way religious. Less formal spring customs than Easter were the mischief traditions of April Fool, when any trick on someone had to be played before noon, and 'Mischief Neet', on 30 April (though 31 March, April Fool's Eve, was also reserved for mischief in other parts of the valley). There were evenings of half-expected japes such as removing doors and gates from hinges, tapping on windows with a button on a thread, and so on. Generally they were annoying but pretty harmless pranks, except where some social antagonism existed. These, however, were not the only Mischief Nights observed in the Calder valley, and we shall come across another in autumn.

The new season was also celebrated locally on Spaw Sunday, the first Sunday in May, when people would flock to certain natural springs whose waters were reputed to be beneficial for health. After the darkness, poor air and restricted diet of winter, the spring waters, often with a sulphur or chalybeate content, were part of the detox regime of their day, as was the celebrated local dish of dock pudding, made with young wild bistort leaves, sometimes with nettles and ransoms as well. The iron of the wild greens was a restorative after

---

[1] E. Cass, *The Pace-Egg Plays of the Calder Valley*, London: FLS Books, 2004; E. Cass, 'What is the Pace-Egg Play?', *Northern Earth*, 2006, 106, pp7-12

a long winter. One of the most popular springs locally, attracting hundreds of people on Spaw Sunday, and doubtless the one to which Midgley residents would go, was a little way downstream from Catherine House Bridge, hard by the river at the foot of Spa Wood in Luddenden Dean.[2] In May 1978, well dressing was introduced into the village as part of the Methodist chapel's Spring festival; four of the village's wells were decorated and blessed (Figure 1). The practice never quite became a custom, lasting only until 1980, but well-tended gardens at two of the town wells testify to a lingering care and respect.

Figure 1   Well dressing on Towngate, Midgley; a transient tradition

The fourth Sunday in May was the anniversary celebration of the Sunday School, 't'charity' as it was known; the whole village spruced itself up, in person, at home and in graveyards, for on these occasions Midgley people who had moved away would try and come back to see old friends and family, and it was important to put on a good show. Related to this event were the Whit Walks, formal processions which took place throughout the North of England, with banners and hymns, ending with a feast and games at the school or designated field.

---

[2] W. Turner, *A Spring-time Saunter: round and about Bronte land*, 3rd ed., Halifax: Halifax Courier, 1913; facsimile reprint, Leeds: M.T.D. Rigg Publications, 1986, pp9-12; J.A. Heginbottom, 'Early Christian Sites in Calderdale', *Transactions of the Halifax Antiquarian Society*, 1988, pp1-15; *Hebden Bridge Times*, 9 May 1883

Midgley village itself does not appear to have had a proper rushbearing ceremony,[3] although Harwood mentions a small village fair or feast 'always called the Rushbearing' on the first Thursday in August,[4] the day following a more customary rushbearing in Luddenden. Such ceremonies were more usual in Anglican churches, and the rushbearings at Mytholmroyd and Luddenden in August, which Midgley folk would have attended, were larger affairs.[5] Rushbearings, or Thumps, as they were often known locally, were precursors of the annual Wakes Week, which flourished particularly in industrial surroundings. The nearest approach to this in Midgley seems to have been the annual excursion to Blackpool run by Oats Royd Mills, which became known as 'the pasty trip' because bilberry pasties would often be made for the day's packed lunch.[6]

The next major event of the year, historically, was Plot Night on or near 5 November (never known as Guy Fawkes Night in Yorkshire in deference to Fawkes' family, who were otherwise a respectable county clan), but before we say more on this event we should pause to reflect again on the self-renewing qualities of folklore. One of the preparatory meetings for the contributors to this book was held on 31 October, 2006, and our discussions were interrupted by a group of adults, children and youths, dressed in an assortment of costumes, and disguised with masks; the trick-or-treaters had arrived!

Hallowe'en is by no means a modern festival, and Hallowtide is an important date on the esoteric side of the Christian calendar. However, Hallowtide customs have largely been displaced in Britain since 1605 by the Gunpowder Plot memorial events. This is not so, of course, in other countries, where the salvation of the British state from a devastating terrorist attack was not a particular cause for celebration or commemoration. Hallowtide traditions have therefore persisted outside Britain, as both a religious and secular observance; but it was in the secular context of the United States that trick-or-

---

[3] Until the 18th century, rushes, sometimes mixed with herbs, were commonly used as a floor covering for warmth in churches. The annual renewal of rushes had become a ceremonial event involving a procession accompanying the rush-laden cart to church by the early 18th century, especially in Lancashire and Cumbria, though it soon developed variations in style from the sombre to the boisterous - the latter becoming more common as time wore on, and continuing even after churches no longer required rush floors. The shift towards a carnival atmosphere does not seem to have been an effect of the transition from a practical to symbolic festival. See S. Roud, *The English Year*, London: Penguin, 2006, pp238-40

[4] H.W. Harwood, *Glimpses of Midgley History*, n.d., West Yorkshire Archive Service (Calderdale), MISC 78/54, Chapter 22, p21

[5] See e.g. *Hebden Bridge Times*, 9 August 1882; *Todmorden News*, 16 August 1882

[6] Harwood, *Glimpses of Midgley History*, Chapter 22, pp21-22

treating developed into the custom we see today in this country: a custom whereby householders are invited to give a cash or food treat to their uninvited visitors or suffer some nuisance. The nuisance is supposed to be some minor annoyance, but occasionally is more severe, and tantamount to harassment, giving newspapers, and others assuming some moral authority, cause to denounce the tradition.

What we have in trick-or-treating is therefore a twofold return to the cycle of calendar customs; for not only has Hallowe'en returned as an observed festival (with all its other more traditional associations of magic and the supernatural, and the passage of spirits between worlds), but so has the autumn's 'Mischief Neet'. This was, traditionally, 31 October, and like the antics of the spring celebrants, and today's trick-or-treaters, was not only deplored by responsible personages, but would sometimes go over the top in targeting certain members of the community.[7] The annoyances of today's Hallowe'en should not therefore be seen as further evidence of youth's increasing moral decline, as is often portrayed, but as the latest manifestation of an old custom giving licence to rough and sometimes malicious exuberance.

Once safely through the darkness and dark deeds of Hallowe'en, we move on to the fire and warmth of Plot Night. The people from Lydgate and Scout Head held a communal fire near the pinfold at the top of Frank Lane, but other neighbourhoods also held their own (the Four Lanes district held theirs in Green Lane), and there was rivalry between them as to whose fire would last longest. Effigies were burnt at some fires, and doubtless this would also involve some rivalry. Several weeks in advance, boys would go 'progging' (collecting) for wood, and storing their collection as securely as possible in yards and outhouses, as fuel theft was a real possibility. A few days before the event, groups would go around town begging for donations of wood or coal, and sang or recited the Midgley Plot Nominy. H. W. Harwood remembered this in two versions; the shorter one ran as follows:[8]

> Little Jackie Lantern 'e gate-catched
> down in a cellar hoil striking a match
> a stick or a stake for King George's sake!

---

[7] .M.F. Roberts, *A Study of the Folklore and Folklife of the Calder Valley, with Special Reference to the Pace Egg Play*, M. Phil. Thesis, University of Sheffield, 1991, pp102-105. Roberts thinks Mischief Night is 'one of the most interesting traditions occurring in the Calder Valley, as I have found evidence of its celebration on three separate, widely divergent dates' and observes that 'All the dates are however within a week of a major festival associated with either the supernatural or with pranks'.

[8] The longer one, too long to reprint here, is in Harwood, *Glimpses of Midgley History* Chapter 22, pp24-25

Pray a cob o'coil or ought you've a mind
to chuck up Midgley bonfire hoil.

Plot Night was also a night for treacle parkin and toffee, the latter in the late nineteenth century as a 'toffee-join' to which all contributed their own home-made product.[9] And so the year turned round to Yuletide; a more substantial feast for those that could afford it, and a wealth of observances that marked the 'blessed season'.

The primary festival of the year throughout the country is Christmas and New Year. In the run-up to the festival, some reports have mentioned a fairly distinctive Midgley wassailing custom, best described by Harwood:

> I only ever saw children once going around with a 'wassail bough' (commonly called a 'wesley-bob'). This consisted of two hoops from a butter tub, criss-crossed one into the other, and covered with coloured tissue paper like a Pace-Egger's helmet, with small decorations hung down inside. They sang the traditional song, 'here we come a-wassailing, among the leaves so green...'

How frequent this actually was in Midgley, however, must be open to question, as Harwood's remark implies that he only saw it once.[10]

Throughout the Christmas and New Year period, Midgley villagers would have shared traditions familiar across wider areas of the country and still in large measure extant today. These general Yuletide customs have been so well documented elsewhere that we need not dwell on them here. There are, however, less familiar and more local traditions associated with this time of year. One very local belief was that Churn Milk Joan, a boundary stone on Midgley Moor that we will return to below, turns thrice at the sound of church bells ushering in the new year (some people say the bells of Mytholmroyd, others those of Sowerby). Similar tales are told of standing stones in other parts of the country, on a variety of occasions, so although the locations are unique, the tale type is not. In this case, it is possible that the turning legend was imported to celebrate the replacement of a single bell in the church with a peal of six in 1875.[11]

---

9 H.W. Harwood, 'As Things Were', *Transactions of the Halifax Antiquarian Society*, 1968, p.20; Harwood, *Glimpses of Midgley History*, Chapter 22, pp23-25; F.H. Marsden, 'Some Notes on the Folklore of Upper Calderdale', *Folklore*, 1932, 43(3), pp249-272

10 Harwood, *Glimpses of Midgley History*, Chapter 22, p25

11 Although legends rarely contain dateable references, there are occasions when we can reach an approximate or earliest possible date; for instance, the installation of the six bells *may* imply that the

Another regional feature of a traditional Yuletide was a curious sweeping custom, which for some was disquieting. On New Year's Eve, communities in this part of the Pennines, stretching across to East Lancashire, might well get a visit from mummers - not, in this case, performers of a mumming play, but local people, usually with blackened faces and cross-dressed or in other disguise, carrying cleaning equipment. Women might wear men's jackets turned inside out. They would suddenly enter houses carrying brooms and, ignoring the occupants, proceed to sweep the hearth, and never a word would be said - instead they would simply hum (hence the name, 'mumming') while they came in, worked and left the house, pausing only to collect some cash from the householders.[12] This custom was common in the childhood of many people I have spoken to, and they invariably have remarked how such a visit was highly unsettling, like having visitors from another world - as it should be, because the turn of the year is, like Hallowe'en, another occasion when uncanny forces are thought to be too near at hand. This meaning is underscored by the symbolism of blackened faces, cross-dressing and the focus on the cleansing (renewal) of the hearth. Renewal, making a fresh start, was and remains a key element of Yuletide and New Year customs, from the refiring of the Yule Log to making New Year Resolutions, to the appearance of a dark-haired stranger (the lucky bird) after midnight on 1 January to the New Year communal dinner enjoyed by many groups and societies.

A somewhat moveable event appears to be Luddenden's Mayor-Making, one of various 'mock mayor' traditions around the country. Such events, often held at the same time as local elections, parody the pomp and pretension of the real thing, and the local representative of the custom was instigated at the Lord Nelson Inn in 1861. The originators had a certificate and chain of office made up especially for the Mayor of Luddenden, and a 'snug' beside the bar was set aside as the Mayor's Parlour, with its own Mayor's Seat. Visitors to the village might be invited to sit here, when the chain of office would be placed over their shoulders; J. H. Stephenson recalled being given this honour in 1945, when he was Mayor of Halifax, though he did not say whether he then had to comply with the first duty of his office - to buy drinks for everyone! The

---

story does not predate this event, or at least the consecration of St Michael's Church (with a single bell) in 1848.

[12] This information has been gleaned from a number of personal communications over several years from local audiences; B. Pegg, *Rites & Riots: folk customs of Britain and Europe*, London: Blandford, 1981, pp73-74

custom has lapsed and been revived on several occasions, and is currently a popular affair, though minus the original chair.[13]

Customs marking significant points in the year provide an annual rhythm, locating community life and solidarity within a known matrix of performance. They are a way of marking time, and communities also evolve ways of marking space, forming a 'mental map' of their territory.

Figure 2   *Robin Hood's Pennystone on Midgley Moor*

Another aspect of folklore with which Midgley, and upper Calderdale generally, is relatively blessed is narrative lore. I have collected a number of place legends from the area and, perhaps surprisingly in a society where the printed word is so dominant, most of them were first told to me orally in the last quarter of the twentieth century.[14] With regard to our township, these

---

[13] Letters, *Evening Courier*, 11 May 1950; 'A pint and a good book', *Evening Courier*, 21 March 1977. The Lord Nelson has played a strong community role in the village, hosting one of Britain's earliest village libraries, founded around 1776-81 and including in its membership such luminaries as Branwell Bronte and William Dearden. The library was wound up in 1923, but some of its books are still held by Halifax's Central Reference Library. The pub is also notable for having window terminals featuring, instead of more traditional and folkloric motifs (discussed elsewhere in this chapter), the initials of Gregory Patchett, who purchased the property in 1634.

[14] J. Billingsley, *Folk Tales from Calderdale Vol 1*, Mytholmroyd: Northern Earth Books, 2007

narratives relate to the prominent landmarks of Midgley Moor: Robin Hood's Pennystone, Churn Milk Joan and the Miller's Grave.

Robin Hood's Pennystone (Figure 2) is a massive boulder of unknown provenance that stands a little way across Midgley Moor. This may once have been part of a prehistoric cairn. It is one of several stones in the area that have an association with Robin Hood. In this case, it and another similarly named stone at Wainstalls were cast across from the Sowerby hillside while Robin Hood was digging. Its name might suggest that it was once used as a 'pennystone' or 'plague stone' - a meeting point at times of pestilence, a point on the edge of the township where traders would do their business with townsfolk. Any money changing hands would be passed through vinegar poured into a basin, to disinfect it. This boulder has a suitable basin on its crown, and may once have been used in this fashion. It is, however, doubtful whether 'pennystone' in both these local examples originally referred to this custom, or to a bygone local pastime, 'pennystone', a form of quoits played with rocks, which was most unpopular among owners of dry stone walls.[15]

So perhaps it was not the plague, but just the pennystone name and its echo of plague customs elsewhere that inspired someone, at some time, to start a new money-exchange custom on Midgley Moor, at a point rather more convenient for local residents, and rather easier to find, namely a 7 feet tall monolith called Churn Milk Joan (Figure 3). This monolith, a boundary stone from the turn of the seventeenth century,[16] has attracted lore and custom to it like moths to a

Figure 3   Performing the money-exchange custom at Churn Milk Joan.

---

[15] A complaint made by the citizens of Halifax in 1539 was that "here is, contrary to the King's Acts, certain that doth play at the pennistone, the which is an unlawful game, and pulls down men's walls and breaks their stones contrary to the King's Acts...". Pennistone is in the source described as "a sort of quoits played with stones - detrimental... to stone fences" [*Halifax Guardian Historical Almanack* 1913, pp82-3]. Further details in Billingsley, *Folk Tales from Calderdale Vol 1*, p59

[16] D. Haigh, 'Fax Fallacies', *Transactions of the Halifax Antiquarian Society*, 1991, pp125-135

flame. Its name is attributed to a legend of a milkmaid, Joan, who went to collect milk or buttermilk (locally known as 'churn milk') and was overtaken by a severe snowstorm on her return across the moor; she died at the spot now marked by the stone. Variants of this tale are known: Poet Laureate Ted Hughes, for instance, who was born in Mytholmroyd in 1930, heard that she didn't succumb to the elements, but was killed by foxes.[17] Another local informant, who grew up in Mytholmroyd in the 1950s, told me the story he heard was that Joan was a witch or prostitute who gave favours to men on the moors, and was murdered by one of them. In addition to these tales, it is said that the stone turns round three times at the sound of the bells of St Michael's Church, Mytholmroyd, at New Year; and local children of the 1930s and later, according to members of the Mytholmroyd History Society, would hold hands and dance around the stone to make wishes.[18] The most popular custom here, however, is the money exchange, and as we will see, there is more to this than a simple customary observance.

The Miller's Grave is a prehistoric mound, and the most obvious remnant of what appears to have been a Bronze Age 'ritual landscape'.[19] The most common story explaining its name involves a miller named Lee, who apparently committed suicide at Mayroyd, near Hebden Bridge, perhaps around the end of the eighteenth century. Those dying in this way were denied burial in consecrated ground and were customarily interred at a crossroads; in this case, it was Four Lane Ends, on Heights Road at the foot of Midgley Moor. However, Lee's soul would not rest, and so disquieted the locals that one night they gathered to exhume the body, and bore it over the moor to the old mound, where it was re-interred. If they hoped that would solve the problem, they were wrong, because Lee continued to 'walk' until his body was accepted into Heptonstall churchyard. Another story tells of a miller walking home from market across the moor; he was set upon, robbed and slain, his body concealed in the old mound.[20]

Such tales may be understood both as history and as legend, and form an important part of local tradition. The construction of narratives around places forms part of a community's 'cognitive map'; the map that they have within their heads of their own territory. Knowing the stories identified one as a

[17] T. Hughes, 'Churn-Milk Joan', in *Elmet*, London: Faber and Faber, 1994, p56

[18] This information has been gleaned from a number of personal communications over several years from local audiences; Billingsley, *Folk Tales from Calderdale Vol 1*, p62

[19] This is illustrated in Chapter 2, Figure 5.

[20] R. Law, 'Evidences of Prehistoric Man on the Moorlands in and around the Parish of Halifax', *Halifax Naturalist*, 1897, 2(7), pp1-2; Billingsley, *Folk Tales from Calderdale Vol 1*, p53

member of that community, as inheritor of its traditions, and hopefully in time as a transmitter also. This process also helped incorporate the place within the local community, by giving it a character. There are other functions that may also be played out in folklore, for instance, the pennystone tradition, which now involves taking any coins which one may find on top of Churn Milk Joan and replacing them with coins to equal or greater value from your own pocket in order to ensure good fortune in the future. This is not just an echo, probably imported from elsewhere, of deal-making at times when the plague was rife; it was also a way of teaching children, here and now, that when you make a deal, you never simply take, but always treat the other side equally or better, to ensure you receive similar respect and the good fortune that inevitably follows. This custom may have shifted to Churn Milk Joan from the appropriately named Robin Hood's Pennystone, the rock basin of which is more conveniently positioned; possibly because Churn Milk Joan is not only nearer settlement but also lies on a more commonly used route across the moor, and thus afforded regular opportunity to reinforce this moral message.[21]

Similarly, whatever the factual truth of the matter may be, the story of Miller Lee's reburial in the ancient mound of Miller's Grave, speaks of old beliefs and practices relating to the burial of those who had taken their own life. Until 1823, the law required that they should be denied a Christian service and buried in the public highway, frequently with a stake through the body, to prevent 'walking'.[22] This usually occurred at a crossroads, traditionally held to be places where the otherworld intersected with our own, i.e. they were liminal points, held to be 'between worlds', and hence appropriate for those who had transgressed spiritual laws. Both the Miller's original resting place - Four Lane Ends, on Heights Road west of Foster Clough - and the tumulus were recognised as such liminal points. Whether the Miller had actually been staked we do not know. The story does not give this information, and no

---

[21] It should be noted that while the form or idea of this money exchange custom is traceable to plague times, the earliest written reference to it at Churn Milk Joan that I have yet seen is in W.B. Crump, *The Little Hill Farm*, London: Scrivener Press, [1951], p76, placing it in the 1930s; Ted Hughes's 'Churn Milk Joan' also refers to it as a recollection from his 1930s childhood. As the earliest references appear to date from the 1930s, this is the latest possible origin for the custom; but as those references are plainly unaware of it being a recently generated custom, we need to allow time for the process of 'forgetting'. I suspect the latest date of origin for the custom would be around the time of the 1914-18 War, but the popularity of folklore among local gentlemen antiquarians of the late nineteenth century might make that a more likely origin.

[22] J. Simpson and S. Roud, *A Dictionary of English Folklore*, Oxford: Oxford University Press, 2000, pp84-85

documentary evidence relating to the event has been found; however, both crossroads burials and staking are recorded from Halifax.[23]

Otherworld traditions are also revealed in measures taken to preserve houses and households from misfortune and malignity. A very common feature in the old farmhouses of the Calder Valley are stone heads, typically placed at doorways, beside windows and in gable ends. These threshold points are also held to be liminal, accessible to otherworld and magical influences, and therefore were considered suitable places to apply folk magic. The carved head employed in this position would not have been a realistic human likeness, as to do so would have rendered the image too close to the 'real' world; the preferred image was the 'archaic head', no more than a naive template for the human face. As such, we again encounter liminality, for this is

a face at the edge of human likeness, and therefore considered able to communicate with beings similarly located at the edge of our consciousness.[24] Dean House has such archaic heads at its windows, while such a carved head has been found at New House Farm; Oats Royd (Figure 4) demonstrates the tradition, in having small caricature heads in the gables, but in this

Figure 4   An archaic head at Oats Royd

---

[23] The usual site chosen in Halifax for such burials appears to have been the crossroads at the bottom of Parkinson Lane, once known, after one such burial, as Goldsmith's Grave. Reports indicate at least three people were laid at this point. T.W. Hanson, 'Some Halifax Houses: Parkinson House', *Transactions of the Halifax Antiquarian Society*, 1923, pp1-20 at p3

[24] The tradition associating severed and carved heads with boundaries between this world and the next can be traced back into prehistory, and appears to have periodically re-emerged since then. One of the most significant re-emergences of the liminal head motif was in the 17th century, and the Calder and Aire valleys of West Yorkshire seem to have been the heartland of this resurgence. J. Billingsley, *A Stony Gaze*, Milverton: Capall Bann, 1998. J. Billingsley, *Archaic Head Carving in West Yorkshire & Beyond*, MA thesis, University of Sheffield, 1993 (available in Central Reference Library, Halifax). Many archaic heads are still to be found in Calderdale, and a gazetteer is included in the thesis, and in the files of the Halifax Antiquarian Society; the author and the HAS would be glad to hear of others.

case the faces show the beginnings of the drift towards the realistic style that became accepted in the eighteenth and nineteenth centuries.

Figure 5   *'Devil's arrow' label stops or terminals at Oats Royd*

A similar protective device is often found in association with archaic heads. The drip mouldings above windows and doors, designed in the days before houses had eaves troughing to throw rainwater away from the walls, often have decorative terminals or label stops in which a number of motifs recur. The most typical is the heart or arrow shape (Figure 5), often found on its side or reversed. These were once known as 'devil's arrows'. Folk terminology reveals that, like the archaic head, they had an apotropaic (evil-averting) role beyond their decorative function.[25] There is a strong overlap with the heart symbol found on gravestones from the similar seventeenth and eighteenth centuries, and again concentrated in West Yorkshire and the Calder Valley.[26] The heart symbolised the soul in Christian thought, and there seems to have

---

[25] L. Ambler, *Old Halls & Manor Houses of Yorkshire*, London: Batsford, 1913, p26
[26] P. Brears, 'Heart Gravestones in the Calder Valley', *Folk Life*, 1981, 19, pp84-93

been a local cross-over between the older and ultimately pre-Christian association of the human head as the seat of the soul with the contemporary Christian symbol. The motifs came together in heart-shaped heads, such as the one high on the wall at the top of Woolshops, Halifax, in decorative allusions to facial features with the heart shape (seen in gravestones in Heptonstall and Halifax churchyards), in the dual occurrence of heads and heart or arrow shapes at thresholds, and in what is probably a later incorporation, though carrying on the development of the tradition, in a heart symbol placed in the gable end of a cottage in Naylor Lane, Midgley (Figure 6).[27]

Figure 6   *The gable heart in Naylor Lane*

Other decorations found on local houses are also associated with a protective function. The diagonal cross, frequently called St Andrew's Cross, in fact derives from the ancient *dag* rune, used as a protective symbol in Viking traditions; the roundel is aimed at deflecting the evil eye; and the spiral, such as those at the foot of the fireplace in the White Lion Hotel, Hebden Bridge, is a protective against fire.[28]

Among the otherworldly characters that such devices are aimed at is the boggart, a species of the 'little people' that could be quite helpful to humans,

---

[27] Billingsley, *A Stony Gaze*, pp121-126

[28] Other 'house luck' devices known locally include old shoes and used underwear like petticoats and chemises, often placed in chimney flues; rowan sprigs, usually placed in the roof space; cats, immured in walls and subsequently mummified; and more common objects such as naturally holed stones (hag stones) and horseshoes. The author would be very glad to hear of any similar items in the area as part of ongoing research into the folklore of the Calder Valley.

especially around the house, or may turn bad (indeed, Dobby the house-elf in J. K. Rowling's Harry Potter books is characterised in a way very similar to boggart traditions), in which case its mischief could be quite spiteful. Boggart accounts from previous centuries have much in common with what we might today call ghosts or poltergeists. Favoured haunts of boggarts were bridges and gates, once again liminal locations, though they were capable of ranging further afield. A horse that suddenly shied for no apparent reason was said to have 'tekken t'boggart', to have been spooked by a boggart. Once numerous in the northern counties, the former supposed haunts of such beings are now mostly revealed in placenames and legends, such as at Boggard House (now known as Ellen Royd). At one stage, this house had part of the old font of Luddenden Church (broken and removed from the church during the Parliamentary period, but now restored to the chancel) in its garden. It was called the Boggart's Chair. In its damaged state, it resembled a seat and the tale grew up that it was a stone that had been worn into its shape by the house boggart sitting on it.[29]

A carved archaic head placed over the doorway of the Old Sun Inn in Haworth in 1973 is reputed to have solved a haunting problem in the pub.[30] If so, we can only note that Kershaw House and Brearley's Grove Inn, other reputedly haunted hostelries in old Midgley township, do not have such protection.[31]

We are obviously not very far away, at this point, from the world of magic and witchcraft, and Midgley was no more a stranger to such affairs than the rest of the world. Indeed, the Rev. Thomas Hawkins, in 1808, saw fit to deliver and publish two sermons on 'The Iniquity of Witchcraft', deploring the prevalence of fortune-tellers, healers and cunning folk in the Warley and Luddenden area.[32] Cunning folk were magical practitioners, skilled to varying degrees in activities such as healing, identifying thieves, recovering lost items, fortune-telling, psychotherapy, inducing love and removing a witch's spells. For such specialised services, there were few alternatives, if any, and cunning folk could build up significant reputations and clienteles - Hawkins notes that a cunning man who had just set up in Luddenden enjoyed queues of up to thirty people.

---

[29] T. Sutcliffe, 'A Tour in Midgley', *Transactions of the Halifax Antiquarian Society*, 1928, p117. Curiously, another Ellen Royd, in Elland, was once known as Boggarts House and had a stone called the Boggarts Chair in its garden (A. Rinder, *A History of Elland*, Elland, 1987, p65).

[30] Billingsley, *A Stony Gaze*, pp163-164

[31] *Evening Courier*, 30 October 1987; 27 October 2001; 2 April 2005; 12 May 2005

[32] T. Hawkins, *The Iniquity of Witchcraft, Censured and Exposed*. Halifax, 1808

Cunning folk should not be seen as witches, though there were plenty of clergymen who were keen to portray them as such, since, like Hawkins, they saw any supernatural act not expressly sanctioned by God as a connivance with the Devil. Cunning folk were more apt to work on behalf of clients who had been bewitched, or, in the local parlance, had 'had hurt done them'. Their rites often consisted of a strange mixture of half-remembered Roman Catholic ritual language, mixed with spirit invocations, hellfire imprecation and a set of remedies and actions derived from some more archaic time. Common dispensations would include a talisman, involving magical sigils, or a charm, written on paper that would then be secreted in some appropriate place around the body or house.[33]

A slander case in Todmorden in 1862 concerned two women from Mankinholes, one of whom repeatedly called the other a witch and at one time asked a neighbour to mind her house while she went to Luddenden to procure a horseshoe. As there would have been no shortage of horseshoes in the

---

[33] Hawkins in *The Iniquity of Witchcraft, Censured and Exposed* reproduces part of such a written charm that was shown to him: "In the name of Jesus Christ, I call upon thee through power will command such creatures, Drimoth, Bellmoth, Lymock, I conjure you up to fetch me back the watch of J— C—, that was stolen on the ninth day of August, 1807, in the house of man, to bring the matter to true light, and to confess the said watch and to the party the owner, to have his watch again in so short time as may be pleasing and acceptable to the Almighty. God will have the whole matter made known in this order without any further trouble unto the parties. I. G. H. name of the angels Satan and Agemon, that you attend to me in the hour acceptable to the Almighty God, and send unto me a spirit called Sagrigg, to torment the thief both day and night that he do fulfil my command, and desire to fetch back the watch *in nomen de patri an filii....* I by these creatures shall make them to yield through God's help, to their sorrow, by the authority of the Omnipotent, the Father, the Son, and the Holy Ghost, and by the holy virgin Mary mother of our Lord Jesus Christ, and the holy angels and archangels, and of St. Michael and St. John the Baptist, and in behalf of St. Stephen and all the martyrs, St. Sylvester and all the confessors, the holy virgins, and all the saints in heaven and earth. Unto whom there is given power to bind all those spirits to bring the thief to judgment, that have stolen the watch. And here, we do excommunicate, damn, curse, and bind with the knots and bonds of excommunication all the thieves, male or female, that have committed this theft or mischief to J— C—, of Causeyfoot, or have accepted any part thereof to their own use. Let them have part with Judas who betrayed Christ, Amen. Let their children be made orphans. Cursed be the thief, be they in the field, in the grove, in the woods, in their houses, barns, chambers, and beds, that have stolen the watch.   And cursed be they in the church, the church yard, in eating, in waking, in sleeping, in drinking, in sitting, kneeling, standing, lying, in all their works, in their body and soul, and in their five wits. And cursed be the heart, back, liver, bowels, and spleen. And cursed be their head, and their arms, and the hands which took the watch. And cursed be their flesh, and cursed be their bones, and the marrow that is within their bones. And cursed be they - by the milk of the virgin Mary. I conjure thee Lucifer, with all thy soldiers, by the Father Son and Holy Ghost — that the thief rest not day nor night, till thou restore the watch again to J—C—, acceptable to Almighty God — Bring them to destruction — And let the torments of hell be strong upon them for ever. Amen."

Mankinholes district at the time, we can only assume that she was after a 'special' horseshoe that might remove the suspected spell.[34]

The popular demand for cunning magic and house talismans in areas of medicine and well-being, where neither doctors nor priests were held likely to be of practical assistance, is further testimony to how strong has been the popular belief in other dimensions of reality that could intrude into everyday life. We have already spoken of liminal places, and boundaries involve an extension of the liminal concept.

Boundaries of all kinds were important in tradition, and Churn Milk Joan owes its location to a boundary dispute between Midgley and Wadsworth at the end of the sixteenth century. Boundary perambulations, common in other parts of the country, were erratic in this area, but in August 1778 and other years, members of Heptonstall Grammar School walked the Wadsworth boundaries.[35] Eighteenth century dates visible on the Greenwood Stone and extremely faintly on the west face of Churn Milk Joan may be attributable to these ceremonial 'beating-the-bounds' walks. After lapsing for a while, boundary perambulations were again recorded in Wadsworth in May 1874, when a number of encroachments were found. In 1898, a boundary walk followed a revival of the Court Baron by Thomas Riley, Lord of the Manor of Midgley, at the Clarence Inn, Brearley.[36]

There are boundaries in life, too, and we must mention local rites of passage, which celebrated the major stages of life, such as birth, marriage and death, and subsidiary points like coming of age, motherhood and retirement. Customs at such times mark well-defined stages in a life, boundaries between one status and another, and are again generally widespread elsewhere. Old Midgley residents, for instance, have affirmed the men's custom of wetting (or 'weshing') the baby's head, i.e. standing a round at one's local pub, and that gifts of a silver coin, spoon or jug were placed in the baby's hand to express a wish for its future prosperity; these customs still persist, though in attenuated form.[37]

---

[34] *Todmorden Times*, 9 August 1862

[35] J.H. Ogden, 'A Moorland Township', *Transactions of the Halifax Antiquarian Society*, 1904, pp37-51 at p38-40; Haigh, 'Fax Fallacies', pp128-131

[36] For 1874 see *Todmorden & Hebden Bridge Historical Almanac* 1875, p13; For 1898 see Hebden Bridge Local History Society Archive, NC14, p65

[37] Other birth presents recorded in Britain included salt, as a protection from evil influences; bread, to confer freedom from hunger; and matches - this surprising gift apparently symbolised strength and good health.

When it came to marriage, we know that Midgley folk might bar the road where the wedding party was to pass - the newly-weds could only continue onwards by paying a toll. At the other end of married life, as it were, a Midgley man, Samuel Hey, was indicted for selling his wife at Halifax Market Cross in November 1833. The purchaser was a neighbour, from which we might assume that an affair had been in progress and the sale was probably to everyone's mutual satisfaction - especially as Hey returned sixpence of the ten shillings he received as 'luck money'.[38]

When someone died, it was customary to 'bid' people to the funeral or memorial service, by sending a bidding card. How often you were so 'bid' was in some measure a mark of local status, and such cards, often ornate, were sometimes framed and displayed in parlours, which also memorialised the deceased within their own community. Funeral parties were given 'burying buns', sponge cakes wrapped in piece of paper for sharing with family at home and ale as they left the house.[39] For a year afterwards, spouses were expected to wear full mourning; in the second year, it was half-mourning, and by the third year after a death, such requirements were dropped.

To keep death at bay, there were ideas about health. Children might be made to wear a red silk thread around their neck as proof against not only drowning, but also the common cold; though a red silk bag containing two hazel twigs was a more general prophylactic. In later life, rheumatism might be combatted by carrying in one's pocket a potato or a small stone about the size of a penny.

Lore concerning the world of nature makes a curious collection. For instance, it was considered unlucky to kill a cockroach or crow, to rob a magpie's (or in local dialect, 'pyenot's') nest, or to have a peacock's feather in the house (for fear of attracting the evil eye). Any coins in one's pocket were turned over on hearing the first cuckoo of spring. It was custom, too, that when a beekeeper died, someone should solemnly inform the bees in their hives; without such respect, it was thought the bees would fly away and swarm elsewhere. And on bee swarms, H. W. Harwood recorded the rhyme:

> A swarm of bees in May is worth a load of hay
> A swarm of bees in June is worth a silver spoon
> But a swarm of bees in July isn't worth a fly

---

[38] *Yorkshire Notes & Queries,* 1909, 5(12), p276

[39] The Rev H Wild, sometime member of clergy at Heptonstall, recalls his first experience of a bidden funeral, in *Holiday Walks in the North Countree,* Manchester: John Heywood, [1912], pp138-140

However, of this kind of material there is much more than we have space for here. Much of such lore in Midgley was shared with neighbouring Pennine communities, communities that shared the kind of economic and social conditions found here; some would have wider currency in northern England and perhaps beyond. This is the context of folklore in Midgley, 'the village where birds fly backwards',[40] as it is anywhere else.

The study of folklore is complex and wide-ranging. By its very nature, it is rarely to be sought in the documents that are usually preferred by historians as primary sources. Its primary sources are as likely to be found sitting in a room with your grandparents, or in a pub with a group of local people, as sitting in a library surrounded by books and papers. Much of historical folklore has been lost because it was not written down, and those who could tell us about it are no longer with us.

Nonetheless, there is much material to be found in old books and papers, but it is invariably interleaved with material on other subjects, or buried in a biographical account. Diaries and other documents relating to social history can provide pieces of the folkloric jigsaw; accounts of trades and industries, schools, churches and chapels can reveal some of the traditions associated with their history; and so on. Collecting folklore is being ready to come across snippets of information from almost any historical or biographical source; and equally, being ready to accept that for many people, the minutiae of everyday life that folklore typically deals in was not questioned, and has not been seen as worthy of record.

In these days of fragmenting communities, there is a need to remember and pass on the 'done things' of our lives, and to be aware of the things we do and say now that might one day be understood as ideas and habits that are characteristic of our time, a time that will be past.

However, it can be difficult to recognise our own folklore, the cultural idiosyncrasies that we ourselves maintain, because it is often so everyday and even humdrum. It is far easier when common sense begins to be overtaken by time, because then it stands out. Few people remarked on the tradition of 'donkey-stoning' the threshold when it was current in Midgley and across the North of England, but now it is no longer the 'done thing', we can recognise it as part of cultural tradition. The washdays, when streets were closed to traffic

---

[40] *Flying the Calderdale Way*, Halifax: Halifax Evening Courier, 1988, p42

by lines of laundry stretched between the facing houses, have similarly vanished. So have, surely to no one's regret, the cock-fighting that once took place in Midgley. Lark-singing is another pastime whose disappearance few in our more ethically-minded modern society may mourn. More to be regretted is the loss of traditional sports such as billets, knur and spell and road bowls.[41] All these sports attracted spectators in great numbers and provided a focus for enthusiastic gambling. Dialect is another aspect of cultural tradition that now attracts attention were we to hear it on the streets of Midgley, but it was not so long ago when it was the one speaking without dialect that would court notice.

It is because traditions become so much more visible when they are out of fashion that we get the impression that folklore is something in the past, and in a perpetual state of terminal decline. Yet while the decline is inevitable in a world of greater mobility and weaker community ties, it shows no sign of being terminal, as we can see from this review of folklore in Midgley past and present. We are constantly creating and discarding folklore, and constantly thereby renewing our sense of community and shared values. Mixed with the nostalgia, then, must be an awareness of moving forward.

---

[41] Road bowls was played with stone discs, each about 2-4" in diameter and 1-2" in thickness, and was played on hardened road surfaces. It had two main variants; competitors would choose a start and finish line, and compete to see who could cover the distance in the shortest number of rolls, or the contest might simply consist of attempting the longest single distance. Harwood, in *Glimpses of Midgley History*, Chapter 23, p2, recalled making them himself and finding them in wall crevices in the village, though he is not forthcoming about whether he actually played them!

CHAPTER 13

The Midgley Pace Egg Play: An Overview

Veronica Gregory and Jane Clyde

The Pace Egg play is one of the few examples of traditional folk drama in the country. It is still performed by young men to large audiences on Good Friday morning in the centre of Midgley village.

> Fool: (in a loud voice)
> Room! Room! Brave gallants. Give us room to sport.
> For in this room we wish to resort-
> Resort, and repeat to you our merry rhyme,
> For pray you remember 'tis Pace Egg time.
> (Bell to ring and drums)
> A ring a ring, I enter in,
> I hope this famous fight to win,
> Whether I rise, stick stand or fall,
> I'll do my best to please you all.

Although various versions of the Pace Egg play have been performed across the West Riding and Lancashire, the Midgley play is a tradition which evokes strong affectionate memories for many residents, especially the elderly. Its identity is seen as strictly 'of Midgley' and as such, quite distinct from any other version. Discussion of the play among those who were once involved concerns appropriate dialect, delivery, costume and the players. Far from being a straightforward play or piece of slapstick, it has captured the interest of many historians who have raised questions about its origins, and its significance.

Arguably the most important account of the history of the play is by H.W.Harwood and F.H. Marsden. There is a wealth of detail and references in their work which has an 'Introductory Study' followed by the text of the Midgley version of the Pace Egg.[1]

---

[1] H.W. Harwood & F.H. Marsden (eds), *The Pace Egg – The Midgley Version*, Halifax: the authors, 1935; reprinted Halifax: David Bland, 1977

Harwood's account is based on his own memories of the play before it ceased performance in the early 1900s, and its revival in the 1930s. Apparently Marsden requested the play from Harwood and also made contact and subsequent performance arrangements with the British Broadcasting Corporation involving Harwood as producer.

Figure 1   Pace Egg players outside Ellen Royd in the early twentieth century

H. W. Harwood 1885-1967

Henry William Harwood was responsible for the 1935 publication of the Midgley version of this play in conjunction with Frank Hawksworth Marsden Together they wrote 'The Pace Egg – The Midgley Version'.

Henry Harwood was a native of Midgley, born on 24 May 1885.[2] In his early years he was a half-timer in a Calder Valley mill. He was an avid reader, learned shorthand writing, and for some years ran the village newspaper, 'The Midgley Intelligencer'. Apart from the war years, 1914 -1918 he worked for the local Halifax newspaper and for the Yorkshire Observer, and retired in 1957. He became a member of the Halifax Antiquarian Society and wrote numerous articles of local interest. He died in 1967 aged 81.

---

[2] 'In Memoriam, Henry William Harwood', *Transactions of the Halifax Antiquarian Society*, 1967, pp vii-xi

F.H.Marsden 1887- 1939

Frank Hawksworth Marsden was the initiator of the revival of the pace-egg play whilst English master at Sowerby Bridge Grammar School. He trained at Sheffield University[3] where he gained an MA on the dialect of the West Riding. He was a member of the Folklore Society. He obtained a hand written copy of the play from Henry Harwood and was successful in interesting the BBC and the play was first broadcast at Easter 1931 and again a year later. This was the stimulus that revived the play as a street performance in Midgley. He died in 1939 aged 52.

HW Harwood and FW Marsden 'The Pace Egg – the Midgley Version' Private publication 1935

The first four pages which, according to Harwood, Marsden wrote[4], drew from Marsden's idea that originally it was a version of a Mummer's Play. Marsden recounted many instances where these plays occurred and made specific links with end-of-winter activities. He suggested that at one time there may have been another version of the Pace Egg which was performed on All Souls Day in Cheshire and was known as 'The Soul Cakes Play'[5] but in Midgley it was performed at Easter, hence Pace Egg (from Pasch meaning Easter).

Marsden further considered the source of the text of the play, which he suggested to be 1788, possibly based on Johnson's 'History of the Seven Champions of Christendom',[6] printed in 1596. He was of the opinion, furthermore, that 'the actual theme of the play was of immemorial antiquity'. The theme was of a combat between two antagonists, the slaying of one followed by resurrection. This could also pose a further question – does this bear any similarity to the life of Jesus Christ - Christians versus Jews - the Crucifixion and the Resurrection?

His considerations explored more distant ancient Egyptian and Semitic practices and plays which seemed to have some links with Midgley's Pace Egg play, not just thematically but also with echoes of the text. However, this assertion is not substantiated and other authors have drawn different conclusions.

---

[3] E.Cass, *The Pace-Egg Plays of the Calder Valley*, London: FLS Books, 2004, p22

[4] Cass, *The Pace-Egg Plays of the Calder Valley*, p11

[5] Harwood & Marsden, *The Pace Egg – The Midgley version*, p1

[6] Harwood & Marsden, *The Pace Egg – The Midgley version*, p3

Marsden's conclusion (assuming this is the final part of his contribution), was that the Good Friday Midgley performance gave witness to one of the oldest, if not the oldest, play in the world.

Harwood's contribution (page 5 onwards)

The Midgley Pace Egg play was different from that performed in other villages according to Harwood. He began by exploring how and why the Pace Egg play was performed in Midgley. His personal recollection was of a number of seasonal customs occurring throughout the year in the village often with specific singing rhymes or chants. He called them 'a cycle of celebration'.[7] He also suggested that due to poor communication between one district and another, village customs were preserved and became a familiar culture.[8]

However, in Julian Harber's review of a later work, there is evidence from a diary kept by William Greenwood of Carrbottom, near Cornholme, a Yorkshire handloom weaver, of an entry for Good Friday April 2 1825, about his pace-egging companions.[9] This seems to be the earliest written reference to pace egging.

Harwood compared the early days of the performances to the ritual of Christmas singing, when groups of young males competed to perform in places where they would receive the best reward (i.e. money). It seemed that from around 1885 males aged between 16 and 20 undertook the same character role (but they were sometimes as young as 11 as Harwood himself was), and were thence known locally by the part they played. Although the acting lacked enthusiasm, it was noted that the costumes were carefully and beautifully crafted. Recollections from former players suggested that some type of dancing accompanied the Midgley play. One question which could be asked is why were the actors predominantly male even during the twentieth century? Was this still the overtones of the 'tradition'?

Great detail of the individual costumes was described by Harwood. Sketches of the costumes and one headdress can be seen in the Appendix. No reference was made to the actual makers but recollections from audio recordings provide evidence of some of the costume makers.[10] The Midgley Pace Egg

---

[7] Harwood & Marsden, *The Pace Egg – The Midgley version*, p5
[8] Harwood & Marsden, *The Pace Egg – The Midgley version*, p5
[9] J. Harber, Review of E. Cass, 'The Lancashire Pace-Egg Play: A Social History', FLS Books 2001, in *Transactions of the Halifax Antiquarian Society*, 2005, 13, pp148-152 at p151
[10] Hebden Bridge Local History Society Archive, *Midgley Oral History Recordings 1977*. See Appendix

helmet was thought to be a survival from other village festive occasions when people dressed up.

In 1840, William Walker and sons of Otley printed a play text entitled 'The Peace Egg' thus suggesting its popularity. Harwood attempted to date it from the illustrations used of dancers from the Nelson period.

Harwood noted that the Walker and Sons published text (1840) served to stabilise the play in Midgley in a logical form, whereas the other oral versions altered in format. He argued that this stability removed original and local references. He did, however, make comparisons between the Midgley versions of the play and the chapbooks of that time and infers that the little local additions were remembrances from the past.

Figure 2   *BBC broadcast of the play in 1934 at Lacy Hey Farm, by Midgley School pupils*

At the end of the play there were some sung verses, but Harwood was not able to say where the specific neighbourhood tune came from (tune on p23 of the play text) or if the verses were sung by all the players or one or any of them. Old players were also noted to have recollected that additions giving a political slant were used where appropriate.

It appeared that the Good Friday performance had been the custom in Midgley. It was thought to be unlucky to perform it after noon due to the influence of the Church regarding the time of the Crucifixion of the Lord.

There were recollections about the swords used by the players, both wooden and metal, and an account of an old family sword used in the play 1896-1987 that was donated by a Midgley survivor of Waterloo.

.....and the rust spots on the blade were solemnly believed to be blood stains.[11]

Harwood recorded that the play was performed up to the First World War when it ceased for a time. It was revived in 1931, certainly due to the efforts of Harwood and Marsden, and broadcast to the BBC Northern Region listeners, performed by adults who had taken part in the play in their youth. An account was also given of the involvement of Midgley school in this venture and how the continuity of the play was established due to their efforts.

Within the last decade a number of articles and books have been written about the play. Three of these are discussed on the following pages.

Julia Smith 'Fairs Feasts and Frolics – Customs and Traditions in Yorkshire [12]

Julia Smith was born in Bradford where she lived all her life. She qualified as a chartered librarian but retired shortly after her marriage to bring up her family. She maintained her interest in writing and became a regular contributor to Pennine Magazine eventually becoming a member of the editorial board.

The Pace-Egg is only one of a whole series of customs and traditions that carry on to this day. Not only does she give eye-witness accounts, but she examines the available material for the origins and the reasons for their continuation. Her information is presented in an interesting and engaging format. She compares the differences between two local places, Midgley and Heptonstall, with Brighouse and Hoyland near Barnsley. Her main focus is on Midgley and she has tried to establish when the tradition or play first started in this village. She suggests the difficulty in trying to give a date is due to the fact that originally it was mainly an oral tradition. She proposes that 'it was a continuous tradition in the village from at least 1800'. [13]

---

[11] Harwood & Marsden, *The Pace Egg – The Midgley version*, p23

[12] J. Smith, *Fairs Feasts and Frolics – Customs and Traditions in Yorkshire*, Otley: Smith Settle, 1999, pp14-18

[13] Smith, *Fairs Feasts and Frolics – Customs and Traditions in Yorkshire*, p16

She has drawn her facts from various sources – written and oral – and this gives the reader her conclusions about the history of the tradition up to fairly recent times.

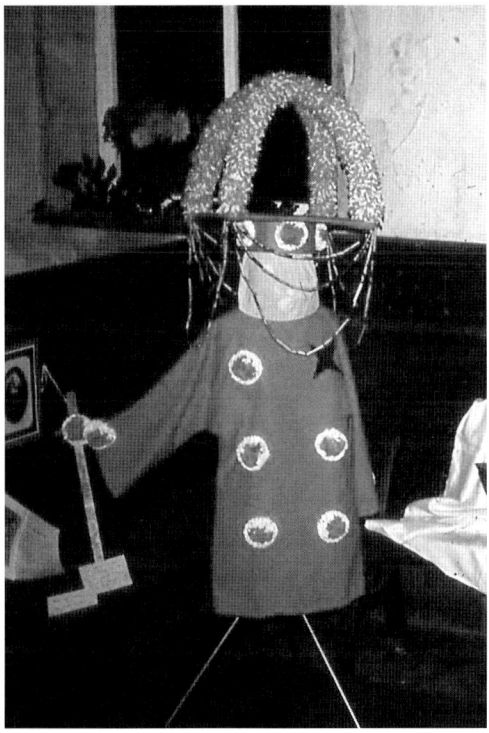

Apart from the play itself, she has also investigated the costumes and traditional style headgear worn by the players. She draws attention to the headgear being a form of disguise for the participants in the first instance, as the play may have originally been a form of bringing good luck and recognition would break this superstition. She does not get involved in trying to source the play from pagan beginnings except to merely hint that the 'good luck' aspect could have echoes of ancient pagan rites. Although this is a fairly brief account of pace egging, it contains many references that may be useful as starting point to pursue this fascinating tradition further.

Figure 3   Costume made for the Midgley School Centenary in 1977

The Works of Eddie Cass

The two remaining accounts of the pace egg to be discussed are by Eddie Cass, who retired as a bank manager in 1993 and then started his academic career. He completed his doctorate on the literary content of the *Cotton Factory Times* in 1996. His post-doctoral work at the National Centre for English Culture and Tradition at the University of Sheffield was spent researching the pace-egg play in Lancashire and resulted in the publication by the Folklore Society of 'The Lancashire Pace-Egg Play: A Social History'. Dr Cass saw his first performance of the Midgley version of the pace-egg play in 1968 in Luddenden and following the publication of his first book decided that the Midgley play merited a full-length study. 'The Pace-Egg Plays of the Calder Valley' was published in 2004.

'The Lancashire Pace- Egg Play – A Social History'[14]

This book has been roundly applauded as an excellent scholarly account of the Pace-Egg in a wider social and historical context with relevance beyond Lancashire. It also contains admirable detail of different versions as performed in Lancashire villages and towns. However, Cass's examination of historical context is also relevant to Midgley.

In his introduction Cass identifies the Pace Egg as the hero-combat type of folk play, which was attached to a calendar custom at Easter. Its function was a form of begging, a 'legitimised wealth transfer transaction'[15] by which young people and adults gained money and food at feast times. He then goes on to suggest that 'there is no clear historical evidence that the play has meaning.'[16] As Pauline Greenhill comments in her review of the book, - 'the concept that any practice, traditional or otherwise could be without meaning seems bizarre particularly when the practice has as long a history as the Pace Egging.'[17]

In another review of this book, Peter Millington also picks up on the point of function, offering the view the Pace Egg played a role in sustaining community spirit, but adds that Cass is not sure of this, claiming its function was self gain (legitimised wealth transfer transaction) and also fun.[18] After examining both function and meaning and reaching his conclusions, which he accepts may be reductive, Cass states:

> ….it is important to understand that (such) origins do not affect the function of the play, the purpose for which it was performed.[19]

He goes on to say that his study focuses on these functions.

In Cass' opinion, these plays date from the late eighteenth century, since there is no firm evidence that they existed before this. He goes on to refute very firmly the myth or ritual theory of the play's origins, once popular at the beginning of the twentieth century. 'Today, most historians find such theory

---

[14] E. Cass, *The Lancashire Pace-Egg Play: A Social History*, London: FLS Books, 2001

[15] Cass, *The Lancashire Pace-Egg Play: A Social History*, p1.

[16] Cass, *The Lancashire Pace-Egg Play: A Social History*, p3

[17] P. Greenhill, Review of E. Cass, 'The Lancashire Pace-Egg Play: A Social History', *Western Folklore*, 2002, Summer

[18] P. Millington, Review of E. Cass, 'The Lancashire Pace-Egg Play: A Social History', *Folklore*, 2002, 113(2), pp273-274

[19] Cass, *The Lancashire Pace-Egg Play: A Social History*, p6

of survivals (of pagan rituals) untenable given the lack of evidence'.[20] He examines this issue again in 'Pace Egg Plays of the Calder Valley' in which he states 'nowadays, no serious play scholar believes in a Pre-Christian origin for folk plays'.[21]

There are, however, important and interesting alternatives to Cass's views on the origins of the play. Michael Haslam has suggested that the metre of the play, fourteen syllables to a line, is a typical metre of the medieval pageant.[22] This metre was already in use by 1600 and it is unlikely that someone in the eighteenth century would write anything in this style without a living model. The characters in the play are also to be found as principal characters of the medieval pageant. Furthermore, St George, Hector and the Turk, and the Black Prince can be found in Thomas Nashe's 'Summer's Last Will and Testament' (written in the 1590s), and in the same work there is reference to Sir Richard Tosspot. It seems unlikely that in the eighteenth century people just happened by chance to resurrect the characters of medieval pageant!

Cass is at pains to point out the difficulty experienced by historians when faced with a variety of theoretical propositions about the origins of plays like this, and that 'firm evidence' is needed and not speculation.[23] Whilst admiring the stringency of such an academic approach, it is difficult to dismiss the strong possibility that there may well be some continuity between these earlier references and the Pace Egg play.

Assumptions that the play contains themes of resurrection and revival have rested upon the Easter timing of the play, but the exchanges between The Doctor and Slasher are dismissed by Cass. He interprets The Doctor's miraculous revival of Slasher as nothing more than entertaining mockery of quack doctors who make excessive promises as to the efficacy of their potions! Cass concludes that there is no attempt to resurrect and that there is nothing in the play to imply a resurrection theme.[24]

---

[20] Cass, *The Lancashire Pace-Egg Play: A Social History*, p2
[21] Cass, *The Pace-Egg Plays of the Calder Valley*, p4
[22] Personal communication from Michael Haslam, poet of Foster Clough, January 2007
[23] Cass, *The Lancashire Pace-Egg Play: A Social History*, p6
[24] Cass, *The Lancashire Pace-Egg Play: A Social History*, p22

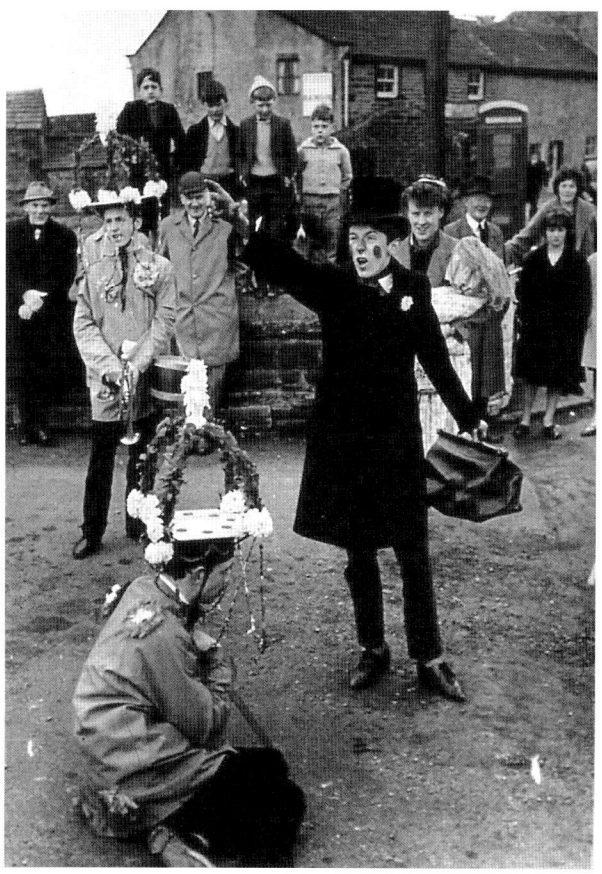

Figure 4   Doctor and Slasher

However, given the play's performance at Easter rather than any other time of year, the link with other Pace Egg traditions, - egg painting and rolling and so on, described by Cass in considerable detail, it is perhaps surprising that he ascribes no significance whatsoever to other seasonal themes of resurrection, renewal and rebirth within the play.[25]

Cass's wider investigations support Harwood's account that the performers in the nineteenth century were teenagers and young men. In the early part of the twentieth century, performers were occasionally younger; for example Harwood himself performed the Pace Egg when he was only eleven years old. As with mumming plays, the performers were also exclusively male, and this seems entirely consistent with much earlier traditions; women for example, did not perform in Shakespearean times. This is a reflection of what was considered seemly and respectable behaviour for young ladies. Only in the early twentieth century are there reports of performing bands which included women.

Who was in the audience? Cass writes that 'current research suggests that the mumming play custom may have evolved from a seasonal house-visiting tradition onto which the play was grafted.' Groups of people in disguise would entertain their hosts, have their disguise removed and then receive food and drink as a reward. Cass then examines the possible development of the play, referring to the existence of core texts and examining the link to

[25] Cass, *The Lancashire Pace-Egg Play: A Social History*, pp8-11

street and travelling theatre, local fairs and gatherings of large numbers of people who attracted performers and entertainers.[26]

He ultimately places the play in the context of rural paternalism which then transferred to industrial communities.

> This paternalism within the factories was an extension of the mill owner's role in the family and the central place which the mill owner, his house and factory occupied within a small community.[27]

Julian Harber makes the interesting observation that, although urban paternalism may have been the case in some locations, it is unlikely to be the case for Midgley:

> which for much of the nineteenth century was amongst the most radical and implacably undeferential villages in the Yorkshire Pennines

He continues:

> (It) might be more usefully seen as a part of a vigorous popular culture of domestic outworkers and small farmers which persisted well into the factory age.[28]

This is an interesting point since it recognises the fact that the significance of the play from place to place may vary, dependent upon cultural, structural and occupational differences.

In his previous study, Cass examined the play and its performance in considerable detail across Lancashire, far beyond the remit of this particular overview, which has taken for its focus the play and its performance specifically in Midgley, West Yorkshire. An examination of the similarities and differences between Lancashire and the pace egg elsewhere, and the influences that lie behind any differences, would be an interesting study.

In 2004, Dr Cass published another volume on the pace egg play. This is 'The Pace Egg play of the Calder Valley'. This is undoubtedly the single most authoritative account of the Pace Egg play in the Calder Valley and the Midgley play in particular. Cass draws on an impressively wide range of

---

[26] Cass, *The Lancashire Pace-Egg Play: A Social History*, pp18-19
[27] Cass, *The Lancashire Pace-Egg Play: A Social History*, p36
[28] J. Harber, Review of E. Cass, 'The Lancashire Pace-Egg Play: A Social History', p151

sources taking full account of the Harwood booklet, but also incorporating the previously unrecorded reports of living authorities on its more recent history.

He identifies the Pace Egg play as the 'hero-combat' type of folk (mummers) play. It also incorporates the 'death and resurrection' theme as identified by earlier scholars as distinct from the 'sword – dance' type of play and the 'plough plays' typical of other parts of the country.

As in his earlier book, Cass dismisses the myth or ritual theory described by Sir James Frazer in 'The Golden Bough 1890'. He also regrets the 'continuing popularity of the idea of pagan origins of these plays'. He is emphatic on this point but does concede to R. Hutton's view that:

> the collapse of the theory of pagan origins has created more problems than it has solved in the quest for the origin of Mummers' plays.[29]

He goes on to propose that they may have evolved from a seasonal house – visiting custom on to which the performance of a play was later grafted, and involved social interaction with the hosts, suggesting its function was solely that of entertainment. What is persuasive about Cass's idea is that such phenomena must surely have existed and persisted because they linked to other customs and provided some expression of social cohesion and that they fulfilled some sort of social function. However, as Cass points out, it is not clear when the play became integrated into other social customs, since early records are absent. He cites evidence that records of customs circa 1642 provide documentary evidence for dramatic activity at the parish level, but that these plays were not a precursor of the plays that we know today.[30] Perhaps this should not, however, be seen as proof that the play did not exist in some form before the eighteenth century. Proving a negative is always difficult, but if history tells us anything it tells us that ideas, norms and customs evolve, and do so in terms of their function and meaning, and categorical assertions to the opposite court correction. In the discussion of Dr Cass's earlier book we have raised the possibility of earlier origins.

Cass tells us that in the nineteenth century the plays were performed by groups of young male workers in return for food and drink or money at seasonal feasts as a 'legitimised wealth transfer transaction'. As Cass reflects, if

---

[29] R. Hutton, *The Stations of the Sun: A History of the Ritual Year In Britain*, Oxford: Oxford University Press, 1996 p79

[30] Cass, *The Pace-Egg Plays of the Calder Valley*, p6

this were the sole reason for their existence, it would ignore the possibility of a wider social function perhaps serving to express community identity.[31] This explanation perhaps makes best sense of the immediately available evidence, but this doesn't have to be the play's *sole* function. One can also agree with Cass' reservations as it raises other questions. One could speculate that there must have been many other more lucrative sources of cash for the impecunious but enterprising young man at that time; what they would have gained would have been no more than tips from relatively small audiences. Thus these plays had a more important social significance and performing actually conferred some social status, as individuals were often thereafter known by their role, as Harwood pointed out.

Cass also considers reasons for the decline of the plays in the late nineteenth and early twentieth century, and takes account of Harwood's explanation of changes in attitudes of the working class in the late nineteenth century, alternative entertainment becoming available, and early twentieth century changes in the law on street begging. 'Out of this attitude came a kind of looking down upon the act of pace-egging as something to be despised'.[32] These suggestions are convincing since this would lead to changes in both the communities' and the performer's perceptions of the acceptability of these activities in the local social context. Clearly the perceived 'rightness' of these plays had been central to the support they gained from the community audiences they were intended for.

Cass provides a very detailed account of Harwood's involvement in the history of the play, firstly with Marsden as a chronicler, and secondly as a major influence on the play's survival from the early 1930s.

When these plays were eventually revived by Harwood and Marsden in the 1930s, their function would be very different, since they were no longer a genuinely spontaneous activity driven by the community members, but were to be organised under the aegis of educated historically-aware individuals (teachers and journalists) who were keen to revise old folk traditions. Children at Midgley School performed the play and then it was transferred to Calder Valley High School in 1950.[33] This has ensured its survival to the present day. However, once under the control of adult authority figures, it can

---

[31] Cass, *The Pace-Egg Plays of the Calder Valley*, p6
[32] H.W. Harwood quoted in Cass, *The Pace-Egg Plays of the Calder Valley*, p7
[33] Cass, *The Pace-Egg Plays of the Calder Valley*, Chapter 3

no longer be seen as a spontaneous expression of any sort, whether economic need or social cohesion.

Figure 5   The Doctor, as described by H.W. Harwood in 1935

Cass examines some of the changes in costumes and accessories described by Harwood. While the materials used were cheaply available, the costumes were distinctive and richly decorated, and beyond the competence of the young performers themselves. This would suggest a greater role for the adults in the community than the accounts have suggested, which would suggest that, prior to its revival, the play was more fully integrated into the larger community than has been recognised. Cass reports Harwood as saying that the 'Midgley helmets were probably a picturesque survival from the days when on all festive occasions village people freely used to decorated costumes and finery….'[34] again suggesting close links between the play and other community activities, especially if the costume or parts had been handed down from performer to performer. Certainly, the oral history of the play from the 1930s confirms that the girls of the village made the complicated helmets.[35] It also seems that variations in costumes and accessories reflected additions which occurred for ad hoc reasons. For example, a bugle and bugler entered the play in 1931, in order to signal key points in the action, but the bugle faded from the play even though the bugler remains in a minor role. Such examples confirm that the play was flexible and could and would be adapted according to what was thought appropriate and what was available.

Cass records other differences in costume from Harwood's day to the present. For example, The Doctor in the 1930s was dressed in a style suggesting 'mock gentility, rather loudly with check trousers, a long black frock coat, spats and a

[34] Cass, *The Pace-Egg Plays of the Calder Valley*, p15
[35] Hebden Bridge Local History Society Archive, *Midgley Oral History Recordings 1977*. See Appendix

beribboned top hat'.[36] More recently The Doctor has been dressed in an overcoat and boxer shorts in 2002 and, in 2003, a medical white coat. These variations make sense, as they reflect a contemporary exaggerated stereotype, embellished to increase humorous effect. It would be entirely reasonable to imagine that changes and embellishments have always been incorporated into such plays and depended upon what was available to the performers, and what would be thought amusing and entertaining by the audience at the time. Plays which have social meaning for the performers and their audiences would surely reflect social and cultural change. So why did the text remain so remarkably consistent in different communities for so long if the play was as random and meaningless as Cass suggests?

Cass's contribution to the historical account of the Pace Egg play is enormous, especially in terms of the collection and documentation of evidence from many diverse sources. Cass' books are comprehensive, extremely well researched and include contemporary oral primary sources for this first time. He is painstaking and presents an impressive amount of detail.

But his books raise as many questions as they answer. Couldn't the play have served functions beyond the economic one considered? Couldn't the origins of the play be traced further back, to the sixteenth century for example? What was the meaning of the play to those who performed it in the eighteenth and nineteenth century? Why did something, which involved not just the performers, but an active and involved audience, persist in its natural form (prior to its endorsement by an educated elite) for so long?

It is certainly the case that the more we have read about the Pace Egg the more mysterious and uncertain its history seems to be. Maybe some of these questions will be revisited by interested individuals in future. One thing is certain, for many local residents today the performance of Pace Egg play at Easter still has real significance. As Julian Harber reported in his review of Eddie Cass's 'Lancashire Pace-Egg Play', a local resident observed that 'it is not really Easter until you have seen the pace-eggers!'[37]

---

[36] Harwood quoted in Cass, *The Pace-Egg Plays of the Calder Valley*, p16
[37] J. Harber, Review of E. Cass, 'The Lancashire Pace-Egg Play: A Social History', p152

Appendix: Transcriptions

Introduction

Whilst we were investigating the Pace Egg play Peggie Horsfield gave us access to some aspects of oral history covering a range of topics. These were recordings made as part of the celebrations for the Centenary of Midgley School. Amongst these were conversations between Midgley residents about the Pace Egg play. As these conversations were authentic recollections of events they had experienced we realised the importance of this primary source of historical evidence. These were some of the actual people who had been involved in the 1931 revival of the Pace Egg play in one way or another.

We are deeply indebted to Peggie Horsfield for, in the first instance, instigating the recordings and recording the interviews, and secondly for allowing us access to the recordings, which she also took part in. Peggie has been so generous with material and also with spending the time to identify the voices of the people who were unknown to us. She has given us descriptions about the people who were interviewed as well. The interviews were recorded during 1977. The following are the transcriptions from two of her recordings. Thanks to the generosity of Peggie Horsfield and Bob Pegg, copies of the original recordings are deposited in the Hebden Bridge Local History Archive.

Hebden Bridge Local History Archive, Midgley Oral History Recordings, OH 6, Tracks 30-31

Begins with reminiscences about playing football.

Alice : I left (school) the year the Pace Egg started. Really Henry William Harwood. I just left that year.... I was in it that year.

Peggie : How did you take part?

Alice : We didn't. We just used to follow it round. The girls didn't take part at all.

Peggie: Did you help to make the costumes?

Alice : No, no. We didn't do anything like that.

Donald: I remember the Pace Egg when I should be about five or six, before I went, well just after I went to school. Down at Well House. There used to be ever so many of t'gangs coming round, doing the Pace Egg. I used to be terrified of the Old Toss Pot.

(laughter)

Well I was only a youngster you know, stood on the steps at Well House. I remember them quite well, long before Calder High School started. They were Midgley boys.

Bob : There were several gangs of them?

Donald : Oh yes! Just like when we used to go sweeping.

Discussion about 'sweeping' follows.

Figure 6   Tosspot, as described by H.W. Harwood in 1935

Hebden Bridge Local History Archive, Midgley Oral History Recordings, OH 9, Tracks 4-6

[Track 4 begins with a discussion about school days (continuation of Track 3 topics) (Pace Egg conversation begins).

Constance: When it were t'Pace Egg I did some sewing. When it were t'next   Pace Egg it used to take us nearly twelve months to make all t'outfits.

Joan: There were Eileen Midgley, Annie Butters, you and I that used to make them Pace Egg outfits. We made them right from scratch. Didn't we Constance?

Constance : Yes we did!

Bob : You made them new every year?

Constance: Every year. We made them new. And the Midgley Pace Egg belongs to Midgley,

Joan: Yes it does!

Constance: And whereever they take it up, anywhere else and make any do about it, it belongs to Midgley does Midgley Pace Egg.

Joan : Yes it does!

Constance : And I will not, d'you know it annoys me when I see stuff written down in t'papers, y'know, because I mean there's none of them that can do it like Henry Broadbent and them did it.

Joan : No there isn't. It's a fact that, love. I mean we used to know every word at one time didn't we? Every word! And then we went down making sandwiches for when they came back.

Joan: And weren't we proud when the BBC came that time when we'd made all the uniforms and outfits and you know, back at the Lacey Hey.

Bob : Can you tell us again how you made the costumes? Because it wasn't, the tape wasn't on just then.

Joan : Well, they were stiff cardboard weren't they Connie? Tops.

Constance : Hats.

Joan : Yes hats, squares of stiff cardboard and then, then that fit sort of round the head, it was cardboard but it was pliable, it weren't as thick was it? And we used to cut 'em, cut 'em fairly tall and then cut along top like that and staple 'em to the top of those, with a stapling machine top of big ones, and then we covered them all with 'em crepe paper, didn't we?

Constance : Mmm, mmm.

Joan : And then beads, they used to be sort of four sides to 'at and then they were four lengths of beads wasn't there, down 'at and these were

Figure 7   *Photograph of the 'hat'; typical of those made by village girls for the revival of the play*

all made out of newspaper. We used to roll those on knitting needles and then varnish 'em, y'know, varnish long lengths and then cut 'em into strips and thread 'em on bands. They were all made out of newspaper wasn't they, the beads.

Peggie : You rolled them first, then cut them up afterwards?

Joan : Afterwards yes, we, y'know, rolled them on knitting needles, y' know how I mean, very tight.

Bob : Were they coloured at all? Apart from being varnished?

Constance : No.

Joan : No! They wasn't was they Connie? They were sort of left as they were, a darkish varnish.

Constance : But they looked like beads. Yes, mmm.

Bob : I suppose the varnish would soak in. Tell me, how did you learn to make the headdresses in the first place?

Figure 8   Cast wearing hats and 'smocks' with rosettes

Joan : Well it was Mr Hopkinson, wasn't it? It were 'im that sort of designed them. And then the tops , sort of the tops they was all different colours.

Constance : Yes.

Constance : They made those out of – er -----. Well it was just material. What did they call that shiny material, Peggie?

Peggie : Sateen.

Joan : All that shiny material, sateen, different colours. Cos Black Prince had to have a black one didn't he but others, it was all bright oranges. Wasn't it?

Constance : Yes and red, red and white.

Joan : Rosettes, we sort of used to cut round saucers didn't we, ever so many sizes and then fringe 'em all, scissors round edge and put a smaller one in t'middle and stitch them all on.

Constance : Yes. Mmn.

Joan : And then there were sort of four ont 'ats, ont' crown of 'ats.

Constance : Yes.

Joan : I'd like to have a go at making a hat again wouldn't you?

Peggie : How did you make them?

Joan : Those was wires Peggie. Y'know. They were sort 'em of, there was four holes at each corner, y'know. They were a, like a copper wire that was put over like that, and fastened int' middle at top and then they were all covered in crepe paper. We used to cut that in lengths and fringe it, didn't we. And pack it with 'em plaited wire with tissue paper before we put us ----, to make it really fat like that. Y'know pack it all with tissue paper and stitch it on and then cover it over with it.

Joan : Yes, I'd like to make a hat again.

Peggie : And the characters themselves, apart from the Black Prince, they hadn't a particular colour?

Joan : Yes, St. George used to be in red and white, y'know, and er mmn ---.

Peggie : And what about the others?

[Sandwich break! Mint and currant pasty discussion.]

Joan : I don't think others had a particular colour, had they, Connie?

Constance : Well, it was orange.

Joan : It was oranges and --- and of course there was the doctor. The Toss Pot.

Peggie : Did you make any particular pattern, or anything like that?

Constance : No, not really love. No. It were a sort of sack weren't it? It used to make them.

Joan: And fat eggs in a basket.

Bob : That's for Toss Pot?

Constance : Eeh, at one time I could have er gone all through it.

Joan : Well, I still have my book. I loaned it Freddy from t'BBC up at er ----

Joan : Yes.

Bob : You've seen the Calder High boys do it? A revival.

Constance : No. I have but er -----

Bob : A revival? I wonder what you thought?

Figure 9   *'I'm a valiant soldier, Bold Slasher is my name'*

Constance : Well I've seen somebody do it but I don't know who it was.

Constance : An' er, the well outfits aren't' same.

Constance : No they're not.And they don't talk right. You see they say, for instance em ---

> Here am I an old coffee grinder,
>
> I've lost mi wife and cannot find 'er.
>
> If onny of you see her, you mun turn her back,
>
> She's two brokken legs and a hump on her back.

Well you see they don't talk like (right?) That is the way it should be said. Y'know.

Bob : Give us a bit more!

Constance : I am the Black Prince of Paradine,

> Born of hairy mairn.
>
> So-o-on I'll fetch St. George
>
> And all his lofty courage dairn.
>
> If that be he that dost stand 'ere,
>
> To slay mi only son
>
> Though he be sprung from royal bluid
>
> I'll make it run like Noah's fluid.

Well y'know they wouldn't say anything like that! It would be 'Noah's flood, blood! They wouldn't say it like that! It was really broad talking, but that was it 'cos I mean but Peggie has recorded it here with t'old lot. They've all been, Sammy Shepherd and George Broadbent and all them lot. They've been here to record it.

Joan : 'Cos Sam Shepherd were t 'Toss Pot when they broadcast it, wan't he?

They wouldn't have Billy Swindells though for be the doctor, would you?

> (Lots of laughing.)

Peggie : The Farrer sisters ….she said they would do it before it was ever done at school, they used to love to listen to it because it was in broad Yorkshire because they weren't allowed to speak like that at home. She thought it was wonderful. But it was wonderful to listen to, to watch and take part in it because they couldn't speak broad Yorkshire at home. Whereas at home they were supposed to speak properly.

Constance : No, I haven't heard it done as good as what it used to be like. It's same as I've said before, it belongs to Midgley

CHAPTER 14

Public Houses 1760 to 1990

Richard Davies

Everyone with an interest in local history will be aware that Midgley was once part of the Manor of Wakefield and appears as 'Micleie' in the Domesday Survey of 1086. Little is known for a long time thereafter, though we may assume there was a settlement on the present site, a staging post on the old road to Burnley and beyond. At about 750 feet the village occupies a plateau between Brearley Wood and Midgley Moor; subsistence farming, spinning and handloom weaving would have provided a modest livelihood. But in the eighteenth and nineteenth centuries all of this changed: the Turnpike Road along the Calder Valley was authorised by Act of Parliament in 1760 and the old packhorse route became less attractive. The Rochdale Canal was completed in 1804 and the Lancashire and Yorkshire Railway opened in 1841. Now domestic industry faced irresistible competition from the water and steam powered mills. Peel House Mill in the Luddenden Valley and the Oats Royd complex (founded 1847) employed hundreds of workers. Some people had a little money to spend and, for a time, locals might choose between an astonishing number of beer shops and public houses.

So when and why did the licensed trade flourish in Midgley village? Although action was taken in 1736 to prevent the sale of cheap gin, and local Justices had the power to control the issue of licences, they were 'surrounded with numbers of pettifogging attorneys and solicitors who (watch) their steps'[1] and in most areas they rarely intervened effectively. During the early nineteenth century enthusiasm for regulation grew: the propertied classes craved an orderly society, Poor Law costs rose year on year,[2] employers demanded a sober workforce and a new evangelical zeal was in the air. But the brewers had an influential voice, farmers wanted a market for barley and hops and libertarians opposed any restrictions. The Beer Act (1830) served their interests well. Now any person named in the Rate Book might open his house as a beer shop on payment of two guineas in local excise - no Justices' Licence was

---

[1] *Distilled Spirituous Liquors - the Bane of the Nation*, London: Roberts, 1736
[2] 1750: £619,000, 1818: £8,000,000 – 13s 3d per head of the population.

needed. The results were dramatic: by 1838 an extra 45,717 beer sellers were plying their trade. Brewers would pay the beer shops' excise fees in order to have outlets and often encourage applications for spirit licences too. The workman:

> now (had) to run the gauntlet through three or four beer shops, in each of which are fellow labourers carousing who urge him to stay and drink with them.[3]

The period between 1830 and the outbreak of the First World War is the time when Midgley's numerous watering holes would have flourished.

Not everyone welcomed the consequences of this. H W Harwood complained that:

> It was drink first thing in the morning and drink late at night .... the poor women and children had to exist as best they could.[4]

There were 'midnight carousels, all-night sittings, long extended weekends and lax, loose ways'. Sport centred around the 'lowest of public houses': when the pigeon shooting, rabbit coursing, cock fighting, billeting and knur and spell matches were over, the 'hard drinking' would begin. Midgleyites who attended the Heptonstall Palm Fair 'would have a fight ..... with someone, or they would fight one another'. We may be sure that local Methodists[5] denounced these indulgences, and the Band of Hope was active, but there were still six pubs in Midgley[6] when Queen Victoria died.

The earliest public house in Midgley was almost certainly the Lord Nelson Hotel, formerly the Scout Head Inn, the last building in the village at the western end of Towngate. 'Hotel' seems rather grand, since the building is of modest proportions and, as has already been noted, there would have been little other than local traffic passing by once the Turnpike Road along the valley had been completed. John Widdop, victualler, was at the Lord Nelson in 1845,[7] William Walker was the inn-keeper in 1881[8] and Benson Bailey was

---

[3] *Select Committee on Inquiry into Drunkenness among Labouring Classes of United Kingdom: Report*, House of Commons Parliamentary Papers, Session 1834 (559), VIII (315)

[4] H.W. Harwood, *History of Midgley*, 1903-4, West Yorkshire Archive Service (Calderdale), Misc 78/52, pp15-16

[5] Providence Methodist New Connection Chapel. Opened 12th December 1883 to replace an earlier building

[6] Not to mention the 'Howld-thi-tongue houses: 'easy of access, evasive of the law' where men might drink till (the) barrels ran dry'. Harwood, *History of Midgley*, West Yorkshire Archive Service (Calderdale), Misc 78/52, p127

[7] All references to this rely on *Walker's Directory of the Parish of Halifax*, Halifax: J.U. Walker, 1845

there in 1901, along with his wife and their children Benjamin, John, Emily, Leonard, Herbert and Clifford. Five of the six were working: there were two quarrymen, an iron moulder, a dress maker and a mule spinner. The pub closed in 1932.

Figure 1   The Lord Nelson Hotel, Scout Head, Midgley

A Bluebell Inn may have stood on the opposite side of Chapel, or Pinfold, Lane but the site has been cleared. The History of Methodism[9] points to 'Bluebell Field or Close. The Bluebell Inn stood where the ruined houses now face Towngate'. 'There is no doubt there was an inn although apart from tradition and one reference in the township accounts I have found no evidence'.[10] That one reference reads '1810. Going recruiting to the Blue Bell 2s'. 'The three houses (at Blue Bell) were demolished just before the end of the nineteenth Century, and the third down the road was the inn'. A paragraph in

---

[8] This information is from the Census Enumerators' Returns, held at the Public Record Office, Series RG. Microfilm copies are available locally in Halifax Central Library

[9] H.W. Harwood, *History of Methodism in Midgley, near Halifax*, Halifax: Halifax Printing Works, 1933, p18

[10] Harwood, *History of Midgley*, West Yorkshire Archive Service (Calderdale), Misc 78/52, p14

the Halifax Courier on 21 January 1913 mentions a headstone which 'had a bell roughly carved in relief, the bell being painted blue'. This, however, cannot be traced and an unsigned letter in Calderdale Archives says that 'the deeds do not refer to the fact that the Bluebell was an Inn'.

Figure 2   The Delvers' Arms

The Delvers' Arms was on the south side of Towngate in what are now cottage properties at numbers 9, 10 and 11. Vikki Egerton records that 'the licence was transferred from the cottage at the west end of Lacey Hey ...a former inn under the name of the Knur and Spell.[11] 'Delvers' reminds us that there was a number of stone quarries in the area. T and J Walton are listed as stone merchants at Foster Clough in 1845, while Robert Midgley of Booth was both butcher and stone dealer by trade. The Delvers' Arms closed on August 1910.

The Weavers' Arms was only a few doors away. At first it was called the Horse and Shoes, but the name was changed in 1866. John Calvert was the licensee when the Weavers' closed in 1906.

The Shoulder of Mutton on the other side of the road had a longer history. An inn called Broad Door Stones occupied the site in 1813, but a new inn and four cottages were built when Richard Patchett bought the property in 1836.[12] In 1845 George Bedford was victualler. William Hoyle had taken over by 1881,

---

[11] V. Egerton, *Luddenden Saga: a Brief History of a Yorkshire Village*, Cleckheaton: Amadeus Press, 2002

[12] J.H. Patchett, 'The Patchetts of Midgley', *Transactions of the Halifax Antiquarian Society*, 2003, pp39-55 at p46

and he was still there twenty years later, but his sons Sam, a joiner and builder, and John, a plumber, had moved on. The Shoulder of Mutton survived as one of Whitakers' tied houses until it closed in May 1956.

Figure 3   The Shoulder of Mutton

The Royal George was next to the Co-op in Lydgate. David Broadbent, a woollen spinner, may have held the licence in 1881. The George closed in 1919. The property opposite, since demolished, was of interest. Access to some of the houses was along a balcony, so that locals would speak of the 'grandstand' The block also contained the Co-operative Hall, which would have provided social and educational facilities.

The Sportsman stood where Thorney Lane diverges. When it closed in 1990 it was selling Tetley's ales. The one remaining pub which we can confidently identify is the Bird in the Hand at High Lees Head. When it closed in 1894 it was deemed to be 'a disorderly place'.[13] In 1881 William Ratcliffe, beer seller and farmer, was there.

---

[13] Harwood, *History of Midgley*, West Yorkshire Archive Service (Calderdale), Misc 78/52, p124

Figure 4   Gentlemen outside the Royal George on Lydgate

The Sportsman marks the eastern end of old Midgley village in which seven (or maybe eight) public houses have been found: two others lay within easy walking distance. The Travellers' Rest, since demolished, stood at the junction of Solomon Hill and Rails Lane. William Fletcher, surveyor, occupied the property in 1881. The Travellers' closed in 1938 and became an Air Raid wardens' post and point of sale for National Savings stamps during the war years.[14]

The Woodman Inn in Booth village was less than a mile away. Robert Midgley, victualler, was there in 1845 and Albert Wadsworth, joiner and inn-keeper in 1881. The Woodman finally closed its doors in February 1949. For a time there was also a public house at Upper Foot: this prospered 'during the period when the Lancashire and Yorkshire Railway was being built'.[15] William Whitaker, beer seller, lived there in 1845.

---

[14] I am indebted to Peggy Horsfield whose knowledge and recollections of Midgley village have proved invaluable.

[15] T. Sutcliffe, 'A Tour in Midgley', *Transactions of the Halifax Antiquarian Society*, 1928, pp113-157 at p115-116

There were beer houses in Midgley too. James Pickles, beerseller, was at Han Royd in 1845, and James Shaw was a beer seller and shopkeeper in Rails Lane at the same time. In 1881 Alfred Howarth had the Lydgate beer house, and it may be that the Springfield Working Men's Club was licensed. A library was set up there in 1897.

And if Midgley hadn't enough to offer then Luddenden was just down the road. There were five inns there. William Clay had bought the White Swan in 1785. He would have had responsibility for the 'Luddenden Library', established in 1781, since its stock was kept here. Like the Scout Head Inn, the pub was renamed in honour of Lord Nelson after his great victory at Trafalgar. Thankfully, it is still open today.

The Wolf Inn stood nearby on the other side of the river. It was from here, according to local folk lore, that a Highlander made a daring escape in the aftermath of the '45 Rebellion. The Murgatroyd Arms was round the corner. It had the only spirit licence in Luddenden. Henry Patchett carried on the trade of undertaker there, and funeral catering was a speciality. Vikki Egerton also mentions the Bridge End Hotel and the Ship Inn.[16]

Figure 5   The Royal George at Lydgate (right) and the Sportsman (end)

---

[16] Egerton, *Luddenden Saga: a Brief History of a Yorkshire Village*, p25

Figure 6   The Traveller's Rest is the first building on the left. On the right is Diamond House, at the top of Old Lane, home of Alderson, plumbers

Five of Midgley's seven pubs closed their doors for the last time in the period between 1894 and 1932, and the small beer houses seem to have faded away. As a result of legislation, the licensed trade was being more effectively regulated, and statutory opening and closing times were now in place Publicans and customers faced prosecution if there was 'drinking after hours'. Then, in 1956, the Shoulder of Mutton ceased trading. Finally, in 1990, the Sportsman closed its doors for the last time and a thriving village community was curiously left with not a single public house to call its own.

CHAPTER 15

'A Wild and Unchristian Place'

Sam Welch

In the mid-eighteenth century the renowned preacher, William Grimshaw, described Midgley as a 'wild and unchristian place'. Compared with Halifax and other areas in the Calder valley, it does indeed appear that early non-conformity did not have a strong presence in Midgley. However, as the imposing façade of the Providence Chapel reinforces, following the visits of Grimshaw and his like, protestant non-conformity took a strong hold in the township. This chapter will look at the scant evidence of early non-conformity in Midgley compared with the wider area; explore the reasons for the growth of non-conformity from the mid-eighteenth century onwards with a particular regard to the chapels in Midgley and Booth; consider the wider impact of non-conformity on village life; and finally, chart the decline of the chapels through the twentieth century.

The story of non-conformity starts with the English Reformation in the mid sixteenth century. Almost immediately a tension arose between the protestant Church of England and those who fell outside it. These were on the one hand Catholics, who continued in their allegiance to the Church in Rome and on the other, more radical Protestants who either had doctrinal or, more often, constitutional objections to the established church. While this latter group initially hoped to change the Church of England from within, by the mid seventeenth century there were some who would no longer conform to the established church. These nonconformists have included Independents, Presbyterians, Baptists, Quakers and Methodists.

The non-conformist cause has fluctuated over time. The first period of significant non-conformity developed out of the Tudors' and Stuarts' attempts to forge a religious settlement and was represented primarily by Puritanism. Puritan opposition can be seen as culminating in the Civil War in the mid seventeenth century, which in turn released a wave of religious radicalism during the political and social turmoil of the late 1640s and 1650s. Religious radicalism suffered a significant set back with the restoration of King Charles

II in 1660, but it struggled on and eventually benefited from the religious concessions and freedoms that culminated with the Toleration Act in 1689.

The next great period of non-conformity coincided with the social and economic turmoil in the late eighteenth century and nineteenth century. This time the established church was seen as inadequate to meet the spiritual needs of the growing urban population. Movements such as the Methodists gained ground on the basis of their lay structures, the popular appeal of their preaching and emphasis on education that would allow followers to access the Scriptures themselves. This 'evangelical revival' shaped the pattern of Christian religious observance well into the twentieth century.

Early non-conformity

Halifax and the Calder Valley have had a long history of non-conformity. It has been suggested that this was due to a medieval Lollard tradition in the area, but J.A. Hargreaves argues that this is much more likely to be a consequence of the cloth trade which exposed people to outside influences and made them more responsive to new ideas.[1] The strong Protestant and Puritan presence in Halifax and the surrounding area was reflected by the vicars of Halifax (the Parish covering the whole of modern day Calderdale) with the eighteenth-century historian, John Watson, identifying Christopher Ashburn as the first protestant vicar in 1559.[2] By the end of the sixteenth century Puritanism had taken a strong hold. John Favour, vicar from 1593-1623, was a prominent Puritan and he and his successors sought to place people with similar views as curates in the different chapels, such as Luddenden, within their control.[3]

Even after the Civil War there is some indication that some of the vicars of Halifax were on the radical wing of the church. This is demonstrated, for instance, by the contrast between two vicars of Halifax, Richard Hooke and Edmund Hough, who were incumbent from 1662–88 and 1688-90 respectively. Hooke was a robust adversary of radicals such as Oliver Heywood, to the extent that on one occasion he refused to share a meal with him at Shibden Hall because, according to Heywood's account, he 'was bound by his canons

---

[1] J.A Hargreaves, *Halifax,* Edinburgh: Edinburgh University Press; Lancaster: Carnegie Publishing, 1999, p43

[2] J. Watson, *The history and antiquities of the parish of Halifax in Yorkshire,* London: Lowndes, 1775, p366

[3] Hargreaves, *Halifax,* p47

not to eat with an excommunicate person'.[4] Hooke's successor, Edmund Hough, was a close friend of Heywood and is reported on one occasion to have preached at the Old Church in Leeds where he 'was looked upon as a non-conformist'.[5]

In keeping with the national trend, it is likely that religious radicalism and non-conformity increased in the Halifax Parish in the mid-seventeenth century. This is well evidenced by the Episcopal Return of 1669, which refers to 'divers meetings of Quakers, Independents and Presbyterians' in the chapelries of Cross Stone, Sowerby and Coley, two conventicles of Independents in Halifax and 'numerous' other meetings of Quakers in Halifax, Sowerby, Illingworth and Ripponden.[6] This growth of non-conformity was resisted with, at times, concerted persecution of religious radicals, who were arrested and fined for holding and attending meetings and for their refusal to pay church fines and tithes. This is graphically illustrated by an account by John Watson of the life of a dissenting preacher, Matthew Smith, who preached mainly in Warley and Mixenden in the late 1660s and 1670s:

> The Civil Magistrates being at that time severe with non conformists as held any public assemblies he was obliged to preach privately often at night and to hide themselves from their resentment; and though parties of soldiers were frequently detached to secure him he was always fortunate enough to elude their vigilance and at last when times were more settled, he had a flourishing congregation.[7]

The Presbyterians rejected the hierarchy of the established church, and the role of bishops in particular, preferring their churches to be run by elected lay people. They appear to have had a significant presence locally with a key role being played by Oliver Heywood during the second half of the seventeenth century. Heywood began an itinerant ministry following his ejection as minister in Coley in 1660 and later established a licensed meeting in Northowram, though his licence was then revoked. As is reflected by his contacts with the vicars of Halifax, he was clearly a well-known local figure and he appears to have provided leadership to non-conformists in this area and further afield. Indeed, John Hargreaves argues that Oliver Heywood was

---

[4] E.W. Crossley, 'Two Halifax vicars: the wills and inventories of Richard Hooke and Edmund Hough', *Transactions of the Halifax Antiquarian Society*, 1904, pp113-127 at p116

[5] Crossley, 'Two Halifax vicars: the wills and inventories of Richard Hooke and Edmund Hough', p122

[6] Quoted by C.F. Stell, 'Calderdale Chapels', *Transactions of the Halifax Antiquarian Society*, 1984, pp16-35 at p18

[7] Watson, *The history and antiquities of the parish of Halifax in Yorkshire*, p514

crucial to the survival of Yorkshire Dissent during the period 1660 – 1688[8] and W.J. Shiels describes him as 'the pre-eminent figure in northern nonconformity' in the period leading up to 1688.[9]

The Independents closely resembled the Presbyterians in advocating the independence and autonomy of each local church. The Quakers, however, went significantly further by effectively downplaying the role of the ministry and scriptures and favouring instead direct individual revelation. There appear to have been Quakers in the Halifax and Calder Valley area from as early as 1652-53, when a meeting was established in Brighouse and a William Dewsbury preached in Halifax.[10] There is also evidence of Quakers in Mankinholes around 1652-53,[11] which also became the site of another established meeting.

In 1689 the Toleration Act allowed (protestant) non-conformists a degree of tolerance and the ability to worship openly. At this point there were seven dissenting congregations in Halifax Parish which included Oliver Heywood's congregation in Northowram.[12] Subsequently the Presbyterian meeting at Northgate End in Halifax was established and by 1715 this meeting had 600 adherents. In total, there are estimated to have been 2,000 dissenters in the Parish.

In the period immediately following the Toleration Act, non-conformity appears to have continued to grow. In 1703, the itinerant preaching of William Mitchell and David Crossley from Heptonstall led to a Baptist meeting being established at Stansfield and subsequently Baptists took over a Presbyterian meeting at Eastwood. By 1725, Daniel Defoe reported that there were sixteen meeting houses in the parish 'which they also call chapels, and are so having bells to call all the people, and burying grounds to most of them, or else they bury within them'.[13]

The early years of the eighteenth century may, however, have been the high water mark for this first period of non-conformity. In 1743, the Vicar of

---

[8] Hargreaves, *Halifax*, p49

[9] W.J. Shiels, 'Heywood, Oliver', in *Oxford Dictionary of National Biography*, Oxford: Oxford University Press, 2004

[10] Stell, 'Calderdale Chapels', p20

[11] W.P. Thistlethwaite, *The Quaker meeting of Mankinholes/Todmorden*, [the author], 1989

[12] Hargreaves, *Halifax*, pp50-51

[13] Quoted by Stell, 'Calderdale Chapels', p16

Halifax, George Legh, made a visitation return to Archbishop Herring of York and reported that of 6,200 households in his parish there were:

> 300 Presbyterian families; scarce any Baptists or Independents; 60 Quaker families; Very few Papists.[14]

The Presbyterians had seven meeting houses (in Halifax, Elland, Mixenden, Warley, Sowerby, Northowram and Stansfield) and the Quakers three, with a new meeting house under construction in Halifax. Assuming that there was a decline, this would be consistent with national trends as, noticeably with the Quakers, the relative freedoms that came with the Toleration Act tended to replace the radicalism and proselytising nature of the earlier years with a more closed and introspective approach.

Despite significant non-conformist activity in Halifax Parish during the seventeenth and early eighteenth centuries, it appears that there was less non-conformity in the immediate area around Midgley. This is most strongly evidenced by the lack of any reported meetings in the area, although there is some evidence of non-conformists living in the township, even if they travelled out of the area to practise their religion.

There is some evidence of Quakers living in the Midgley area with Pearson Thistlethwaite[15] highlighting two prominent local Quakers who attended the Halifax meeting. These are Henry Broadbelt, who died in 1702 and Henry Wadsworth, who died in 1678. Wadsworth, who was described by Oliver Heywood as a 'great Quaker, very rich',[16] spent most of his life in Warley but latterly lived at Kershaw Hall. It may, however, be that these two identified Quakers in Midgley were exceptional. While it is inevitably difficult to prove a negative, a review of early Quaker records such as the 'Record of the Suffering of the People of God called Quakers within Brighouse Monthly Meeting ...'[17] which normally provides an accurate picture of where Quakers lived, does not appear to have any references to people from the Midgley or Luddenden area. It also appears, especially in the early 1700s, that the Halifax Meeting, which

---

[14] S.L. Ollard and P.C. Walker (eds), *Archbishop Herring's Visitation Return 1743 Volume III*, Leeds: Yorkshire Archaeological Society Record Series, 1929, vol 75, pp31-32

[15] P. Thistlethwaite, 'Local Quakers and their meeting houses', *Transactions of the Halifax Antiquarian Society*, 1986, pp25-37at pp33-34

[16] T. Sutcliffe, 'Visit to Warley', *Transactions of the Halifax Antiquarian Society*, 1913, pp195-254 at p233 p231

[17] Leeds University. Brotherton Special Collections, Carlton Hill Archive, *A Record of the Suffering of the People of God called Quakers within Brighouse Monthly Meeting in the County of Yorke, 1658-1718*, Manuscripts: MS Dep. 1979/1 L14

in probability local Quakers would have attended, was not particularly active.[18]

A further source of evidence for non-conformity in Midgley is the 1743 return to Archbishop Herring by the Curate of Luddenden, John Grimshaw[19] (at the same time as the return by Vicar Legh, for the whole parish). Grimshaw reported that of 311 families in the chapelry, fifty-three were Presbyterian, four Quaker and two 'Anabaptist' (i.e. Baptist); although he confirms that there were no meeting houses in the chapelry. The number of Presbyterian families is significant because even though the figures given by the Vicar and Curate may not be entirely accurate, this suggests that around 17 per cent of families in the chapelry were Presbyterian against a figure of 5 per cent across the parish (while at around 1.3 per cent of families in the chapelry the proportion of Quakers was pretty close to that across the whole parish). The difficulty here, however, is that the chapelry of Luddenden took in more than Midgley and the figures may well reflect the Presbyterian meetings in Warley and Mixenden – Mixenden had a congregation of 400 at that time which was the largest for all the local Presbyterian chapels.[20]

It is probably only possible to speculate as to why there appears to have been less active non-conformity in Midgley. The first reason may well be a matter of geography, because if it is accepted that there were some non-conformists locally but no meeting places, it could simply be that Midgley's relative isolation, backing as it does on the high moor land, meant that it was easier for early non-conformists to travel out to meetings than to draw other adherents in.

The second possible reason for less active non-conformity may also be linked to geography, but in this case the social consequences of geographical isolation. It is likely that there were preconditions for religious radicalism taking hold in an area, which included access to external ideas that would cause people to challenge existing norms and practices, and having a sufficiently open society to outweigh the counter-pressure of social cohesion and family and kinship bonds. While on the one hand people in Midgley would probably have had access to radical thinking through the textile trade

---

[18] Leeds University. Brotherton Special Collections, Carlton Hill Archive, *A Record of the Suffering of the People of God called Quakers within Brighouse Monthly Meeting,* Manuscripts: MS Dep. 1979/1 L14; Leeds University. Brotherton Special Collections, Carlton Hill Archive, *Minutes Book of the Brighouse Monthly Meetings,* 1688-1728, Manuscripts: MS Dep. 1979/1 Q1-Q3

[19] Ollard and Walker (eds), *Archbishop Herring's Visitation Return 1743 Volume III* , pp149-150

[20] Stell, 'Calderdale Chapels', p21

and markets in Halifax, the relative isolation of the village and prominence of a few main families may have held most religious radicalism in check.

Linked to this it is worth noting that for thirty years, until his death in 1684, William Farrar of Ewood, just below the village of Midgley, was a Justice of the Peace and appears to have been happy to prosecute Quakers. For instance in the 'Record of the Suffering ... within the Brighouse Monthly Meeting ...' there is a report that;

> John ffirth of Sowerby in the parish of Ealand or Halifax and countie of Yorke was taken by Michall ffrior of Warley a Bailiff and brought before William Farrar of Ewood and Thomas Hawton who were called justices of the peace who committed him to Yorke Castle till the 14th day of the fifth month 1683 ...[21]

Earlier there is a reference from 1670 to an Edward Hullon of Blacktree in Bradford who was jailed and fined by William Farror who' in view of the dates that Farrar served as a JP, is probably the same person. This evidence is not conclusive, but allows speculation as to whether the fact of a member of a prominent local family being a JP, may have exerted some specific local control. It is also interesting to speculate about the relationship between Henry Farror and another wealthy local man, Henry Wadsworth.

The final possible reason for less active non-conformity in Midgley may be the role of the local church. The local church was represented by the Chapelry of Luddenden and it is possible that, if this established church was broad enough in its doctrine and observance, it may have provided very particular and local circumstances that would reduce non-conformity. Unfortunately, there appears to be very little information about the curates of Luddenden, for instance, John Watson gives a partial list of the curates and then only highlights two of these as notable;[22] but if the local church reflected the diversity that has already been mentioned among the vicars of Halifax, this may be a possibility.

The Evangelical Revival

In his History of Halifax, the former incumbent of Rippponden, John Watson, listed the 'other places of Worship' in 1758:

---

[21] Leeds University. Brotherton Special Collections, Carlton Hill Archive, *A Record of the Suffering of the People of God called Quakers within Brighouse Monthly Meeting,* Manuscripts: MS Dep. 1979/1 L14

[22] Watson, *The history and antiquities of the parish of Halifax in Yorkshire,* p437 and pp453-528

Presbyterian Meeting Houses. North Gate --- Hill End in Mixenden --- Warley town --- Sowerby town --- Northowram town --- Elland town --- Eastwood Chapel in Stansfield.

Quakers. Meeting House in the township of Rastrick --- Clayfields in Barkisland --- Shoebroad in Langfield --- Wards End in Halifax.

Methodists. Church-Lane in Halifax. Four-Lane-Ends in Sowerby

Anabaptists (as they are called) Rodhill End in Stansfield --- Slack in Heptonstall --- Wainsgate in Wadsworth.[23]

It appears that, in the fifteen years following Vicar Legh's return to the Archbishop, the number of chapels had again increased and this, combined with the significant addition of two Methodist chapels, points to the start of the second great period of non-conformity, namely the Evangelical Revival.

The Evangelical Revival is generally linked to the growth of Methodism, which in turn started in the early 1740s with the preaching of John and Charles Wesley. John Wesley first preached in Halifax in 1748 and other preachers linked to the growth of Methodism came into the area, too, such as the peddler preacher William Darney (popularly known as 'Scotch Will') and George Whitfield. However, there were also more local preachers who had a significant impact on non-conformity in the Calder Valley and more specifically on Midgley – in particular William Grimshaw and John Fawcett.

William Grimshaw was born near Preston in Lancashire in 1708 and became a Church of England clergyman. Following eleven years as curate in Todmorden, he was appointed in 1742 as perpetual curate of Haworth, which remained his principle home till his death in 1763. Grimshaw had a connection to Midgley through his marriage in 1735 to Sarah Sutcliffe, the daughter of John Lockwood of Ewood Hall. Sarah died after four years of marriage but Grimshaw maintained a connection with Ewood Hall[24] and it also appears that his two children by Sarah continued to live there. The Midgley area clearly remained important to Grimshaw because, on his death, his body was carried over the moors to be buried in St. Mary's Church in Luddenden.

Grimshaw was described as an 'alarming preacher' and set off a popular revival at Haworth to the extent that on occasions he had to preach in the churchyard.[25] Initially he had little to do with the growth of Methodism

---

[23] Watson, *The history and antiquities of the parish of Halifax in Yorkshire*, p452

[24] H.W. Harwood, *History of Methodism in Midgley, near Halifax*, Halifax: Halifax Printing Works, 1933

[25] J. Walsh , 'Grimshaw, William' in *Oxford Dictionary of National Biography*, Oxford: Oxford University Press, 2004

Figure 1   William Grimshaw

around him, but in 1744, following a religious vision, he started to link up with it. Grimshaw was visited in Haworth by Charles and John Wesley in 1746 and 1747 respectively and also formed an unlikely relationship with William Darney leading to local comment that 'Mad Grimshaw is turned Scotch Will's clerk'.[26] These contacts appear to have overcome Grimshaw's reluctance to go beyond his own parish and he quickly became an itinerant evangelist covering

---

[26] W. Myles, *Life and writings of the late William Grimshaw*, 2nd ed., London: Thomas Cordeaux, 1813, p18, quoted by Walsh, 'Grimshaw, William' in *Oxford Dictionary of National Biography*

a large area within a fifteen mile radius of Haworth. Thus it was that in 1747 he wrote;

> This evening I am venturing, by divine assistance, upon a public exhortation in a wild, unchristian place called Midgley, about 4 miles west of Halifax, where of late I have had a great part of my residence.[27]

John Walsh[28] argues that Grimshaw represents an interesting phase in the development of Methodism and describes him as a 'half-regular' clergyman who linked early Methodism with the later evangelical school in the church. He built a Methodist chapel in his parish to maintain gospel preaching in the event of his being succeeded by a non-evangelical minister, but in his later years was also disturbed by the drift of Methodism away from the established church. This said, he played a significant role in stimulating the growth of Methodism and, although drawing some followers away from other groups, such as the Baptists, provided support to other key local figures.

One such figure was the Baptist Minister, John Fawcett (1740–1817). Fawcett owed much to Grimshaw's preaching at Haworth[29] and other Methodist preachers, but in 1776 he moved to Brearley Hall to open a college for men to train for the Baptist Ministry. Subsequently, some twenty years later, he moved to Ewood Hall, which had already become the actual college location. Like Grimshaw before him, Fawcett became a leader among local non-conformists and he became an active champion for a range of education, philanthropic and religious works in Yorkshire and Lancashire.[30]

An insight into the impact that evangelical preachers had can be gleaned from the account by John Fawcett the younger which describes a visit from George Whitfield to Ewood.

> Intelligence of their coming having been announced in the neighbourhood, an immense concourse was assembled. A temporary booth was erected in a field near the house, for Mr. Whitfield and the other ministers. Not only the field, but the woody land above it, was covered with crowds collected from different parts. An unusual solemnity pervaded the vast multitude, and at the close of

---

[27] Quoted in Harwood, *History of Methodism in Midgley*, p5
[28] Walsh, 'Grimshaw, William' in *Oxford Dictionary of National Biography*
[29] J.A. Hargreaves, 'The Revival of Old Dissent: Baptists and Independents in the Parish of Halifax 1743 – 1851', *Transactions of the Halifax Antiquarian Society*, 2001, pp79-99 at p81
[30] R. Collinge, *A History of Luddenden Methodist Chapel*, [Luddenden: the author], 1978

the service the 100th Psalm was sung and concluded with Mr. Grimshaw's favourite doxology, 'Praise God from whom all blessing flow'.[31]

This account is quoted by H.W. Harwood, who goes on to report that the volume of sound produced by the voices of thousands, while it re-echoed through the vale below is said to have had such an effect 'as no language can describe'.

The fact that the son of a Baptist should describe the preaching of a Methodist in the presence of an Anglican clergyman highlights the fact that, while different groups were essentially in competition with each other for followers and resources, there was still a strong bond and links between the main non-conformist sects. Dr Frank Baker describes Grimshaw, for example, as having exercised a 'greater influence among the Baptists, than among other dissenters'[32] and Harwood quotes a Connexional reference from September 1827 which again links Baptists, Independents and Methodists;

> We held a meeting at Midgley at which place we have a neat and commodious chapel … A venerable Independent minister of Booth, opened with a prayer and Mr. Fawcett, son of the sainted Dr. Fawcett presided, and it is said that he gave a humorous and appropriate address.[33]

Methodism was clearly the most successful of the non-conformist movements in the Halifax area. During the eighteenth century the growth of Methodism was steady but not spectacular with 1,000 Methodists recorded in 1786, but there was a rapid expansion following the Great Yorkshire revival in 1793-94.[34] There was then what Hargreaves describes as a 'phenomenal expansion' of Methodism up to the mid-nineteenth century.[35] As the largest non-conformist sect, the growth is reflected by the fact that in 1843 the Denominational Survey by Edmund Baines identified 110 Non-Conformist chapels in the Parish with accommodation for one third of the total population, which was twice the number that could be accommodated in the twenty-two Anglican Churches.[36]

---

[31] Quoted in Harwood, *History of Methodism in Midgley*, pp7-8

[32] Quoted in Hargreaves, 'The Revival of Old Dissent: Baptists and Independents in the Parish of Halifax 1743 – 1851', p88

[33] Quoted in Harwood, *History of Methodism in Midgley*, p24

[34] Hargreaves, *Halifax*, p100

[35] Hargreaves, 'The Revival of Old Dissent: Baptists and Independents in the Parish of Halifax 1743 – 1851', p79

[36] Hargreaves, *Halifax*, p100

The growth of Methodism in and around Halifax was not without obstacles – the most obvious of which was a tendency for Wesleyan Methodists to argue and for significant portions of the congregation to break away. In Halifax, around half of the Wesleyans seceded in 1762 and joined the newly re-emerging Independents (or Congregationalists) and in 1797 another quarter broke away to join the Methodist New Connexion, who opened the Salem Chapel in Halifax in 1798 and Hanover Chapel in 1836.[37] Generally the splits were driven by organisational rather than theological issues – the secession to the New Connexion was largely driven by the way that Wesley increasingly 'assumed what was virtually a dictatorship'.[38] This was in turn demonstrated by his continued insistence that communion could only be received in an established church, in the face of an increasing desire among Methodists to receive this in their own chapel and from their own minister.

The Evangelical Revival also had a positive impact on other non-conformist groups. In particular, the Independents and Baptists became, as Hargreaves puts it, 'imbued with a new expansionist energy'[39], although the Presbyterians became increasingly marginalised. The Independents, now increasingly referred to as Congregationalists, grew throughout the early nineteenth century, becoming by 1851 second in numerical strength to the Wesleyans. The link between the growth of Methodism and the re-emergence of the Independents can be partly attributed to the fact that the initial congregation in Halifax had broken away from the Wesleyans. However, more generally, W.B. Trigg argues that 'the particular brand of Independency which flourished so abundantly in these parts in the nineteenth century … was indebted far more to Wesley and his followers than to the non conformists of 1662, both for its theological doctrine and its conduct of public worship'.[40]

The Baptists also experienced a revival, though it is noteworthy that they appear to have fared better in the upper Calder Valley, which was in many ways their earlier heartland around Heptonstall and Eastwood, whereas the Independents (Congregationalists) were stronger nearer Halifax. The growth of the two sects is demonstrated by the increase from 4,265 Baptists in Halifax Parish in 1800 to 6,323 in 1851; and from 4,310 Independents to 10,063 in the same period. In 1851, the Baptists had eight places of worship with 2,231

---

[37] Hargreaves, *Halifax*, p100
[38] Harwood, *History of Methodism in Midgley*, p16
[39] Hargreaves, 'The Revival of Old Dissent: Baptists and Independents in the Parish of Halifax 1743 – 1851', p80
[40] Quoted by Hargreaves, 'The Revival of Old Dissent: Baptists and Independents in the Parish of Halifax 1743 – 1851', pp88-89

sittings in Halifax and 4,092 in Todmorden. In the same year the Independents had seventeen places of worship with 8,948 sittings in Halifax and 1,120 in Todmorden.[41]

While the role of the Evangelical Revival and work of the evangelist preachers should be acknowledged as significant factors in the massive growth of non-conformity in the late eighteenth and nineteenth centuries, another key factor was the massive social and economic upheaval of the Industrial Revolution. Industrial migration and urban expansion led to a level of social breakdown for which the established church, especially in large and relatively remote parishes such as Halifax, was ill prepared.[42] Non-conformist churches with a strong emphasis on education could flourish in this vacuum; not that these churches should be seen as an exclusively working-class phenomenon. The Independents in particular had wealthy supporters and the building of churches and schools was only possible through the growth of industrial capital.[43]

The Midgley and Booth Chapels

In contrast to the first period of non-conformity in the seventeenth and early eighteenth century, the growth of non-conformity associated with the Evangelical Revival clearly took hold in Midgley township. The legacy of this period still has a physical presence, with the former Methodist New Connexion Chapel still standing at Scout Head (albeit now converted to flats). There was also a substantial Congregationalist Church in Booth, until its demolition in 1980.

While the development of the Midgley and Booth chapels cannot be directly linked to the visits of the itinerant preachers, it is clear that their evangelism sowed the seeds that would flourish in these churches. It is also possible to identify a causal chain between Grimshaw's links to Ewood and the establishment of the New Connexion Chapel, because his presence and then memory meant that high profile preachers, such as Wesley, continued to visit. This is demonstrated by an entry in John Wesley's diary for 1766 where he writes:

---

[41] Hargreaves, 'The Revival of Old Dissent: Baptists and Independents in the Parish of Halifax 1743 – 1851', p80
[42] Hargreaves, *Halifax*, p99
[43] Hargreaves, 'The Revival of Old Dissent: Baptists and Independents in the Parish of Halifax 1743 – 1851', p95

> I rode to Ewood. The last time I was here, young Mr. Grimshaw received us in the same hearty manner as his father used to do; but he too is now gone into eternity…[44]

In total, Wesley came to Ewood ('which I still love for good Mr. Grimshaw's sake') nine times; his last visit being in 1782.[45]

In 1774, John Sutcliffe, a young man of twenty one who worked for the Lockwood family at Ewood, established a Methodist Class there. This was the year of one of Wesley's visits so it is likely that Wesley's preaching and connection was a catalyst. Five years later, Sutcliffe moved to Piniel Top (Pin Hill Top) in Midgley and, though there are no records till as late as 1817, Harwood speculates that the Methodist Class and prayer meetings continued there.[46] Sutcliffe also established Methodist Classes in Luddenden and although it appears that membership and activity fluctuated (almost ceasing in 1799)[47] in 1808 there were seven classes drawing members from Midgley, Luddenden, Warley, Mount Tabor and Luddendenfoot. In 1808, these Classes merged to form the Luddenden Wesleyan Chapel. It is a useful reminder of the turbulent times in which the chapel opened, that both ministers were at the time subject to Luddite death threats following their preaching against them and an instance when the Reverend Bunting refused burial to a rioter.[48]

In 1818, a Midgley weaver and farmer William Boardall, and Warley farmer George Hartley, led a break away from the Luddenden Wesleyan Chapel to join the Methodist New Connexion based at the Salem Chapel in Halifax. Salem Chapel had already resolved to find somewhere to preach in Midgley and in the same year the building of the Methodist New Connexion Chapel commenced with Hartley acting as one of the trustees and both appearing to play a key role in its operation. The Union Chapel was erected at the cost of £400 at Scout Head, a little nearer to Towngate than the later Providence Chapel.[49]

The development of the Union Chapel was not immune to developments around it and membership of the church fluctuated; from thirty-seven members in 1820, to a low of seventeen in 1834, recovering to fifty-two in 1841.

---

[44] Quoted in Harwood, *History of Methodism in Midgley*, p7
[45] Harwood, *History of Methodism in Midgley*, p7
[46] Harwood, *History of Methodism in Midgley*, p9
[47] Collinge, A *History of Luddenden Methodist Chapel*
[48] Collinge, A *History of Luddenden Methodist Chapel*
[49] Harwood, *History of Methodism in Midgley*, p20

The chapel was also troubled financially, especially in the 'hungry forties' at which time repayments on loans stopped and the Connexional Chapel Fund needed to make a grant. While the building was extended slightly in 1861, with the addition of a vestry and a recess for an organ, the loans for the initial construction were not paid off until 1870.

By the second half of the nineteenth century the chapel was stronger and the demands on the building greater as it proved a focus for village life in Midgley. In 1875, fundraising to build a new chapel started and on 11 March 1883 the last service was held at Union Chapel, which was then demolished. After six months, during which time services were held at the Cooperative Hall, on 12 September 1883 the new Providence Chapel was opened. This was a larger and grander building with six classrooms to hold twenty people each, a big room to hold 300 and a chapel with 'accommodation for 500, or 700 at a pinch'.[50] The total cost of the building was £1,420 which was part funded by a £500 loan. It is a measure of the chapel's growth that this was cleared by 1893.

In 1761, before even the setting up of the first Methodist Class in Midgley, a group of Independents came together to build a one-room church in Booth. Their leader in this was James Crossley, who was born in 1731 and lived in Upper Saltonstall. Crossley was a convert of George Whitfield and was 'nurtured in the faith by William Grimshaw'.[51] However, following a recommendation from Grimshaw to John Wesley of Crossley's suitability for the ministry, Crossley broke with Methodism for what were described as a variance in 'their views on certain theological questions and on matters relating to church governance'.[52] Instead Crossley became the Minister of the rapidly expanding congregation in Booth until shortly before his death in 1782.

In 1828, the first purpose-built chapel was built and in 1830 the church had seventy-four members. In 1851, a new school was added and then in 1869, a little in advance of the similar development with the New Connexion Chapel in Midgley, a larger 'New Church' was opened at a cost of £4,000.[53] This church remained in use until its closure and subsequent demolition in 1980.

---

[50] Harwood, *History of Methodism in Midgley*, pp45-46

[51] Hargreaves, 'The Revival of Old Dissent: Baptists and Independents in the Parish of Halifax 1743 – 1851', p91

[52] C. Teasdale, *Historical sketch of Booth Congregational Church, Halifax*, Halifax: Ashworth & Sons, 1919, p5

[53] Teasdale, *Historical sketch of Booth Congregational Church, Halifax*, p11

Figure 2   *Providence Chapel, Midgley*

The chapels at Midgley and Booth clearly dominated their local communities and, accordingly, it is worth considering the membership of these chapels and the larger role that they played in their respective communities. In the case of the New Connexion Chapel in Midgley, the first indication of who the key members were is the list of trustees for the Union Chapel dated 13 February 1819. Of twenty one trustees, nine came from Halifax and were all linked to the Salem Chapel. Of the remainder, four are described as coming from Warley (including George Hartley), five from Midgley and one each from Luddenden and Denholme. The Halifax-based trustees are described as a gardener, two drapers, a carder, a wiredrawer, a shopman, a car maker, a flour dealer and a grocer. The remainder are two farmers, two weavers, four cotton manufacturers, an innkeeper and a cloth dresser. The remaining trustee was Edward Wilkinson from Lacey Hey who was the vendor of the land the chapel was built on (although Henry Murgatroyd, later of The Greave in Midgley, also had an interest in this).[54]

By 1874, the trustees were composed of nine weavers, two farmers, two bootmakers, a carter, a school master, a butcher, a porter, a cloth miller, a warehouseman and the Superintendent Minister. Significantly, Harwood describes them all, with the exception of the Minister, as Midgley men, though in fact one of the trustees is described as being from Elland.[55]

---

[54] Harwood, *History of Methodism in Midgley*, pp19-20
[55] Harwood, *History of Methodism in Midgley*, p27

Another interesting source, which this time gives a profile of the whole congregation, is a collection of favourite quotations chosen by members of the congregation and published as a 'Midgley Miscellany' in 1907. This gives the names and approximate address for each contributor and out of 204 just over four-fifths come from the immediate Midgley area. After Midgley, nine came from Hebden Bridge, three from Halifax, three from Brighouse and two from Warley. The remainder came from further afield, such as Rochdale, Oldham and in one instance, Pennsylvania. As to their choices, other than a smattering of attributed quotations from the Bible and the likes of Tennyson, Longfellow and Walter Scott, the majority are either popular sayings, such as 'Love one another'; favourite hymns; or comic – 'Many are called, but few get up, especially on a cold morning'.[56]

An essential component of the chapels' contribution to their communities was the provision of education. In 1820, John Boardall, son of William Boardall, was illiterate and it is more than likely that his father and many of the other founding Methodists were also unable to read. The Union Chapel Sunday School was set up in 1817, before even the chapel was built, and a reading society was introduced on 1 January 1819. In 1828 the Sunday School had 170 scholars and fifty-nine teachers; by 1859 there were 291 scholars (but only twenty-one teachers). This said, as a reminder of the wider social and economic context in which the chapel operated, in 1848 the number of scholars had dropped to 105.[57] When the Sunday school transferred to the Providence Chapel there were forty-two teachers and 269 scholars.[58]

The impact of the chapels' educational missions (this was as strong with the Congregationalists in Booth) should not be underestimated given the poverty and deprivation of the residents of the township at that time. We can only speculate as to the impact this had on radicalising the community as they were able to access new ideas and sources of information, but it is clear that there were close links with the Co-operative movement. Furthermore, with the introduction of a Mutual Improvement Society in 1859, a forum was created for the robust exchange of views and exploration of issues. Harwood describes this as part of the 'radical Midgley' tradition and writes of the relaunched society in 1902:

---

[56] *The Midgley Miscellany*, Midgley: Providence Methodist New Connexion Church, 1906
[57] Harwood, *History of Methodism in Midgley*, p33
[58] Harwood, *History of Methodism in Midgley*, p48

While it lasted there was plenty of eloquence in the lecture room and not a few national problems were authoritatively settled.[59]

The decline of the Midgley and Booth chapels

Just as the nineteenth century saw a phenomenal growth in non-conformity and the chapels playing a key role as centres for the community, the twentieth century saw a terminal decline for both the Providence Chapel in Midgley and the New Church in Booth. For both chapels the immediate causes were the same; a declining attendance and consequent loss of income, coupled with the deterioration of the fabric of the chapels.

The start of the decline can perhaps be seen at the start of the twentieth century. In Booth, the Congregational church celebrated the jubilee of the New Church in 1919 and as part of this, the then minister, the Reverend C. Teasdale, produced the Historical Sketch for the Jubilee of the Booth Congregational Chapel.[60] This slim pamphlet gives an historical account of the development of the chapel in Booth, but then, having reflected on the 'abnormal conditions' since the start of his ministry in 1916, Teasdale goes on to emphasise the importance of sustaining the church in the face of the challenge of modernity;

> There is a great danger lest the pressure of present day life and the love of pleasure push aside the more vital things of the spirit.[61]

Teasdale also expresses concern about the local lack of opportunities for young people, causing them to leave in order to find work elsewhere and becoming exposed to people of different religious persuasions.

Fourteen years later, in his History of Methodism in Midgley,[62] H.W. Harwood has some similar concerns. He compares the world at the time that the Providence Chapel was opened, when 'Midgley was still a comparatively closely knit social unit', and the present day where young people are compelled 'for economic and other causes' to leave the village. He reports that this trend, combined with the fact of families being smaller, had led to a more rapid turnover of officers and leaders in the previous twenty-five years than in the ninety years before.[63]

---

[59] Harwood, *History of Methodism in Midgley*, p55
[60] Teasdale, *Historical sketch of Booth Congregational Church, Halifax*
[61] Teasdale, *Historical sketch of Booth Congregational Church, Halifax*, p18
[62] Harwood, *History of Methodism in Midgley*
[63] Harwood, *History of Methodism in Midgley*, p48

Key milestones in the decline of the chapels were the two World Wars. In a 'Scrapbook' by Mr D. Craven, the impact of the Second World War is mainly seen as restricting activities and of also making the Midgley Chapel seem 'to grow quite self contained and even more independent than hitherto'.[64] Craven then describes a moment of optimism post war, albeit that this was not realised, as the social changes further impacted on membership:

> However, we in this village along with the whole world celebrated the cessation of hostilities in 1945 and we thought that things would really begin to hum and to develop in our activities in Midgley. As it happened, however our hopes and aspirations were not to be realized. In the Sunday school many of the pre war helpers did not renew their office for various reasons and on account of the movement of the population we lost approximately 25 scholars in about 6 months.[65]

In Booth, the post war years saw a rapidly aging congregation. This is reflected in the Minute Book for the annual meeting in 1952, which records the report by the minister, Mr. Sunter:

> Mr. Sunter then gave an account of church life and appealed to members to be patient: He thought members might think him slow in bringing young people in to the church but this was much harder than it sounded ...[66]

There were also concerns about the lack of men in the congregation. It is indeed noteworthy that whereas in 1962 the officers of the church were split equally between men and women, by 1982 all the officers were women.

Financially, Booth Congregational Chapel appears to have been reasonably strong and indeed was seeking to build an alternative venue for their meetings until the plans fell through in 1986. The Methodists in Midgley, however, struggled to maintain their building. In the 'Scrapbook' D. Craven writes of the trustees (of which he was one):

> While this august body did endeavour behind the scenes to keep the property in a reasonable state of repair and habitable it was the eternal question of faith versus finance which decided many of the issues in the last analysis.[67]

---

[64] West Yorkshire Archive Service (Calderdale), *Continuation of Scrapbook by Mr. D. Craven (1943 – 1970)*, n.d. [but presumably after 1983], MISC 967, p24

[65] West Yorkshire Archive Service (Calderdale), *Continuation of Scrapbook by Mr. D. Craven (1943 – 1970)*, p25

[66] West Yorkshire Archive Service (Calderdale), *Minute book of Booth Congregational Church*, 1952–89, MISC 822; entry for 5 January 1952

[67] West Yorkshire Archive Service (Calderdale), *Continuation of Scrapbook by Mr. D. Craven (1943 – 1970)*, p25

He also identifies a tension between trustees and an advisory congregational meeting (an arrangement that was 'peculiar to Midgley') 'which superseded many of the decisions which the Trust may in their wisdom have taken... This was a case of democracy raising either its sublime or ugly head above the activities of the Trust'.[68]

While there was a late revival due in part to the exceptional organisational abilities of Arnold Edwards between 1970 and 1986, in June 1994 the chapel newsletter starkly points out the fact that the weekly running costs for the chapel were £108.75 and income £46.37.[69] With only around twenty members, the decision was finally taken to merge with the Luddenden Methodist Church. The final service in Midgley was held on 30 October 1994.

The closure of the chapels in Midgley and Booth marked the end of 350 years of non-conformity in this area. Perhaps because of its relative isolation, the people of Midgley may not have played as prominent role in the early period of non-conformity as other neighbouring areas. However, once the old bonds of family and kinship were loosened by the rapid social and economic change associated with the start of the Industrial Revolution, the people of Midgley and surrounding areas were strongly drawn to the vigorous evangelism of the new non-conformist churches. As central institutions in village life, these shaped not only the patterns of religious observance, but also the education and aspirations of local people and perhaps this aspect is the most significant impact of Midgley's history of non-conformity.

---

[68] West Yorkshire Archive Service (Calderdale), *Continuation of Scrapbook by Mr. D. Craven (1943 – 1970)*, p26
[69] West Yorkshire Archive Service (Calderdale), Booth Congregational Chapel, *'Special Edition'* *newsletter*, 1994, June, MISC 967/18

CHAPTER 16

Self-help

Shirley Fielden

Introduction

In the 1830s and 1840s, the inhabitants of Midgley were living in a desperate situation. Handloom weavers were under inexorable competitive pressures that were forcing down the work payment they received. Mills were springing up in the valleys and many parents were beginning to send their children to work in the mills in order to supplement their declining income.[1]

John Fielden of Todmorden wrote:

> I well remember being set to work in my father's mill when I was little more than 10 years old; my associates too, in the labour and recreation are fresh in my memory. Only a few of them are now alive; some dying very young, others living to become men and women; but many of those who lived, have died off before they attained the age of fifty years, having the appearance of being much older, a premature appearance of age which I verily believe was caused by the nature of the employment in which they were brought up.[2]

It is interesting to note that, while John Fielden was little more than ten years old, children younger than he had to work in the factories. Between 1839 and 1842 a succession of poor harvests, causing higher food prices, contributed further to the plight of the villagers, some having to sell their meagre possessions in order to survive.

In 1834, the Poor Law Amendment Act or the New Poor Law, as it became known, was introduced. Under the old system each parish or township was responsible for its own poor. Although workhouses existed, relief was not conditional on people entering the workhouse. Under the New Poor Law, existing workhouses were closed and new 'Union Workhouses' were built in which conditions were such that paupers would live in conditions worse than any criminal. It is no wonder that the New Poor Law was hated amongst the

---

[1] The impact of industrialisation and child labour is discussed in Chapter 17
[2] J. Fielden , *Curse of the Factory System*, Halifax: Milner, 1836, p39

working classes who would accept any job regardless of pay rather than submit to the workhouse. The Midgley workhouse (Figure 1) closed, having only had a few inmates living there during its existence as a workhouse. The first meeting of the Board of Guardians of the Poor for the Halifax Union was held at Cheapside, Halifax on the 17 February 1837. There were twenty-eight members present, one member representing Midgley. At this meeting, a chairman and clerk to the board were appointed for the purpose of registering births and deaths. The Halifax Union was divided into ten districts, Midgley becoming part of the Luddenden District. The union workhouse, known as St. John's Hospital, had been purpose built in Gibbet Street, Halifax, at a cost of £12,000, and was opened on the 25 March 1840. From this date onwards inmates of workhouses in surrounding townships and parishes were transferred into the new building. Inmates were put into cells, husbands and wives were split up. Conditions were horrendous.[3]

Figure 1   *New Heath (Earth) Head before renovation. The workhouse for Midgley township until 1834*

The 1830s and 1840s seem to have been a period when crime was rife in Midgley. Crime was such that evidence can still be seen in Midgley of villagers having to protect their property with shutters, which were firmly closed at night to prevent break-ins (Figure 2). Stocks were still used for minor offences such as drunkenness. The stocks of Midgley are still to be seen in Towngate, and have been recently renovated, the stoops being original. The

---

[3] J.G. Washington, 'Poverty, Health & Social Welfare: The History of The Halifax Union Workhouse and St. John's Hospital- 1834-1972', *Transactions of the Halifax Antiquarian Society, 1997*, 5, pp77-98 at p79-80

records of the Wakefield House of Correction show that a disproportionate number of inmates came from upper Calderdale, Midgley having a particularly bad reputation.[4] It is little wonder that the villagers of Midgley needed to protect themselves both from poverty and crime. In these circumstances, there was little option but to provide help for themselves.

Figure 2   Shop at Turn Lee, Midgley. Note the shutters by the near window

Friendly Societies

The general aim of friendly societies was to provide insurance against sickness, pay for funeral expenses and bring members into closer social contact. A study of the practices of friendly societies in this period throws some light on the way in which the 'industrious classes' sought to let a little entertainment and colour enter their drab lives. In the early years the convivial activity of the societies was of the utmost importance and, while it was less important in 1875, it was still regarded as an essential part of the life of any self-respecting society. The ritual of initiation, the good fellowship of the lodge room and celebrations of the annual 'club day' meant much to members.[5] Nationally, the years between 1835 and 1845 were a very difficult

---

[4] B. Jennings, *Pennine Valley: a History of Upper Calderdale,* Otley: Smith Settle, 1992, p95

[5] P.H.J.H. Gosden, *The Friendly Societies in England 1815-7*, Manchester: Manchester University Press, 1961, p10

period for the working men of many industrial districts and it witnessed the rapid growth of a number of working-class organisations of self help and self defence, including the Chartist movement.[6]

The strengthening of the friendly society movement was claimed to be one of the aims of the Poor Law Amendment Act and of the policy which guided its administration. Soon after the act was passed, the poor law commissioners began to claim that this desired effect was, in fact, being achieved. The Act was said to have led to the immediate formation of new societies.[7] The probability that it was the Poor Law Amendment Act which led to the rapid increase in friendly societies after 1834 is strengthened when the conditions of trade and employment are considered. Gayer, Rostow and Schwartz in their study of fluctuations in economy, show that the years between 1836 and 1842 saw no burst in prosperity which might have been an alternative reason for the rapid increase in the number of friendly societies.[8]

Although there is no direct local evidence to suggest that the Poor Law Amendment Act was responsible for the growth of friendly societies, it may be that the Jacob's Well Lodge of the Peaceful Dove Society was formed in Midgley with the object of saving its members from the workhouse. The Census of 1841 does not give places of birth for the inmates of the workhouse, so we are unable to say how many, if any, inmates came from Midgley. The Census of 1851 shows that there were only three inmates of the Halifax Union Workhouse born in Midgley. The Census of 1861 shows there were seven inmates. Sadly, two of these were an eighteen year old worsted twister from Bradford and her baby of 'under 1 month' who was born in Midgley. What happened to them? Without further enquiry it must be left to the reader to contemplate. The Census of 1871 tells us that there were five inmates born in Midgley. By 1881 it would appear that there were no inmates born in Midgley resident in the Workhouse.

The friendly societies generally throughout the country were all maintained by the subscription of members. They met socially in local inns. The members all had to be of good character as is evident from the 'Rules of the Peaceful Dove Society'. Annual General Meetings were held with audited accounts.

---

[6] Gosden, *The Friendly Societies in England 1815-7*, p33

[7] *Poor Law Commissioners for England and Wales. First Annual Report*, House of Commons Parliamentary Papers, Session 1835 (500), XXXV (107), p31

[8] A.D. Gayer, W.W. Rostow and A.J. Shwartz, *The growth and fluctuation of the British economy, 1790-1850 : an historical, statistical, and theoretical study of Britain's economic development*, Oxford: Clarendon Press, 1953, Vol 1, pp275-6, 300-3

The accounts were available at any time for members, or people interested in a society, to inspect. Membership cards and rule books were issued to new members. Annual returns were sent to the Registrar of Friendly Societies.

The Peaceful Dove Friendly Society

In 1840, the first meeting of the Jacob's Well Lodge, No 49 of the Halifax United Order of the Peaceful Dove Friendly Society, met at the Shoulder of Mutton Inn, Midgley.[9] The purpose of the society was to insure sums of money to defray the expenses of burial for deceased members, members' deceased wives and also deceased members' widows, who contributed 1s per quarter.[10] The officers of the society were a grand master, a deputy grand master, a district secretary, a correspondence secretary and a district treasurer, plus a committee that was elected annually. Admission to the society was as follows:

> No one of ill health or with periodical complaints.
> No one of bad character or who frequents bad company.
> No one with habitual intoxication or a quarrelsome behaviour.
> No one who has left any other society in a dishonourable manner.[11]

Members had to produce a 'surgeon's note' for fourteen days in order to draw benefits, unless they had special permission from the committee. In 1883 it was agreed with the Yorkshire Penny Bank that funeral expenses could be paid by cheque.[12]

It is quite noticeable from the membership lists between 1840 and 1881 that members were young; working men aged between eighteen and forty.[13] Comparing the Census of 1851 with the membership book, there were thirty-one male members of the population who had joined the Peaceful Dove Society. By 1871, there were ninety-two male members of the community who were members of the Society. Interestingly, in 1871 membership amongst the male inhabitants of the centre of the village of Midgley was twenty-six, over half of the male population aged between eighteen and forty. Clearly, Midgley's friendly society was very popular with village residents.

---

[9] Illustrated in Chapter 14, Figure 3

[10] West Yorkshire Archive Service (Calderdale), *Rules of the Peaceful Dove Society*, 1858, TU 7/16

[11] West Yorkshire Archive Service (Calderdale), *Rules of the Peaceful Dove Society*, 1861, TU 7/18/217

[12] West Yorkshire Archive Service (Calderdale), *Minutes of the Committee of Management, Peaceful Dove Society*, 1883, JM814-5, pp3-4

[13] West Yorkshire Archive Service (Calderdale), *Proposition Book of the Peaceful Dove Friendly Society, Jacob's Well Lodge*, 1840-1957, JM 805

Figure 3   *An early page (1847) from the proposition book for the Midgley Friendly Society*

Figure 4   *Black Rock, the home of James Fletcher, a forger who became the twenty-sixth member of Midgley's Peaceful Dove Friendly Society when he was initiated on 13 February 1847 (see Figure 3)*

Figure 5   *Doves Rest, Midgley*

Funds were raised by each member paying a subscription. Other monies were raised by entrance fees, levies, fines, donations or the sale of rules. Interest on investments was applied to carry out the objects of the society and to pay the expenses of management according to the rules. Funds of the society which were not wanted for immediate use were invested by the trustees of the society in Post Office Savings, the Yorkshire Penny Bank or in the purchase of land and buildings. In 1883, property was owned in Todmorden, Halifax and at Smithy Fold, Midgley. In 1885, two houses in Sackville Street, Hebden Bridge were purchased and in 1886 properties at Springfield Terrace, Midgley were also purchased. In 1887, the committee decided that the property at Smithy Fold was to be completely rebuilt, changing its name to Doves Rest.

There appeared to be great camaraderie within the society, members referring to each other as 'brother'. Records available show that, from 1883 onwards, an annual dinner was held each year, the landlord of the Shoulder of Mutton being asked to provide a meal, beer and entertainment. Members paid a nominal sum and the remaining cost was met from society funds. In 1884, 160 dinners were ordered. In 1887, the order was for 170 dinners and forty-eight gallons of beer, while in 1888, 180 dinners and forty gallons of beer were ordered.[14] It is more than likely that the annual dinner had been held for some years prior to 1883, although there does not appear to be any surviving recorded evidence of this. It is interesting to note that in 1851 there were thirty one members of the Society but by 1888, 180 dinners had been ordered for the annual dinner. The society appears to have grown significantly. The society continued until 1957, just one year after the Shoulder of Mutton had closed.

Juvenile Burial Society of the Peaceful Dove

The object of the society was to provide sums of money to be paid on the death of a member to provide a decent funeral. Any person from three months to sixteen years of age could become a member of the society. His or her guardian would apply to the secretary or the grand master of any of the lodges of the order and, if no objection was made, then the candidate would be entered on the books of the society. In some cases, a doctor's certificate had to be produced if the secretary or officer of the lodge thought it necessary prior to admission as a member. A male member, on attaining the age of sixteen, could enter any lodge of the order and, if he had been a member for two years or more, the lodge would pay 2s 6d towards his entrance fee. Female members and male members over sixteen who were unable or unwilling to transfer to a lodge could remain members of the society by paying the full contribution and were thus entitled to full death benefit.

Every member had to pay the secretary on the meeting night the sum of ½d. per week. From these weekly contributions, 1s 8d would be paid to the management fund and the remainder would be paid into the general fund for the purpose of paying funeral expenses. Penalties, in the way of fines, were made if members did not keep up their payments. Levies would be made on members if the management fund was over spent. No money would be paid on the death of a member until the production of the death certificate.[15]

---

[14] West Yorkshire Archive Service (Calderdale), *Minutes of the Committee of Management, Peaceful Dove Society,* 1840-1957, JM814-5

[15] Rules of the Juvenile Burial Society in Connection with the Halifax United Order of the Peaceful Dove Friendly Society, Halifax,1933

Prosecution of Felons

On 25 April 1838, a meeting was held at the house of Mrs Bedford, innkeeper of the Shoulder of Mutton in Midgley, to form a society for the more effectual prosecution and prevention of felonies, misdemeanours and other offences, especially wilful and malicious injuries and damage to property. On 13 June 1838, it was resolved that articles and rules for the government of the society be signed by every person becoming a member, subject to such additions or alterations as may from time to time be agreed upon. Membership was restricted to the five townships of Midgley, Warley, Sowerby, Erringden and Wadsworth. People obviously felt the need to protect themselves from the lawlessness of the area. Meetings were held quarterly and members paid 1s per share to the fund and 3d was to be spent on liquor among the company present.

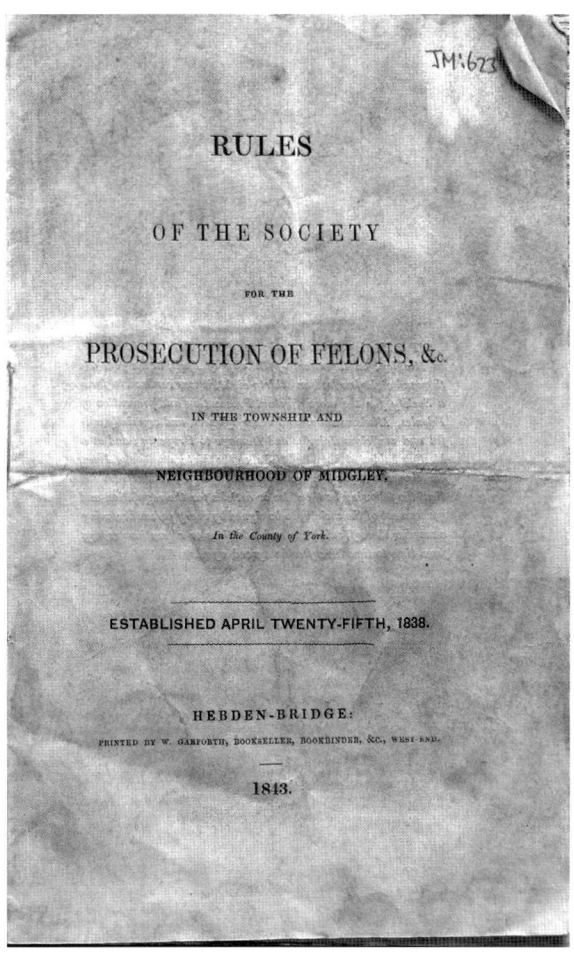

Figure 6   *The rule book of the Midgley Prosecution Society*

The Society was managed by a committee and appointed officers. No one could be admitted as a member without the approval of the committee members present at the relevant meeting. At every annual general meeting a secretary, with a salary, and a committee consisting of twelve members were chosen. At any meeting of the committee, the members attending would have 6d each allowed for refreshment, paid by the treasurer. Protection was not only available for the person, property and workplace where they lived, but also for members with extensive concerns, or goods in mills and warehouses. In these instances members had to either pay a larger subscription or buy more shares in the society.

Figure 7   A poster advertising the Jacob's Well Lodge in 1910

Any member having property stolen or receiving an injury had to report it immediately to the president or secretary of the society who would immediately convene a meeting of the committee. The member was obliged to pursue all proper measures for discovering the offenders and bringing them to justice (observing the directions of the committee). If approved by the committee, then the member would receive all the necessary charges and expenses incurred by him. Any person committing a misdemeanour would be excluded from the society. Six months notice in writing had to be given for anyone wishing to leave. In the case of a member dying, his wife or relation would be admitted as a member with the approval of the committee.[16]

Midgley Co-operative Society

The history of the Midgley Co-operative Society has already been well documented. HW Harwood's centenary history of the society written in 1961 tells us that the Society was formed in 1861:

> in a former schoolroom at Smithy Fold, the site of the present Doves' Rest. When the Co-op was decided upon there were only poor people in Midgley village and it is but justice to say that the brave men who decided to trade amongst themselves did not lack enterprise.[17]

> One hundred years on the small seed planted by the men in Smithy Fold reflects how well they planned. There had been honest trading. Its members were people of widely differing religious and political views, poor and moderately well-to-do – all formed a common bond within the society. Here indeed was the start of the modern day communal centre.[18]

Although the Co-op was formed relatively late, it has strong connections to the earlier self-help societies; its first meeting place was Smithy Fold where the Peaceful Dove Society owned property, and several of its leading members had been Chartists.[19]

Conclusion

The Friendly Societies, Prosecution Society and Co-operative Society of Midgley were the self-help groups of their era. They grew from the need of the

---

[16] West Yorkshire Archives (Calderdale), *Rules of the Society for the Prosecution of Felons in the Township and Neighbourhood of Midgley. Established April Twenty Fifth 1838,* 1838, JM:623
[17] H.W. Harwood, *The Midgley Story: 100 Years of Co-operation*, Midgley: Midgley Co-operative Society, 1961, p2
[18] Harwood, *The Midgley Story: 100 Years of Co-operation*, p16
[19] Chartism is discussed in Chapter 18

Figure 8   *A Midgley Co-op procession outside the Sportsman Inn on Lydgate*

people to help themselves in times of adversity. The societies consisted of the ordinary working people of Midgley whose main source of social life was built around the events organised by the societies. The building of the Co-op hall, opened in 1871, was a boon to the community, the hall in its lifetime having many uses from holding a Sunday School anniversary to being a centre for the Yorkshire Penny Bank, not to mention the numerous concerts and dances which were held there. It was even a day school before the one at Lane Ends was ready.[20]

From their early beginnings, the societies went from strength to strength. It would appear that the same people were members of the various societies. We can tell from the list of members of the Peaceful Dove Society that they were also members of the Co-operative Society and, although we have no record, it seems likely that they were also members of the Prosecution Society. Their strength banded them together. Their hopes and foresight served them well in obtaining a better standard of living for themselves and future generations. It is a great tribute to their fortitude and determination that they rallied together to improve their lot. Those of us whose ancestors were born in the area must remember that it is only three or possibly four generations ago that our forebears, living in appalling conditions, took the initiative to raise themselves up out of the mire. How different it might have been for us had they not.

---

[20] Harwood, *The Midgley Story: 100 Years of Co-operation*, p9

CHAPTER 17

'Sacrificed at the Shrine of Avarice' ?
Child Labour and the Growth of the Factory System

Ian Bailey

The Beginning of the Factory Age

The process of industrialisation in the West Riding began towards the end of the eighteenth century and led to the creation of mass employment in factories. The consequence for textile production was a rapid expansion of cotton, woollen and worsted mills, especially in the Pennines. This caused the demand for hand woven cloth to fall and consequently reduced the wages of those who produced textiles by handloom weaving. In the early nineteenth century, textiles was the third largest category of employment in the country and was the overwhelmingly dominant means of earning a living in the township of Midgley.

In the early stages of industrial development, especially when factory technology was limited to water powered spinning mills, handloom weavers and factories worked side by side with spinning mills, with the latter often employing weavers to weave their yarn into cloth. The Luddenden Valley developed along these lines in the early part of the nineteenth century and there were eight water-powered textile spinning mills in existence by 1831. The first was Dean Mills (Figure 1), a cotton spinning mill built in 1792 alongside an existing paper mill. The others were built to spin worsted yarn in a rapid expansion of the industry between 1819 and 1831. Their water supply was supplemented from Cold Edge dams, constructed as a joint venture of the valley's mill owners. As technology developed, power looms were introduced and output was increased by the building of large steam-powered mills. The cotton industry was affected first, in the early decades of the nineteenth century, whilst worsted production followed by around 1850.

The transfer of textile production from handloom weaving to factory production had an enormous impact on domestic life. Handloom weaving

Figure 1   *Dean Mills, where paper and cotton had been produced from the eighteenth century*

was a trade performed at home and involved the whole family: husbands, wives and children as young as ten could all be fully-operational weavers. What is more, children well below the age of ten were expected to make their contribution towards the family budget. Historians have been slow to realise that child labour was very much the norm in the past and it is against this background that the employment of children in factories must be viewed.

Whilst handloom weaving was hard labour-intensive work, the domestic weaver could choose when and how long to work, free of any master. But it was work that was unprotected by trade guilds or unions. Indeed, that was what had attracted many into the trade in the first place. Consequently, they were particularly vulnerable to the impact of industrialisation and they suffered tremendous economic hardship as the price of the cloth that they had the capacity to produce fell below a living wage.

Factory Conditions

The new mill owners preferred to employ children and young women because they were cheaper. Equally, parents welcomed the additional income that their children brought. The earliest sector of the industry where child labour made an impact was spinning, primarily because the spinning process was the first to go into factories. Long hours for children as young as six were common. Typically, production began at 5.30 in the morning and:

> did not end until seven or eight o'clock; and in the last hours of which children were crying or falling asleep on their feet[1]

However, it should be remembered that they had probably been working these kind of hours at home. What was new was the fact that they were now gathered together in factories and that this pattern of employment could be clearly seen by outside observers for the first time. As economic circumstances changed, wives and children found work in the factories while husbands were left at home to make whatever they could of their faltering trade. Whilst once heading the household, husbands were now faced with relying on their wives and children's wages to maintain the family budget.

Especially in the early days of the factory system, some mills became infamous for their harsh conditions, not just because of the long hours but because the young children were often treated with unrelenting brutality. Robert Blincoe recalled his experiences in factories in Derbyshire and Manchester in harrowing detail. He and his fellow young apprentices were 'flogged with belts, the metal buckles cutting into the flesh' and were subjected to an overlookers' trick where they would 'hang weights from the children's shoulders and then insist that they work encumbered for the rest of the day'.[2] He described how, during his time as a child worker there was seldom a time when a part of his body was not bruised. He developed bandy legs and walked stooped for the rest of his life.

Understandably, contemporaries were outraged by reports of such shocking conditions. This outrage provided fuel for the factory reform campaign. However, it would be a mistake to assume that all mill owners were guilty of such cruelty and careful study of the available evidence must be made before drawing conclusions.

---

[1] E.P. Thompson, *The Making of the English Working Class*, London: Gollanez, 1963, p373
[2] J. Waller, *The Real Oliver Twist*, 2005, Cambridge: Icon Books, p150

Campaign for Reform

The impact of factory labour became a major issue for reformers and Huddersfield's Richard Oastler initiated a campaign to introduce regulation to prevent the exploitation of factory workers, especially children. He wrote to the Leeds Mercury in 1830, when he likened the factory system to infantile slavery and declared 'poor infants you are sacrificed at the shrine of avarice'.[3] But the campaign for a ten hour day with age restrictions became a bitter struggle between reformers and factory owners. Many felt that reducing the working day would drive up prices and make them uncompetitive. They also saw nothing wrong with the employment of young children. During the newspaper debate that Oastler had provoked, Halifax manufacturers responded by claiming that:

> those between the ages of seven and fourteen are capable of undergoing long and continued hours of labour ... For confirmation of this we would appeal to all medical men in the district[4]

A series of parliamentary investigations was undertaken in order to assess the nature and impact of factory conditions. In 1832, Michael Sadler, an MP who campaigned for reform, produced a report with evidence from interviews with factory operatives. Samuel Coulson of Leeds described how his young daughters were required, at times, to work from three o'clock in the morning until half past ten at night. This enabled them to get just three hours sleep before getting up for the following day's work. And when one of them lost a finger in an accident, pay was stopped immediately.

George Crabtree, an associate of Oastler, also gave some graphic accounts of the barbaric attitude of some mill owners in the Upper Calder Valley. He toured the area in 1833 and on one occasion spoke to Rev. Devine about Sutcliffe Wilcock, an eleven year old employed at Hinchliffe's Cragg Vale Mill. He recalled that:

> the day before he died he worked seventeen hours; at night he was ill, and was obliged to be carried home by his father, he could not eat his supper, was put to bed; about four o'clock he lifted up his head and, looking towards the window, asked his brothers if they could see the lights up in the mill, for he was afraid of being late, he laid down his head and never spoke more, he was found dead in his bed!![5]

---

[3] R. Oastler, letter to the *Leeds Mercury*, 20 September 1830
[4] Master Spinners of Halifax, letter to the *Leeds Mercury*, 5 March 1831
[5] G. Crabtree, *A Brief Description of a Tour Through Calder Dale*, Huddersfield: J. Hobson, 1833, pp18-19

Legislation

The agitation for change resulted in the gradual introduction of better working conditions. Whilst a succession of factory acts to regulate the cotton industry began in 1819, the woollen and worsted industries that predominated in Yorkshire were not covered until the Act of 1833. This restricted the minimum age at which children could be employed in a textile mill to nine years old and required under-thirteens to have two hours schooling whilst working forty-eight hours a week. It is worth noting that, at least in this respect, children who worked in factories had some advantage over their contemporaries in that they had some compulsory schooling half a century before this became universal. Under-eighteens were restricted to a twelve-hour day or sixty-eight hours per week. However, there was considerable opposition to reform and pressure from some factory owners led to the reduction in the minimum age to eight in the subsequent Act of 1844. This Act did, however, increase the requirement for school attendance to three hours per day and restrict their working hours to six and a half hours a day. A doctor's medical examination was also required for each child employee. The ten hour day for all workers was not achieved until 1874, forty-four years after Oastler's letter to the Leeds Mercury.

The Impact on Midgley

Documentary evidence relating specifically to Midgley is available from three principle sources. The Factory Inquiry Commission of 1834 asked factory owners to volunteer information regarding the age, pay and conditions of their employees. The second source of information is the census where the returns for Midgley Township in 1841 and 1851 have been analysed for evidence of employment patterns amongst heads of households and their children. The final source of evidence is the child employment register from Murgatroyd's mill that was required, after the 1844 Factory Act, to record all children under thirteen. The availability of these sources enables us to take a balanced and informed view of conditions in local mills.

The Factory Inquiry Commission

The factory owners of the four most intensive textile-producing areas of the country, which included Yorkshire, were sent a questionnaire in 1833. This asked a series of twenty-seven questions on the conditions under which they operated their mills. These included the number, ages and wages of all employees, working hours, use of corporal punishment and views on introducing legislation on working hours. Returns were voluntary and many mill owners refused to participate. But the rate of return for the factories along Luddenden Valley was exceptionally high by national standards with seven out of eight mill owners responding. They provide a fascinating insight into the conditions of employment in the Midgley area.

The returns confirm that mill owners had a preference for young workers. Nearly two-thirds were under fourteen and over 90 per cent were under twenty-one (Figure 3). There was also a tendency to employ girls. The hours were long, typically over seventy per week with a necessity to vary them according to the level of water supply. The longest working week in the Halifax area was at Whitworth & Company's Peel House Mill (Figure 4), which was recorded as being seventy-eight hours.[6] The pay for a child under ten at this mill was 2s a week; ½ d per hour. A pint of milk cost 1½ d.

Not surprisingly, Whitworth was against legislation to restrict child employment and commented:

> As to the health of children in country factories, they are as healthy as any other part of the community, and in a deal better circumstances.[7]

Indeed, all respondents were cautious about factory reform, being especially concerned for the need to maintain flexibility to allow for the unreliability of water power. All were against the proposed restriction to a ten hour day, although some proposed eleven or twelve hours. None of them admitted to sanctioning corporal punishment. This is in contradiction to the widespread reputation of mill owners, some of whom refuted the accusations that they were especially cruel. One Yorkshire owner replied:

> there has been too much said on this subject as, in no mills that I have ever worked in, had a tenth of the corporal punishments been inflicted as is to be found in the best public schools of our land.[8]

The full extent of factory cruelty is impossible to determine, but such comments do remind us that society's attitude towards violent punishment was very much harsher then than it is today.

---

[6] C. Spencer, 'Child Labour in the Early Textile Mills', *Transactions of the Halifax Antiquarian Society*, 1991, pp109-123 at p116

[7] *Royal Commission on Employment of Children in Factories. First Report*, House of Commons Parliamentary Papers, Session 1833 (450), XX (C1), p345

[8] *Royal Commission on Employment of Children in Factories. First Report*, House of Commons Parliamentary Papers, Session 1833 (450), XX (C1), p338

The returns of the Luddenden Valley mills were typical of the Halifax area and comparable with Akroyd's in Halifax, Greenup's in Sowerby Bridge and Walker & Edmondson in Mytholmroyd (situated where Grange Dene Medical Centre currently stands). They all show a high proportion of children within their workforce. But one Upper Calder Valley mill bucks this trend; John Crossley in Hebden Bridge employed only three children under ten and he advocated legislation to make the minimum age ten years old. Around two thirds of his workforce were over sixteen. This illustrates the difficulty of broad generalisations; behind the horror stories there were clearly some employers with a more enlightened attitude. Caution is needed, therefore, and we must not assume that every factory upheld a cruel regime.

Of the seven textile mills in the returns for the Luddenden Valley, four were situated on the upper part of the river around Wainstalls. This was entirely within the Warley Township and their geographical location makes it unlikely that Midgley inhabitants would have worked there. By considering the three mills in the lower section of the valley, it can be estimated that fewer than two hundred people from Midgley were employed in the textile mills (Figure 3). This is around 10 per cent of the working population; by 1834, the factory system had just begun to have an impact on Midgley. It was, however, still in its infancy with the overwhelming majority of the population making a living in other ways. But where industrial development had taken place, the preference for child labour was very clear.

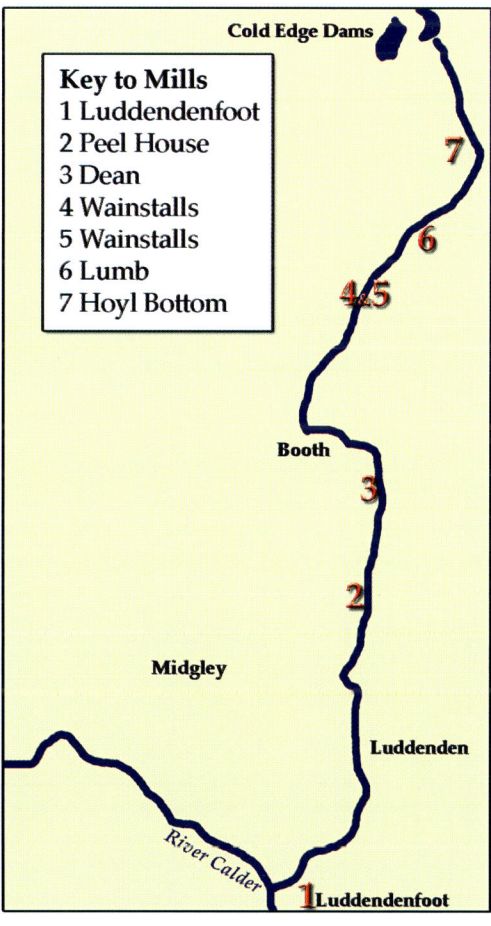

Figure 2 Textile mills in the Luddenden valley. The mills are referenced by number to the return details given in Figure 3

Mill Details						Workers					Wages		
						Total	Children under 14		Female		Under 10	Adult Male	Adult Female
Map Ref.	Location	Purpose	Built	Power	Hours per Week	No.	No.	%age	No.	%age	s d	s d	s d
Mills in the Midgley Township Catchment Area													
1	Luddendenfoot	Worsted Spinning	1827	Water/Steam	76	125	76	61%	71	57%	2 3	17 0	6 0
2	Peel House	Worsted Spinning	1819	Water	78	48	34	71%	33	69%	2 0	17 0	6 0
3	Dean Mill	Cotton Spinning	1792	Water	72.5	32	17	53%	22	69%	1 6	16 0	6 0
	Midgley Total					205	127	62%	126	61%			
Other Mills													
4	Wainstalls	Worsted Spinning	1821	Water	70	93	70	75%	51	55%	1 11	20 0	5 6
5	Wainstalls	Worsted Spinning	1831	Water	63	19	14	74%	13	68%	2 0	N/A	6 0
6	Lumb	Worsted Spinning	1828	Water	67	20	15	75%	10	50%	2 6	22 0	9 0
7	Hoyl Bottom	Worsted Spinning	1829	Water	70	15	9	60%	10	67%	3 6	N/A	6 0
	Grand Total					337	226		200				
	Average				71	48	32	67%	29	61%	2 3	18 5	6 4

Figure 3   *Summary of returns for Luddenden Valley mills in the 1834 Factory Inquiry Commission*

Figure 4   *Peel House Mills, where the working week was seventy-eight hours in 1833, the longest in the Parish of Halifax*

The Census

In 1841, the dominant occupation of heads of households in Midgley was handloom weaving and factory work was a minority occupation. Half of all households in the township were headed by a handloom weaver whilst very few were mill workers. However, the total number of Midgley people employed in the mills stood at 262, a modest rise since 1834. The mill owner's preference for employing the young continued, although the age profile had shifted away from children towards young adults. For example, only thirteen under-tens are recorded in 1841 compared to forty-seven in the Midgley employment area in 1834. This reflects the impact of the 1833 legislation that introduced a minimum age of nine years for employment in the textile industry.

Further employment trends emerge when considering the different geographical locations within Midgley township. The village of Midgley is located on a hillside away from the rivers that housed the water-powered mills, whilst the rest of the population of the township was predominantly located in riverside settlements. The township's population was split roughly

LOCATION	YEAR	POPULATION	HEADS OF HOUSEHOLD OCCUPATIONS			MILL WORKERS (as a percentage of total in age group)			
			Handloom Weaver	Mill Workers	Other	AGE			
						8-9	10-12	13-15	16-20
Midgley Village	1841	1,231	67%	0%	33%	5%	13%	31%	22%
	1851	881	44%	11%	45%	50%	69%	70%	58%
	Change	-28%							
Other Areas	1841	1,434	38%	8%	54%	12%	30%	50%	41%
	1851	1,512	20%	10%	70%	41%	55%	75%	59%
	Change	5%							
Township Total	1841	2,665	50%	5%	45%	12%	24%	43%	34%
	1851	2,393	30%	10%	60%	44%	60%	73%	59%
	Change	-10%							

Figure 5   Summary of census information: occupations by year, area and age group

equally between the two areas. The village was dominated by handloom weaving and a pattern of child labour had not emerged; few under-thirteen year olds were employed in mills. In the other areas, however, there was a transfer away from handloom weaving into factory work, especially amongst the young. In 1841, the factory system was gaining ground in the valley bottoms, but employment remained limited to the immediate area. The village, on the other hand, was reliant on a dying trade with its consequences of economic hardship. The 'hungry forties' hit the inhabitants of Midgley village very hard indeed.

By 1851, the population of Midgley township had fallen due to a significant depopulation of the village, a reflection of the distress suffered by handloom weavers. Amongst heads of households, handloom weaving had declined significantly over the previous decade, although it remained stubbornly high in the village, where it continued as the most common occupation. Few of them had found employment in the mills, even in the other areas of the township. In the village, the majority of the handloom weavers from 1841 were no longer living in the township; either they had migrated or died. The vast majority of those remaining continued to be weavers and only one of them found employment in a factory.

However, factory employment expanded significantly amongst the rest of the population; over five hundred people were working in the mills in 1851. This was over a quarter of the township's population with little difference between the village and other areas. Significantly, the expansion was facilitated by a large increase in child labour; the majority of eight to fifteen year olds were working in the mills. The numbers were even more dramatic amongst the children of the village handloom weavers; nearly all their children over eight were factory employees. By 1851, a clear pattern had developed throughout Midgley township; adults were at home, children were in the mills. A major reason for this was the founding of the Oats Royd Mill by John Murgatroyd in 1847.

The Impact of Oats Royd Mill

The Murgatroyds' worsted spinning factory was entirely steam powered, free from the constraints of water power, which facilitated a location away from the river on the hillside between Midgley and Luddenden. By the time that Oats Royd Mill was built, child labour in worsted mills was regulated by two acts of Parliament. Children could not be employed under the age of eight. As the mill expanded, it provided employment for an ever-increasing number of

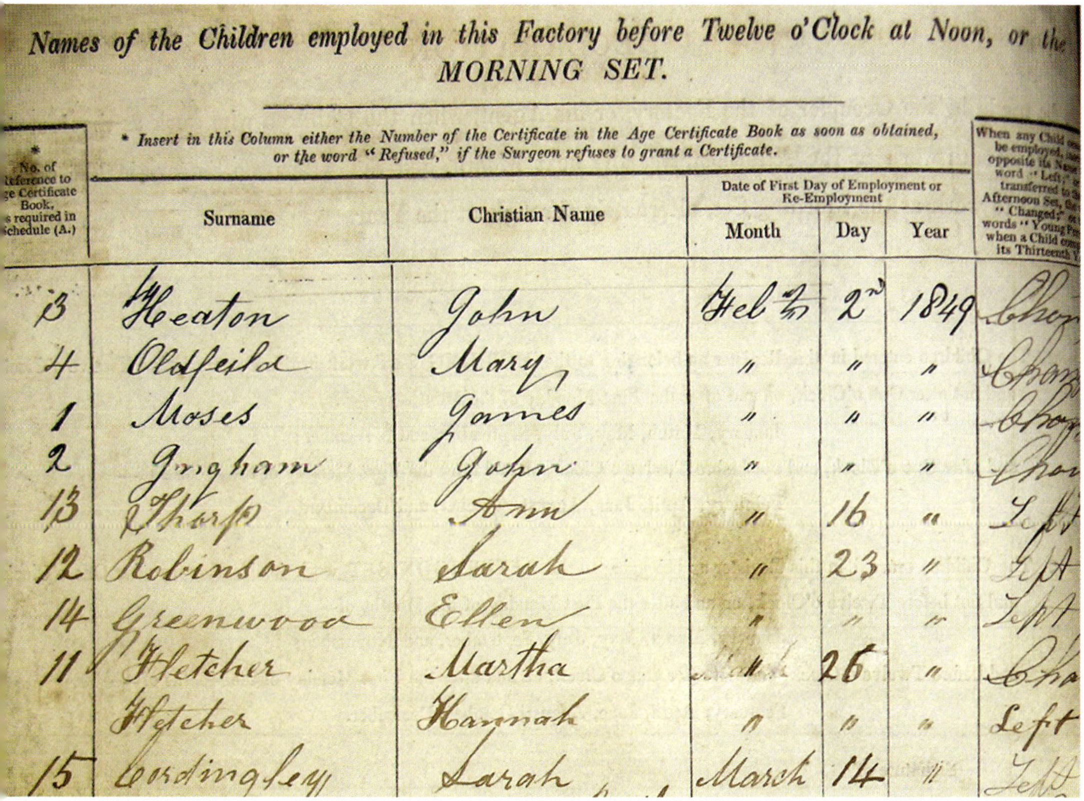

Names of the Children employed in this Factory before Twelve o'Clock at Noon, or the MORNING SET.

* *Insert in this Column either the Number of the Certificate in the Age Certificate Book as soon as obtained, or the word "Refused," if the Surgeon refuses to grant a Certificate.*

* No. of Reference to Age Certificate Book, as required in Schedule (A.)	Surname	Christian Name	Date of First Day of Employment or Re-Employment: Month	Day	Year	When any Child be employed, ... opposite its Name ... word "Left;" ... transferred to the Afternoon Set, the ... "Changed;" ... words "Young P... when a Child comp... its Thirteenth Y...
3	Heaton	John	Feb[y]	2nd	1849	Chang...
4	Oldfeild	Mary	〃	〃	〃	Chang...
1	Moses	James	〃	〃	〃	Chang...
2	Ingham	John	〃	〃	〃	Chan...
13	Sharp	Ann	〃	16	〃	Left
12	Robinson	Sarah	〃	23	〃	Left
14	Greenwood	Ellen	〃	〃	〃	Left
11	Fletcher	Martha	〃	26	〃	Cha...
	Fletcher	Hannah	〃	〃	〃	Left
15	Cordingley	Sarah	March	14	〃	Left

gure 6 *An extract from the Murgatroyds' child employment register in 1849*

Midgley children. The meticulously-kept statutory child employment registers (Figure 6) for Oats Royd Mill survive and demonstrate this expansion; in 1851, 91 of the 249 Midgley village children aged between eight and thirteen worked there. Employment was especially high amongst children of handloom weavers. By 1861 this had expanded to 166, half of the children eligible for factory work that were living in the village. All were medically certified as was required and the records indicate that Murgatroyds' were keen to abide by the spirit as well as the letter of contemporary factory legislation.

Whilst the parents, both husband and wife, remained trapped in the dying days of handloom weaving, their children were provided with employment at the local factory and made a vital contribution to the family budget. When Murgatroyd founded his mill, he had a readily available workforce from a village in decline and employed children and young people whose parents must have welcomed the lifeline that the wages of their offspring represented.

The Half Time System

From 1844, children employed in factories had to attend school for three hours a day and were allowed a maximum of six and a half hours factory work. This became known as the half time system and it lasted until 1921. In Midgley, Murgatroyds' child employees went to John Naylor's school at Smithy Fold. There was one set that went to school in the morning, whilst another went to work. In the afternoon they swapped around. This arrangement continued until 1877, when the new Midgley Board School opened at Lane Ends.

Legislation, however, did not protect every child from overwork. In 1907, the Head Master, Mr Gibson (Figure 7), wrote in his diary:

> Lancelot Bailey is habitually late and always tired and sleepy in the afternoon. I have ascertained that he works from 4.30am to 9am and in the evenings from 5 to 8pm.... He tells me he has not had any breakfast and has passed the night in the fields.[9]

Almost certainly, Lancelot Bailey was not working in a mill but represents the abuses of child labour that could still take place in the unregulated world of casual working.

---

[9] Midgley County Primary School , *The Centenary Journal*, 1977, pp3-5

H.W. Harwood was a half timer who attended Midgley School at the turn of the nineteenth century. By then, the minimum age for factory work had been raised to eleven. He recalls that a simple exam and medical had to be passed before entering factory work and then again at thirteen when they became full timers. He notes that nearly every child in the village went to work, most going to Oats Royd or Peel House (unlike himself, who went to Sykes & Co. in Brearley). He also points out how proud they were in their work and that they were neither brow beaten nor subject to the likelihood of serious injury.[10]

Figure 7   Mr Gibson (front left), Midgley School Head Master between 1880 and 1912, with his staff

The End of Child Labour?

In the early years of Oats Royd Mill, children provided much of the workforce, being employed primarily in the spinning process. By the 1860s, the proportion of children in the workforce was very much less, even though the numbers of them had risen. It is not yet clear why an ever larger proportion of adults were employed, but it may well be that, as Murgatroyds' expanded their weaving production, there was increasingly a need for the employment of skilled adult workers. It may be significant that the final phase of the

---

[10] H.W. Harwood, *The Half Time System*, West Yorkshire Archives (Calderdale), HAS/B 21/28

development at Oats Royd Mill was the addition of the extensive weaving sheds in 1887.

Murgatroyds' wages books of 1871 illustrate this final phase in the transfer of employment into the mills.[11] Entire families worked there; father, mother, sons and daughters were all paid as a family. The factory system initially broke up the family unit, but ultimately brought it back together. Child labour was a dominant feature in Midgley throughout the Victorian age and to beyond the First World War; legislation did not prevent it nor was it meant to, but it did improve conditions as factory work became an accepted necessity of working class life.

Figure 8   *The lower part of Luddenden Valley at the height of its industrial development. Murgatroyds' Oats Royd Mill is at the top right*

---

[11] West Yorkshire Archives (Calderdale), *Murgatroyds' Wages books*, 1871, JM 41

CHAPTER 18

Home-made Bombs and a Circulating Library:
The Midgley Radicals in an Age of Unrest

Ian Bailey

No Right to Vote

When the trading of slaves was abolished in 1807, the leader of the abolition movement, William Wilberforce, was elected to parliament as one of two MPs for Yorkshire. Midgley's two thousand residents were amongst those living in this huge constituency – but only twenty-seven of them registered votes in the open ballot (Figure 1).

Residence.	Name and Description.	Freehold.	W	L	M
Midgley,	Aked John, tanner,				1
	Barstow Matthew, cornmiller,				1
	Brown Thomas, corndealer,		1	1	
	Bracken Jona. papermaker,				1
	Crosby John, worstedmanufac.				1
	Casson Thomas, butcher,		1		1
	Ditherington Eli, cot. manuf.				1
	Eastwood John, cottonmanuf.		1	1	
	Foster William, publican,		1	1	
	Foster Wm. cottonspinner,	*Thornton*			1
	Foster Thomas, innkeeper,		1	1	
	Garnett John, weaver,				1
	Howarth Wm. tanner,		1	1	
	Hellowell Henry, cottonspin.				1
	Lockwood John, farmer,		1	1	
	Melling John, whitesmith,	*Gisburn*	1	1	
	Murgatroyd Jas. cottonmanuf.		1	1	
	Parker John, manufacturer,			1	
	Ratcliffe John, yeoman,				1
	Sunderland, Wm. butcher,	*Erringden*			1
	Shackleton Wm. farmer,		1	1	
	Savill Richard, farmer,	*Clayton West*			1
	Sutcliffe Demas, hawker,				1
(High Lees,)	Sutcliffe Wm. weaver,				1
	Sutcliffe Joseph, liquormerch.	*Halifax*	1	1	
	Tatham Joseph, farmer,				1
	Woodhead W. Roberts, weav.		1	1	

Figure 1   *The Poll Book of the 1807 election. Each of the twenty-seven Midgley voters had up to two votes and could choose between William Wilberforce (W), Henry Lascelles (L) or Viscount Milton (M)*

Two hundred years ago, representation in politics was restricted to a privileged few. The right to vote was determined by land ownership and, as a result, only the wealthy were entitled to a parliamentary vote. The overwhelming majority of the country consisted of the landless poor or tenants who had no right to determine their member of parliament. There were two political parties: the Tories who appealed predominantly to the landed gentry and the Whigs (Liberals) who represented the upwardly mobile entrepreneurs who built businesses such as the textile mills. Neither represented the interests of the working classes nor did they have any inclination to allow them the franchise.

When the Napoleonic Wars ended in 1815, the optimism brought about by peace was quickly shattered as the country plunged into deep recession. The poorest suffered first and in the harshest way. In Midgley, the main occupation was handloom weaving and, as the price of cloth plummeted, life became a desperate struggle for survival. The political response of the nation's poor was to demand the right to fair parliamentary representation. In August 1819, the ironically named 'Peterloo' massacre signalled the beginning of a long and bitter struggle to introduce universal suffrage. But, as the dragoons charged the unarmed protesters at St Peter's Fields in Manchester, the authorities signalled their steadfast determination to resist.

In 1832, the Great Reform Act was introduced but did little to satisfy the campaigners. It was a bitter disappointment as the franchise was barely changed. With the revised property qualification requiring ownership of property worth at least £10, or leasehold property worth £50, the majority of people were still left unable to vote. The experience of the township of Midgley demonstrates the severe limitations to the so-called reform. In the census just a year earlier, the population of Midgley was recorded as being 2,409 and yet the electoral register for 1832 numbered just fifty-two, six of whom did not even live in the township but qualified on the basis of owning property there (Figure 2). A vote was allocated according to the location of qualifying property, not the residence of the individual. In this county constituency, the value of the property required to qualify was: 40s freeholders, £10 copyholders or £50 leaseholders. Three other Midgley residents were entitled to vote in other local townships, bringing the total of Midgley voters to forty-nine. This equates to just 8 per cent of Midgley's adult men having the opportunity to vote for the two MPs in the new West Riding

Christian Name and Surname of each Voter, at full Length.	Place of Abode.	Nature of Qualification.	Street, Lane, or other like Place in the Township where the Property is situate, or name of the Property, or Name of the Tenant

MIDGLEY TOWNSHIP.

Aked James	Kershaw House	Occupier of Land	Kershaw House
Aked John	Ellen Royd	Freehold House and Land	Ellen Royd
Aked Richard	Ellen Royd	Freehold House and Land	Dry Carr
Alderson Richard	Lower Ewood	Occupier of Land	Lower Ewood
Alexander Lewis	Hopwood-Hall, Halifax	Freehold House and Land	Upper Hanroyd, in occupation of T. Fletcher
Boardal John	Lydgate	Occupier of Land	Lydgate Farm
Brown Thomas	Brearley Mill	Freehold House and Mills	Brearley Mills
Bracken Jonathan	Dean Mills	Freehold House, Land, and Mills	Dean Mills
Carr James	Langroyd Hall, near Colne, in the County of Lancaster	Freehold House and Land	High Lee Head
Cockroft Richard	Ewood	Occupier of Land	Ewood
Casson Thomas	New House	Freehold House and Land	New House
Crowther William	High Lees	Freehold Houses	High Lees
Crowther Charles	Lydgate	Freehold Houses	Lydgate
Clayton James	Brearley Hall	Occupier of Land	Brearley Hall
Crossley John	Hollin Top	Freehold House	High Lees
Eastwood John	Mill House	Freehold House and Land	Mill House
Fawcett John	Ewood Hall	Occupier of Land	Ewood Hall
Foster John	Brearley	Freehold Malt Kiln	Brearley
Foulds Thomas	Oats Royd	Freehold House and Land	Deanhouse
Foster James	Mill-field End	Freehold House and Land	Millfield-End
Greenwood William	Dean House	Occupier of Land	Dean House
Greenwood Thomas	Carr House	Freehold Houses	Carr House
Greenwood James	Scout Head	Freehold Houses	Scout Head
Greenwood James	Bloomer Gate	Freehold Houses	Green Royd
Greenwood Thomas	Hirst Wadsworth	Freehold Houses	Midgley
Harwood William	Rough, Wadsworth	Freehold Houses	Mill House Lane
Howarth Timothy	Hob Lane, Sowerby	Freehold Houses	Luddenden
Hawkins Reverend Thomas	Warley Town	Freehold House and Land	Goose Nest
Holland Thomas	High Lees	Freehold House	High Lees
Illingworth Timothy	Broad Fold	Freehold House	Luddenden
Murgatroyd Hartley	Greave	Freehold House and Land	Greave
Midgley Robert	Booth	Freehold House and Land	Booth
Parker William	Stoney Springs	Occupier of Land and Mill	Stoney Springs and Brearley Mills
Patchett Henry	Mytholmroyd	Occupier of Land and Mill	Mytholmroyd
Parker John	Mirfield	Freehold House and Land	Brearley Hall
Ratcliffe John	High Lee Head	Freehold House	High Lees
Ratcliffe James	Pasture	Freehold House	High Lees
Scott John	Lydgate	Freehold House	Lydgate
Smith Thomas	Luddenden	Freehold House	Bank Bottom
Sutcliffe David	White Lee	Occupier of Land	White Lee
Sutcliffe Reverend Thomas	Luddenden	Freehold Houses and Land	Pepper Hill
Thomas William	Acre	Freehold Houses	Lane Top
Thomas William	Midgley	Occupier of Land	Great House
Titterington Ely	High Lees	Freehold House and Land	High Lees
Thomas John	Mount Pleasant	Freehold House and Land	Mount Pleasant
Taylor John	Midgley	Freehold House	Midgley
Taylor James	Midgley	Occupier of Land	Lacey Hey
Thomas William	Hathershelf, Sowerby	Freehold Houses and Land	Lower Hanroyd
Walker James	Brier Hey	Leasehold Houses and Land	Brier Hey
Wormald Timothy	Luddenden	Freehold Houses	Luddenden
Whitaker William	Upper Foot	Occupier of Land	Upper Foot
Wilcock Mark	High House	Occupier of Land	High House and Tray Royd

Figure 2   The Electoral Register of 1832, listing just forty-six Midgley Residents. Fifteen qualified to vote on the basis of occupation of property worth £50 or more.

constituency. This figure was in line with the rest of the Parish of Halifax, where it had risen from 6 per cent prior to the act.[1]

Furthermore, the imposition of the new Poor Law in 1834 that took control of parish poor relief from the townships to Poor Law unions, which amalgamated several townships, was bitterly resented and added fuel to the growing hunger for mass protest. The economic situation in the textile regions of the country grew ever more desperate as mills worked by children made adult domestic weaving increasingly unremunerative. This was a foretaste of the 'hungry forties'.

The Founding of 'Radical Midgley'

The combination of desperation, lack of state support and a tradition of independence from ties to the landed gentry (unlike many agricultural areas in the south of England, where labour was effectively bonded to the

Figure 3   *The Midgley Radical Association held its first anniversary dinner in 1838 in the Shoulder of Mutton pub, which is to be seen on the left of the photograph*

---

[1] J.A. Hargreaves, *Halifax*, Edinburgh: Edinburgh University Press; Lancaster: Carnegie Publishing, 1999, p104

The Six Points
OF THE
PEOPLE'S
CHARTER.

1. A VOTE for every man twenty-one years of age, of sound mind, and not undergoing punishment for crime.

2. THE BALLOT.—To protect the elector in the exercise of his vote.

3. NO PROPERTY QUALIFICATION for Members of Parliament—thus enabling the constituencies to return the man of their choice, be he rich or poor.

4. PAYMENT OF MEMBERS, Thus enabling an honest tradesman, working man, or other person, to serve a constituency, when taken from his business to attend the interests of the country.

5. EQUAL CONSTITUENCIES, securing the same amount of representation for the same number of electors, instead of allowing small constituencies to swamp the votes of large ones.

6. ANNUAL PARLIAMENTS, thus presenting the most effectual check to bribery and intimidation, since though a constituency might be bought once in seven years (even with the ballot), no purse could buy a constituency (under a system of universal suffrage) in each ensuing twelvemonth; and since members, when elected for a year only, would not be able to defy and betray their constituents as now.

Figure 4   The People's Charter giving details of the Chartists' demands

landowner) contributed to a desire amongst the people of Midgley for radical politics. The age of 'Radical Midgley' arrived and in September 1837 the Midgley Radical Association was founded. Their meeting place is reputed to have been the 'Old Radical Hole' at Smithy Fold, situated at what is now Dove's Rest in the centre of the village.[2] Major events were also held at the Shoulder of Mutton pub on Towngate (Figure 3) and attracted speakers such

[2] H. W. Harwood, *Glimpses of Midgley History*, n.d., West Yorkshire Archive Service (Calderdale), MISC 78/54, Chapter 18, p23

as Benjamin Rushden to boost membership.[3] The association's chairman was John Naylor, a thirty-nine year old handloom weaver who lived at Smithy Fold and later ran a school there for the children who worked at the mills.[4] He presided over a meal at the Shoulder of Mutton that celebrated the association's first anniversary in September 1838 when, despite the infiltration of conservative operatives, it was attended by 'happy villagers' until midnight.[5]

Midgley and the Chartist Movement

When the People's Charter was published in May 1838 (Figure 4), the residents of Midgley were already organised to support the national campaign for a massive change to parliamentary representation. The first Chartist petition was presented to parliament in July 1839 with an estimated 500,000 signatures. It was overwhelmingly rejected by 235 votes to 46. As a result, the Chartist campaign grew stronger and, by the time that the second petition was presented on 1 May 1842, it reached its peak. Despite its three million signatures, Parliament again rejected it, this time by 287 votes to 46.

The most charismatic leader of the Chartist movement was Fergus O'Connor, an energetic Irishman and powerful orator who founded the National Charter Association (NCA). He set up a newspaper, the Northern Star, which quickly established itself as the primary means of recording and promoting Chartist activity. At its peak, it had a circulation of fifty thousand, comparable to that of The Times. In the years preceding the second petition, it reported a number of events in Midgley. Its tone was decidedly populist and it was not afraid to criticise local elites. When James Aked from Kershaw House, a worsted manufacturer and the township's chief constable, reduced his weavers' wages by up to 10 per cent he was described as, 'a great enemy to the Chartists, a liberal whig, corn law repealer and a great friend to the new Poor Law and Bastille system.'[6] The newspaper was keen to promote the success of local NCA groups and described Midgley as a place where, 'Chartism is assuming a very healthy appearance here, which promises to vie with any other village in the great and glorious cause of universal liberty'.[7] It also gave details of large open air meetings that became a trademark of the campaign. On 2 May 1842, the day after the second petition was rejected, a procession marched through

---

[3] *Northern Star*, 21 April 1838
[4] Information derived from the Censuses of 1841 and 1851
[5] *Northern Star*, 29 September 1838
[6] *Northern Star*, 25 May 1840
[7] *Northern Star*, 17 April 1841

Midgley on its way to the Mount Skip at Wadsworth Moor where there was, 'one of the largest meetings in the neighbourhood for many years with upwards of 7,000 people'.[8] It seems that there was strong support for Chartism in Midgley.

The Plug Plot

After the failure of the second petition, the strength of feeling erupted into the region's largest and most violent mass protest. In August 1842, thousands of men and women took part in marches that included one that began in Lancashire and went down the Calder Valley before ending in a mass demonstration in Halifax. On the way, the protesters forcibly entered mills where they drew the plugs from the boilers to render them unusable. This became known as the Plug Plot, one of the most notable events during the whole of the Chartist campaign. The route took them through the township of Midgley; from Mytholmroyd, where they camped overnight, then along to Brearley and through Luddendenfoot.

igure 5   Yew Trees, home to Eli Hoyle who was found guilty of participating in the Plug Plot

[8] *Northern Star*, 7 May 1842

Perhaps the most notorious incident in local Chartist activity was when a large group of rioters attacked cavalry men of the 11th Hussars at Salterhebble as they returned from escorting prisoners to Elland station. According to the Halifax Guardian, the local Tory newspaper that devoted several pages to condemning the protest, the 'women armed with tremendous bludgeons were even more violent than the men'.[9] Despite this, none of the thirty-nine people arrested after the soldiers fired on the rioting crowd were women. But one of them was a Midgley man, William Jackson, a twenty-four year old weaver from Tray Royd.[10] He was committed to York Castle, but was acquitted at his trial and so escaped punishment.[11] Another Midgley resident who was arrested in Halifax during the Plug Plot, Eli Hoyle, was a twenty-two year old weaver who lived at Mill Field End in 1841 and Yew Trees in 1851. Although found guilty, he avoided a custodial sentence and was discharged, 'on entering into recognizences of £20 and one surety of £10 ..... to keep the peace for twelve months'.[12]

Riot in Midgley

One further incident reported in the Halifax Guardian was the arrest of four men for 'riot in Midgley on the 15th, and stopping the mill of Mr T Hirst'.[13] Three of these men were neighbours from the area of Luddendenfoot in Midgley township. Joseph Broadbent, a factory overlooker, and John Gibson, an engineer, were both in their mid-thirties, whilst John Whitaker was an agricultural labourer of around twenty years old, according to the Census of 1841. However, the witness statement of Benjamin Naylor (Figure 6), suggests that he was a mill worker at the time of the Plug Plot.[14] The details of their contribution to the Plug Plot are described in a series of three witness statements that were prepared for their trial in York. Thomas Hirst was the manager of Jonathan Bracken's Dean Mill (Figure 7), Benjamin Naylor was a twenty-six year old weaver who worked there, and William Shaw was visiting the mill from Sowerby. Although the evidence relates to Dean Mill in particular, it also includes reference to other mills in the valley.

---

[9] *Halifax Guardian*, 27 August 1842

[10] The age and occupations are taken from the Censuses of 1841 and 1851. In the case of William Jackson, there are five people of the same name in 1841 but William Jackson of Tray Royd seems most likely to be the Chartist from the details available.

[11] *Halifax Guardian*, 27 August 1842

[12] *Halifax Guardian*, 27 August 1842

[13] *Halifax Guardian*, 27 August 1842

[14] The age, place of residence and occupations are taken from the Census of 1841. In the case of Joseph Broadbent, there are three people of the same name in 1841 and two in the case of John Whitaker, but these seem the most likely candidates from the details available.

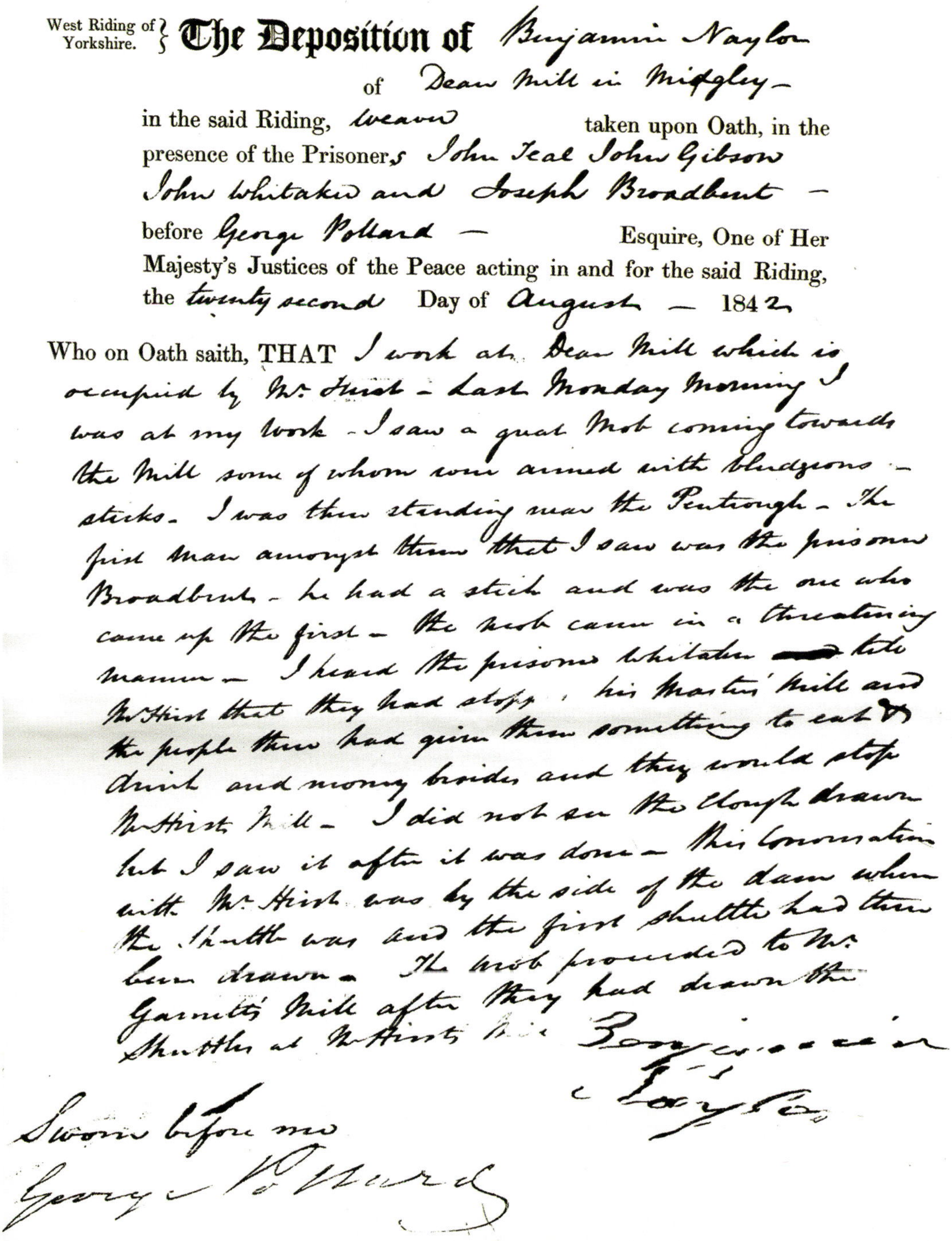

West Riding of Yorkshire. } **The Deposition of** *Benjamin Naylor*

of *Dean Mill in Midgley —*

in the said Riding, *weaver* taken upon Oath, in the presence of the Prisoner*s* *John Teal John Gibson John Whitaker and Joseph Broadbent —*

before *George Pollard —* Esquire, One of Her Majesty's Justices of the Peace acting in and for the said Riding, the *twenty second* Day of *August —* 184*2*

Who on Oath saith, THAT *I work at Dean Mill which is occupied by Mr Hirst – Last Monday morning I was at my work – I saw a great Mob coming towards the Mill some of whom were armed with bludgeons – sticks. I was then standing near the Pentrough – The first Man amongst them that I saw was the prisoner Broadbent – he had a stick and was the one who came up the first – the rest came in a threatening manner – I heard the prisoner Whitaker tell Mr Hirst that they had stopp. his Master's Mill and the people there had given them something to eat & drink and many besides and they would stop Mr Hirsts Mill – I did not see the Clough drawn but I saw it after it was done – this Conversation with Mr Hirst was by the side of the dam when the Shuttle was and the first shuttle had then been drawn – The mob proceeded to Mr Garnetts Mill after they had drawn the Shuttles at Mr Hirsts Mill*

Benjamin Taylor

Sworn before me

George Pollard

Figure 6   *The witness statement of Benjamin Naylor from the trial of four men, three living in Luddendenfoot, who were convicted for taking part in Plug Riots at Dean Mills, Booth on 15 August 1842*

Early in the morning of Monday 15 August 1842, a threatening crowd of around 150 men armed with sticks and bludgeons left the main demonstration at Luddendenfoot and proceeded up through Luddenden to draw the shuttles (sluice gates) at the several mills that were situated in Luddenden Dean, rising towards Cold Edge dams. When an advanced party arrived at Dean Mill, the fourth mill up Luddenden Dean, between nine and ten o'clock, they had already been drawing plugs for over five hours. These men went back to disable John Ambler's Peel House Mill (Figure 8) before returning with more protesters to repeat the process at Dean Mill. After completing the job, they proceeded up the valley, firstly to Nathaniel Garnett's mill and then onwards towards Cold Edge Dams.

Before disabling a mill they sought out the owner or manager to gain information to assist their exploits and were prepared to be threatening in order to get it. At some mills the protesters received the support of at least some of those they met; 'they had stopped his masters mill and the people there had given them something to eat & drink and money besides'.[15] But at others the mill management were prepared to stand their ground. When the protesters threatened to break the windows of Dean Mills, its manager Thomas Hirst replied, 'in this hot weather we could do as well without windows as much as with them'.[16]

Figure 7   Dean Mills, below Booth

---

[15] The National Archives, Assizes: Northern and North-Eastern Circuits: Criminal Depositions and Case Papers, *Witness statement of Benjamin Naylor*, 22 August 1842, ASSI 45/66

[16] The National Archives, Assizes: Northern and North-Eastern Circuits: Criminal Depositions and Case Papers, *Witness statement of Thomas Hirst*, 22 August 1842, ASSI 45/66

Figure 8   Peel House Mills where the Plug Plotters visited on 15th August 1842

All four of the defendants were found guilty and each of the Luddendenfoot men were sentenced to three months imprisonment with hard labour. By the time of the Census in 1851, none of them was living in Midgley township. John Gibson was a gas works labourer living in Skircoat Green whilst Joseph Broadbent was a worsted factory overlooker living in Akroyd's model village of Copley. Perhaps they were blacklisted by local mill owners and were forced to move elsewhere.

Chartism after 1842

The defeat of the second petition was a bitter blow to the Chartist movement and its leadership began to fracture. Fergus O'Connor was popular with the Chartist followers but not its fellow leaders. He became increasingly separate from them and in 1845 he began to concentrate on his new idea, the Chartist Land Plan. The idea was to raise money to build idyllic villages in the countryside where people could escape from the industrial squalor and enjoy a subsistence lifestyle alongside fellow Chartists. Participants bought subscriptions and when enough money had been raised a village was built. Subscribers drew lots and the lucky winners moved to a new life. It proved to be extremely popular and seventy thousand people each bought five pound subscriptions. But just 250 people actually settled in only six villages before the scheme went bankrupt.

One of O'Connor's leadership rivals was William Lovett and he became increasingly interested in self improvement for the working classes, particularly education. However, O'Connor continued the policy of petitioning Parliament and led it to a third and final petition. This was instigated in 1848, but less than half of the expected five million signatures were actually raised and, again, Parliament predictably rejected it.

Confidence in O'Connor was severely damaged after this defeat. In 1852, he was certified as insane after assaulting various MPs, committed to an asylum and died three years later. Ernest Jones became the leading figure in the movement and he even began a Chartist newspaper, the People's Paper, to replace the defunct Northern Star. But the Chartist movement never recovered and its popularity waned before finally being wound up in 1860. It was not until 1918 that the Chartist demands for universal male suffrage were finally met.

Midgley Chartism in the Final Years

The last reference to Midgley in the Northern Star was in July 1842. Furthermore, a recent study of the Chartist Land Plan has found few subscribers from Midgley. Just eight can be traced to the township, but none of these lived in the village, mostly being from Mytholmroyd.[17] This is in stark contrast to further up the valley at Todmorden where there were ninety one subscribers.[18]

So, what happened to this hot bed of Chartism after the Plug Plot? It is tempting to conclude that the Midgley Chartists simply ceased to be active; after all, it was a small village and many other groups in small localities disappeared at this time. But the People's Paper reveals something quite to the contrary. In one of its earliest editions it reported that James Finlan had visited Midgley and commented that:

> The Midgley Chartists are well organised; they muster strong. Their locality has been in existence for 15 years … and are in an excellent and promising position.[19]

Local NCA meetings continued and Midgley was one of the few places in the Upper Calder Valley to send delegates. The names of James Clayton, John

---

[17] Private communication, Anne Kirker, 2006
[18] L. Croft, *John Fielden's Todmorden,* Todmorden: Tygerfoot Press, 1994, p72
[19] *People's Paper*, 24 July 1852, p2

Fletcher, William Fletcher, James Greenwood, William Greenwood, James Jackson, John Naylor, James Thorpe and John Walker were given as the Midgley representatives at various meetings during 1852 and 1853. Some of these men were also members of Midgley's Friendly Society, an indication of the connections between the village's various community institutions.[20] In 1852, there was also a weekend camp held on Midgley Moor where a large audience was reported.[21] Clearly, the Midgley Chartists continued to exist, although perhaps not as followers of Fergus O'Connor.

igure 9   *A pike head found at the Shoulder of Mutton, Midgley*

Why the break with O'Connor?

It is possible that the Midgley Chartists followed one of the other, less popular leaders. In particular, it could have been William Lovett, a promoter of self help, particularly education. One person represented Midgley at Chartist conventions throughout the entire Chartist period; the school master, John Naylor, who operated his school from Smithy Fold where the Chartists met. The integration of schooling and Chartism seems to be confirmed by the Peoples Paper in 1852 as:

---

[20] West Yorkshire Archive Service (Calderdale), *Proposition Book of the Peaceful Dove Friendly Society, Jacob's Well Lodge*, JM805
[21] *Peoples Paper*, 17 July 1852 p5

Figure 10   *Well Lane below Lacy Hey, where home-made bombs were reputed to have been exploded*

their meeting rooms they use for the education of young men in the secular principle; they have a circulating library[22]

However, it is quite possible that Midgley's desertion of O'Connor was because the Midgley Chartists found his Land Plan too tame. They may have preferred physical force, as they had a reputation for direct action. The involvement of some in the violence of the Plug Plots has already been noted but the local historian H.W. Harwood, who was born just one generation after Chartism, makes a number of references to the use of weapons:

Midgley men made weapons for themselves out of bars of iron, scythes and the like, and it was related to me long ago that they experimented with home-made bombs in the form of gunpowder in bottles which they exploded by way of experiment in Well Lane below Lacy Hey! On two recorded occasions lead had been stolen by them from the roof of Luddenden Church for the making of bullets.[23]

[22] *Peoples Paper*, 24 July 1852 p2

[23] H.W. Harwood, *The Midgley Story: 100 Years of Co-operation*, Midgley: Midgley Co-operative Society, 1961

These men armed themselves with pikes…and had regular drill.[24]

When the government began to take strong action against rebellious Chartists, the Midgley men buried their pikes in Stock's Field (the field behind Town Syke).[25]

In 1839, the Halifax Guardian estimated that there were seven hundred Chartists in the neighbourhood of Halifax armed with muskets. It reported that these 'deluded radicals' held a 'meeting at a public house in Midgley at which a number of firearms were ordered.'[26]

Weapons were also found in the years after the Chartists. In 1883, James Alderson's men were repairing the inside of the barn at Far Laithe (between Thorney Lane and Broadfold) when they found two eleven-inch bladed daggers wrapped in an old rotten rag. They had handles intended for a shaft to be fitted.[27] Weapons have also been found in more recent times. When new owners of the former Shoulder of Mutton pub, a known Chartist meeting place, were refurbishing the premises they found an old pike head stored above a doorway (Figure 9).

The Impact of Midgley Chartism

When the Chartist movement was wound up in 1860, Midgley had been active in the campaign for electoral reform for twenty-three years; an entire generation had been brought up with it. It had provoked strong passions and Midgley men were prepared to take up arms and attack mills to achieve their aims. They were also prepared to break their ties with the movement's most popular leader and assert their independence. But there was also an educational element, as a school was part of the local movement as well as a library. Chartism was more than a campaign for electoral reform; it was a community institution that was amongst the strongest in the country.

Although Chartism ceased to exist, the Midgley Chartists continued to build the village community. Harwood wrote that 'some of them became the founders of the Midgley Co-operative Society in 1861'.[28] Its first president was James Clayton, a forty-two year old weaver from Thorney Lane, who had been

---

[24] H. W. Harwood, *Glimpses of Midgley History*, Chapter 18, p23

[25] H. W. Harwood, *Glimpses of Midgley History*, Chapter 18, p23

[26] *Halifax Guardian*, 30th March 1839

[27] *Halifax Guardian*, 23rd June 1883 p.5

[28] H. W. Harwood, *Glimpses of Midgley History*, Chapter 18, p23

Figure 11   The Midgley Co-operative Society's 'Grandstand' which contained both houses and a 500 capacity hall. The Co-op was founded by former Chartists in 1861.

a Midgley delegate at a West Riding Chartist meeting in 1852.[29] The Co-operative Society began at Smithy Fold, the 'Old Radical Hole' where the Chartist used to meet. After just one year it had attracted 166 members, around half of the households in Midgley village.[30] The Midgley Co-op continued for over one hundred years, during which time it built a new shop at Lydgate, houses and an impressive hall for village social events with a capacity to seat 500 people (Figure 11).

Nationally, the Chartist Movement may have failed in its objectives, but the Midgley Chartists made a huge contribution to their community and were fundamental in improving the township during some extremely harsh times. Furthermore, despite all the set backs, they never gave up. Midgley was one of the few villages in the country that could claim to have been there at the beginning and there at the end.

---

[29] *People's Paper*, 1852

[30] West Yorkshire Archive Service (Calderdale), *Report of the Midgley Co-operative to 15 November 1862*, TU 110/2/2

CHAPTER 19

The Luddenden Valley Railway

Richard Davies

The people of Midgley would surely have celebrated the Coronation of Queen Victoria in June 1838, but they cannot have anticipated the extent to which their lives would change during the long years of her reign. A short walk along Heights Road in 1839 would have provided a fine view of the great earthworks being completed as the Manchester and Leeds Railway moved relentlessly forward. Along Rails Lane, the early development of Oats Royd Mill would soon be under way.

Contracts to build the Sowerby Bridge to Todmorden section of the Manchester and Leeds Railway had been advertised in May 1838, and the line along the Calder Valley was opened on 5 October 1840. Those locals who were not in a position to profit as the work went ahead would have been relieved to see the labour force disperse. In July 1839 the Manchester Courier had reported a 'desperate affray' between English and Irish labourers which had, at the second attempt, been contained by the militia. At first there were only 3 trains a day between Leeds and Hebden Bridge, with a journey time of one hour fifty minutes, but when Summit Tunnel opened in March 1841 traffic increased eight-fold.

The immediate local impact of the railway would have been limited, since most people worked at spinning or weaving in the home, or in the quarries, mills and fields nearby. Self-sufficiency was their aim - chapels, a church and several schools were all within easy walking distance. John Ambler, worsted spinner of Peel House, would walk from Luddenden to Manchester on market days,[1] though few locals would have cause to make journeys of this kind.[2]

---

[1] T. Sutcliffe, 'Peel House in Warley', *Transactions of the Halifax Antiquarian Society*, 1920, pp53-62 at p61
[2] A. Holt, A *Pennine Pioneer*, Littleborough: George Kelsall, 1999, p26. The Manchester and Leeds Railway would not allow one man to carry three pieces (of cloth). They said this contravened the forty pounds luggage allowance for passengers.

However, the railway would have been a talking point. The gregarious Branwell Bronte became Clerk in charge at Luddenden Foot station in April 1841.[3] The excursion trains proved to be an early success and a trip from Sowerby Bridge to Hull in August 1844 attracted almost 2,000 passengers, and Scarborough soon became a popular destination.

By 1850, most of the main lines had been opened and some amalgamations had taken place. Potential investors would have become wary when the irregularities associated with George Hudson 'the Railway King'[4] came to light. But the benefits of railways were so apparent that it would not be long before new plans were being made. Branch railways would come next – partly to draw goods and passengers on to the main network, and partly to take fuel, food and raw materials to nearby towns and villages, and workers, if needs be, to their place of employment.

A scheme to build a railway alongside Hebden water as far as Walshaw Dean, which might eventually have been extended to Keighley, seems to have made little headway, but the Lancashire and Yorkshire Railway Company (the product of several amalgamations pre-1847) was soon surveying other local routes. In partnership with the Great Northern Railway they secured parliamentary approval for the Halifax and Ovenden Junction Railway in June 1864,[5] and pressed on with their own plans for the Ryburn branch from Sowerby Bridge to Ripponden, sanctioned in 1865, but not finally opened until 1878. A short line from North Dean (Greetland) to Stainland was completed three years earlier. The Lancashire and Yorkshire Railway (L & Y) also took an interest in a proposed Luddenden Valley railway, from Luddenden Foot to an initial halt by Holme Bridge at the foot of Jouler (Jowler). The unlikely story of this railway may be followed in some detail.

---

[3] J. Wells, *The Eleven Towns Railway: the Story of the Manchester and Leeds MainLine,* Keighley: Railway & Canal Historical Society, 2000, p 87. He lodged at Brearley Hall (1841 Census). Luddenden Foot was 'a small roadside place. The station was a rude wooden hut' and Branwell 'spent his time at the pubs of the Calder valley'. F. Grundy, *Pictures of the Past* quoted by J. Barker in *The Brontes,* London: Weidenfeld & Nicholson, 1994, p367

[4] The driving force behind railways in the north. At one stage he controlled almost half the railways in England. He aimed to 'mak all t'railways cum t'York'. G. Biddle and O. S. Nock, *The Railway Heritage of Britain,* London: Studio Editions, 2000, p11

[5] This eventually provided the Keighley connection via the Queensbury triangle. Queensbury station became the junction for three services: Halifax (North Bridge) – Keighley, Halifax (North Bridge) – Bradford Exchange, and Bradford Exchange – Keighley.

Local interest prompted a first survey of a possible Luddenden branch in 1863. This led to a meeting in June when Mr J.E. Norris, solicitor and clerk to the Midgley Board of Health, proposed that a company should be formed. On 13 October 1864 directors of the L & Y agreed to subscribe half the required capital and the Luddenden Valley Railway Company was incorporated on November 10 1864. It was agreed that plans for the line should be deposited with the Clerk of the Peace in Wakefield and that 'printed copies of the Act or Bill would be deposited in the Private Bill Office of the House of Commons on or before 23 December'. The plans, along with a Book of Reference,[6] were completed in November and a Subscription Contract and Agreement signed on 14 December. Share capital of £22,000 would be raised, of which the L &Y would take up half; their three directors would be joined by local manufacturers and landowners William Ambler, James Eastwood and William Murgatroyd the younger. John Marshall says that the 'Luddenden Valley Railway Bill passed Standing Orders in February 1865…but failed to achieve a Second Reading on grounds of sparsity of population',[7] but this cannot have been the case since Royal Assent was granted on 26 May that year.[8] However, no engineering work was ever carried out, and after the first ordinary meeting of shareholders on 19 September 1865 the trail gradually goes cold.

Throughout the planning process, any potential opposition would have had to be identified. In such circumstances parliament would apply a 'public interest' test but, as the railway network expanded, only the opposition of substantial and well-connected groups and individuals was at all likely to prevail. The committee of management of the Luddenden Valley Railway was originally made up of six of the most influential mill owners in the valley, and when a schedule of subscribers for the company shares was drawn up they and members of their families proposed to buy £8,500's worth of the £11,000 in shares for which an offer was invited. Of the committee only Robert Thompson, a corn miller at Luddenden Mills, had not committed himself to an investment, whilst a newcomer, Joseph Priestley Edwards of Fixby Hall, Huddersfield was willing to subscribe £2,000. This may well have had some bearing on the outcome of the whole project, since he had bought the Castle Carr estate at the head of the Luddenden valley and if it had ever seemed

---

[6] West Yorkshire Archive Service (Wakefield), *Luddenden Valley Railway, plan and section*, 1864, QE20/1/1864/ Plan 15
[7] John Marshall, *Lancashire and Yorkshire Railway*, Newton Abbott: David & Charles, 1969, Vol 2 p117
[8] An Act to incorporate a Company for making a Railway to be called the Luddenden Valley Railway, 26 May 1865, 28/29 Victoriae Reginaea Cap xxiii

Figure 1   *The proposed route of the Luddenden Valley Railway, shown on the first edition six inch to one mile Ordnance Survey Map of 1851 (scale reduced)*

possible that the railway might encroach on his estate he would wish to protect his interest. Even small landowners might have seen a profit in the venture, since compensation for loss of rights of way or the sale of land along the line could have seemed attractive. A Court of Referees sitting in the House of Commons would reach a decision when disputes arose: when the Manchester and Leeds Railway was built the company paid out £44,628, less than a third of the £146,448 claimed. Environmental issues rarely arose, although William Wordsworth complained bitterly when the Kendal and Windermere Railway was built.[9]

Those who proposed the Luddenden Valley Railway scheme, and were prepared to invest their money, would have believed that they stood to benefit directly.[10] 'Such an undertaking might become an element of considerable profit'.[11] 'There is an increasing trade carried on in the thriving woollen manufactories of the Luddenden Valley'. The Amblers (Peel House Mills), Calverts (Wainstalls), Eastwoods (Mill House and Pepper Hill) and the Murgatroyds (Oats Royd) were worsted spinners and manufacturers. The Brackens (Dean Mills) were paper makers, and Robert Thompson was a corn miller. Other employers, not directly involved with the planned railway included the Hoyles at Holme House Mill, John Rothwell, machine maker, and James Ogden, spindle maker, both at Holme House Bridge Mill. 'All the landowners throughout the line had promised their support'.[12] It was pointed out that 'heavy and increasing stone traffic over the township roads... was becoming a burthen to the ratepayers'.[13] Great savings would be achieved in transporting stone and coal. It was claimed that 'upwards of 30,000 tons of stone passes annually between the proposed termini of the line...and a first-class stone field of 400 acres (is) as yet unopened'.[14] J.E. Norris calculated that 'the coal conveyed up the valley for the exclusive use of the manufacturers

---

[9] 'Is there no nook of English ground secure from rash assault?' W. Wordsworth, *On the projected Kendal and Windermere Railway* in The Complete Poetical Works, London: Macmillan and Co., 1888

[10] The Lancashire & Yorkshire Railway, for example, paid a dividend of eight and three-eighths per cent in 1872. M. Robbins, *The Railway Age*, Harmondsworth: Penguin Books, 1965, p65

[11] Prospectus for the Luddenden Valley Railway Company, 1864

[12] West Yorkshire Archive Service (Wakefield), *Book of Reference, Plan and Section for the Luddenden Valley Railway Company*, 1864, QE 20/1864/15. Landowners listed were the Lancashire and Yorkshire Railway, the Rochdale Canal Company, Todmorden Turnpike Trust, William Whitworth, Hon Wellington Henry Stapleton Cotton and John Napper and Richard Greville, George Sutcliffe, The Local Board of Health, Robert Thompson, James Eastwood and John Eastwood, John Murgatroyd, Jonathan Bracken and Richard Bracken, Dyson Thomas, and Jonathan Calvert.

[13] Prospectus for the Luddenden Valley Railway Company, 1864

[14] Prospectus for the Luddenden Valley Railway Company, 1864

Schedule

Name and Surname of Subscriber.	Description of Subscriber	Place of Abode of Subscriber	Usual Signature of Subscriber	Amount Subscribed	Amount paid	Seal	Name of Witness date of Signature
John Ambler	Worsted Spinner	Peel House Luddenden	John Ambler	500		(SL)	W. Thomas 20 Decr 1864
John Murgatroyd	Ditto	Oaks Royde Luddenden	John Murgatroyd	1000		(SL)	W. Thomas 20 Decr 1864
Robert Thompson	Corn Miller	Luddenden	Robert Thompson	1000		(SL)	W. Thomas 20 Decr 1864
James Eastwood	Worsted Spinner & Manufacturer	Luddenden	James Eastwood	500		(SL)	W. Thomas 20 Decr 1864
John Eastwood	Worsted Spinner & Manufacturer	Luddenden	John Eastwood	500		(SL)	A.C. Foster 24 Decr 1864
William R. Eastwood	Worsted Spinner & Manufacturer	Luddenden	William R. Eastwood	500		(SL) (SL)	A.C. Foster 24 Decr 1864
William Murgatroyd Jr	Worsted Spinner & Manufacturer	Luddenden	Wm Murgatroyd Junr	1000		(SL)	W. Thomas 20 Decr 1864
William Ambler	Worsted Spinner & Manufacturer	Luddenden	William Ambler	750		(SL)	Jno R. Newby 24 Decr 186.
James Ambler	Worsted Spinner	Luddenden	James Ambler	750		(SL)	Jno R. Newby 24 Decr 186
Jonathan Bracken	Paper Manufacturer	Luddenden	J. Bracken	1000		(SL)	Jno R. Newby 24 Decr 186.
Richard Bracken	Paper Manufacturer	Luddenden	R. Bracken	1000		(SL)	Jno R. Newby 24 Decr 1864
Joseph Priestley Edwards	Esquire	Treasby Park near Huddersfield	J.P. Edward	2000		(SL)	J.E. Norris 28 Decr 1864

Figure 2   Schedule of subscribers to the Luddenden Valley Railway

was 40 tons per diem'.[15] Coal would have been carried for ¾d per ton per mile, plus an additional farthing per mile if company wagons were used. Stone could be charged at one and one-fifth of a penny per ton. The Act of Incorporation made provision for passenger services,[16] but no stations or halts are shown in the plans or sections which were submitted with the original application to Parliament in the previous December. If passengers had ever travelled along the line, they would have paid one and four-fifths of a penny first class or nine-tenths of a penny in third.

The Luddenden Valley Railway would have left the L & Y main line roughly 200 yards beyond the western end of Luddendenfoot station. The River Calder, the Rochdale Canal and the Todmorden turnpike road would all have to be bridged: a three-arched viaduct offered the most obvious solution. This would be formed of a 65 foot arch over the river (height above water 25 feet), an arch to have 'between the abutments a clear space of not less than forty feet' across the canal (height again 25 feet),[17] and a 35 foot arch with a height of

---

[15] Inaugural Public Meeting of interested parties 10 July 1863, *The Halifax Historical Almanack* 1864, p17
[16] An Act to incorporate a Company for making a Railway to be called the Luddenden Valley Railway, 1865 s.39
[17] An Act to incorporate a Company for making a Railway to be called the Luddenden Valley Railway, 1865 s.54. Only details of the canal bridge are contained in the Act., other details are from the plan (note 6)

16 feet over the turnpike road. The railway would meet the rising ground on Luddenden Lane above the Red Lion Inn,[18] and the lane itself would be diverted so that it ran between the railway and the Luddenden Brook, until it resumed its original course by Lane House.

The line would now head north, with Kershaw House, Carr Well, New Box House and Box House on its western flank. Midgley New Road and High Street would be crossed on the level, but a bridge was needed when Old Lane was reached (25 foot arch; height 15 feet). Oats Royd Mill was to the west, as were Dean House and Booth Ebenezer Chapel. On the eastern side lay Peel

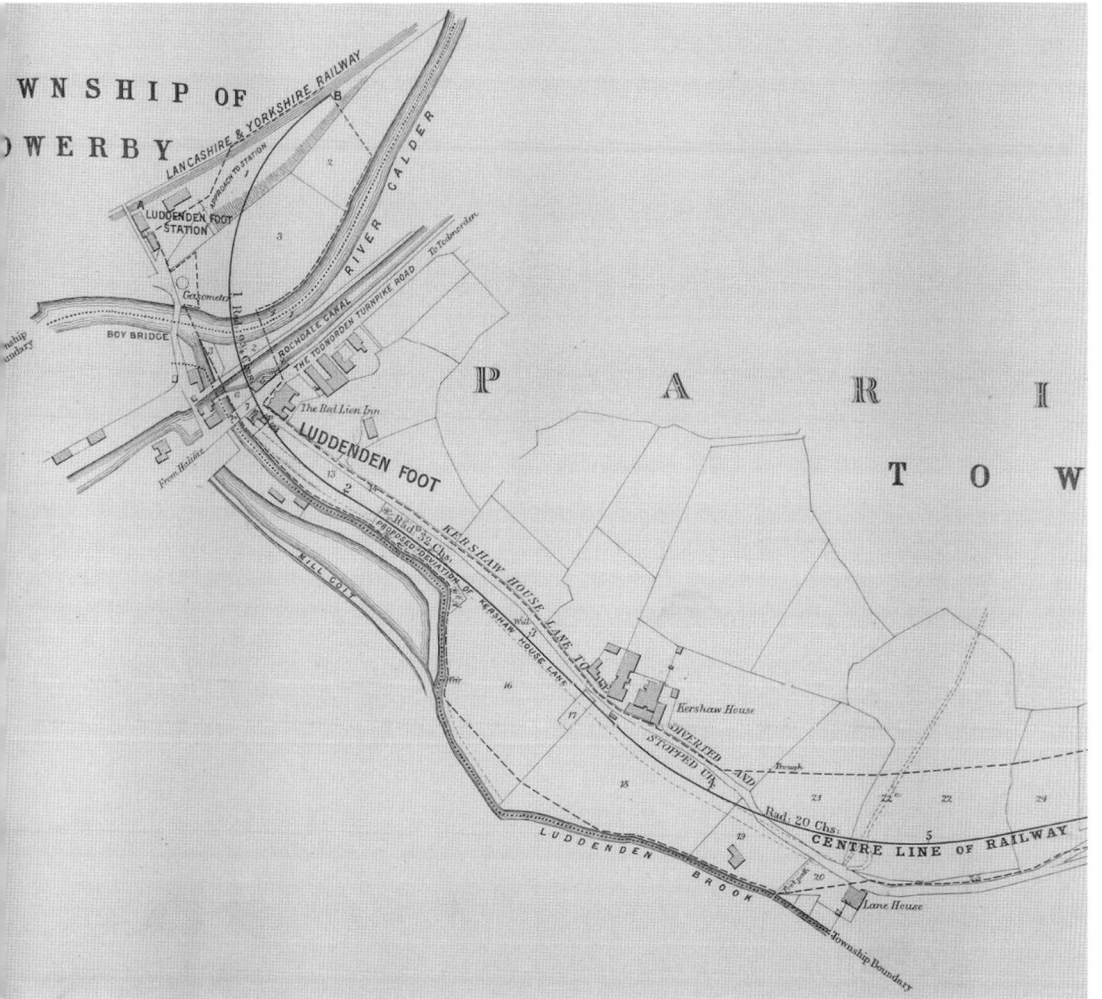

igure 3   Plan for the first section of the railway, beginning at Luddendenfoot

---

[18] Later rebuilt as the General Rawdon and latterly renamed the Coach & Horses

House Mill, Dean Mill and the cottages at Goit Side. The Luddenden Brook was not to be bridged, so one supposes a culvert would have been necessary.[19] The plan dated November 1864 marks a clearance of 3 feet 6 inches over the stream. The terminus would have been on the meadow below Little Holme House. At this point it was 484 feet above sea level, and the railway had risen 178 feet along the course of 1 mile 7 furlongs (almost 2 miles).

Figure 4   The proposed route crossed Old Lane here below Box House, Luddenden

This leads on to what is perhaps the most intriguing part of the story. The original prospectus aimed to raise £50,000 in £10 shares but, by the time the Act to incorporate the company was passed, the capital sought was just £22,000. It is clear that a significantly less ambitious scheme was now being proposed. 'Mineral branches' were no longer part of the plan;[20] the two and a half mile link via Wainstalls to Fly Flats and a further short line to Moor End had been abandoned. This was probably wise, since Wainstalls is 500 feet above the terminus at Little Holme House, and Fly is 300 feet higher still. Gaining this ground would have involved the use of an inclined plane. Two systems were quite widely used in mining and quarrying areas.[21] Track or

---

[19] The wholesale destruction of the culvert in front of Brook Terrace during the flood of May 1989 suggests this would have been a rather risky arrangement.

[20] Prospectus for the Luddenden Valley Railway Company, 1864

[21] In North Yorkshire and Derbyshire successful examples include the Ingleby Incline on the Rosedale Railway and the Hopton and Middleton Inclines on the Cromford and High Peak Line.

Figure 5   Holme House Bridge, where the railway would have terminated

*Figure 6   Holme House Bridge, from the opposite side to Figure 5, showing the
              ironworks that was there in 1864*

tracks would rise steeply, at an angle which ideally could be maintained, and
wagons built to the railway gauge would be raised and lowered by cables
which passed over a substantial drum. A steam-driven winding engine would
power the drum – alternatively two cables wound in opposite directions were

used so that laden wagons going down the incline would wind empty wagons back to the top. Beyond the drum house, a considerable length of ordinary railway, which might have been locomotive or horse hauled, would have been required, and it is hardly surprising that such an ambitious part of the project should be abandoned at an early stage.

Shareholders Meetings are recorded from 31 December 1866 through to 30 June 1870,[22] but no work was ever begun on the line. The £10 shares remained part-paid, and an authorised mortgage of up to £7,300 was never raised. The end came quite quickly. On 7 May 1870 the Directors of the Luddenden Valley Railway, being supported by at least three-fifths of the shareholders, made application to the Board of Trade for leave to abandon the railway. No objections had been raised, with posters announcing the proposed closure having been displayed on the 'principal outer door of the parish church of Halifax and at Luddenden church'.

> Your petitioners have not commenced the said railway, and it has been found that such railway cannot be made with advantage either to the promoters thereof or the public.... In consequence of the badness of trade they are unable advantageously to advance the necessary capital for the construction of the said railway…the whole of the share capital has not been subscribed and….the time has expired for the compulsory purchase of land, and owners are unwilling to sell by agreement.[23]

In light of these representations the Board of Trade authorised the abandonment of the railway on 26 September 1870. Expenses of £1,552 having been met, and further liabilities having been noted, a balance of £336 remained.

From a present day perspective the original plans for a railway seem unrealistic. Although some local mills expanded,[24] the Luddenden valley would never develop as a major industrial area, nor would its population increase dramatically. Long before Dr Beeching intervened, the four branch railways which were actually completed in Calderdale had all closed. If a Luddenden Valley Railway had ever been built it, too, would have failed eventually.

---

[22] The National Archives, *Luddenden Valley Railway Company*, 1867, BT 285/252. Board of Trade: Companies Registration Office: Railway Companies Securities Act 1866: Returns
[23] The National Archives, *Luddenden Valley Railway: abandonment*, 1870, MT 6/69/6. Board of Trade Warrant, 26 September 1870
[24] Notably Oats Royd Mill. C. Giles and I. Goodall (eds), *Yorkshire Textile Mills 1770 – 193,* London: HMSO 1992, p100

CHAPTER 20

The Murgatroyds: a Study in Paternalism

Eileen Furey and Patricia Lester

The West Riding of Yorkshire, and the North of England generally, provide many examples of small, semi-rural communities whose growth is linked to the establishment of a single-family firm. In this chapter, we will attempt to illustrate how, in the second half of the nineteenth century, the economic development of Midgley and its township were closely bound up with the establishment and continued success of Oats Royd Mill, owned by the Murgatroyd family.

In rural mill villages in the nineteenth century, most mill owners had to provide the basic housing needs of their employees to enable them to attract a sufficiently large labour force. However, a number went beyond this basic provision in that they provided a wide range of welfare, social and recreational facilities. This was in direct response to the growing social, moral and economic problems posed by increasing industrialisation of the workplace, as mills and factories gradually usurped the family home as the major workplace. Many employers installed the 'working family' model, headed by the male husband and father, into the workplace, with themselves as the head of the 'family', giving birth to a growing paternalistic relationship between employer and employee.[1]

Well-known examples of such paternalism include Saltaire, Bradford, where a complete model village was built, and Ackroyden and Copley on the outskirts of Halifax, where smaller-scale versions were established. Whereas these examples represent an all-embracing form of paternalism, where employers attempted to have complete control over employees, not only in their work but also in their leisure, the relationship that developed between the Murgatroyd family firm of Oats Royd and the Midgley community was less controlling. It was, therefore, more typical of the wider paternalistic

---

[1] For a fuller account of the issues which gave rise to the paternalistic movement see J. A. Jowitt (ed.), *Model Industrial Communities in Mid-Nineteenth Century Yorkshire*, Bradford: University of Bradford, 1986, pp5-15

movement.[2] Unlike Saltaire, where employees were denied alcohol in the village and had to attend church on a Sunday, Murgatroyds did not impose such conditions on their workers. They did, however, provide them with housing and recreational facilities.

The Murgatroyds living at Green Edge, Warley, were the forebears of the founders of Oats Royd Mill. These Murgatroyds had established their presence in the early domestic textile trade in the Halifax area as early as the seventeenth century.[3] By 1787, John Murgatroyd of Green Edge, Warley, and James Fowles of 'Oates Royd', are listed as cloth merchants operating from the new Halifax Piece Hall, where they rented room 28A in the Arcade.[4]

At this period many major towns in the West Riding had cloth halls for the sale of finished pieces of cloth. Leeds built the Mixed Cloth Hall in 1758, Huddersfield followed in 1766 and Bradford was built in 1773.[5] When the present Halifax Piece Hall (Figure 1) was first opened in 1779, a

Figure 1   *The Halifax Piece Hall*

[2] C. Pearce in Jowitt, *Model Industrial Communities in Mid-Nineteenth Century Yorkshire*, p102

[3] S. Wade private communication 2007

[4] http://www.piecehall.info/ [Accessed on 13 April 2007 – page entitled Piece Hall in the 18th century]

[5] H. Heaton, *The Yorkshire Woollen and Worsted Industries*, 2nd edn., Oxford: Oxford University Press, 1965, p270

subscription for the new building was £28 per room. The records of occupants are incomplete, but it is likely that the Murgatroyds were there from the start given their involvement in the trade. Built during a period of rapid expansion of cloth production, when Halifax was the most important producer of worsted cloth, the Piece Hall provided a major market place for producers and merchants to trade. By 1854, however, very little cloth trading was still taking place in the Piece Hall. As the scale of industrialisation gathered pace, the hall was no longer required, as small-scale manufacturers were superseded by larger companies that sold their products directly to the buyers.[6]

During the 1830s, John Murgatroyd's son, also John (and future founder of Oats Royd Mill), working from Green Edge, Warley, had cloth woven by over 164 hand-loom weavers, who lived as far apart as Stansfield, Heptonstall and Erringden to the west, with Midgley, Mytholmroyd and Wadsworth providing weavers closer to home, and Ovenden and Warley nearby.[7] Similarly, John Foster of Black Dyke Mills, Queensbury, in Bradford, began his career as a worsted manufacturer by employing workers in the domestic system. He bought wool and raw materials such as soap and oils and was organising the activities of as many as 700 weavers by 1836.[8]

Between 1833 and 1840, there was a steady increase in the number of cloth pieces sold by Murgatroyds, both locally to merchants in the Halifax area, and further afield to merchants in Bradford, Leeds, Huddersfield, Manchester, Birmingham and London. Local buyers included James Aked and Son, Kershaw House; William Appleyard and Son, Wainstalls, George Holdsworth of Shibden; John Foster of Denholme, who bought lastings and J. Butterworth of Shelf who bought damasks, lastings and serge. Cloth was sent to William Watson of Hebden Bridge to be dyed, and soap was purchased from R.R. Gregory and Bros. Lastings were used in shoe manufacture and a considerable trade developed with the shoe manufacturers of Staffordshire.[9] In 1836, plaids and lastings were sold to merchants located in Manchester, mainly the Italian merchants Novelli Casacuberta & Co and several Prussian merchants. These merchants moved to Bradford in the 1840s as it became increasingly important as a centre of the textile trade and John Murgatroyd & Son (hereafter

---

[6] http://www.piecehall.info/ [Accessed on 13 April 2007 – page entitled Piece Hall in the 19th century]
[7] S. Wade private communication 2007
[8] E. M. Sigsworth, *Black Dyke Mills: A History*, Liverpool: Liverpool University Press, 1958, p142
[9] West Yorkshire Archive Service (Calderdale), *Miscellaneous Documents 1833-1834*, JM 620

Murgatroyds') continued to sell cloth to them throughout the nineteenth century from the mill established at Oats Royd.[10]

By 1842 John Murgatroyd was living at Oats Royd. The mill register of 1844, an obligatory legal document, records him as the occupant of the bottom room of Mill House Mill in Luddenden, and employing five thirteen-year olds at that time. Interestingly, the record for holiday time indicates that, unlike nowadays, half a day was given for 'plott night' on the fifth of November indicating, perhaps, an early interest in the welfare of his young employees. John Murgatroyd's forward thinking is also indicated in his early adoption of new technologies; the mill was using steam power even though, at that time, the take-up of steam in the industry was relatively slow, possibly because of the investment required.[11]

By 1846, John Murgatroyd was in a position to buy the Oats Royd and Thorney Lane estates in Midgley from James Winstanley of Liverpool and he began building his first purpose-built steam-powered mill near Luddenden.[12] Unconstrained by the necessity for waterpower, he was able to position the mill on the hillside above Luddenden Brook, the boundary between Midgley and Warley Townships.[13]

Figure 2   John Murgatroyd by Patrick Branwell Brontë, 1841

---

[10] West Yorkshire Archive Service (Calderdale), *Cash Book 1869 -1874,* JM 272
[11] C. Giles & I.H. Goodall, *Yorkshire Textile Mills: the Buildings of the Yorkshire Textile Industry 1770 – 1930,* London: H.M.S.O., 1992, p15
[12] S. Wade private communication 2007
[13] See Ordnance Survey map of 1851 at end of book

Figure 3   An early print of Oats Royd Mill, as it would have appeared after 1851

This first mill was built as a three-storey spinning mill of seventeen bays and included an engine and boiler house. The economic influence of the mill went beyond production at the mill itself; its building and subsequent additions provided much-needed employment for a variety of skilled trades such as masons, glaziers and carpenters; notwithstanding the deteriorating circumstances of hand-loom weavers, who found it increasingly difficult to earn a living once the mill was running.

Millwrights and engineers were also gainfully employed at Murgatroyds'. Timothy Bates & Co of Sowerby Bridge was paid a total of £1,210 in 1848-9, probably in payment for the first steam engine employed in the mill. It is also likely that a bill for £380 3s 10d, which itemised walling, flagging and ashlar for the engine bed, referred to stone extracted from local quarries and would have involved local stoneworkers.[14] In 1841, according to the Census Enumerators' Returns, twenty-two men in Midgley township described themselves simply as stonemasons or delvers.[15] By 1851 this had increased to twenty-seven, eleven of whom were masons, six labourers, nine delvers and one a dresser, giving some indication of the growth of stone-related trades.[16]

---

[14] West Yorkshire Archive Service (Calderdale), *Cash Book 1848-185,* JM238

[15] This information is from the Census Enumerators' Returns, held at the Public Record Office, Series RG. Microfilm copies are available locally in Halifax Central Library

[16] This information is from the Census Enumerators' Returns, held at the Public Record Office, Series RG. Microfilm copies are available locally in Halifax Central Library

Murgatroyds' also employed professional classes of worker such as architects at different times during the nineteenth century. One such architect was Thomas Dearden, who was employed on the first buildings from 1848 to 1851. Another Dearden, John, was employed for five years between 1865 and 1870. In the later part of the century, T. Lister Patchett began working for Murgatroyds' and remained with them until 1905, a total of twenty-one years.[17]

By 1855, there had been two major additions to the original 1847 mill that greatly increased the working capacity of the mill. Firstly, a ten bay extension was constructed, making twenty-seven bays in all, followed in 1855, by another mill to the north end of the original 1847 mill.[18] This illustrates the growing success of John Murgatroyd's business and its increasing importance in the township. The continued development of mill buildings on the Oats Royd site represented a major investment in the area on the part of the Murgatroyds. An entry in the account books for 1855-57, during which time Mill No 2 and the warehouse were built, attribute an amount of £3,180 11s 8d, a substantial amount at the time, as 'money paid for mill building'.[19]

As the business expanded in the late fifties and early sixties, it became necessary to build on the other side of the road. Between 1858 and 1863, the combing shed and Mill No 3 were completed. The Weavers' Book of 1859-1864 also reveals that the shortage of mill space had forced Murgatroyd's to commission weaving at Samuel Ramsden's of Ovenden on thirty looms. The latter were returned to Murgatroyds' between 1863 and 1864.[20]

Up to this time, the remnants of domestic handloom weaving had operated alongside the factory system. The 1851 Census illustrates how the two systems were working side-by-side. Whereas Matthew Ackroyd from Lane Ends, Midgley, head of household, was listed as a handloom weaver, his son, Matthew, aged fourteen, was listed as a 'factory operative, woollen'. In another example, John, forty-four, and Jane Widdop, forty-five, of Scotland, Midgley, were described as handloom weavers while their sons Thomas, nineteen, and William, twenty-two, were power-loom weavers. In addition, both Mary, fifteen, and John Widdop, thirteen, were factory operatives. Their

---

[17] West Yorkshire Archive Service (Calderdale), *Estate Records 1846-1925*, JM547
[18] Giles and Goodall, *Yorkshire Textile Mills 1770-1930*, p100
[19] West Yorkshire Archive Service (Calderdale), *Cash Book 1848-1857*, JM238
[20] West Yorkshire Archive Service (Calderdale), *Weavers Book 1859-1864*, JM 73 with reference to Samuel Ramsden

sister Sarah, aged ten, was a 'factory operative and scholar.' It would appear that young people and children were employed as mill operatives rather than established handloom weavers in the early stages of factory production. After 1860 there is little evidence of domestic production.

Combing by hand continued for some time because the process was difficult to mechanise. Until Samuel Cunliffe Lister patented his combing machine in 1858, Murgatroyd's employed hand combers. In 1858, Murgatroyds' paid £1,000 for the use of the patent for Lister's combing machine, which facilitated full mechanisation of the process and led the way for further expansion.[21]

Figure 4   The complete Oats Royd Mill complex

The final phase of expansion took place between 1885 and 1887 with the building of a combing and a weaving shed, together with an engine-house. After 1887, there were only minor alterations to the complex, including such things as the installation of electric lighting. The only textile processes not carried out on site were finishing and dyeing of raw wool, yarn or pieces. The

[21] S. Wade private communication 2007

new weaving shed caused great excitement as indicated by a celebratory meal, or 'rearing supper', for contractors, architects, foremen and representatives of the firm at the Shoulder of Mutton Inn in 1888.[22]

Overall, the period of 1856-1905 saw considerable investment in plant, machinery, six reservoirs, and housing for employees. In addition to this, the firm at first rented, then in 1851 bought, warehousing in Brook Street, Bradford.[23] As Bradford became the centre of wool trading, it would have made economic sense for Murgatroyds' to invest in such warehouses. The merchants who moved from Manchester in the early part of the nineteenth century had become well established in Bradford by this time. The Bradford Observer in 1836 reported that, 'manufacturers are removing to Bradford as fast as they can get accommodated with room'.[24] By 1861, more than 40 per cent of Bradford worsted merchants had foreign names, reflecting the importance of the export market for the worsted industry. By the 1870s, Murgatroyds' was selling increasing amounts of yarn and cloth for export via the Prussian merchants of 'Little Germany' in particular. These merchants, Schlesinger, Behrens, Schuster, Albrect and others, held monthly meetings and sent their sons to fight in the Franco-Prussian War of 1870.[25] The importance of this export business to Murgatroyds' is illustrated by a £10 donation in August 1870 via Heymann & Alexander 'for the relief of the wounded in the Prussian Wars'.[26] Given that the prevailing public mood at the time was to support the French rather than the Prussians, the donation was interesting:

> Most English followers of events on the continent felt pity for France in its desolation and above all for Paris, the hunger and despair of the siege, the internecine destructiveness of what followed. London alone sent £80,000 worth of provisions to the starving.[27]

In the 1870s, there is evidence that other companies were struggling to sustain the expansion of previous years and were unable to pay for goods purchased from Murgatroyds'.[28] However, the firm was now established as the major employer in the Midgley area. A statistical summary dated March 1875, shows the scale of manufacturing at the Oats Royd Mill: 345 power looms were in

---

[22] West Yorkshire Archive Service (Calderdale), *Scrap Book 1876-1982,* JM 848

[23] West Yorkshire Archive Service (Calderdale), *Warehouse in Brook Street Bradford 1864-1899,* JM 557

[24] Sigsworth, *Black Dyke Mills: A History,* p25

[25] Sigsworth, *Black Dyke Mills: A History,* p65

[26] West Yorkshire Archive Service (Calderdale), *Cash Book 1869-1874,* JM273

[27] A.N.Wilson, *The Victorians,* London: Hutchinson, 2002, p345

[28] West Yorkshire Archive Service (Calderdale), *Cash Book 1874-78,* JM273

operation (this had increased to 379 by 1887); 8,236 doubling spindles; 12,538 spinning spindles and nine combing machines.[29]

That the mill was a major employer in 1875 there is no doubt. Figures for the morning shift of employees number fifty-eight males between thirteen to eighteen years: 215 males above eighteen years and 384 females above thirteen years. The numbers of children under thirteen years are listed as sixty-seven males and sixty females. In the afternoon shift there was a decrease in female operatives over eighteen to 289 and an increase in males over eighteen to 247. The numbers for children under thirteen were similar to the morning shift: sixty males and sixty-two females. The morning shift employed a total of 787 operatives, while the afternoon shift employed a total of 723.[30]

The wages record of 1881 outlines the variety of employment opportunities available at the mill.[31] These included overlookers, spinners, woolsorters, drawers and combers, winders, reelers, twisters, warpers and machinists. Warehousemen, mechanics and oilers and stokers were also employed. In addition, wool and cotton had to be brought up the hill from Luddendenfoot and there were horses to be cared for in the early days.

Figure 5   *Carthorses outside the stables at Oats Royd*

---

[29] West Yorkshire Archive Service (Calderdale), *Statistical Survey of Number of Machines at the Mill*, 1875, JM638

[30] West Yorkshire Archive Service (Calderdale), *Statistical Survey of Number of People Employed at the Mill*, 1875, JM638

[31] West Yorkshire Archive Service (Calderdale), *Wages Record 1878-1883*, JM44

The position of overlooker was a highly regarded post and the 'Overlookers' Assistant' handbook illustrates the level of knowledge and skill required.[32] The level of responsibility attached to the position was such that the wage of an overlooker was one of the highest. In the 1887 wages record, William Thomas of Providence earned 66d per day and received £2 15s 0d over the fortnight. Miles Parker earned 42d a day and a fortnightly wage of £1 15s 0d while Joseph Maud earned 44d a day and £1 16s 8d a fortnight.[33] The differences in amounts could be explained by the different sizes of the various sheds the overlookers had responsibility for, as well as differences in seniority. One of their duties was to oversee the management of the children and young people working for Murgatroyds'. The handbook advised the overseer to:

> study and make himself acquainted with the different tempers and dispositions of such as are placed under his care, and adapt his conduct and proceedings with them accordingly. For some children are of a tender and soft disposition, such will require coaxing and encouraging, rather than coercion and threatening… but under all circumstances be firm and keep good-tempered and so conduct yourself towards your hands as to gain their esteem and respect, for a great amount of good may result from a good understanding between overlookers and those that are placed under them.[34]

Increasingly, whole family units were employed at Oats Royd, among them the Prior family of Yew Trees, Midgley, who were all employed as spinners at the following daily rates:

Elizabeth Ann Prior	19½d
Phoebe Prior	16d
Jeanette Prior	3d
Samuel Prior	7d

The male members of the Sharp family of Lane Ends, Midgley, were employed in various jobs at Murgatroyds' and paid fortnightly:

Richard Sharp woolsorter	£1 19s 0d
Thomas Sharp spinner	12s 6d
John William Sharp spinner	13s 9d
Herbert Sharp delver	5s 5d

---

[32] T. Bailey, *The Managers' and Overlookers' Assistant*, Bradford: J. Lund, [ca. 1860], pp14-15
[33] West Yorkshire Archive Service (Calderdale), *Wages Books 1883-89*, JM45
[34] Bailey, *The Managers' and Overlookers' Assistant*, p7

In common with many Midgley families the Sharps rented their home from the firm, in their case for 4s.[35]

Families from outside Midgley township were attracted by the employment opportunities offered by Murgatroyds'. The Census returns of 1851 and 1861 illustrate how many families and individuals began to move into the township, firstly from Halifax, later from Todmorden, Lancashire and Lincolnshire and, increasingly from Ireland.[36] It is possible that increased employment opportunities in Midgley township, and in particular at Oats Royd in 1847, were already having an effect on population towards the end of the 1840s. Harwood reports that Midgley Poor Rate overseers wrote to a Midgley man in Lancaster asking him to return as,

> manufacturing in our township is very greatly improved and workmen scarce… we are determined to fill up the empty houses in our township with our own poor as much as possible.[37]

This need for workers continued into the middle of the twentieth century when families moved into Midgley from the north of Yorkshire, where the firm had advertised extensively. In a brochure produced around that time, Murgatroyds' emphasised the attractive location of its mill complex, together with the fresh air and pleasant working conditions.[38] Indeed, those people in the locality who were employed at the mill remember working there with some fondness.

Throughout the nineteenth century, wherever industry developed away from centres of population, it was common for manufacturers to provide workers' housing. Murgatroyds' was typical of medium-sized firms in that they provided the basic housing needs of their workers, either through building houses or renting rows of cottages from other landowners. The first row of cottages they built was adjacent to Oats Royd Mill at Providence (Figure 6).

Subsequently, as the firm expanded, more building took place. In Midgley village, the physical layout of the village was substantially altered by the building of twelve cottages at Lane Ends and thirty cottages on Thorney Lane.

---

[35] West Yorkshire Archive Service (Calderdale), *Wages Books 1878-83* JM44

[36] This information is from the Census Enumerators' Returns, held at the Public Record Office, Series RG. Microfilm copies are available locally in Halifax Central Library

[37] H.W. Harwood, 'Midgley Gleanings', Transactions *of the Halifax Antiquarian Society*, 1951, pp111-118 at p118

[38] John Murgatroyd & Son, *Promotional Brochure*, n.d. [1950-60?], Private collection S.Wade

In common with most mill owners of the time, these cottages were rented out rather than sold to the workers. By 1861, at least ninety-one families were having their rent deducted from their wages.[39] By the end of the century, the Murgatroyd family, according to the Certificates of Contract for Land Tax in 1897, owned a substantial number of properties including public houses, farms and farm cottages and houses. The certificates show that Pasture, Clough, Greenhouse, Ferney Lee, Hollin Top, High House, Height, Gate House, Brownhill, Acre, Thorney Lane and Lydgate were among the farms belonging to John Murgatroyd. In addition, he owned cottages and properties at Dean House, Luddenden and Booth. The purchase of the Castle Carr estate alone in 1895 brought a further twenty-one farms into the Murgatroyd estate.[40]

Figure 6   Providence Place photographed in the first half of the twentieth century

In 1881, cottage rents varied from 2s to 8s a fortnight: Yew Trees was one of the cheapest properties to rent at 2s 4d, while Church Hill, Luddenden commanded a rent of 8s. Lane Ends tenants were paying on average 4s 6d and Thorney Lane rents were 3s.[41] Rents for the farms varied considerably. In 1867 Brownhill and Acre Farms were let to Samuel Farrer for £32 to be paid in two

---

[39] West Yorkshire Archive Service (Calderdale), *Wages Book 1861-1873*, JM44
[40] West Yorkshire Archive Service (Calderdale), *Estate Records 1823-1889*, JM548
[41] West Yorkshire Archive Service (Calderdale), *Wages Book 1878-1883*, JM44

equal half-yearly instalments. High House Farm was let for £56 a year to John Shackleton, Height Farm for £20 to William Driver, and Thorney Lane Farm to Samuel Thomas for £40. All the farms had to be kept in good repair and, each year, some part of the land had to be spread with Burnley or Clitheroe lime to the value of four pounds with Murgatroyds' paying half. To keep the land in good fettle, the tenancy agreement stipulated that tenants were not allowed to turn more than one-sixth of the pasture land in any one year and could not sell or part with any hay, grass or straw. A penalty of twenty pounds was payable if this edict was disobeyed.[42]

The provision of basic housing needs was part of the paternalistic approach to employer-employee relationships that developed in England gradually over the latter half of the nineteenth century. The movement gained momentum after the Chartist uprising of the 1840s and came to reflect a different approach to industrial relations. In the 1850s, a small group of West Riding manufacturers went beyond this simple provision. J.A. Jowett in his introduction to 'Model Industrial Communities in Mid-Nineteenth Century Yorkshire' argues that:

> following the demise of the Chartist threat in 1848, a whole range of paternalistic issues were forthcoming. Prominent amongst them were features such as works brass bands, factory and community cricket teams, works trips, works dinners and social welfare facilities.[43]

Jowitt quotes from the Bradford Observer:

> We advert with the greatest satisfaction to the recent pleasure trips and festivities of our manufacturers and their workpeople…. It shows that there are masters truly alive to the welfare of their workpeople….

Although this is undoubtedly true, the further comment by the newspaper throws some insight into why there was a change of approach in how to treat workers.

> We have tried to govern too exclusively by force or fear, at great expense and not with the most satisfactory result…But there is no fear of failure: - a railway trip to Skipton, and a good English dinner to the workpeople in any one of our great factories, is a better guarantee of the public peace than a regiment of soldiers.[44]

---

[42] West Yorkshire Archive Service (Calderdale), *Tenancy Agreements etc 1823-1889*, JM 548
[43] Jowitt, *Model Industrial Communities in Mid-Nineteenth Century Yorkshire*, p9
[44] Jowitt, *Model Industrial Communities in Mid-Nineteenth Century Yorkshire*, p13

The Murgatroyd firm was one of those which went beyond providing for the basic needs of its employees. The recreational ground at Turn Lea, Midgley, and the cricket ground at Booth were both donated to the local community by the family. Annual seaside outings to destinations like Blackpool, Rhyll and Scarborough, for a subsidised fare of 3s per person, were a hugely popular feature of working life at Murgatroyds'. Accompanied by the works brass band, the workers and their families would walk down to the station at Luddendenfoot to catch their train. The band again serenaded them as they walked from the station at Blackpool. The Halifax Courier reported in 1890 that:

550 excursionists…. quite filled the streets and alarmed all in Blackpool….At 8p.m. the big drum gave a signal in the street for home and the band played up to the station.[45]

Brass bands were a regular feature of the popular culture of the day. In 1867, the Oats Royd Brass Band had fifteen members, all of whom had to keep their newly acquired instruments, on loan from the firm, in good repair. Instruments were expensive items to purchase and were

Figure 7   *Poster advertising the 1876 annual excursion to Blackpool for Oats Royd employees and their families. Note the amendments for the following year's excursion to Scarborough.*

---

[45] I. Bailey, *Escape from the Mills: Textile Mill Outings in the Halifax Area Before the Second World War,* [unpublished]

well beyond the means of the workers of the time. Typical costs were: cornet £9 9s 0d; baritone £11 11s 0d; euphonium £14 14s 0d; tenor trombone £10 10s 0d. The firm of F. Besson & Co of London, who were the principal suppliers to the famous Lancashire and Yorkshire brass bands, supplied some of the instruments and others were purchased more locally from Joseph Higham of Manchester. The instruments were engraved, as were the brass buttons of the uniforms, with the firm's initials, JM. Brass band concerts were very popular and the Oats Royd Brass Band played in a variety of venues, for instance in March 1890 at Midgley Co-operative Hall for the Midgley Old Folks Tea, and further afield at Dewsbury, Colne, Rawtenstall, Glossop, Ripponden, Elland, Brighouse and Wyke. The firm also paid for tuition and sheet music. Committee members met at the Lord Nelson, Luddenden.[46] By 1949, when the new works canteen was opened, works outings, dinner dances and parties were well established as an integral part of working life in the mill.

The Murgatroyd family, as did other family concerns, involved themselves in public life and established themselves as local benefactors. They not only provided recreational grounds, but also had a long association with the church and schools in the township. They provided the organ and stained glass window in St Mary's Church, Luddenden, and donated the war memorial site to the village. Cashbooks from the 1860s onwards show regular payments to Luddenden National School and Midgley School Board. The former benefited from regular payments amounting to £5 on average every term and Midgley School also received regular contributions when it opened.[47]

Although the family firm prided itself on its good relations with its employees, it would have been unusual if there had not been some disputes. A letter from the Power-Loom Weavers' Association in 1893, asking for a meeting about a proposed reduction in wages, attests to this. In reply, John Murgatroyd gave a typical mill owner's response at the time, agreeing to meet with his workers but not with any outsiders. In reply, the Weavers' Association said they had:

> no desire to see the firm if they could settle the job with their workpeople. They had never forced themselves into any employer's office and never would.[48]

---

[46] West Yorkshire Archive Service (Calderdale), *Oats Royd Mills Brass Band 1864-1891*, JM857

[47] West Yorkshire Archive Service (Calderdale), *Cash Book 1869-1874*, JM273 and *Cash Book 1874-78*, JM273

[48] West Yorkshire Archive Service (Calderdale), *Weavers' Dispute 1893*, JM646

Longevity of employment was to become a feature of working at Oats Royd, an indication perhaps, of the high regard felt between employer and employee, as present ex-employees testify. D. James, in his survey of paternalism among Keighley mill owners, argues that:

> the growth of affection and esteem which was built up over the years between a master and his workforce had much to do with the fact that many of the manufacturers lived among their employers for much of their lives and were seen as an integral part of the local community. As a result many workers would stay with the same employer for many years.[49]

The fact that the Murgatroyds lived amongst their workers for successive generations is probably one reason why they were able to maintain good working relations. From the 1870s, there was a tendency among successive generations of family mill owners to move away from the mill location, which meant less involvement with the work force. Jowett gives the example of Crossley's, Halifax where, in the 1840s, John Crossley's widow lived in the mill yard, but her grandson eventually moved away to live at Somerleyton Hall in Suffolk.[50] The Murgatroyds, however, always lived within walking distance of the mill, first at Oats Royd, then Broadfold Hall and finally at The Greave, and participated fully in the various functions put on by the firm for their employees.[51] Family occasions were also an opportunity to create a bond with the workforce as, for example, in 1901 when John Murgatroyd, son of the founder, paid his workpeople 1s 6d for every year they had worked for Murgatroyds', in celebration of his son's marriage. Employees in turn presented the latter with a clock and a pair of horses. Later, in 1906, to celebrate his daughter's marriage, the workers were paid 1s per year for continuous service. On another occasion, during the coal strike of 1912 when work had to stop, Murgatroyds' paid 5s a week to all the millhands earning 15s and under, while the half-timers received 2s 6d. This was paid on three separate occasions.[52]

The Murgatroyds were proud of the fact that successive generations had worked at the mill[53], reflected in the fact that, in 1927, five of their employees won £10 in the Yorkshire Observer long service competition. The winners were: Miss Ellen Barren, sixty-six years service; Mr Milford Rushworth, sixty-

---

[49] D. James in Jowitt, *Model Industrial Communities in Mid-Nineteenth Century Yorkshire*, p107
[50] Jowitt, *Model Industrial Communities in Mid-Nineteenth Century Yorkshire*, p14
[51] West Yorkshire Archive Service (Calderdale), *Scrap Book 1876-1892*, JM848
[52] Information obtained from a diary kept by John Ratcliffe's father who was overlooker and/or mill manager at Oats Royd Mills, 1901-1904. Original in care of great grandson.
[53] John Murgatroyd & Son, *Promotional Brochure*, n.d. [1950-60?], Private collection, S.Wade

six years; Miss Sarah Greenwood, sixty-four years; Mr Joseph Barnes, sixty-two years; Miss Sarah Patchett, sixty-one years. [54]

Figure 8   *Winners of the Yorkshire Observer long service award, 1927.*
Left to right: Ellen Barren, Milford Rushworth, Sarah A Greenwood,
Joseph Barnes, and Sarah Patchett

When John Murgatroyd, the founder, died in 1880, an illuminated address of condolence to his wife, paid for by the workers at the time, showed how highly regarded he was. In it they say:

> We, on behalf of the workpeople of Oats-Royd Mills, Midgley, desire to express our sincere and heartfelt sympathy with you in the sad and deeply deplored event, the removal by death of your worthy husband, our late and beloved Master. His removal is a sad calamity not only to you but also to us his workpeople, who ever found in him a Master worthy of the name, kind-hearted

---

[54] West Yorkshire Archive Service (Calderdale), *Scrap Book 1876-1892,* JM 848

and considerate towards the poor working man. He has been a staff on which the whole neighbourhood could with safety lean for daily bread.[55]

Although today we would find the level of deference and respect illustrated here unusual, the sentiments shown in this address, and repeated in numerous testimonials, are written with honesty, affection and sincerity. John Murgatroyd's son, it would appear, was no less well thought of, as indicated by his obituary in *The Halifax Daily Courier* in 1921.

> Mr Murgatroyd knew the whole of his employes (sic) personally and so long as they could walk to the mill and attend reasonably to duty, they were assured of a position. Some have been employed there well over 50 years. In times of sickness, "Mr John," as he was always described by the staff and workpeople, invariably went to visit them, and by little gifts and kindly word rendered much thoughtful service.[56]

The mill continued to be a wholly Murgatroyd concern until 1954 when it became part of the Worsted and Woollen Mill Group, Guiseley, and became, as such, one of the largest manufacturing groups in the country. As a result of changing trade patterns in the 70s and 80s, the mill finally closed in 1982. It was, for many people, the end of an era.

Sigsworth, in his introduction to 'Black Dyke Mills: a History', maintains that the elements of success in manufacturing are an ability for organisation and risk bearing, in addition to a sufficient labour force to populate a busy mill.[57] While we would consider both of these elements pre-requisites for success, the example of the Murgatroyds at their Oats Royd factory would indicate that, in addition, the philosophy behind paternalism could also account for the success of smaller family firms such as Murgatroyds'. The relationship between employer and employee is always going to be a complex matter and the fundamental fact that can never be disguised or forgotten is that a manufacturer's economic power over his employees is almost total.[58] The paternalism illustrated here gives some indication that, when the welfare of the workforce is taken into consideration, it is to the benefit of both employer and employee. In this way, a major manufacturing base was established in Midgley township, changing its face forever, and giving rise to stable employment for the inhabitants for over one hundred years.

---

[55] *Illuminated Address.* Private collection, S. Wade
[56] *The Halifax Daily Courier and Guardian*, 22 June 1921
[57] Sigsworth, *Black Dyke Mills: A History*, Introduction
[58] D. James in Jowitt, *Model Industrial Communities in Mid-Nineteenth Century Yorkshire*, p108

CHAPTER 21

Thorney Lane Transformation

Ruth Wilson

In 2005, the new owner of a house in one of the terraces in Thorney Lane was working on some alterations when he found a 1901 penny in the roof and showed it to me. Knowing nothing about the history of Midgley, I wondered whether the house was already there in 1901. And what about the other terrace I could see across the road? Who had built them here? When and why? Could I find out about some of the people who had lived in them in 1901 or earlier? What was there in Thorney Lane before the terraces? Soon after this I heard about the Midgley History Group and so there was no excuse for not trying to find the answers to some of my questions.

Thorney Lane turns off the main street of Midgley village, running roughly to the north. I concentrated on the stretch beginning at the present number 40 (on the east side of the road), including Thorney Lane Farm, and stopping just before Gate House Barn (on the west side).

Before and After

There are no terraces on the first edition six inch Ordnance Survey map surveyed in 1848-50, just a structure at Lane Top (which no longer exists as a place name) and two buildings called 'Thorny Lane' in the area of the present farmhouse (Figure 1). By the time the second edition six inch Ordnance Survey map was surveyed in 1888-1894, the farm was now surrounded by three terraces and Lane Top had disappeared, although there was still a small structure in that area (Figure 2).

Things were essentially unchanged when the (undated) photographs (Figures 3 and 5) were taken, probably in the 1920s or 1930s. In Figures 4 and 6 we can see Thorney Lane as it is today. The only building which has remained constant (though not unchanged) throughout the entire period is the farm and it was certainly already there in 1782 when it was owned by James Hemingway, a member of the family from whom the Murgatroyds bought

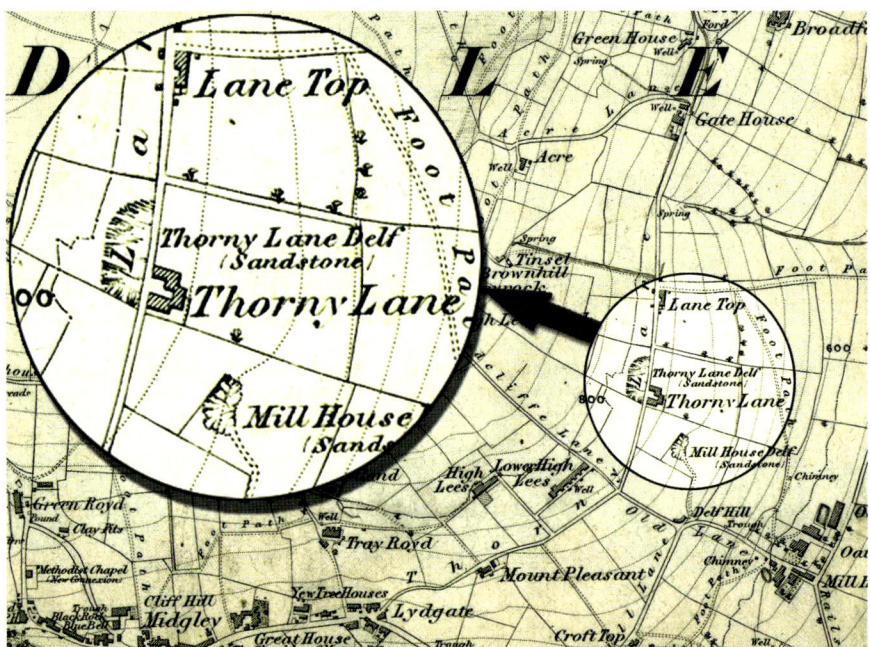

Figure 1   First Edition Six Inch Ordnance Survey Map, surveyed
                  1848-50 and published in 1851, sheet 230

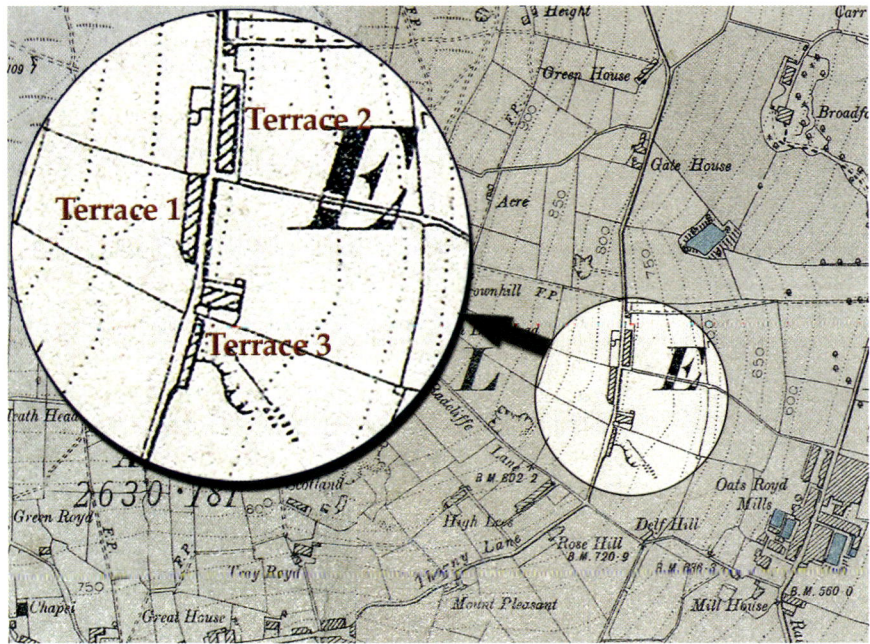

Figure 2   Second Edition Six Inch Ordnance Survey Map,
                  surveyed 1892 and published in 1894, sheet 230

Oats Royd House and land in 1846.[1] This purchase marks the start of the story of the three terraces because John Murgatroyd went on to establish Oats Royd Mills in 1847 in the nearby Luddenden valley. They were quickly successful, with a 'massive expansion' between 1850 and 1890,[2] and so in 1851 John Murgatroyd built a terrace of houses for his new workers at Oats Royd, close beside his mill. Soon after this he began to look for another site suitable for further housing.

The first terraces arrive

When Oats Royd Mill finally closed in 1983, a huge archive of documents was transferred to the West Yorkshire Archive Service and so we have an undated 'Specification for the carpentry and joinery work of ten cottages intended to be built at Thorney Lane by John Murgatroyd'.[3] These are now numbers 1 to 10 on the west side of the road: I have called them Terrace 1 (Figure 7)

When the Census Enumerator walked along the lane in 1851 there were no new buildings, but Terrace 1 had been completed by 1857 because, in that year, William Patchett of Luddenden signed a contract[4] to build twenty more (Terrace 2) and it specified that the windows and cupboards must be the 'same as at Thorney Lane'. Terrace 2, now demolished, contained numbers 11 – 30. Patchett received his final payment in April 1858, so the second terrace arrived quite quickly and all thirty houses were finished, and twenty-seven occupied, at the time of the 1861 Census.[5]

Terrace 1 was 'through houses' and Terrace 2 'back-to-backs', a type of housing which started in the late eighteenth century and was developed 'particularly in the Upper Calder valley'.[6] Numbers 11 to 20 (at the front, facing west) backed onto numbers 21 to 30 (facing east): back and front shared a common spine wall and were built under a single roof.

[1] S. Wade, Private communication, 2007

[2] C. Giles & I.H. Goodall, *Yorkshire Textile Mills: the Buildings of the Yorkshire Textile Industry 1770 – 1930*, London: H.M.S.O., 1992, p215

[3] West Yorkshire Archives Service (Calderdale), *Specification for the carpentry and joinery work of ten cottages intended to be built at Thorney Lane*, n.d., JM 549-554

[4] West Yorkshire Archives Service (Calderdale), *Contract for carpentry and joinery for 20 cottages at Thorney Lane*, 1857, JM 551

[5] This information is from the Census Enumerators' Returns, held at the Public Record Office, Series RG. Microfilm copies are available locally in Halifax Central Library

[6] L. Caffyn, *Workers' Housing in West Yorkshire 1750 – 1920*, London: H.M.S.O., 1986, p16

Figure 3   *An undated photograph of Terrace 1 (left) and Terrace 2 (right) from the south*

Figure 4   *View of Terrace 1 (left) from the south taken in 2007*

Figure 5 *An undated photograph of Terrace 3 (right) with Terraces 1 (left) and 2 (right) in the background. Taken from the south.*

Figure 6 *View of Terrace 3 (right) with Terrace 1 (left) in the background. Taken from the south in 2007*

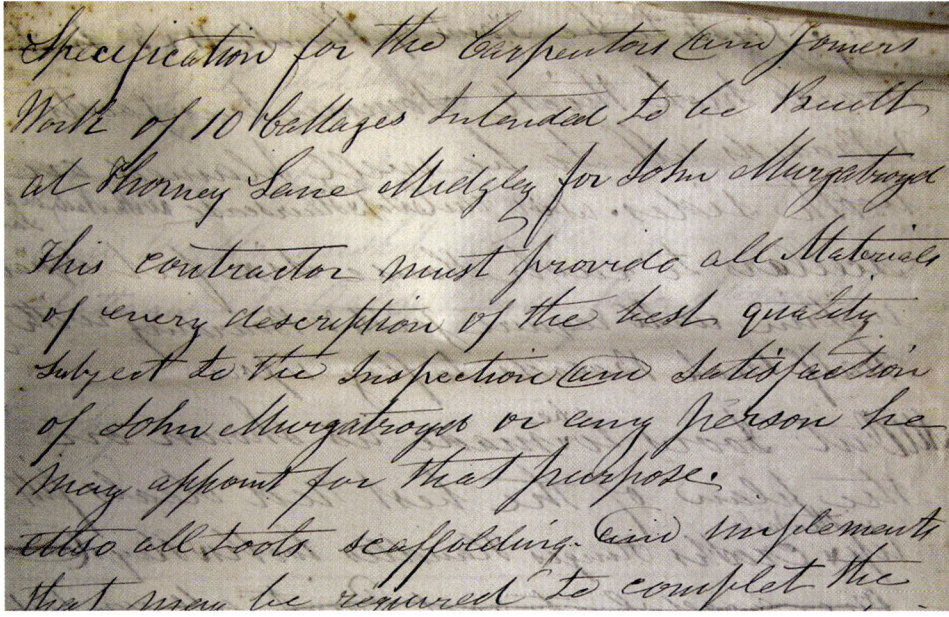

Figure 7   *Specification for carpenters and joiners work at 1 to 10 Thorney Lane*

Back-to-back houses were cheaper to build, economising on land and building materials. They were criticised by housing reformers in the later nineteenth and early twentieth century as overcrowded, ill-ventilated and unhealthy, although the worst conditions were caused by the density in which they were packed together in towns and cities by private speculative builders. However, several former residents of Terrace 2, still living in the area, have very happy memories of life there. So how do the criticisms apply to John Murgatroyd's Terrace 2?

Housing provided by employers in West Yorkshire was generally well-built.[7] After all, it represented a capital investment and, in some cases, included a philanthropic element. Indeed some local mill-owners created model villages near their mills, like Akroyden, Copley and West Hill Park in Halifax. Where did John Murgatroyd fit into this spectrum? Did he, in his haste to accommodate an increasing workforce, lower his standards between Terrace 1 and Terrace 2? We have only the carpentry and joinery specifications for both (none of the other trades) and a contract for gas fitting[8] but, using these, a comparison has been attempted. In both cases, the contractor 'must provide materials of every description of the best quality'.

---

[7] Caffyn, *Workers' Housing in West Yorkshire 1750 – 1920*, p68
[8] West Yorkshire Archives Service (Calderdale), *Estimate for gas fitting from James Alderson*, 1865, JM 549-554

Terrace 1	Terrace 2
Gas fitted in 1865 2 lights per house + 1 slide pendant	Gas in 1865 3 lights per house + 1 slide pendant
1 bedroom	1 bedroom + a garret
2 sash windows at front	2 sash windows + rollers for blinds 1 extra sash in 10 of the houses
Back window in bedroom	No back windows
No skylights	1 skylight per house (in garret)
Floorboards 1 inch thick 'All to be of the best red deals'	1 inch thick 'of good red deal'
Rails to each staircase	Rails to stairs, including to garret
Cellars 6 feet square	Cellars approx. 8 feet x 7 feet
Coat of good red paint on doors and good paint on windows	All doors & windows to have a coat of good red paint
Windows & cupboards	'Same as those in T Lane'
Roof ribs, door thicknesses	No differences
'Plain' doors inside & out	Outside door 'panelled in best St Petersburgs Deals' Garret door in 'best St John spruce deals'

As far as can be seen, therefore, from this limited information, it does not seem that, at least for the woodwork, Murgatroyd's second terrace was markedly inferior. In fact, at some time before 1901[9] he must have felt that it was Terrace 1 which was now below his desired standard, and the houses were extended at the back, adding a second bedroom and a scullery.

We have the architect's drawings from 1963,[10] when modern kitchens and bathrooms were installed, and in these we can see the original layout and the pre-1901 extensions (Figure 8). There are no comparable drawings for Terrace 2 as it was demolished at around this time. However, when he came to plan his third development in Thorney Lane, Murgatroyd decided to build to a dramatically higher standard.

---

[9] On the 1901 25" OS map the cottages have already been extended.

[10] West Yorkshire Archives Service (Calderdale), *Proposed alterations to 1-10 Thorney Lane, Midgley*, 1963, JM774

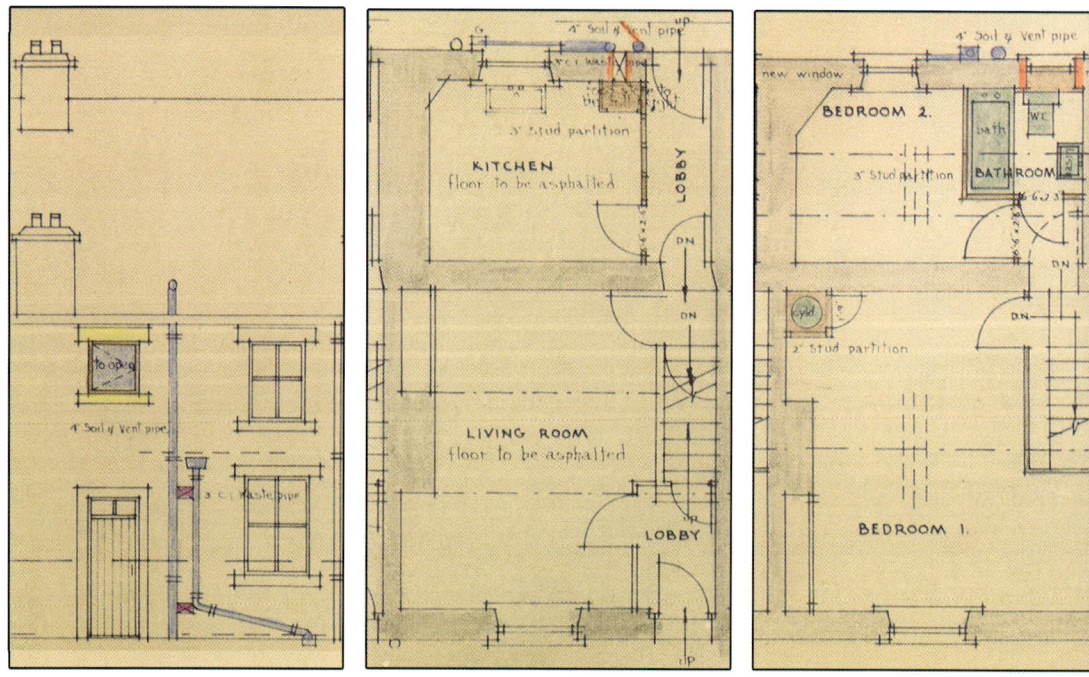

Figure 8   Architect's drawings of Terrace 1 made in 1963 when bathrooms were installed. Rear elevation (left), ground floor (middle), first floor (right).

The final terrace

Oats Royd Mill continued to expand, new sections being added between 1885 and 1887: at its peak in the early 1900s, 1,500 people were employed. It was at this point, after a gap of thirty-five years, that the 'New Houses' (still so described locally) were completed, south of the farm on the east side of the road, in 1894. They are the present numbers 34 to 40 (Terrace 3 on Figure 2) . This time he employed an architect, T Lister Patchett of Halifax, and indeed these houses are still of interest to architectural experts.

In 1982, Lucy Caffyn studied number 38 (the least altered internally) and commented that 'they may have been intended for the higher levels of workers (managers etc.) or else the builders had enlightened ideas about housing standards'.[11] In 1986, she produced 'Workers' Housing in West Yorkshire 1750 – 1920' for the Royal Commission on Historical Monuments, a standard reference work on the topic, and so was well-placed to make such comparisons. She points out that there was a growing recognition in the 1870s and 1880s of the desirability of improving the quality of workers' housing.

[11] Personal communication. L. Caffyn, *Handwritten notes, plans & section for 34-40 Thorney Lane*, 1982

Murgatroyd's contractor was instructed to 'clear away the present cottages and outbuildings, together with the back fence walling, garden walling, flagging and other work'. The slaters were to 'carefully take off slates and ridges to present roofing of buildings required to give place to new work'.[12] He had bought the land in 1879, 'in Messrs. Eastwood's Liquidation', and, although the map documenting that transaction shows no buildings to the south of the farm, there were in fact one or two old cottages there (Figure 1). In the 1891 Census two unoccupied houses are listed near the farm: these will be the ones awaiting demolition.

Terrace 3 was modernised in 1955 when new kitchens and bathrooms were installed but the architect's drawings from that time[13] also give us a picture of the original layout (Figure 9). An excellent set of specifications, tenders and bills[14] survives for Terrace 3, the 'Seven Through Houses' in Thorney Lane.

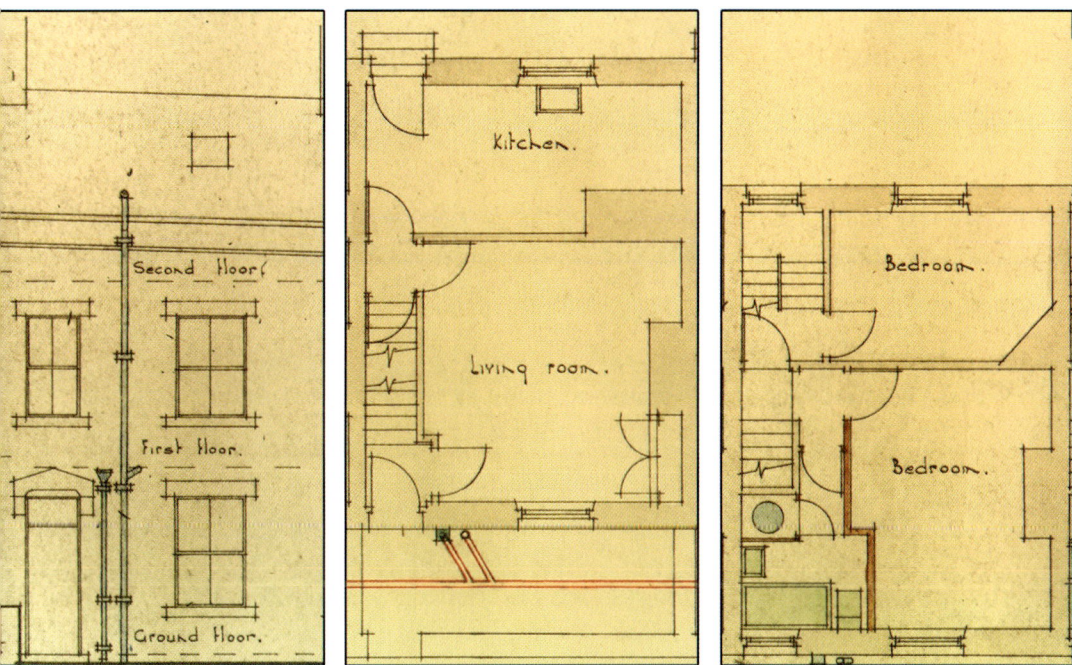

Figure 9   Architect's drawings of Terrace 3 made in 1955 when bathrooms were installed

---

[12] West Yorkshire Archives Service (Calderdale), *Specifications for Seven Through Houses for Excavators, Masons & Bricklayers*, 1892, JM 574-575

[13] West Yorkshire Archives Service (Calderdale), *Proposed improvements for Nos. 34-40 Thorny [sic] Lane*, 1955, JM 767

[14] West Yorkshire Archives Service (Calderdale), *Specifications for Seven Through Houses for Excavators, Masons & Bricklayers*, 1892, JM 574-575

Tenders were invited to be at the 'offices of the Architect, George Square Chambers, Halifax at on or before 12.00 noon on Friday, 22nd April 1892'. There were three bids for the work of the excavators, masons and bricklayers, seven for the slaters and plasterers, six for the plumbers and glaziers and four for the carpenters and joiners. It was clearly an attractive job for local firms.

Murgatroyd was not looking for all the cheapest tenders here: he chose the most expensive slater and plasterer (Thomas Alderson of Luddenden), and neither Thomas Pickles of Luddendenfoot (excavator and mason) nor Edwin Marsland (carpenter and joiner) had submitted the lowest tender. For these houses 'new stone will be provided by the proprietor' which reminds us that there were several quarries nearby, including one on Thorney Lane itself and from 1872 this quarry had belonged to Murgatroyd.[15] As we have details for only the carpentry and joinery work in numbers 1 to 30, it is not possible to make direct comparisons for the other trades, but here are some examples of the quality specified for 34 to 40. They were much bigger houses of three floors, with fireplaces in both bedrooms and both attics, a feature described by Lucy Caffyn as 'most unusual'.

The carpenters were to work in 'good, red memel timber' (a quality material from the Baltic town of Memel) and the joiners in 'good yellow pine sound, well-seasoned, free from sap, large knots, shakes and other defects'. Front and back doors were 2 inches thick with four panels, the front to have 'beaded transome & overlight with a mold planted across each front door transome'. In the living room there were cupboards with 'ebonised knobs & latches', sets of three drawers and some shelving, plus, at the top of the first flight of stairs, 'folding cupboard doors, beaded with brass knobs & locks'.

The wallstones are to be 'slightly tilted forward to keep out the weather'. This is a very clear reference to the practice of 'watershot' walling which is very common throughout the Pennines, although this is a rather late occurrence of it.

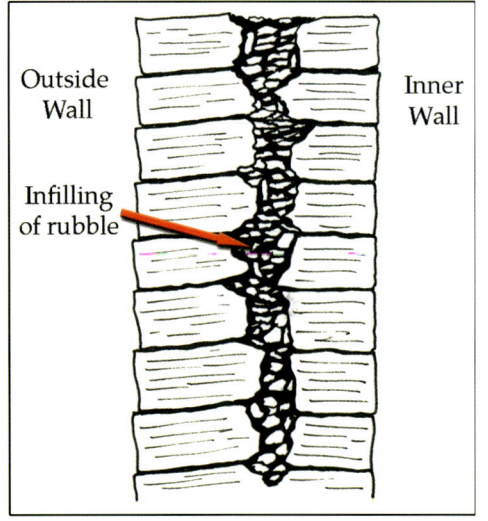

Figure 10   Watershot walling

---

[15] West Yorkshire Archives Service (Calderdale), *Valuation of the Township of Midgley 1865 plus Supplements*, 1872, HSB 5

The sculleries to have '5 inch slopstones, properly dished and drilled'. Slopstones were the forerunners of modern sinks, but much shallower: these seem to have been quite deep. The sculleries also had waste pipes from the sinks to an outside drain. Neither of these features was expected 'in the older type of house which was to be seen down to 1890'[16] in Midgley. Roofs were of 'good grey slate … to a lap of not less than 3 and a half inches' with 'redwood pegs … laid on good red laths'. Inside, 'best Baltic laths & hair mortar' were covered with '2 coats of plaster' except the cellar which was whitewashed.

The rooms had cornices and 'to each ceiling a centrepiece 2'6" in diameter in enriched plasterwork to an approved design'. Gas was fitted in all rooms and the contractor was to provide 'to each living room and sitting room … a good strong bronze sliding pendant with brass burners' and 'bronze gas brackets and burners' in the scullery, bedrooms and attics. Glass in the windows and skylights to be 'free from waves, twists and other defects' and laid in 'good old tough putty'.

This terrace has purely decorative features. The front doorheads are to be 'hollowed, splayed and filletted' and the front windowheads 'splayed, filletted and stopped'. Caffyn's report mentions the windows 'with coved lintels and projecting, chamfered cills' and the doors with 'fanlights and pointed lintels, moulded and given the effect of corbels'[17]. However, the lavatories, were still outside, in two blocks at either end of the terrace as in the earlier houses. Between September 1893 and March 1894 the contractors received their final payments and by March 1895 all the houses were occupied.

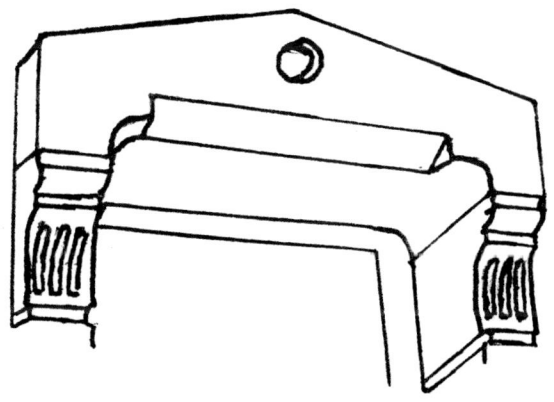

Figure 11   The decorative door lintel of Terrace 3

[16] H.W. Harwood, *Glimpses of Midgley History*, n.d., West Yorkshire Archive Service (Calderdale), MISC 78/54, Chapter 21, p 3

[17] Personal communication. L. Caffyn, *Handwritten notes, plans & section for 34-40 Thorney Lane*, 1982

Perhaps the rents Murgatroyd charged most objectively confirm the differences between his three terraces. We have a Rent Book[18] from 1895 to 1900. Terrace 1 cost 5s per fortnight (except number 1, which is slightly smaller). In Terrace 2, numbers 11 – 19 were 3s, number 20 was 5s (it had an extra room in 1901) and numbers 21 – 30 were 3s 6d. In 1898 the New Houses in Terrace 3 cost 8s except number 34 which was slightly bigger and cost 9s.

The most expensive houses in the Rent Book – and the only ones costing more than Thorney Lane – are Dean House New House (11s 6d) and No1, South Carr, New Road, Luddenden (10s). The cheapest are Pasture (1s 6d) and part of Gate Head, Luddenden (2s).

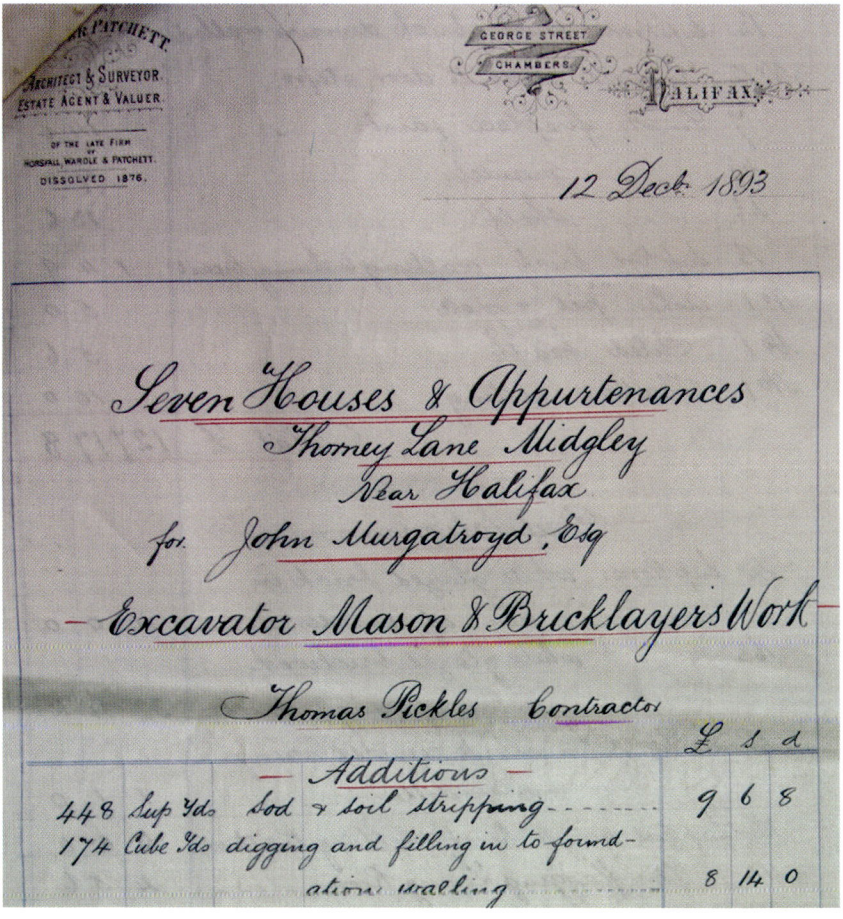

Figure 12   One of the bills for Terrace 3 from Thomas Pickles of Luddendenfoot

---

[18] West Yorkshire Archives Service (Calderdale), *Midgley Rent Book 1895-1900*, JM 280

New neighbours

Samuel Thomas at Thorney Lane Farm saw all the terraces going up. What did he think of the transformation of Thorney Lane? His father, another Samuel, was already farming there in 1830.[569] Samuel himself was born at the farm in 1845, and lived there for at least fifty-five years. The family combined running the farm (18 acres in 1851 and 16 in 1861) with working at Oats Royd. Samuel was, no doubt, on friendly terms with some of his new neighbours (his son Albert, for instance, had moved into one of the terraces by 1901) but we can imagine his reaction to the Thorney Lane Roughs who, in 1882, left large stones and umbrella wires in a field ready for harvesting to spoil the scythes, and shortly before 11 October went through the village challenging people, 'Come out and you shall smell hellfire, at once: we neither care for young Jack or old Jack'.[570]

Who came to live in the first thirty new houses?

For a picture of the newcomers we have to look at the Census for 1861. Many were from nearby villages and none from further afield than Halifax. Using the places where they had lived immediately before coming to Thorney Lane, there were two families from elsewhere in Midgley, ten from Warley, eight from Wadsworth, one from Heptonstall and the rest came from Halifax. Three properties were unoccupied in 1861 and one family had two houses, using part of the second as a grocery shop. Altogether, 170 people were living in the two terraces, which gives an average of 6.3 per household. In one of the back-to-backs was a family of eleven (parents plus nine children) and a group of nine lived in one of the houses in Terrace 1: there were, however, two households with only two residents. Parents and their children composed most groups living together, but the Census also recorded a sister-in-law, two parents-in-law, a step daughter, a grandchild and a grandfather.

Almost everyone worked at Oats Royd Mill, as you would expect, the largest group being forty-four worsted spinners and thirty-six worsted weavers. There were two overlookers, one in each terrace, and twenty-two in other wool or worsted occupations. Cotton was also processed at Oats Royd and four Thorney Lane people worked on that as did one mixture weaver. Three men worked at the quarry, a husband and wife ran the grocery shop, and one

---

[569] W. Parson and W. White, *Directory of the Borough of Leeds, the City of York and the Clothing District of Yorkshire*, Leeds: the authors, 1830, p478

[570] *Hebden Bridge Times*, September & October 1882 especially 11 October 1882, p6. I am indebted to John Billingsley for this information

iron moulder, one joiner, one clogger, one machinist, one cart driver, one cordwainer and one highway labourer were also recorded.

As families grew up and some people moved out, the residents of 1 – 30 began to come from a wider area. In 1871 there were new people from Thornton, Bradford, Lancashire and Derbyshire: by 1891, people from Pocklington, Folkestone and Stroud had moved in and more variety in jobs developed. In 1871 we have a 'Knitter' (aged seventy-nine), a woolsorter and local preacher, a stoker and a butcher: in 1881 a dressmaker, a paper maker, a gamekeeper and a plasterer: in 1891, a tailor's apprentice, a journeyman tailor and tailoress, a pupil teacher at the board school, two more dressmakers, and one newspaper reporter.

Who arrived with the 'New Houses' of 1894?

We have John Murgatroyd's rent book covering the period 1895 to 1900 and, apart from that, we have to wait for the Census of 1901. The clerk at Oats Royd Mill was methodical and started his indexed rent books with the thirty houses in Thorney Lane, in number order, followed by all the firm's other properties in Midgley. He obviously could not slot the new houses into his neat system and had to start a new page for them, at the back. It shows considerable movement: number 34 had had five different tenants by 1901 as had number 38, and number 36 had already had four changes by 1900. Only number 40 kept its original tenants until at least 1901.

In the 1901 Census only five of the houses were inhabited. Mary Addison, a widow of fifty-nine, was from Ayr in Scotland, but all her six children (youngest aged twelve) were born in British India. John Widdup came from Warley and his wife from Lincolnshire: all their children (except Joseph, aged one) were born in Leeds. Joseph Round from Dudley in Worcestershire and his wife, from Lincoln, had lived in Newark, Nottinghamshire where their older children were born but had moved to Halifax at least five years before. Annie Horsfall, wife of William from Midgley, came from Penrith, Cumberland. In the Wilkinson family both parents were local (from Sowerby and Midgley) and their five year old had been born in Mytholmroyd. Four of the tenants were men who had married wives from outside Yorkshire and, in three cases, these families had already moved areas once or twice. Perhaps this shows, although in a very small sample, the increasing mobility of the workforce and the attraction of Oats Royd Mill for families from further afield.

		HOUSES								

The undermentioned Houses are situate within the Boundaries of the

[or Township] of	City or Municipal Borough of	Municipal Ward of	Parliamentary Borough of	Town or Village or Hamlet of	Urban Sanitary District of	Rural Sanitary District of	Ecclesi
idgley					Midgley	Lud

ROAD, STREET, &c., and No. or NAME of HOUSE	HOUSES In-habit-ed	Un-in-habited (U.) or Building (B.)	NAME and Surname of each Person	RELATION to Head of Family	CON-DITION as to Marriage	AGE last Birthday of Males / Females	Rank, Profession, or OCCUPATION	WHERE BORN	
Thorney Lane	1		John Sutcliffe	Head	Mar	32		Worsted Weaver	Midgley in the C. of York
Do			Emma Do	Wife	Mar	30	Do Black Weft Minder	Wadsworth Yk
Do			Emma Do	Daur		6	Scholar	Pellon Halifax Do
Do			Sarah A Do	Do		2		Midgley Do
Do	1		John Widdop	Head	Mar	69	Worsted Weaver	Wadsworth Do
"			Marah Do	Wife	Do	71		Do Do
"			Dan Do	Son	Unm	40	Mason	Do Do
"			Eliza Do	Daur	Do	34	Worsted Reeler	Do Do
"	1		Nathaniel Bridley	Head	Mar	44	Butcher	Par of Halifax Do
"			Sarah Do	Wife	Mar	34		Do Do
"			Maranda Do	Daur	Unm	26	Mill Hand	Do Do
"			Sam Do	Son		21	White Smith	Do Do
"			Mary J Do	Daur	Do	18	Mill Hand	Do Do
"			Sarah A Do	Do	Do	14	Do	Do Do
"			Matilda Do	Do		11	Do	Do Do
"			Hannah Do	Grau Do		2		Do Do
"	1		Garnett Hartley	Head	Mar	30	Worsted Weaver	Ovenden Do
"			Achsah Do	Wife	Do	34	Do Reeler	Do Do
"	1		Joseph Maude	Head	Mar	36	Iron Overlooker	Midgley Do
"			Mary Do	Wife	Mar	36	Weaver	Wadsworth Do
"			Ann E. Do	Daur		11	Scholar	Midgley Do
"			John W. Do	Son		9	Do	Do Do
"	1		Mary Schofield	Head	W	34	Worsted Weaver	Do Do
"			Grace E. Do	Daur		9	Scholar	Do Do
Total of Houses... 6				Total of Males and Females... 8 / 16					

Figure 13   Census Enumerator's Returns for 1881 for part of Thorney Lane, including Garnett and Achsah Hartley's house

Did Murgatroyd intend to let the larger houses to larger families?

The Widdups had eight children and a boarder, but the Horsfall household was only three adults and a boarder. The Wilkinsons had two sisters-in-law and a niece living with them as well as their son: the remaining two households were of seven people and six people. Two houses had boarders, but then at this time there were two boarders, two sisters, two mothers-in-law, one niece and five grandchildren living with families in the older terraces. The five occupied houses had thirty-three residents, giving an average of 6.6, which is slightly higher than the 5.08 figure for the other terraces in 1901.

Was Terrace 3 for managers?

Not in 1901. In the New Houses were one worsted spinning overlooker, eight worsted spinners, four worsted drawers and five in other textile occupations with a stoker and a carter from the mill. The painter, the tailoress–fustian, the fustian dyer and clerk, and the cotton velvet weaver may have worked elsewhere. At Terraces 1 and 2 most tenants were still mill-workers, but the two overlookers, the school attendance officer, the pupil teacher and the rate collector might have been seen as having higher-level jobs than most of the new arrivals.

Also some people moved between the old and new terraces. In 1901 Miranda Priestley was living with her brother-in-law's family in Terrace 3, but previously her home had been in Terrace 2 for at least twenty years. Eli Fielding, who had previously lived in the new houses, had moved with his family to Terrace 2 by 1901.

Some Thorney Lane families and individuals

James Garnett was born in Midgley in 1821 and in 1841 was living at Lane Top with his widowed mother Mary, his sister Sarah and his older brother John. James, Sarah and John were worsted weavers and were still living with Mary, now aged seventy-three, in 1851. By 1861, James had married Mary Ann, from Wadsworth, and they had moved into Terrace 2 bringing Mary Ann's parents (both seventy-four and retired farmers from Heptonstall) to live with them. She already had a daughter aged fifteen, Sarah, who came with her from Wadsworth and she and James had a daughter of their own – Ellen, aged three. By 1901 Mary Ann (now a widow aged seventy-nine) was still in the same house with Sarah (fifty-five) and Ellen (forty-two), who had both worked at the mill all their lives, James having died between 1881 and 1891. So this family were in Thorney Lane for at least sixty years.

There were probably many romances and marriages amongst the tenants but it is not always easy to work these out owing to the frequency of some surnames and the limited range of popular Christian names. However, Garnett Hartley and Achsah Rushworth have such unusual names that we can trace their story. Both came from Ovenden, Garnett aged ten and Achsah fourteen, with their respective families by 1861. His father was William, a widower with five sons and a daughter, who brought his father (a retired farmer aged eighty-one). Garnett's older brother Henry moved out into one of the other back-to-backs on marrying. He had eight children by 1891 and the whole family (except

Frances Ann, an apprentice dressmaker) worked at the mill. Achsah's parents had three daughters and two sons: her older sister Ellen is recorded by the Census Enumerator as 'Blind' with 'No employment'. All the workers in both households were at Oats Royd except for one of the Hartley brothers – a stone mason. In 1871, Garnett and Achsah are still single and living with their parents, but ten years later (now aged thirty and thirty-four) they are married and living in the Rushworths' old house (Figure 13). Achsah's brother Milford has also married and moved out into one of the other back-to-backs with his young family. By now there is no mention of the other Rushworths, but Milford has named his three year old after Ellen. Garnett and Achsah, who seem to have had no children, worked at the mill. In December 1880, he is listed in the Oats Royd weavers book, which records the fortnightly wages.[21] Each fortnight is recorded on two different pages, probably for two different types of work. Garnett earned 10s plus 15s 2d for the first half of December. In the second fortnight he earned 6s plus 10s 10d. Achsah is in the 1891 wages book, described as a Reeler. In two weeks she earned 17s 2d. Her husband died some time after 1895 and so the 1901 Census records Achsah, a widow of fifty-four, living alone and 'living on own means'.

Finally, there were two interesting individuals in Terrace 2. In 1901, Marion Walton, aged eighteen and born in Midgley, whose family moved to Thorney Lane some time before 1881, was a pupil teacher. William Howarth, a worsted weaver, brought his wife and five children to the new terraces in 1861 and continued at the mill until at least the age of sixty-six. But ten years later, now a widower, he told the Census enumerator of 1891 that he was a newspaper reporter and, in 1901, a 'Correspondant'. A trade directory of 1901 mentions him as the 'School Attendance Officer'.[22] Unlike all the other tenants, who had their rent taken out of their fortnightly wages, he paid in cash for six months at a time.

And what happened to the other Thorney Lane buildings?

In 1871, the Midgley Township Board passed John Murgatroyd's plans for a new farm with two cottages attached and, the following year, for a new barn and mistal.[23] The contractor was instructed to 'pull down the present farmhouse and adjoining building'. Included in the conditions for letting the

---

[21] West Yorkshire Archives Service (Calderdale), *Murgatroyds' Weavers Book*, 1880-81, JM103
[22] *Post Office Directory of the West Riding of Yorkshire*, London: Kelly & Co., 1901, p630
[23] West Yorkshire Archives Service (Calderdale), *Midgley Township Board Minute Book*, 1871-1872, SOW 18. Entry for March 1871, p94

re-built farm to Samuel Thomas[24] was the clause that he must 'permit the peaceable occupation' of the cottages by any tenant approved by Murgatroyd. Perhaps Samuel had been objecting to some of the Thorney Lane Roughs as neighbours? These houses are now numbers 31 and 32, with the farmhouse being number 33.

Built into a wall in the area which was known as Lane Top is a datestone of 1779, which is likely to have come from some demolished buildings there. By 1830 there were definitely four cottages and the owner, at least until 1863, was a member of the Thomas family so they may have had links to the farm. In 1851 there were still 6 handloom weavers at Lane Top (two are described as handloom carpet weavers) as well as five powerloom weavers. By 1861, only William Garnett, a widower of sixty-four, is still working by hand and by 1901 he is described as an agricultural labourer. Indeed, in 1861 there were still two handloom weavers in Terrace 2, aged seventy-one and forty-six. As the lane filled up with terraces, some of the old cottages at Lane Top continued to be inhabited. Only two were recorded in 1881 and by 1891 they had disappeared. The small structure marked in 1895 (Figure 2) must have been used for animals.

Glancing at the sepia photographs of Thorney Lane (Figures 3 and 5) it might be tempting to conclude that life in the later Victorian period proceeded with uninterrupted tranquillity. However, this study shows that nothing could be further from the truth; families came and went with extraordinary rapidity. Equally, the three terraces on which this study concentrates might easily be dismissed as just ordinary houses, yet subject to detailed study together with a surviving archive they have much to reveal about one of the most common types of housing in the district.

---

[24] West Yorkshire Archives Service (Calderdale), *Conditions of the letting of Thorney Lane Farm to Mr Samuel Thomas residing on the same farm*, 1873, JM 563

CHAPTER 22

Village Trades and Services in the Victorian Era

David Cant, Merial Evans, Pauline Ford,
Hannah Palfreeman and Chris Toole

Trade Directories

The earliest trade directory was published in 1677 by Samuel Lees of London, as a list of City merchants. However, it was not until the Industrial Revolution of the late eighteenth century that trade directories appeared in the provinces as a guide to commerce and potential customers alike. Sometimes they covered a whole county and sometimes an individual town, in which case more local information was given. The first trade directory to deal only with Halifax and district was Walkers Directory of the Parish of Halifax, published in 1845.

These books are a valuable resource for researchers, listing tradespeople and employers in categories and in alphabetical order, with their addresses. Many also give a brief history of the area, details of local services (such as transport, carriers and postal services) and names of prominent local inhabitants. Some include maps, street names and advertisements, which are full of interest and information.

Directories, therefore, give an insight into the lifestyle of earlier times, while those of different dates show how local towns or villages changed over a period of years, especially with regard to the development or decline of various trades. It must be remembered, however, that this information may be out of date, inaccurate or incomplete, depending on the ability of the complier and the time taken to research and produce the publication. Nevertheless, trade directories provide a fascinating insight into the life of a community, giving information that is readily accessible and not easily gained from other sources.

As local directories focused on centres of population, the growing urban areas of Mytholmroyd and Luddendenfoot were given separate entries, in addition to Midgley and Luddenden. In order to give as full a picture as possible, all these areas have been included, as parts of both Mytholmroyd and Luddenden lay in Midgley township. Where possible, additional information has been added from the decennial Census.

White's Directory, 1838 [1]

Of the thirty shopkeepers listed, five were butchers and the rest were grocers. Although we can only speculate what goods were stocked by the latter, it seems safe to assume that most foodstuffs would be produced locally and the variety would be limited, especially as only primitive refrigeration was available and methods of preserving were still very basic. As most clothing was homemade at this time, cloth and other drapery items might well have been stocked by some grocers, as no draper's shop is recorded.

There were, surprisingly, eighteen producers of footwear, classed as boot and shoe or clog makers, rather than retailers. This seems a high number, even allowing for footwear being frequently repaired and patched. Some of the trades listed have now virtually disappeared, such as wheelwright, blacksmith, cornmiller, bookbinder and coal merchant. Interestingly, the wheelwright was a woman, Elizabeth Alderson, probably a widow employing workmen. Post offices at Luddenden Foot and Mytholmroyd were both run by women, presumably at home, where letters arrived at 8am and were collected at 5pm. Just two years after this directory was published, a standard charge of one penny per letter was introduced, using the famous Penny Black stamp.

The importance of the textile industry in this area is reflected by the number of people involved in it. There were nineteen worsted manufacturers and five worsted spinners, together with two woollen manufacturers. Numbers for cotton were almost as high; fourteen manufacturers, including two of fustian and three who were only spinners. There were still handloom weavers working in their own cottages under the 'putting out' system, whereby the production of cloth was organised by clothiers, who gave out wool and collected the finished pieces. It is not possible to know exactly what the situation was in the Midgley township, but some manufacturers were certainly based at Brearley Mill, Dean Mill and Mill House. In fact these buildings must have been centres of industry, as several manufacturers are located at each.

Besides those directly employed in the production of cloth, there were seven

---

[1] W. White, *History, Gazetteer and Directory of the West Riding of Yorkshire,* Vol 2, Sheffield: the author, 1838

men with related jobs. There was one representative of each of the following trades: overseer, machine maker, he'd (huddle) maker, spindle and flyer maker, wool comb maker, reed and heald maker, and fustian cutter and dyer. None of the locations for these men mention mills, but only give areas.

In the category of professions, we have just six entries. There are two schoolmasters, at Luddenden and Sowerby respectively; one minister of the Independent persuasion, the Rev Joseph Massey at Booth and the other, a Weslyan, in Sowerby; two surgeons, one at White Lee and the other, James Crabtree of no given address. Exactly what the term surgeon covered in the first half of the nineteenth century is difficult to assess.

All farmers but one are listed in the Midgley section of the directory, although no farms are named and no locality given for five of them, including Martha Garnett, the only woman. Jonathan Stansfield, farming in Erringden, is the exception. Also associated with farming are two cattle dealers.

Tanning seems to have been carried on as family concerns by the Akeds and the Appleyards. Their tanneries can be seen on the Ordnance Survey map of 1851 at Ellen Royd, White Lee and Kershaw House. There were also four quarry owners. On the same map four sandstone delfs are marked at Foster Clough, a number on Low Moor and several more scattered around the hillside, which is not surprising, as all the buildings in the township are of stone. The third industry was carried out by Jonathan Bracken of Dean Mill, who combined his occupation of paper manufacturer with that of cotton spinner.

Altogether ten inns are listed, along with five beer houses, which were private dwellings licensed to sell beer, but not spirits. All the beer houses were run by men, but four of the innkeepers were women. Two of the taverns shared the name of Lord Nelson, one in Midgley, the other in Luddenden, doubtless in celebration of the English victory at the battle of Trafalgar in 1805.

Only four persons seem to qualify as gentry, entered with no trade or occupation. These are Stn (Stephen) Fawcett, gent, of Hanroyd, Mr Jth (Jonathan) Morley of Sowerby and Mrs Hannah Briggs also of Sowerby. While Thomas Foster of Brearley is listed as maltster, his wife or mother has the title Mrs, so appears to be classed as gentry in her own right. No wives are listed for any other tradesman or manufacturer.

White's Directory, 1853 [2]

Forty-one shopkeepers are listed in all. There are sixteen grocers and one butcher at Mytholmroyd and twenty grocers and three butchers in Midgley. Three of the grocers at Midgley are women. One of these, Susanna Eastwood of Luddenden Foot also kept the Red Lion, and at Mytholmroyd Mary Southwell also kept a beerhouse in Wadsworth. Of the eleven grocers who are found in the Midgley Census of 1851, eight appear in the Directory. This is obviously a trade which the compilers felt would be useful to include in their Directory. This was not true of all occupations, as will be shown later in the case of farmers. The one other retailer is a chemist and druggist.

There still is a large number of boot and shoemakers and cloggers: ten boot and shoemakers at Mytholmroyd, of whom four were also cloggers; at Midgley, three boot and shoe makers and four cloggers. There are six blacksmiths, four at Midgley and two at Mytholmroyd; seven joiners, and three tailors. Other trades are: one plumber and glazier; one tinner and brazier; two coal merchants; two station merchants; two post offices; one hairdresser, and one carrier. The wheelwright and bookbinder of the previous directory are no longer there.

The number of manufacturers has decreased from forty-three to twenty-six since the 1838 directory. It seems unlikely that this shows any decrease in the importance of textiles. More probably it means that many of the smaller manufacturers have gone out of business, and the work tends to be concentrated in fewer hands. Those mentioned comprise five cotton spinners and manufacturers; four fustian manufacturers; sixteen worsted manufacturers and one woollen manufacturer. The 1851 Census for Midgley reveals what a network of operatives in the textile trade supported the manufacturers. Over two hundred factory operatives are listed and more than fifty other specifically woollen factory operatives, together with one hundred and twenty power loom weavers. There were also still about one hundred and twenty hand loom weavers. None of this can of course be gathered from the trade directories, as it is not their function. The trades that relate to the textile industry are: machine maker; wool comb maker; reedmaker; fustian cutter; dyer and dyer and finisher.

The number of ministers of religion has risen to four. The Independent

---

[2] W. White, *Directory and Gazetteer of Leeds, Bradford ... and the whole of the Clothing Districts of Yorkshire,* Sheffield: the author, 1853

minister at Booth and the Wesleyan in Sowerby remain. The incumbent of Luddenden and the Rev. Wm. Baldwin (denomination not given) have been added. There are also two schoolmasters, a surgeon and a clerk.

Of the fourteen farmers listed, twelve are in the Midgley section. The farms listed range in area from sixteen acres to sixty acres. Many other farms appear in the Census, but not in the Directory. Some have a smaller area than this, but many have significant acreage, e.g.Thomas Lacy of Ewood Hall, farmer of fifty-six acres, who does not appear.

Two of the tanners remain, as do four quarry owners, and Jonathan Bracken of Dean Mill, paper manufacturer. There is also a stone mason at Hawksclough, and two millers, Hartley and John Murgatroyd and William Thompson.

There are five inns at Mytholmroyd, one of these, the Shoulder of Mutton, being run by a woman, with the only beerhouse also run by a woman. At Midgley there are six inns, two of which are run by women, and five beerhouses, all run by men.

The number of gentry has risen from four to eleven, a sign, perhaps, of increasing prosperity in the area. Those listed for Mytholmroyd are: James Appleyard; Samuel Briggs; Mr. Thomas Uttley Fielden; Mr. George Greenwood; Mr. Robert Halstead; Thomas E and William Walker. Those from Midgley are: Thomas Foulds of Dean House; Samuel Milne of Gordon Bank; Mr. Richard Murgatroyd of Greave House; and John and Thomas Riley.

Kelly's Directory, 1861 [3]

Between 1851 and 1861, the population of Midgley had increased by 17.75 per cent, from 2,438 to 2,871 people, of which 552 were children of eight years of age or less, many of whom were already working, at least part time

By 1861 there were only thirty-two shopkeepers in Midgley and Mytholmroyd, nine fewer than in 1853 but serving a larger population, so one wonders if travel to Halifax had become a viable alternative for specialist shopping. Nineteen Midgley shops sold an unspecified range of goods, probably everything needed in the locality. There were two druggists, three butchers and three drapers. The 1861 Census lists six drapers, some of whom were also grocers.

---

[3] *Post Office Directory of the West Riding of Yorkshire*, London: Kelly & Co., 1861

MIDGLEY is a village on a lofty eminence and a mountainous moorland township, containing a scattered population, and parts of the villages of Mythomroyd, Luddenden, and Luddenden foot; the two latter being principally in the adjoining township of Warley. Midgley township forms a part of the north side of the Vale of Calder, and is in the parish and union of Halifax, Morley wapentake, Halifax deanery, Craven archdeaconry, and Ripon diocese, and the western division of the West Riding. It is 5½ miles west from Halifax, 7 east from Todmorden, 27 north-east from Manchester, and three-quarters north-west from the railway station at Luddenden foot. The church, St. Mary's, in a picturesque dell at Luddenden, is a neat stone structure in the Gothic style, with square tower and 1 bell, and has side aisles and a chancel. The living is a perpetual curacy, worth £170 yearly, with residence, in the gift of the Vicar of Halifax, and held by the Rev. James Nelson, B.A. The Independents have a chapel at Booth, and the New Connexion Methodists at Midgley. Here are also some extensive cotton and worsted mills, and a paper mill. The population, in 1851, was 2,393, and in 1861 it was 2,842, and the acreage is 2,628, nearly half of which is uncultivated. Thomas Riley, Esq. of Ewood Hall, is lord of the manor. The charities amount to nearly £40 per annum, which is distributed weekly in bread among poor widows.

Aked William, esq. Ellen Royd
Appleyard James, esq. White Lee
Clay James, esq, Middle foot
Crossley Daniel, esq. Upper White Lee
Fielding Lewis, esq. Brier hey
Foulds Mrs. Dean house
Jones Rev. David [Independent] Booth
Milne Mr. Samuel, Gooden bank
Murgatroyd Mr. Richard, Greave house
Norris J. E. esq. Brearley
Riley James, esq. Brearley house
Riley Thomas, esq. Ewood hall
Titterington Mr. Thomas, Greave
Wilcock Mrs. Field house

COMMERCIAL.

Ainley George, farmer, Catherine house
Aked James & Sons, worsted manfactrs. Kershaw house & Pellon lane, Halifax
Aked William, farmer, Ellen royd
Alderson James, plumber & glazier, Diamond house
Atkinson Samuel & Son, woollen manufacturers, Brearley mill
Bann John, farmer, Gate house
Bedford George, *Shoulder of Mutton*
Bedford Wm. *Red Lion*, Luddenden foot
Beverley Susannah (Mrs.), stone merchant & quarry owner
Bloomer Thomas, farmer, Dean house
Boardall Abraham, shopkeeper
Bracken Jonathan & Sons, paper manufacturers, Dean mills
Bracken Mary (Miss), shopkeeper, Dean mills
Brown Arthur, *Mill inn*, Brearley mill
Butterworth Wm. blcksmth. Luddenden
Chew Ellis & Son, tailors, Pepper hill
Clayton Joseph, grocer & draper, Spring house, Luddenden foot
Clayton Joseph, plain & fancy worsted & cotton manufactrs. Luddenden foot
Cockroft Richard, academy, Ewood
Crossley Grace & Hannah (Misses), farmers, New heath head
Crossley Thos. wood turner, Hoyle bank
Crowther John, boot & shoe maker, Pepper hill

Crowther William, farmer, Lydgate
Eastwood John (executors of), worsted spinner & manufacturer, Mill house & Pepper hill mills, Luddenden
Fielding Lewis, surgeon, Brier hey
Fletcher Henry, stone merchant & farmer, Handroyd
Fletcher John, farmer, Stoneyroyd
Fletcher Wm. beer retailer, Pepper hill
Foster John, worsted manufacturer, Lower Ewood
Foster William, farmer & wool sorter
Greenwood George, farmer, High house
Greenwood Henry, grocer & post office, Luddenden foot
Greenwood Thomas, cotton manufacturer, Luddenden foot
Greenwood Thos. farmer, Castle Carr
Greenwood Thos. shopkpr. Carr house
Greenwood Wm. clogr. Luddenden foot
Hartley William Henry, beer retailer, Grove, Brearley
Harwood Jas. whitesmith & shopkeeper
Harwood Wm. whitesmith, Railhouse la
Horsfall William & Co. cotton spinners, Delph mill, Luddenden foot
Horsfall Henry Rusher, rent & debt collector, news agent, beer retailer, & agent to Family Endowment life insurance, Luddenden foot
Horsfield John & William, machine makers, Luddenden foot
Horsfield Christopher, farmer, Trayroyd
Horsfield John, sen. joiner & wheelwright, Luddenden foot
Horsfield Jonathan, coal merchant & farmer, New house
Howarth James, boot & shoe maker
Ibbotson John, fellmonger & farmer, Upper Ewood
Ingham William, farmer & cattle dealer, Hawks Clough
Jackson Richd. beer retailer, White Lee
King Samuel, gardener, Lane house
Midgley John, *Woodman*, Booth
Midgley Robert, stone merchant & quarry owner, Booth

Midgley Robert, sen. farmer, Booth
Murgatroyd John, worsted spinner & manfctr. Oates royd mills, Luddenden
Nicholl John, shopkeeper, Luddenden
Ogden & Lumb, worsted spinners & manufacturers, Brearley
Ogden John, spindle & fly maker, Holmhouse bridge
Pickles William, stonemason & shopkeeper, Lane ends
Radcliffe William, farmer & shopkeeper, High Lee head
Rothwell John, machine maker, Holmhouse bridge
Scott John, farmer, Great house
Shackleton John, butcher
Shackleton Thos. farmer, Fearney Lee
Smith James, butcher & shopkeeper
Smith James, farmer, High Lees
Stansfield Wm. shopkpr. Mnt. Pleasant
Stell James, farmer, Lane ends
Sutcliffe Frederick, clogger, Lane ends
Sutcliffe John, beer retailer
Tatham John, farmer, Arrowbut Lee
Thomas David, clogger
Thomas Dyson, sub-post office, boot & shoe maker, & shopkeeper, Luddenden
Thomas Richard, farmer & assistant overseer, Bloomer gate
Thomas Samuel, farmer, Thorney lane
Tillotson John, greengrocer, Luddenden foot
Walker William, coal merchant & shopkeeper
Walton John, stone merchant & farmer
Walton Thomas, farmer
Whitehead Eli, farmer, Broadfold
Widdup Mary (Mrs.), *Lord Nelson* & shopkeeper
Woodhead Robert, coal merchant & joiner, Luddenden foot
Woodhead Wm. boot & shoe maker, Millhouse
Wormald Jonas, clogger & shopkeeper, Luddenden
Wormald Ruth (Miss), *Lord Nelson*, Luddenden

Post Office, Luddenden foot—Henry Greenwood receiver. Letters are received through Manchester; arrive at 7 a.m.; dispatched at 7 p.m. through Halifax; arrive at 12.30 p.m.; dispatched at 9.30 p.m.

Sub-Post Office, Luddenden—Dyson Thomas, receiver Letters are received from Luddenden foot There is also a Receiving Box at Brearley
Railway Station, Luddenden foot—Abraham Hirst, master

Figure 1   The entry for Midgley in Kelly's trade directory of 1861

There are four grocers' shops but the Census lists twenty-six men as grocers as well as several grocers' wives, so it seems that many people combined a grocery business with another trade (particularly textiles or agriculture) which may have confused the compilers of Kelly's Trade Directory. Despite the fact that many families would have grown their own produce, Kelly claims one greengrocer but this is not substantiated in the 1861 Census, in which the only 'greengrocer' is a visitor. Although at least one Co-operative society was established by 1861, there is no reference to one in the 1861 Trade Directory, perhaps because it had only been established in that year..

In Midgley and Mytholmroyd, a wide range of services were provided by forty-nine businesses, although there was some duplication. Even though many families would have patched their own footwear there were thirteen footwear businesses, all of which were in Midgley. They probably repaired shoes and clogs as well as supplying new ones, whether made to measure on the premises or factory-made elsewhere. Other services included six tailors, one hairdresser and crucial to the expansion of trade, the Post Office and the Station. Apart from two joiners, two plumbers and glaziers and a gardener, most of the other contemporary trades have almost disappeared; the whitesmith, blacksmith, wood turner, woodman and the wheelwright. Two farmers declared themselves to be stone merchants, which is hardly surprising given the number of quarries indicated on maps of the area. This is backed up by the 1861 Census, which records over twenty stone barers, delvers, masons and an apprentice as well as five quarrymen and two flag dressers. There were four coal merchants in Midgley but none in Mytholmroyd, yet maps indicate coal yards beside the railway line. Many manufacturers would have been using coal-fired steam power by 1861. Other services were a rent and debt collector and a life insurance agent, John Crabtree of Luddenden Foot, who was also a farmer, newsagent and beer retailer, so it is questionable how successful he was at any of these trades.

There had been a further decline in the number of textile firms listed in 1853, but those that remained may well have been larger, vertically integrated, firms carrying out all processes from the raw material to the finished cloth. There were equal numbers of cotton and worsted manufacturers, with two woollen and one fustian manufacturer. By 1861, these probably all used steam power for some processes. Coal was brought in and finished goods exported to Manchester or Leeds along the Rochdale Canal or by the Lancashire and Yorkshire Railway.

Despite the contraction in the number of textile firms, several spinning firms continued to flourish. There were four cotton-spinning firms, three worsted spinners and one spinning worsted and mixed yarns. These and the cloth weaving firms must have created a demand for spare parts and machine repairs. One spindle and fly maker is listed in the Trade Directory, the Census listing a family of four living at the same address as spindle-makers. One reed maker was listed in Kelly's Trade Directory.

William Henry Hartley was minister of Booth Independent chapel but the Reverend Jones also lived at Booth, his church or chapel unspecified. John Rothwell of White Lee was the only surgeon in the area although there were druggists in Midgley and Mytholmroyd. There would appear to have been three schools; the 'Academy' at Ellen Royd, the 'Ladies Boarding School' at Brearley, but the third a boys' school run as a secondary occupation by a worsted spinner. If the teaching was of secondary importance to the teacher, perhaps he was teaching half-timers.

In the 1861 Trade Directory, there are twenty-three farmers listed which is barely half of the forty-three named as farmers in the Census. However, a majority were small-holders for whom another form of employment was probably necessary. One farmer of twenty-three acres employed 638 hands; however, Emma Ratcliffe was also a worsted-spinning manufacturer. As she was visiting Lacey Hey on the day of the Census, these activities may relate to another part of the country.

Other industries in the area included two quarry owners, two machine makers one boiler composition manufacturer, one pattern maker, an oil refiner, a stearine and grease manufacturer and paper manufacturer.

At a time when many public houses still brewed their own ale, there were no brewers in the area but there were four full time beer retailers and a fifth who combined beer retailing with farming, a news agency and an agency for life insurance. These retail outlets were all in Midgley. In addition, there were seven named public houses listed in Kelly's Directory of 1861. These were the Shoulder of Mutton in Midgley, The Red Lion in Luddenden Foot and four in Mytholmroyd, two of which, the White Lion and the Shoulder of Mutton, were used as holding addresses for Horsfall William & Co and for Sutcliffe, Hollinrake & Sutcliffe, respectively. One wonders whether the firms used public houses as accessible venues for meetings (as had been done in the coaching era) or whether the firms had taken over the buildings as accessible offices, in which case there may no longer have been a public function. Equally, Railhouse In (sic) is listed in connection with Samuel Briggs esq. so this may have been a private residence.

There are nineteen private residents listed in the Trade Directory: fourteen in Midgley and five in Mytholmroyd, of whom none would appear to be armigerous. They all have names common to this locality: Aked, Appleyard, Clay, Crossley, Fielding, Riley and Sutcliffe are some of the families that did not declare a commercial interest by the 1860s, although this is not to gainsay that other family members are working in trade or the professions elsewhere.

Kelly's Directory, 1881[4]

In Kelly's Directory for 1881, the area covered by Midgley township comes under four areas – Luddenden, Luddendenfoot, Midgley and Mytholmroyd. By comparing names and occupations with the Enumerators' Returns from the 1881 Census, it was possible to determine that ninety-eight of the 240 entries in the trade directory were actually in Midgley township.

The largest single group were farmers, with twenty-one names listed, some having a second entry, for example William Dennitt, of Scotland Farm, who was also a quarry owner, or William Radcliffe at High Lea Head, who was also a beer retailer. The Census Return confirms most of the details of the latter, although his name was spelt Ratcliffe. He was sixty-two and living with his son and daughter-in-law. William Dennett was recorded at Springfield Terrace with his wife Betty, not at Scotland. There were other members of the Dennett family living next door – some also involved in quarrying.

More importantly, in the Census Enumerator's Returns there were fifty heads of household who gave their occupation as farmer. It appears, therefore, that the directory was identifying less than half those in this occupational group. However, of the fifty, sixteen had other occupations, including four woolsorters and three quarrymen. The acreage of farms was given in half the cases, ranging from seven or eight acres to the fifty acres of William Tatham of Harrowbut Lee, in the upper Luddenden valley. Many of the smaller farms appear to be family run, and there were only thirty agricultural labourers and a dozen farm servants in the Census Returns.

The next major occupational groups in the directory listing were in the retail

---

[4] *Post Office Directory of the West Riding of Yorkshire*, London: Kelly & Co., 1881

trade, with eighteen entries, and the fourteen inns and beer houses. There were three bootmakers, three coal merchants, two general shopkeepers, two tailors and a draper, and there were also entries for the co-operative stores in Midgley and Luddenden, which had been running for fifteen years by 1881. Their competitive buying power and dividends may have allowed them to undercut the smaller shopkeepers and expand business at their expense.

Comparison of these categories with the Census Returns presents an interesting contrast. Whereas the number of inns and beer shops is very similar, it is clear that far more people were involved in providing retail services, particularly if clothing and footwear are included. The Census recorded nineteen bootmakers, twenty-two dressmakers and nineteen tailors, giving a very different picture from the directory. In addition, there are eleven butchers, ten grocers and four greengrocers, a milliner and two ironmongers; a far more diverse picture, with one hundred and twenty-five people working in these trades.

The textile industry was a major employer in the area by 1881. The Census recorded just under 1,100 people involved in the cotton, worsted and woollen mills and their associated trades, about eighty per cent of those in work. The Census identified twelve mill owners, compared to nine in the directory, and these figures give a representative picture of the importance of the trade to the area. The majority were working in large mills, such as Oats Royd, or the recently established Albert and Greenhill Mills in Mytholmroyd.

Another group of occupations which present an interesting contrast between the two sources is the building trades. The Census identified ninety-three people, the majority delvers, masons and a few woodworkers such as joiners and carpenters. It is difficult, especially in the stone trades, to identify the employers. By contrast, Kelly's directory only identified two joiners, one plumber and one stone merchant, Robert Midgley of Booth. As the quarries at Scotland and Walton Edge would have been in full swing at this time it is surprising they are omitted.

Turning finally to transport, the growing importance of the railway was reflected in the eleven railway workers, the nearest stations being at Luddendenfoot and Mytholmroyd. However, the twenty-five carters, six cab drivers and four coachmen show the horse was still important for transporting both goods and people. In the Directory, however, only John Tillotson, of Luddendenfoot, was mentioned as a cab proprietor, but railway and canal connections were mentioned in the preamble.

Turning now to those listed as private residents, the Directory has seventeen 'private residents', but many of these can be identified from the Census returns as factory owners – for example the Bracken family, whose paper mill at Dean in the Luddenden valley provided employment for around fifty people. The Census has far more information on those who did not work. Thirty-nine 'retired', twenty-five 'annuitants', thirty-one unemployed and 778 scholars are all mentioned in the Census. Clearly, members of the Riley family of Ewood Hall were very conscious of their status; Thomas described himself as 'Lord of the Manor of Midgley', his wife Ellen as 'Lady of the Manor'.

In total, the Census recorded 3,085 people living in the township of Midgley in 1881. The Returns provide a rich source of information, which can be augmented by referring to the trade directories.

Slater's Directory, 1891[5] and Kelly's Directory, 1901[6]

A comparison of the entries in Slater's Directory of 1891 and Kelly's of 1901 allows us to bring the analysis up to the end of the nineteenth century. Employment sectors in the same localities – Luddenden, Luddendenfoot, Midgley and Mytholmroyd – can be compared both with each other and over a ten year period to identify growing or contracting trades. Thus it is possible to trace the development of economic activity and the growth of particular specialist trades to meet a more demanding local population.

As with the period ten or twenty years earlier, the single largest employment type was still the agricultural sector as recorded by the directories. This is a somewhat surprising finding in an area that was at the heart of the Industrial Revolution, but is explained by the fact that individual mill-workers were not listed in the directories, only the manufacturers being mentioned. Some fifty-seven people in 1891 were classified as farmers, but the distribution amongst the locations was markedly different. Twenty-eight farmers were listed in Midgley, twenty-three in Luddenden, six in Luddendenfoot and only three in Mytholmroyd. By 1901, this had changed considerably in some areas; with twenty-nine farmers in Midgley, only one recorded in Luddendenfoot, three in Luddenden and seventy-two in Mytholmroyd. This is such a marked

---

5 *Slater's Royal National and Commercial Directory of the West Riding of Yorkshire,* 11th edn., Manchester: Slater, 1891, pp498 - 505
6 *Post Office Directory of the West Riding of Yorkshire,* London: Kelly & Co., 1901

difference that a question must be asked about coverage. While it could be surmised that agriculture had in fact been replaced by industrial employment in Luddendenfoot, the rise in the numbers in Mytholmroyd is harder to explain. In fact, a comparison of a couple of names shows that farming was as prevalent in Mytholmroyd in 1891 as ten years later, but the entries had been recorded differently. James Mitchell of Nab End is recorded as a farmer in Mytholmroyd in 1901, but entered in the area of Cragg in the township of Sowerby in 1891. Similarly, William Helliwell is entered as a farmer at Cragg Hall in Mytholmroyd in 1901, but recorded at Old Hall in Cragg in 1891. It is certainly true that the formation of Mytholmroyd Urban District Council in 1894 brought into Mytholmroyd tracts of agricultural land and the inhabitants.

There is a very wide range of shops and other service providers in both Directories, which provide a fascinating glimpse of the diversity of social activity in what were semi-rural localities. Butchers and grocers were thriving at the end of the nineteenth century, with a total of sixteen and twenty-six respectively in 1891. This had fallen markedly to nine and twelve by 1901, but what is remarkable for such provincial communities is the profusion of other retailers and service providers. In addition to a blacksmith in each area, drapers' shops, chemists and ironmongers co-existed with the more refined providers, such as dressmakers and confectioners. Sarah Jackson of Luddendenfoot is recorded as a milliner in Slater in 1891. By 1901, Luddendenfoot also had two newsagents (Henry Moses and Albert Drake) and a jeweller (Frank Hoyle). There was a tripe dresser, a tea merchant and a saddler within the township as a whole in 1891 and three fried-fish dealers in Luddendenfoot alone in 1901. As well as tailors, coal merchants and boot and shoe-makers, the area supported John Shaw as a cabinet maker (with a secondary occupation of painter) and John Tillotson as a coach proprietor in Luddendenfoot in 1891. The demand from the gentry families in the Luddenden valley was evidently sufficient to sustain this growing activity. All four locations had Industrial Co-operative Society stores and in all four cases they also acted as coal merchants.

The textile industry continued to feature in trade directories, but not as prominently as in census records, as the majority of those employed were not advertising their services. In 1891, together with a cotton manufacturer, Luddenden has an entry for James Ogden and Sons spindle makers and over the four locations, Slater's records twenty-six entries relating to textiles, including thirteen manufacturers of cotton, wool, worsted or velvet. There is, interestingly, no textile-related entry recorded in Midgley. By 1901, the total of textile-related entries was twenty-four, with three manufacturers in Midgley and one William Sunderland, a rag dealer in Mytholmroyd.

Professional services are well represented. In addition to Anglican, Methodist and Congregational clergy, there are schoolmasters or schoolmistresses in each locality in 1891, together with surgeons, solicitors, managers (including a gas works manager) and, by 1901, a sprinkling of specifically public sector posts such as the collector to the Urban District Council, George Taylor, in Luddendenfoot and the inspector of nuisances, Emmet Smith of Calder Terrace, in Mytholmroyd plus a stationmaster and postmaster. Luddenden also had a police sergeant in 1891.

Other industrial sectors are represented by a small but diverse group, including two canal carriers in Luddendenfoot in 1891, corn millers, iron and tinplate workers and John Wilcock, an oil manufacturer in Mytholmroyd. While the number of public houses (fifteen in 1891 and seven in 1901) is not as great as in earlier times, there is a surprisingly large number of beer retailers; fifteen in 1891 and seventeen in 1901. In 1891 there is a total of forty entries for the gentry or private residents and this had risen to sixty-five by 1901, reflecting the prosperity of the Murgatroyds of Oats Royd Mills and Broadfold Hall, the Titterington family of Greave and the Rileys of Ewood Hall amongst others.

	White's 1838	White's 1853	Kelly's 1861	Kelly's 1881	Slater's 1891	Kelly's 1901
Shopkeepers	30	41	30	44	68	82
Service Providers	37	41	48	41	100	76
Textile Industry	43	26	11	24	13	12
Textile Industry Others	8	7	11	5	13	18
Professions	6	8	6	9	7	32
Farmers	21	14	24	33	60	105
Other Industries	9	10	13	11	9	10
Inns & Beer Houses	17	17	11	17	21	19
Gentry	4	11	19	31	42	65

Figure 2   *Summary of numbers of trades and services from 1838 to 1901*

Summary

An analysis of the trades over the second half of the nineteenth century shows a marked trend towards diversification of the economic base. Several points need to be made at the outset: firstly, that the directories are published by different compilers so the methods and reliability may differ; secondly, the definitions above may not always be internally consistent and thirdly, the geographical coverage may have changed.

Bearing these caveats in mind, a number of key conclusions can be drawn. It is interesting to note the growth of the farming sector across the township – the fivefold rise between 1838 and 1901 to over one hundred farmers is a surprising result. If we believe that boundary changes account for some of this increase in 1901, there is nevertheless still a threefold rise by 1891. Perhaps the real reason for the apparent rise in the number of farmers is increasingly comprehensive coverage on the part of directory compilers in the late Victorian period.

Shopkeepers and service providers also grow significantly and, as explained in more detail above, there is a great variety of shops and services, as befits a more demanding customer base.

The professional classes are pretty stable, at less than ten, until the final ten years of the century, while the classification of gentry, perhaps self-classified as such, also remains stable until 1891. The number of entries for textile manufacturers and other textile-related occupations actually fell or grew only slowly. Some of the forty-three textile manufacturers in 1838 may have been calling themselves gentry by 1891 and the real growth in overall employment in the textile industry may be hidden here, as mill hands were not recorded in the directories.

Entries for other industries remain remarkably stable over the sixty years at between nine and thirteen (with 1881 as an exception to the trend). As a bell weather of social activity, entries for inns and beer houses also remain pretty constant. Although Midgley may have been considered remote and old-fashioned in some quarters, the continued presence of a wide range of professions, industry and services proved the opposite: it was sustaining all the essentials of a modern consumer society.

CHAPTER 23

Reminiscences of Shopping in Mid-Twentieth Century Midgley

Hilary Shackleton

I was born at 30 Thorney Lane, Midgley on 15 November 1937. It was the house rented by my grandparents from Murgatroyds'. We lived at number 22 and Aunty Chrissie was at number 26. Ours was the best place for children to grow up in. We had safe areas for play and wonderful views. Everyone knew who we were and looked out for us. I was fifteen years old when we moved to Luddendenfoot and in those fifteen years I learned about life and how people should live. We didn't need to go far for all our needs.

Our nearest shop was Lister's on the other side of our row. It was the middle house but was also a shop. They sold sweets, pop, some medicines like tapes of Aspros, bread and very little else. The counter was in the 'passage' between the outer door and the stairs. The living room window was also the shop window making their room very dark.

Mrs Robinson had a bigger shop at the bottom of Radcliffe Lane (Figure 1). It

was wooden and had a huge door on rollers which was pushed round the side when the shop was open. At the back of the shop was a small, cosy living area with a wood burning stove, an armchair with cushions and a parrot on a stand. The counter was high and held a tray with a bottle of pop and a few small glasses.

Figure 1   Mrs Robinson's shop on Radcliffe Lane

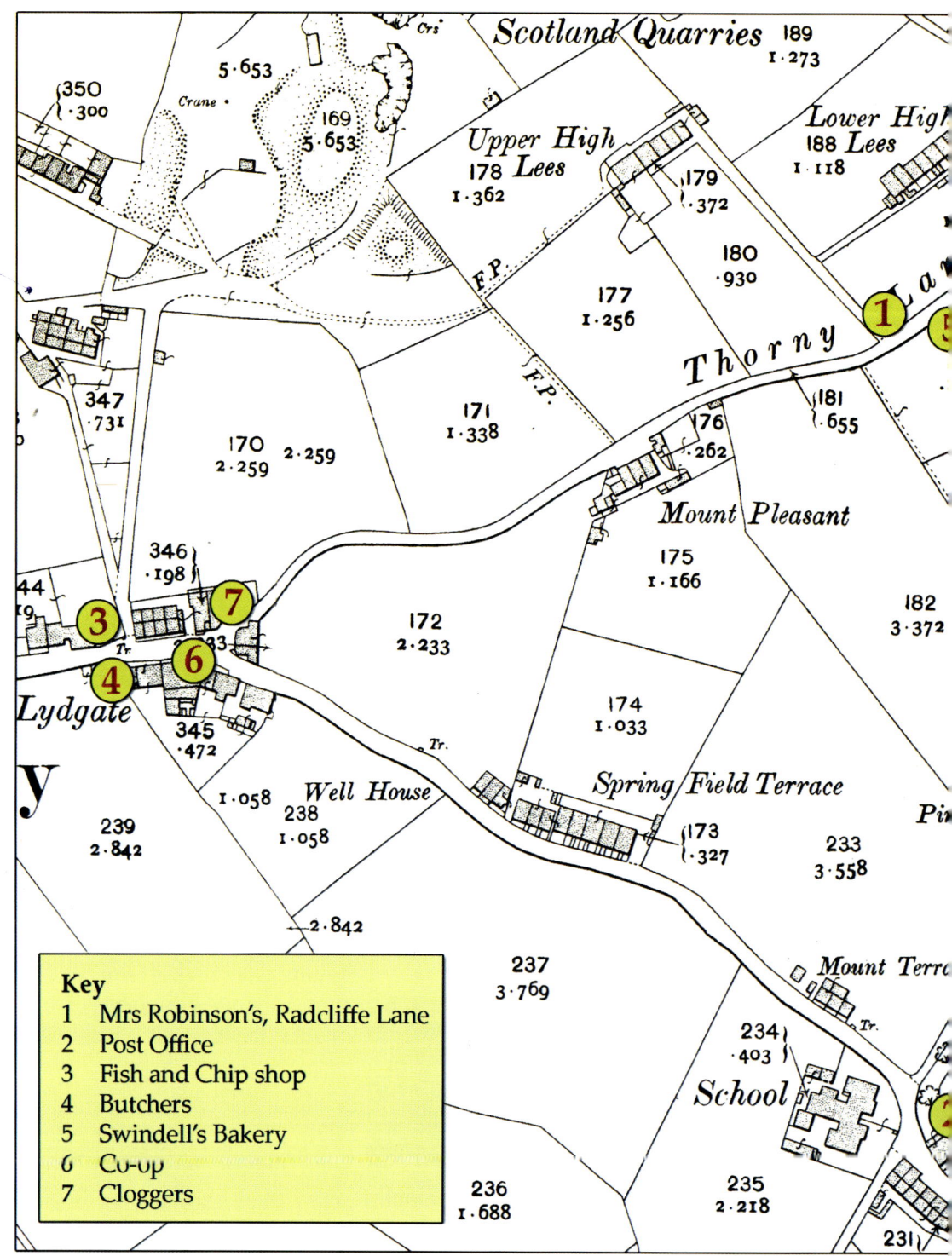

Figure 2   25 inch to 1 mile Ordnance Survey map, Yorkshire, published 1907, sheet 230

These were for penny drinks. The shelves held cans and bottles and packets. They had things like cocoa, treacle, zebo grate polish and shoe polish. There was not much room, but it was much bigger than the Lister's and Mrs Robinson would find any small items like shoe laces and sewing needles behind the counter.

At the post office in Midgley (Figure 3), near the school, Frank Howarth kept

vegetables, bread and the same things as Mrs Robinson. He also had stationery. He delivered weekly to our neighbour, Mrs Tasker, who asked him to bring a Methodist Hymn Book as a present for me so that I could play the hymns on our piano and she could hear them.

At the bus terminus was Mr Eastwood's shop. It too was a typical local shop. Mr Eastwood made penny lollies with wooden sticks to hold. They were extra juicy and we looked forward to buying them when we came from Sunday School.

Figure 3   Midgley Post Office

Doris Crowther made the most wonderfully crispy, battered fish. Always haddock, which could also be bought in the form of fishcakes, to be eaten with chips wrapped in a piece of white paper, then in newspaper (Figure 4). Her shop was near the well at the bottom of Tray Royd Lane (Figure 2). Doris's mother would bring a bucket of cut chips from the living room into the shop always at the right time when Doris ran out. Fish cost 5d. Over the cooking range was an old alarm clock with a piece of paper covering the dial with the words 'No Tick'.

Opposite Doris's shop was the butcher's run by Eric Ogden (Figure 2). There was sawdust on the floor to absorb the blood that dripped from carcasses hanging in the shop. The Avery scale on the counter gave the weight but Eric had to work out the cost of the meat.

Figure 4   The one storey building on the right was Crowther's fish and chip shop

We couldn't buy fish in the village. John Broadbent was our nearest fishmonger. His shop was near the top of Old Lane, the cobbled hill leading down to Luddenden school and church; it was just below Alderson's the plumbers.[1] In the school holidays I went to Broadbent's for fish for our neighbours and Mrs Jennings from Brown Hill Farm. The orders were usually for haddock to cost between 2s and 2s 6d. I walked from Thorney Lane down Cow Lane along Providence and Duke Street to get the orders.

We could buy strawberries, potatoes and cabbages in season from Jim Warriner at Green Houses but our Grandad usually had them too. Grandad grew peas and lettuces. I sometimes had peas in a bag as sweets were scarce, also Quaker oats and sugar, or sometimes, cocoa and sugar. This was a good substitute for chocolate.

Because Grandma and Grandad had a hen run, we had chickens and eggs. Also, Uncle Fred could catch rabbits for Grandma's rabbit pies which she made in a big green enamel bowl in the oven at the side of the Kitchen fire. She made black puddings with the pig's blood from Haig's farm at Green Houses. They were not in skins, but were in basins. Dock pudding was also a

---

[1] This is illustrated in Chapter 14, Figure 6

favourite in April when we collected docks on the dam bank and bilberry pies disappeared much quicker than the time it took to pick them on 'The Slacks'. Grandma's blackberry jam was also a favourite; spread on her oat cakes it was delicious. When she made rhubarb pies with rhubarb from Grandad's allotment by the side of the path on the way to Brown Hill, she would give me a stick to dip in sugar on a saucer. Curd tarts were made with milk from a cow which had calved. All this with only a fireside oven and a gas ring. Grandma also made bread and baked cakes every week. As a very great treat, buns and cakes could be bought at Rose Hill, Swindell's bakery (Figure 2).

Our main source of supply was, of course, the Co-op at Lydgate (Figure 2). Three large windows displayed anything we could need (Figure 5). The first two held groceries. Inside was a row of chairs where customers waited for their turn to be served. Whilst you sat there, the biscuit tins with glass lids faced you; the Lincoln biscuits with little raised blobs, digestives, sparkling nice and oblong shortbreads. Broken biscuits were cheaper. Behind the row of chairs was the counter with the bacon slicer and cheese board with wire for cutting wedges from a barrel shaped cheese. Next was butter, marg., yeast and lard in huge blocks waiting to be cut, weighed and wrapped in greaseproof paper by Eric Horsfield, Leslie Steward or Reggie Smith. They always wore white coats and everyone chatted to them while they served. Aunty Chrissie Singleton worked there for a while. Willie Greenwood was the manager, but he was usually in the office upstairs.

Flour, sugar, currants and other dry goods were weighed in blue paper bags. Two ounces of sweets went into a white kite-shaped paper bag and four ounces fit in a square one. Soft white teacakes, plain or currant, and crusty loaves were wrapped in tissue paper and we carried ours in Grandma's white cotton crocheted bags on days when grandma didn't bake. Large non-food items were kept in the back of the shop. Firewood bundles, broom handles, purple methylated spirits for lighting lamps, paraffin, buckets and mops, hand shovels for coal etc. Almost everything they didn't have they could get and it could be delivered with groceries on a day when coal was not on the lorry. Our vegetables were in open sacks on the floor to the left of the shop floor and there was still soil on them. Apples were individually wrapped in squares of soft tissue paper; very useful in the toilet.

Next to the grocery department was the drapery run by Mrs Luty. Haberdashery filled little drawers. Knitting wool in hanks was a favourite at our house as was crochet cotton. Underwear included navy knickers which had a pocket and elastic in the legs. Liberty bodices, some which buttoned up the front, had rubber buttons which didn't break in the mangle. We could buy socks, lisle stockings, Wellington boots, suspender belts and combinations for grandparents. When we made a purchase the amount spent was recorded on a perforated pad with carbon paper between its sheets. We had to give our number (403) and were given a small ticket. At the end of the financial year we got a share of profits called 'divi' or dividend. On that day there was always a sale in the drapery department where we bought bargains after collecting our cash from the hall above the houses opposite.

Also opposite the co-op was the village cobblers where Frank Schofield mended shoes, boots and clogs (Figure 2). He made clogs, too, and was known as Frank Clogger. He sat at a bench in his leather apron and I loved to watch him from behind his tall counter where I stood on a bench. He would have a row of boot tacks in his lips or bits of match stick that he would put into holes that he made in wooden clog soles, before hammering the tacks through the iron rims like horse shoes, which sparked on the stone cobbles just like in the Lowry song.

In short, we had everything we needed. I was so lucky to have parents, grandparents, aunts and uncles who could make, or 'make do' as we used to say, anything that was necessary for a comfortable and happy life.

Figure 5   *Midgley Co-op, with its three large display windows*

INDEX

Compiled by Nigel Smith

This is a subject index, and therefore does not list every single name and place in the book. Entries have been made for topics and names that have been judged historically significant as well as those for which a useful amount of information is given. Topics or names that are otherwise mentioned in passing are not indexed.

Entries have been made under the most specific heading that has been thought to be helpful to readers. However entries have also been made under major topics dealt with by each chapter. Subheadings and cross references have been provided to help identify more detailed aspects of the topic. Additional description for a heading, such as occupation, has been provided where thought to be useful. This is also presented as a subheading for clarity. Illustrations are not indexed as such and reference should be made to the list of illustrations on page 331.

List of Illustrations

P.Horsfield

Towngate, Midgley, in the early twentieth century

P.Horsfield

A band marches along Duke Street and past the former Traveller's Rest, the first building on the left

Contact Details

The contact details for the major sources consulted in the writing of this book that are open to members of the public are:

West Yorkshire Archive Service (Calderdale)
Central Library
Northgate
Halifax
HX1 1UN
Tel: 01422 392636
Email: calderdale@wyjs.org.uk
Web: http://www.archives.wyjs.org.uk

West Yorkshire Archive Service (Wakefield)
Newstead Road
Wakefield
WF1 2DE
Tel: 01924 305980
Fax: 01924 305983
Email: wakefield@wyjs.org.uk
Web: http://www.archives.wyjs.org.uk

Halifax Central Library
Northgate
Halifax
HX1 1UN
Tel: 01422 392630
Email: libraries@calderdale.gov.uk

Borthwick Institute
University of York
Heslington
York
YO10 5DD
Tel: 01904 321166
Email: bihr500@york.ac.uk
Web: http://www.york.ac.uk/inst/bihr

The National Archives
Kew
Richmond
Surrey
TW9 4DU
Tel: 020 8876 3444
Web: http://www.nationalarchives.gov.uk

The British Library
St Pancras
96 Euston Road
London
NW1 2DB
Tel: 020 7412 7332
Email: Visitor-Services@bl.uk
Web: http://www.bl.uk

Yorkshire Archaeological Society
Claremont
23 Clarendon Road
Leeds
LS2 9NZ
Tel: 0113 245 7910
Email: yas.library@googlemail.com
Web: http://www.yas.org.uk

Other useful sources include:

Hebden Bridge Local History Society
Email: librarian@hebdenbridgehistory.org.uk
Web: http://www.hebdenbridgehistory.org.uk

Midgley History Group
Email: midgleybooks@3-c.coop
Web: http://www.midgley.org.uk/history

List of Subscribers

The following people have kindly supported this book by subscribing to it:

Name	Location
Abbott, Shirley	Todmorden
Annison, Rodney	Luddenden
Armstrong, Alison C	Skipton
Ashdown, Marjorie	Shipley
Ashman, Edward	Jerusalem Farm
Bailey, Adrian	Masham
Bailey, Ernie & Angela	Sheffield
Bainbridge, Howard	Midgley
Baker, A & G	Mytholmroyd
Baldwin, John	Big Six Inn
Ball, Kenneth	Sowerby Bridge
Barber, Carol	Sowerby Bridge
Barker, Stephen & Margaret	Height Farm, Midgley
Baxter, Sharon	Midgley
Beach, Elaine	Stainland
Bellamy, Tony	Berkhamsted
Benson, Alexandra	Foster Clough
Benson, Katharine Gate	Foster Clough
Bestilny, Helen	Minneapolis, USA
Boland, Kim	Germany
Boland, Rebekah	Germany
Booth, Louise & Craig	Todmorden
Botten, Brenda & Jim	Hebden Bridge
Bouckley, Chris & Stephanie	Midgley
Bradbury, Jean	Midgley
Broadbent, David	Green House Farm, Midgley
Buckley, Mike	Dobcross
Burgess, Stephanie	Norland
Button, Ian & Yelena	Linden Road, Halifax
Cansdale, Daphne	Mytholmroyd
Cant, Jenny	Hathershelf
Carter, Nick & Sandra	Midgley
Cawkwell, Christopher	Midgley

Name	Location
Charlestown History Group,	Hebden Bridge
Clark, Audrey & Alastair	Abernethy
Clarke, Ian	Midgley
Clarke, John	Halifax
Clatworthy, Brian & Jeanne	Luddenden
Clyde-Evans, Eleanor	Height Road, Hebden Bridge
Clyde-Evans, Gwen	Height Road, Hebden Bridge
Clyde-Evans, John	Height Road, Hebden Bridge
Cobley (Midgley Descendants), Vickie	Utah and beyond, USA
Cocker, David	Midgley
Cockroft, J&V	Luddenden
Cockroft, K&S	Midgley
Cockroft, R	Luddenden
Collinge, Rodney & Margaret	Luddenden
Compston, David	Midgley
Conquest, Sandra	Low Moor
Cowgill, Jennifer	Otley
Cox, Graham	Sportsman Inn, Midgley
Cox, John	Leeds
Croft, Linda	Todmorden
Crook, Rosie	Midgley
Crossley, Alan	West Linton
Crowther, Jack	Halifax
Crowther, John Anderson	Halifax
Crowther, Stuart	Backhold Hall, Siddal
Davies, Alison	Aberystwyth
Davies, Andrew G	Far Headingley
Davies, Elaine & Dai	Ewood Hall Barn, Midgley
Degnan, Paul	Old Town
Dixon, Dwane	Todmorden
Domstead, Sarah J	Knaresborough
Dyson, Tony	Hebden Bridge
Farnell, Anne & Pete	Midgley
Fawcett, Sheila	Midgley
Ferguson, Mandy	Carnoustie
Fielden, Catherine & Mollie	Todmorden
Finnell, Georgia Jayne	Tray Royd, Midgley
Finnell, Harrison James	Tray Royd, Midgley
Fisher, David	Luddendenfoot

Name	Location
Fletcher, Dan & Hilly	Oats Royd, Midgley
France, Dawn	Heptonstall
Gay, Jenefried	Midgley
Gee, Craig	Midgley
Gibson, Philip	Westercroft, Northowram
Gilyeat, Anna	Midgley
Gilyeat, Kris	Midgley
Gledhill, David R	Streatham, London
Godfrey, Brenda	Hebden Bridge
Goodchild, Jennifer	Wakefield
Graham, Alastair	Hebden Bridge
Graham, Frank	Mytholmroyd
Grant, Alistair & Elaine	Midgley
Greenwood, Alan	Cragg Vale
Greenwood, Howard	Halifax
Greenwood, June Helen	Midgley
Gregory, Julia	Signy Signets, France
Hair, Joseph Paul	Midgley
Halifax Antiquarian Society	Halifax
Hanson, Eric & Wendy	Luddendenfoot
Hargreaves, John	Halifax
Hartley, John	Mytholmroyd
Harwood, Diane	Halifax
Haslam, Michael	Foster Clough
Hawkins, Daniel	Wadsworth Banks
Hawkins, Katherine	Wadsworth Banks
Hawkins, Marilyn & Graham	Wadsworth Banks
Hawkins, Rebecca	Wadsworth Banks
Heaps, George	Midgley
Heaps, Nick & Joy	Midgley
Heaps, Victoria	Midgley
Hebden Bridge Local History Society	Hebden Bridge
Hircock (nee Cox), Adrienne	Stainland
Holgate, Ron & Moyra	Thurlby, Lincs
Holt, Jenny, Robin & Morven	Luddenden
Holt, Peter	Midgley
Hopkinson, Jean & Giles	Stamford
Horsfield, M.E.	Midgley
Horsfield, Rebecca	Breedon-in-the-Hill

Name	Location
Hutchinson, Cynthia	Halifax
Hynes, Joyce	Mixenden
Ingall (nee Barraclough), Jean	New Zealand
Jagger, Patricia	Thornton
Jebson, John & Jean	Langcliffe
Johnson, Beryl	Midgley
Jolley, Frank	Lightcliffe
Jones, Philip	Midgley
Joyce, Bethen	Midgley
Kelly (nee Bridges), Norma	Midgley
Kinder, Susan	Keighley
Kirker, Anne	Rishworth
Kneen, Lawrence & Kaye	Midgley
Knowles, Lynn	Hipperholme
Knutton, Penny & Stephen	Midgley
Lambshead, Mrs Josephine	Midgley
Lester, Wanda	Cottingley
Lihou, Richard	Luddenden
Lloyd, Clive R	Luddenden
Lockett, Kym	Midgley
Lockyer, Phil	Midgley
Loney, Derek	Butts, Mytholmroyd
Longley, Sharon	Midgley
Lucas, Jeff	Brearley
Mallinson, Connie	Booth
Mallinson, Irene	Hebden Bridge
Mallinson, Tony	Booth
McCartney, Brigitte	Luddenden
McDonald, Mr N & Mrs C	Halifax
Midgley, Andrea	Corby Glen
Midgley, Damien	Branston
Midgley, Julian	Huddersfield
Midgley, Michael	Ruskington
Midgley (nee Bridges), Mrs S	Midgley
Midgley, Owen	Rhode Island, USA
Midgley, Robert H	Luddenden
Midgley, Sarah	Bexhill-on-Sea
Mitchell, Winnie B	Friendly
Monahan, Diana	Hebden Bridge

Name	Location
Murgatroyd, Stuart	Birmingham
Mytholmroyd Historical Society	Mytholmroyd
Narey, Kevin John	Woodstock
Narey, Sean	East Morton
Nelson, Margaret	Shifnal, Shropshire
Oldroyd, George	Midgley
Pacey, Arnold	Addingham
Paget, Elizabeth	Leeds
Paskowitz, Jane	California, USA
Patchett, John H	Gomersall
Patrick, Margaret	Queensbury
Perry, Caroline	Menston
Riddle, Sheila	Midgley
Riley, Mandy	Midgley
Robinson (nee Bridges), Mrs V	Midgley
Robinson, Andrew	Halifax
Robinson, Mrs G	Halifax
Robinson, Peter	Liverpool
Saddleworth Historical Society	Uppermill, Saddleworth
Saville, Graham	Foster Clough
Scott, Sandra	Midgley
Sears, Erica	Whitchurch
Shackleton (nee Cox), Hilary	Mytholmroyd
Shannon, Issy	Hebden Bridge
Shore, David & Noelene	Fixby
Sim, David	Midgley
Sleight, Joan	Midgley
Smeenk, Everdien M	The Netherlands
Smith (nee Singleton), Ann	Northowram
Smith, Barry & Eileen	Clifton
Smith, Clare	Hebden Bridge
Smith, Daniel	Hebden Bridge
Smith, David	Queensland, Australia
Smith, Margaret	Hebden Bridge
Smith, Michael	Stoke Fleming
Smith, Rachel	Hebden Bridge
Spencer (nee Bridges), Betty	Midgley
Spencer, Tracy	Queensbury
Strickland, Craig	Midgley

Name	Location
Sullivan, Christine	Todmorden
Sunderland, Molly	Mytholmroyd
Swinscoe, Jean Mitchell	Halifax
Taylor, Angela	Pecket Well
Tetlaw, Molly	Halifax
The Grammer School	Hipperholme
Thomas, Gwynneth	Midgley
Thomas, Matt	Midgley
Thomas, Neil	Midgley
Thorpe, Judi	Marsden
Tighe, Deborah	Midgley
Tighe, Rachel	Midgley
Toole, Chris	Halifax
Toole, Margery	Marple
Topliss, Jeremy	Foster Clough
Tune (nee Hartley), Ethel	Newbury, Berks
Turner, John & Marian	Winchfield, Hampshire
Turner, Laura J	Emsworth, Hampshire
Turner, Louise	Midgley
Uttley, David	Stoodley Glen
Uttley, Max	Wheatley
Waddingham, Keith	Haworth
Wade, Sheila	Ilkley
Walker, Tracy J	Todmorden
Warner, Annette	Fife
Watkins, Liz	Hebden Bridge
Watson (nee Mitchell), Patricia A	Knaresborough
Weir, Richard	Holmfirth
West, Martin & Sheila	Holebank Head
Wheeler, Rose	Midgley
Whitaker, Janet	Burnley
Whiteley, Marilyn	Midgley
Wilcock, Elisabeth	Adel
Wild Rose Heritage & Arts	Hebden Bridge
Wilding, Nick	Slack Top
Wilkinson, Jeff	Calderside
Williams, Graham	Mytholmroyd
Wilson, Heather & Douglas	Todmorden
Wilson, Rachel	Midgley